T0384096

Routledge Revivals

International Commodity Policy

Originally published in 1993, this book provides an excellent analysis of commodity policies internationally during the late 20th Century. It discusses 2 major methods of market regulation: price stabilization – based on buffer stocks or export quotas – and compensatory finance. The authors analyse whether major commodity policies have reached their primary objectives and to what extent they have had economic side effects. Discussion of more general policy issues centres around three international commodity agreements for coffee, rubber and cocoa. The authors also look at the policies adopted by individual nations to regulate commodity trading and assess to what extent they have reached their objectives. A discussion of the intervention of the International Monetary Fund and STABEX assesses the degree of stability they can provide in a highly volatile and variable environment. Nearly 30 years later, volatile world commodity markets are still a major issue in the policy dialogue. Although topics, policy instruments and concepts have changed, this book remains a fundamental contribution to the study of international commodity policy.

International Commodity Policy

A Quantitative Analysis

Roland Herrmann, Kees Burger and Hidde P. Smit

First published in 1993 by Routledge

This edition first published in 2023 by Routledge
4 Park Square, Milton Park, Abingdon, Oxon, OX14 4RN
and by Routledge
605 Third Avenue, New York, NY 10158

Routledge is an imprint of the Taylor & Francis Group, an informa business

ISBN 13: 978-1-032-45904-2 (hbk)
ISBN 13: 978-1-003-37925-6 (ebk)
ISBN 13: 978-1-032-45919-6 (pbk)
Book DOI 10.4324/9781003379256

International commodity policy

The pricing of commodities in the world market is a serious and sensitive business. The instability of world commodity markets has been a central issue in the north-south dialogue. Price stabilization policies and compensatory finance schemes installed as international measures to counter the negative consequences of world market instabilities have also had mixed results. In a world in which commodities and supplies are becoming increasingly scarce it is vital to understand the important issues involved if any improvement is to be hoped for.

International Commodity Policy provides an excellent analysis of international commodity policies during the late 20th century. It discusses two major methods of market regulation: price stabilization – based on buffer stocks or export quotas – and compensatory finance. The authors analyse whether major commodity policies reached their primary objectives and to what extent they had economic side effects.

Discussion of more general policy issues centres around three international commodity agreements for coffee, rubber and cocoa. The authors also look at the policies adopted by individual nations to regulate commodity trading and assess to what extent they have reached their objectives. Finally a discussion of the intervention of the International Monetary Fund and STABEX assesses the degree of stability they can provide in a highly volatile and variable environment.

This volume is an unchanged reissue of the book's first edition in 1993. Nearly 30 years later, volatile world commodity markets are still a major issue in the policy dialogue. Although topics, policy instruments and concepts have changed, this book remains a fundamental contribution to the study of international commodity policy. It will be of great interest to students of commodity policy and economic development and economists in national and international organizations dealing with market stabilization.

Roland Herrmann is Professor Emeritus of Agricultural and Food Market Analysis at Justus Liebig University, Giessen, Germany. **Kees Burger**, 1950–2016, was Associate Professor of Development Economics at Wageningen University and Research, Wageningen, Netherlands. **Hidde P. Smit** is an Independent Consultant on Analysis and Forecasts for the Rubber Economy. He was Secretary General of the International Rubber Study Group in London and Singapore (2005–2009) and Head of the Economic Research Division of the Economic and Social Institute, Free University Amsterdam (1995–2004).

International commodity policy

A quantitative analysis

Roland Herrmann
Kees Burger
Hidde P. Smit

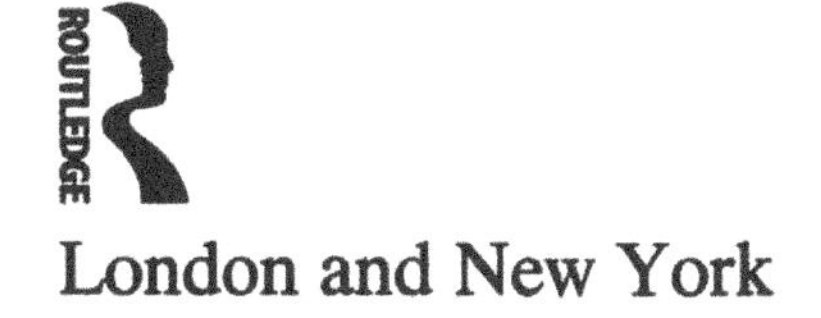

London and New York

First published 1993
by Routledge
11 New Fetter Lane, London EC4P 4EE

Simultaneously published in the USA and Canada
by Routledge
29 West 35th Street, New York, NY 10001

Typeset in Times by Leaper & Gard Ltd, Bristol
Printed and bound in Great Britain by Mackays of Chatham PLC,
Chatham, Kent

British Library Cataloguing in Publication Data
A catalogue record for this book is available from the British Library

ISBN 0-415-05945-3

Library of Congress Cataloging-in-Publication Data
Burger, Kees.
International commodity policy : a quantitative analysis / Kees
Burger, Roland Herrmann, Hidde P. Smit.
p. cm. -- (Routledge commodity series)
Includes bibliographical references and index.
ISBN 0-415-05945-3
1. Commodity control. 2. Price maintenance. 3. Compensatory
financing. I. Herrmann, Roland, 1952– . II. Smit, Hidde P.,
1944– . III. Title. IV. Series.
HF1428.B87 1993
382'.3--dc20 92-37255
CIP

Contents

Figures

Tables

Preface

This study arose from a joint paper we presented at the conference on 'Primary commodity prices: economic models and policy', held at the Centre for Economic Policy Research (CEPR) in London on 16 and 17 March, 1989. A shorter version of the paper was published in the proceedings: see Herrmann *et al.* (1990). In Fall 1989, we decided to extend the analysis of the original version significantly. Historical surveys of agreements and of the economics of stabilization were added, the coverage of financial arrangements of the International Monetary Fund (IMF) and those under the Lomé Convention was expanded and a study of the cocoa agreements and of the Lomé protocols was added to the analysis of the agreements on coffee and natural rubber. We now hope to present a more comprehensive analysis of the impacts of the international stabilization arrangements and thus to provide a broader base for policy conclusions.

Thanks are extended to L. Alan Winters who invited us to present the paper at the CEPR Conference and therefore gave us the opportunity to think about extensions of the study. We are also grateful to the discussants of our conference paper, Philip Daniel and John Spraos, as well as David Sapsford, as an editor of the conference volume, and other conference participants for their helpful comments. The series editor Gordon Gemmill read two drafts of the book and improved the contents and presentation by many critical comments. Helpful comments have also been received from David Elliott, Robert van Schaagen and Jan van Sluisveld. At the University of Giessen, we benefited from the work of Dietmar Weiss whose M.Sc. Thesis provided background material on the commodity protocols (Weiss 1991). Walter Mengel assisted in the quantitative analysis on Chapter 4 and delivered additional background material on the sensitivity of the stabilization impacts of the compensatory financing systems (Mengel 1991). Additionally, Charlotte Hagner,

Frank Plinke and Matthias Schlund assisted in the preparation of the final draft, Karl Schmidt drew several graphs and Margot Hilla typed several versions of Chapters 3–6 and 9. At the Free University in Amsterdam, Arjan Heyma provided valuable computational assistance. Hanneke van Wouwe skilfully unified the text as a whole and took care of the final layout. Many thanks are given to all of them.

Of course, we remain responsible for any remaining errors and insufficiencies.

Roland Herrmann
Kees Burger
Hidde P. Smit
Amsterdam and Giessen

Introduction

For several decades now, the instability of world commodity markets has been a central issue in the north–south dialogue. The proponents of policy interventions argue that excessive market price fluctuations cause negative microeconomic and macroeconomic consequences which can be avoided by stabilization measures. Price stabilization policies, based on buffer stocks or export quotas, and compensatory financing schemes were installed as international measures to stabilize export earnings and to counter the negative consequences of world market instabilities.

Over the years, an enormous literature has evolved on these issues. Arguments for international price stabilization schemes are that pure price stabilization can, 'potentially at least, improve aggregate welfare' (Turnovsky 1978: 143) and that, except for the case of supply-induced fluctuations and a price-elastic import demand, it will contribute to earnings stability (Nguyen 1980) and, hence, to economic growth (Lim 1976). But many authors, for example Newbery and Stiglitz (1981), have argued that compensatory financing is superior as it can stabilize national export earnings directly, whereas market price stabilization does so only under specific conditions. Compensatory financing would not require intervention in international commodity markets and would thus avoid the aggregate welfare losses associated with price-changing commodity agreements.

The analytical literature on price stabilization has dealt with the effects of hypothetical buffer stock schemes which are purely price stabilizing (Behrman 1978a, b; Behrman and Tinakorn-Ramangkura 1982; Nguyen 1980). Other important *ex ante* studies that analyse the impacts of hypothetical market stabilization schemes are Newbery and Stiglitz (1981), Ghosh *et al.* (1987), Gardner (1979) and Williams and Wright (1991). It is typical for those *ex ante* studies to assume stabilization programmes to be well designed and operational and then to proceed with an investigation of the hypothetical impacts on, say, income stability. Similarly, studies stressing that compensatory financing systems are superior to buffer stocks and export quotas have been derived from the assumption of a perfectly stabilizing compensatory financing scheme (Newbery and Stiglitz 1981: 299; Bird 1987). Both branches of the literature lead to assessments that are too favourable compared with the actual performance of commodity initiatives, which are not so ideally designed as is assumed. The literature dealing with *ex post* evaluations of international commodity policies usually contains a detailed description of the arrangements and qualitative judgements on their effectiveness, but does not explicitly model the situations with and without the policy (Gordon-Ashworth 1984; Hoffmeyer *et al.* 1988). Among the exceptions is MacBean and Nguyen (1987b) who combine theoretical *ex ante* considerations on commodity market stabilization with simulation analyses on selected policy instruments.

There is a dearth of studies that evaluate existing commodity policies in a quantitative way, with due consideration of the imperfections that characterize the arrangements and the markets. This is the objective of this book. We analyse whether major commodity policies have reached their primary objectives and to what extent they had economic side-effects. The most important existing compensatory financing schemes and current or recent commodity agreements with price stabilization instruments are covered. On the basis of quantitative analyses on their major impacts, the effectiveness of these commodity initiatives is evaluated. Compared with *ex ante* studies, our approach has the advantage of explicitly incorporating any defects in the design of stabilization programmes or in the way the commodity market operates. In particular, the analysis explicitly accounts for the timing of payments made by compensatory financing schemes, or for the lapse of time between negotiating and the coming into force of an agreement. We show how negotiators have struggled with practical issues like exchange rate changes or choice of currency for the intervention price and we indicate the effects of defective price transmissions between world market and producers. Compared with most *ex post* evaluations, this book provides quantitative information on the effects of the arrangements. The analysis uses a variety of measures for stabilization: reduction of the coefficient of variation, risk benefits, *ex ante* uncertainty reduction both in the short run and on a longer term. Other effects, like transfers induced by the arrangements, are quantified and their redistributive impacts across countries are evaluated.

The study is organized as follows. Part I, 'The politics and economics of commodity agreements and compensatory financing', is an introductory review. Since the major focus of the book is on realized commodity initiatives, we start in Chapter 1 with a survey of 'The history and politics of international commodity agreements and compensatory financing'. In a broad time perspective, the chapter surveys post-war agreements and investigates the relationship between price instability and the existence of agreements. Chapter 2 contains 'The economics of stabilization: a historical survey'. The economic literature on stabilization has developed substantially over time. Development economics literature has moved from MacBean's analysis of 'export instability and growth' to present-day trade shock theory. The microeconomic literature has moved from Marshallian welfare analysis towards the systematic incorporation of expected utility, asymmetric storage functions and separate risk-aversion and time-preference parameters.

Part II of the book deals with the first major option of international commodity policy, i.e. compensatory financing. It is entitled 'Compensatory financing: an economic evaluation of current programmes'. The quantitative evaluation concentrates on three important approaches to compensatory financing: the IMF's Compensatory Financing Facility in Chapter 3, the STABEX system laid down in the Lomé Convention in Chapter 4, entitled 'Commodity-related financial compensation by the European Community', and the cereal import facility as an extension of the traditional Compensatory Financing Facility of the IMF in Chapter 5. The IMF's traditional Compensatory Financing Facility and STABEX focus on export earnings stabilization of developing countries and the cereal import facility combines this with a food-security goal, namely the stabilization of cereal import costs. Chapter 4 also includes two other instruments of development policies by the European Community, namely SYSMIN, which is oriented at the mining sector, and COMPEX, which is supposed to stabilize export earnings of least developed countries which are not signatories to the Lomé Convention.

Part III primarily covers international commodity agreements as the second major option of international commodity policy. Chapter 6 deals with 'The International Coffee Agreement' and evaluates the success of the Third and Fourth International Coffee Agreements in the early 1980s. As we argue that this export quota arrangement was mainly targeted at international income redistribution, the quantitative modelling of these income transfers under the International Coffee Agreement is a key issue of Chapter 6. A special section is devoted to national interests in this agreement; here we investigate the rationale for a country's choice of becoming a member of the Agreement or not. Chapter 7 evaluates 'The International Natural Rubber Agreement' which is the only agreement that has been introduced under UNCTAD's Integrated Programme for Commodities. The stabilization effects of this agreement are quantified by comparing actual data with counterfactual outcomes of a quarterly model. We calculate the reduction in short-term and long-term *ex ante* uncertainty. International income transfers are also computed. Chapter 8 is related to the 'International Cocoa Agreements' of the 1980s. The buffer stock policy under the International Cocoa Agreements was targeted at international price stabilization and its stabilization and transfer effects are investigated by use of an annual world cocoa model. Again, transfers from consumers to producers are calculated. The size of the transfers is enhanced by the lack of price transmission in major producing countries. The extent to which transfers are affected is measured. International commodity policies do not embrace commodity agreements alone but also include other commodity-related initiatives. As an important example, we discuss in Chapter 9 the commodity protocols laid down in the Lomé Convention and provide a quantitative analysis of the impacts of the sugar and beef protocols on objectives of stabilization, redistribution and allocation.

A common feature of Parts II and III is that the effects of major commodity policies are modelled quantitatively. Chapter 10, 'A comparison and evaluation of the arrangements', combines the results and evaluates the various programmes in a comparative manner. Many countries are affected by more than one of the arrangements and the extent of accumulation of benefits is indicated here. Finally, we formulate an answer to the question of whether these types of stabilization arrangements should be continued.

Part I

The politics and economics of commodity agreements and compensatory financing

The emphasis of this book is on a quantitative economic evaluation of international stabilization measures. We shall discuss price stabilization through commodity agreements and export earnings stabilization through compensatory financing. The details of the evaluations are described in Parts II and III of the book and the schemes are compared in a concluding Chapter 10. By way of introduction, Part I is devoted to historical developments in the presence of agreements and in the economists' view of (in)stability.

In most cases in the history of international commodity arrangements, political reality came first and analysis and discussion by economists followed. For that reason and because it is useful to introduce the various types of arrangements first, this part starts off with a review of arrangements and their history. It focuses on the institutional background that will act as a basis for the analysis in quantitative terms in Parts II and III. Such a review was presented in much more detail in, for example, Gordon-Ashworth (1984), Gilbert (1987) and MacBean and Nguyen (1987a). Here we only give a brief summary, because the focus of this book is the quantitative analysis of agreements in economic terms. Chapter 2 reviews the economic debate, looking at both the macroeconomic and the microeconomic side of instability, uncertainty and stabilization.

1 The history and politics of international commodity agreements and compensatory financing

INTRODUCTION

A brief overview of the occurrence of price instability and commodity agreements leads, at first sight, to the conclusion that periods of high price instability are not followed by successful efforts to set up new agreements. The number of active commodity agreements appears very stable over time. In the past, at any point of time some three or four agreements have been operational, but in 1992 only one agreement was left. The overview also suggests that the existence of agreements does not reduce price instability.

This being the case, some sections of this chapter are devoted to general political and economic developments during this century in an effort to assess to what extent the general political and economic context has been conducive to setting up, extending or terminating commodity agreements. The rise and fall of the most significant international commodity agreements is briefly described for each period. An introduction to commodity protocols and compensatory financing schemes is given in the penultimate section and conclusions are presented in the final section.

PRICE INSTABILITY AND THE PREVALENCE OF COMMODITY AGREEMENTS

Owing to colonization, before the Second World War producers and consumers of primary commodities often belonged to countries under the same governments and, as part of the domestic policy, efforts were made to achieve steady availability of raw materials and remunerative and stable prices. The crash of 1929 and the depression that followed, however, created dramatic levels of excess supply and price instability. During the Second World War, J.M. Keynes, the noted economist, suggested that the UK Treasury set up a series of buffer stock arrangements to contribute to reducing what was known as the trade cycle and to promote orderly marketing. Keynes's measure of price instability was in terms of year-to-year percentage price changes. In this section we look at such percentage price changes and introduce the prevalence of commodity agreements for seven important commodities: cocoa, coffee, rubber, sugar, tea, tin and wheat. The political and economic context in which commodity agreements came into existence or fell into inactivity or complete disuse is discussed in some detail in the following sections.

Graphs of nominal prices for the above mentioned seven commodities are shown in Figures 1.1 and 1.2. All prices have been indexed at unity for 1946. It is interesting to see that the four nominal price series in Figure 1.1, for coffee, cocoa, sugar and tin, show some variation during the 1950s and 1960s but appear to be fairly stable when compared with developments during the 1970s and 1980s. Cocoa, coffee and tin reached levels in the late 1970s of almost fifteen times their levels in 1946, while the price of sugar increased up to six times the 1946 level. This is a huge rise compared with the situation of those commodities whose prices are portrayed in Figure 1.2 – rubber, tea and wheat. An interesting feature in this figure is the decline in prices of the three commodities during the 1950s and

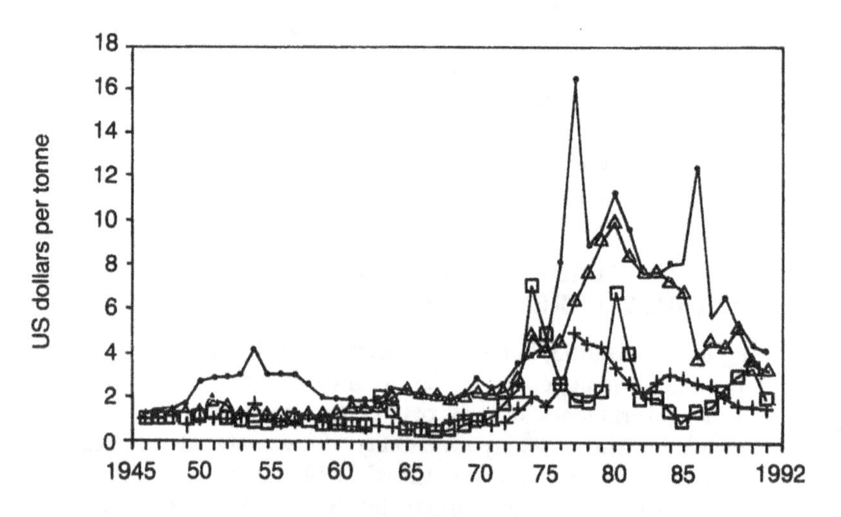

Figure 1.1 Price indices (1946 = 1): —•—, coffee; —+—, cocoa; —□—, sugar; —△—, tin

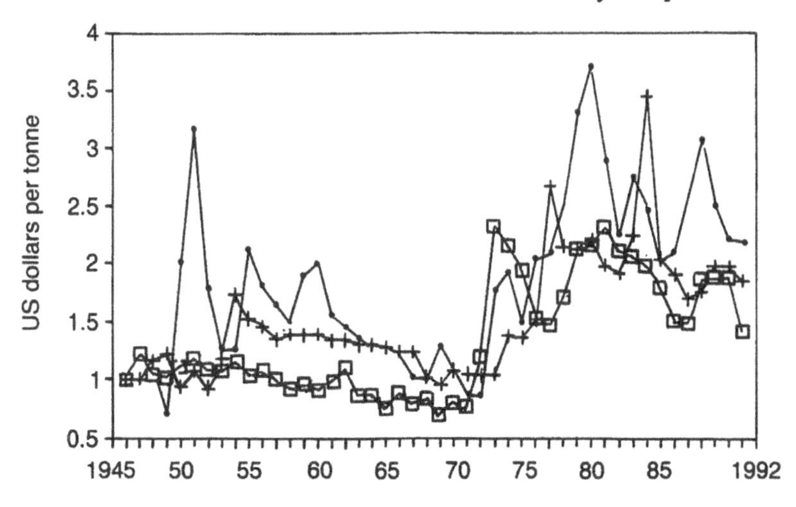

Figure 1.2 Price indices (1946 = 1): —•—, rubber, —+—, tea; —⊡—, wheat

1960s, while reaching levels in the 1970s and 1980s of 'only' two to four times their levels in 1946.

The next question is: during which periods did prices fluctuate most? For that purpose, absolute values of year-to-year percentage changes have been calculated. These are shown in Figure 1.3. From this figure it is clear that prices were very unstable during the first half of the 1950s, while the same applies to the 1970s and to some extent to the latter half of the 1980s.

Is there any relationship between the presence or absence of agreements and the level of price instability? A schematic representation of the presence of agreements for the seven commodities is given in Figure 1.4, along the lines of McNicol (1978). Events in 1929 and the following years have clearly led to commodity agreements (a maximum of five out of seven). However, at no point since then have so many agreements been active. All through the period from the early 1950s to the late 1980s, three or four agreements were functioning. It was at the end of the 1980s that the number dwindled to only one, the International Natural Rubber Agreement (INRA). At first sight at least, the level of instability in prices has not led to a dramatic change in the number of agreements nor has the presence of agreements seemed to have led to greater stability.

In order to look into this matter in more detail, the rise and fall of commodity agreements will be put in their political and economic

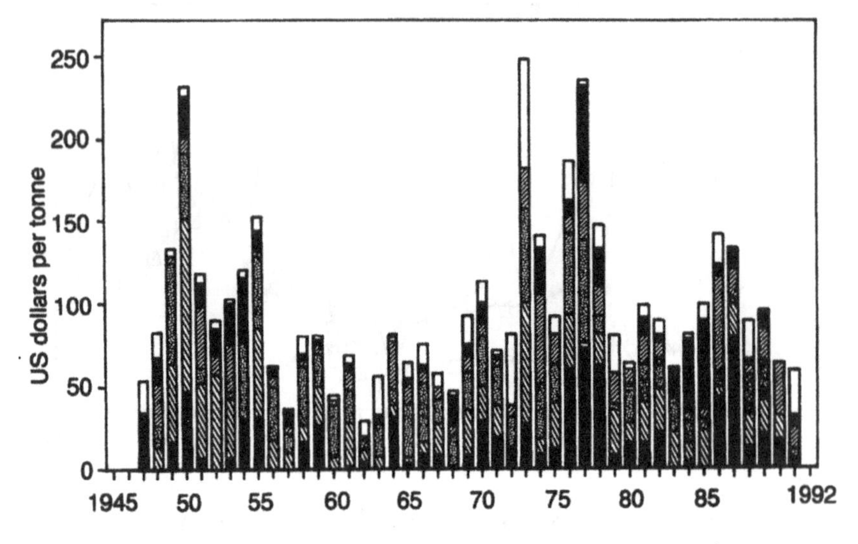

Figure 1.3 Unweighted absolute percentage changes in commodity prices: ■, coffee; ▧, rubber; ▩, cocoa; ▨, tin; ▦, tea; □, wheat

context in the remainder of this chapter in order to assess the more generic aspects of such developments. The century will be split into a number of consecutive periods with similar characteristics as far as attitudes regarding commodity agreements and stabilization arrangements are concerned. We distinguish the pre-war period, the aftermath of the Second World War, the period until roughly 1976 and the most recent time. For each period, whenever appropriate, the birth, life and death of individual commodity agreements will be briefly sketched. For details on many commodities, the reader is referred to J.S. Davis (1946), Law (1975), McNicol (1978), Gordon-Ashworth (1984), Gilbert (1987), MacBean and Nguyen (1987a) and Hoffmeyer *et al.* (1988).

BEFORE THE SECOND WORLD WAR

This period is characterized by a number of specific features. First, owing to colonization producers and consumers of primary commodities often were in one and the same country. Availability of raw materials as well as remunerative and stable prices were in general in the natural interest of both producers and consumers, in particular the colonial powers which ruled both. As early as 1919, at a conference in Versailles, the creation of international agencies to intervene

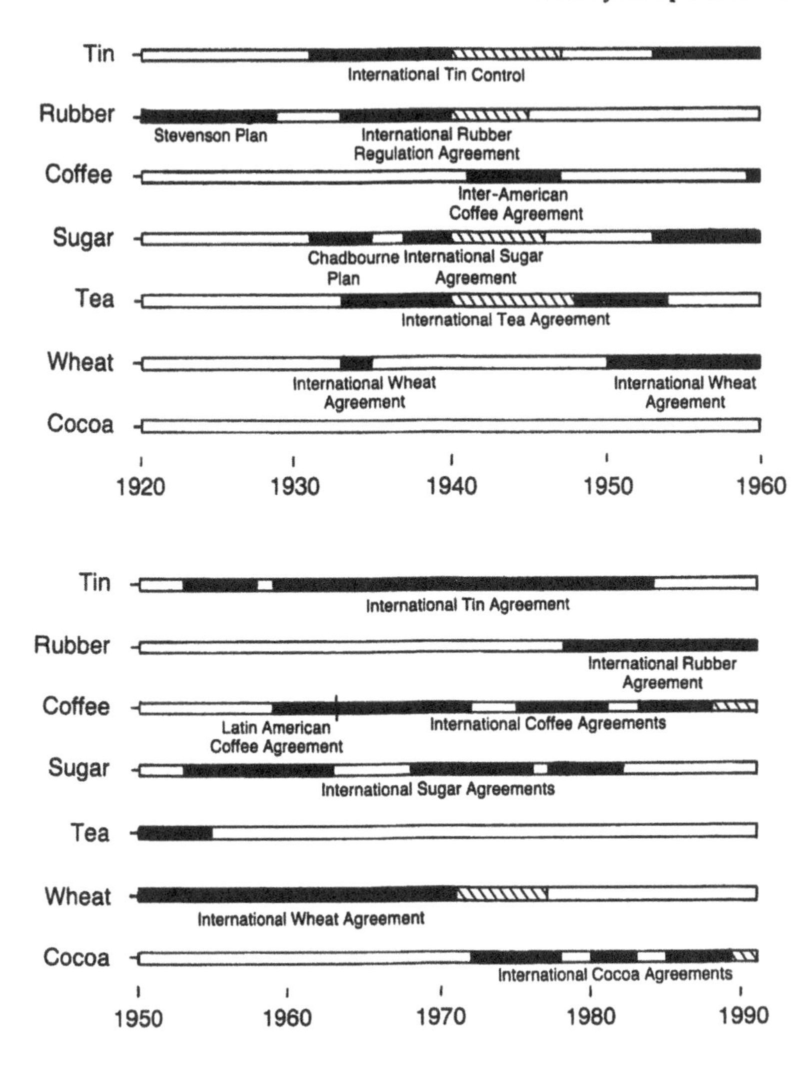

Figure 1.4 Presence of commodity agreements: ■, agreements; ▨, provisions suspended

in commodity markets was considered. During the 1920s, stability and growth had come after the First World War, leading to increases in production capacity for many primary commodities. The crash of 1929 and the consequent depression created dramatic levels of excess supply. This led to a number of agreements during the 1930s, where colonial powers and others tried to restore some order in the markets.

The basic approach is to restrict output. For countries with monopolistic power, this option is readily available. An example is the 'valorization scheme' for coffee introduced by Brazil as early as 1906–7, when prices had dropped dramatically. The scheme continued in one way or another until 1937. Millions of sacks of coffee were burned, in particular in 1933 and 1937. Efforts to obtain agreement with other producers were not successful at the time. Competing coffee-producing countries expanded their production as well as their market share at the expense of Brazil.

The natural rubber market provides an example of monopoly turning into duopoly. Following the rubber boom in 1909–10, the acreage under rubber was rapidly expanded, leading to oversupply. In 1917 and in 1920 the Malayan rubber industry (the British Rubber Growers' Association) set up voluntary restriction schemes, followed by a compulsory restriction scheme in 1922, the Stevenson Plan. The Dutch (East Indies) refused to join. After some increased output by the Dutch in 1926, additional restrictions were imposed by the British, but the resulting increase in prices was more beneficial to the Dutch than to the British. After the crash of 1929, US consumption virtually vanished, and prices dropped from four shillings in 1925 to one and a half pence in 1932. At last, the Dutch became interested in joint control and in 1934 the International Rubber Regulation Agreement (IRRA) was accepted by almost all producers, aiming at regulating exports, stabilizing prices and reducing stocks to normal levels through a system of export controls and the prohibition of new planting. The basic implicit objective according to Davis (1946) was to prevent liquidation of estate companies and to hold in check the gradual encroachment of lower-cost native producers by means of production quotas for estates as well as for native producers.

In the case of tea, as for rubber, the British planters started to control output, but their main competitors, the Dutch East Indies, did not cooperate until after further price falls in the second half of the 1920s. This situation worsened further during the depression. In this period, tea exporters agreed on a system of export quotas with government assistance. The scheme was moderately successful in supporting the price and was followed by further agreements in 1938 and 1943.

The same two colonial powers joined hands in raising the price of tin. In the Bandoeng Pool of 1921, agreements were made on withholding stocks. The agreement was later followed by a private international tin pool operating in the same manner and by successive tin agreements in 1931 and 1933 that had export quotas as an instrument. By agreement in 1935, a buffer stock instrument was added.

Led by the same two powers, but in a more multi-national setting, agreement was reached in 1902 on sugar. Over-expansion of beet production was the main reason for sliding sugar prices, which in turn led to the Brussels Convention of 1902. The Convention prohibited the payment of bounties on exported sugar but permitted the UK and the Netherlands to grant preferential tariff arrangements for their colonial sugar imports. As was the case for many commodities, prices slumped around 1930. This led to the Chadbourne Agreement by exporters in 1931, initiated by Cuba. One additional reason for the fall in prices was the discovery of a new sugar cane variety in Java, which brought a strong increase in yields. The objective of the Chadbourne Agreement was to divide exports to the USA among members of the Agreement. Some 60 per cent of all sugar exporters were in the Agreement. Outsiders such as the British Empire, Japan, Taiwan and the USSR increased their production and thus spoilt the game: the Agreement fell apart in 1935. The 1937 International Sugar Conference made a new start by bringing together producers as well as importers. The 1937 Sugar Agreement that resulted only applied to the free market.

The First International Wheat Agreement came into existence in 1933 to reduce surpluses and increase prices. The major policy instrument was export restraint, while an increase in growing area was prohibited. The Agreement lasted for only one year, however, because Argentina dumped her bumper crop on the market.

THE IMMEDIATE POST-SECOND WORLD WAR PERIOD

Before and during the war, John Maynard Keynes had suggested that the UK Treasury set up a series of buffer stock arrangements to contribute to reducing the trade cycle and to promote orderly marketing. The idea never became very popular, but some interest in commodity agreements was present, as is clear from provisions in the Havana Charter of 1948. The Charter prohibited agreements leading to price fixing, the allocation of market shares or collusion in the instituting of export restrictions. International agreements were permissible exceptions, provided that the aim was price stabilization or the elimination of burdensome surpluses.

The early part of the post-war period was one of shortages in many commodities, as demand was picking up more quickly than supply. However, it was not long before supply overtook demand again. This first led to efforts to set up study groups and similar bodies for various commodities such as cotton, rubber, wheat, tea and sugar. During the Korean crisis, acute shortages emerged for some commodities and their prices soared. Consequently, consumer governments pressed for stabilization agreements and the major countries proposed study groups for a long list of commodities. The emphasis of international attention was increasingly directed towards price stabilization.

Under the Havana Charter, the First International Sugar Agreement (ISA) was concluded in 1953, running from 1954 to 1958 and being dominated by Cuba. In 1959, a second agreement followed.

In 1954, a new Tin Agreement became operational after many years of negotiating. Both export quotas and a buffer stock of 25,000 tonnes were applied. This Agreement covered a relatively hectic period, including unpredictable US stockpile activities and sales by the USSR.

For both coffee and tea, exporting countries joined forces, but only coffee exporters managed some degree of control by export quota. At first only the Latin American coffee producers were involved, but the UK, France and Portugal (with their colonies) joined later. The emergence of Africa as a tea exporter made it impossible to agree on export quotas within the tea community.

Finally, some agreement was reached on wheat. After special post-war controls, a new Agreement was concluded in 1948, excluding Argentina and the USSR. It contained provisions for prices and allocation of export quotas. Within its limited coverage it was fairly successful in supporting the price of wheat (Gordon-Ashworth 1984). With some modifications in the terms and in membership, the Agreement was renewed in 1953, 1956 and 1959. The International Wheat Council, however, considered its direct effects only limited.

THE DEVELOPMENT AID PERIOD

From the middle of the 1950s onward, the focus of commodity policy formulation by commodity-exporting developing countries shifted towards the need to enhance commodity prices as a tool to boost and stabilize foreign-exchange earnings. This approach was well received in many developed countries, where it was seen as a strong instrument to help the poor underdeveloped countries. This evolved as part of the aftermath of the decolonization period. Higher and more stable commodity prices would then be among the tools. International commodity arrangements obtained a place on the international agenda.

During the early part of this period, the predominant idea in development cooperation circles was that the results of growth in export earnings, and thus in national income, would trickle down and by themselves alleviate the living standards of the poor. In addition, the ultimate producers would benefit directly from better prices.

Furthermore, fairly stable exchange earnings and domestic income flows would help governments to satisfy the tremendous need for infrastructural investments, most of which require a large share of imported goods. This was particularly important from the point of view of developed countries exporting capital goods as well as for creating stable supply conditions in developing producer countries. Such a policy orientation was also made possible because of the change in the political environment in the USA in the 1960s under Presidents Kennedy and Johnson. In the latter half of the 1960s, however, the atmosphere changed again, with the Vietnam War capturing most of the attention and Nixon becoming President of the USA in 1968.

UNITED NATIONS CONFERENCE ON TRADE AND DEVELOPMENT

Almost all efforts regarding international commodity arrangements took place under the auspices of or were initiated and organized by the United Nations. The major events of the period in this respect were the establishment in 1964 of the United Nations Conference on Trade and Development (UNCTAD) as a permanent United Nations body and the periodic sessions of the Conference. The United Nations General Assembly in 1974 adopted the Declaration and the Programme of Action on the Establishment of a New International Economic Order, including the need for an Integrated Programme for Commodities (IPC).

In furtherance of this Declaration, UNCTAD, at its Fourth Session in Nairobi in 1976, adopted Resolution 93 (IV) regarding the IPC. The resolution includes in its objectives the intention to create 'stable conditions in commodity trade, including avoidance of excessive price fluctuations' and to protect developing countries 'from fluctuations in export earnings, especially from commodities'.

The commodities to be included under the IPC were, in alphabetical order, bananas, bauxite, cocoa, coffee, copper, cotton and cotton yarns, hard fibres and products, iron ore, jute and products, manganese, meat, phosphates, rubber, sugar, tea, tin, tropical timber and vegetable oils. Provisions were made for the inclusion of other commodities as well. At an earlier stage wheat, rice and wool were also included.

UNCTAD IV agreed in principle on the need for a financial institution, the Common Fund for Commodities (CFC), to support the IPC. Not until 1979 was agreement reached that the CFC was to consist of two 'accounts'. The first account was to be used for financing buffer stocks, while the second account was to be used for other measures such as research and development. Buffer stocking was to be used in particular for ten core commodities: cocoa, coffee, copper, cotton, jute, rubber, sisal, sugar, tea and tin.

It took eight more years before enough countries had ratified the Agreement for it to come into force and for the CFC to prepare for operation. At the time of writing (early 1992), commodity organizations have been designated, the so-called International Commodity Bodies (ICBs), entitled to submit projects to the second account of the CFC. One of the criteria for a commodity organization to become an ICB is that both producers and consumers are members of the organization. The first account of the CFC is still inactive.

The initial political interest and efforts in commodity arrangements came at a time when commodity prices turned from stable low levels into highly unstable and occasionally very high levels, as can be clearly seen from Figures 1.1–1.3. The events during the 1970s made many countries again put adequate and stable supplies of raw materials higher on the agenda. An example was the relative shortage of gasoline and electricity during the mid-1970s in the USA. However, this concern did not change the basic position of the USA as the major consumer of most commodities. Throughout this period the USA in principle rejected the idea of commodity agreements but was prepared to consider support for commodity agreements on a case-by-case basis. This position was later shared more explicitly by countries such as the UK.

Without support from the USA, the International Tin Agreements were extended throughout this period. After successive increases in the target price range, the buffer stock started buying when prices fell in 1967. The export control provisions were activated in 1968 but proved unnecessary as prices rose again.

It was largely for political reasons, in particular after the Cuban missile crisis, that the USA announced its willingness to join a coffee price stabilization agreement in the early 1960s. In 1962 the First International Coffee Agreement (ICA) came into force. A price range was included to trigger market intervention by means of export quotas. The approach was strongly supported by Brazil and

Colombia, who were most eager to preserve their market shares. On the importing side, checks on where the coffee originated were supposed to provide a monitoring and controlling system for the export control system in the producing countries. No complex pricing rules were specified.

Having been reasonably successful in bringing about fairly stable prices, but at the expense of huge stock withdrawals (particularly by Brazil), the Agreement was renewed. The 1968 Coffee Agreement first experienced oversupply due to liquidation of inventories in the USA and huge low-price selling by Brazil. No settlement could be reached on the necessary cutback in export quotas. A steep increase in price owing to the news of a severe frost in Brazil roughly restored equilibrium between supply and demand. The higher prices in the early 1970s, together with so-called unfair undercutting of the North American soluble coffee market by Brazil, caused support to fade and the USA withdrew from the negotiations. Law (1975) claims that the First Agreement strongly increased instability in the market. The Agreement was extended to 1975, but without economic provisions. In the meantime the Agreement was replaced by a few producer arrangements.

The Cuba crisis led the USA to ban all sugar imports from Cuba into the USA. After this major disruption of the sugar market it took until 1968 before a new agreement was reached, including producer-held stock and export quotas as instruments. However, when prices went through the upper limit stocks were hardly released. In 1973, the economic provisions were dropped from the agreement.

Under the auspices of UNCTAD, negotiations were held on an International Cocoa Agreement (ICCA), which was finally concluded in 1972 after earlier talks in 1963 (under the FAO umbrella) had failed. In 1964, five major exporters had started a quota system, but the ICCA contained provisions for both export quotas and a buffer stock. The instruments did not become operational, however, as prices rose sharply in 1973.

THE LATE 1970s AND 1980s

During the late 1970s, it was already clear that the expectations aroused by the numerous UNCTAD meetings would not be met. This created frustration in various quarters, resulting in producers wanting more and quicker action, while supporters of development assistance and cooperation in consuming countries were losing patience and idealism. The frustration was further fed by the recession of the early 1980s.

This recession, combined with high inflation and high interest rates, had a very depressing effect on consumption and inventory demand for commodities. This was enforced by technological development that significantly reduced consumption of raw materials per unit of output of the final product. Producing countries, on the other hand, had dramatically increased productive capacity for most commodities in reaction to buoyant prices in the late 1970s. This resulted in a situation of oversupply in most commodity markets. Consumer stocks were relatively low because of high interest rates, and they remained at that level. As a consequence, prices were kept under serious pressure, leading to a serious and fairly steady drop in prices during the 1980s, as seen in Figures 1.1 and 1.2. This trend weakened the bargaining position of producing countries and reduced the willingness of importing countries to renegotiate existing commodity agreements or to negotiate new ones.

Tin

Following events at UNCTAD and the United Nations General Assembly, the USA and the USSR were among the members of the Fifth International Tin Agreement (ITA). Prices went up sharply in 1976 and 1977 because of the weak supply situation and steady growth in demand. All the buffer stock was sold and the ITA was unable to defend the ceiling of the price range.

The Sixth ITA, concluded in 1980 again along similar lines, became operational in 1982. Until 1985, the International Tin Council (ITC) was almost completely successful in defending the floor price. However, the Sixth ITA had the problem of limited participation, not including the largest consumer, the USA, and the third largest producer, Bolivia. For a number of reasons, including additional supply, in particular from Brazil, prices entered a downward trend. In 1985, the buffer stock manager was no longer able to defend the floor price. For further information the reader is referred to Fox (1974), Robertson (1982), Anderson and Gilbert (1988) and Kimmig (1989). Obviously, only the recent publications cover the collapse of the Agreement.

Coffee

In 1976 the Third ICA was concluded, the economic clauses of which resembled those of the 1968 Agreement. A new feature was the formal introduction of price ranges in combination with an indicator

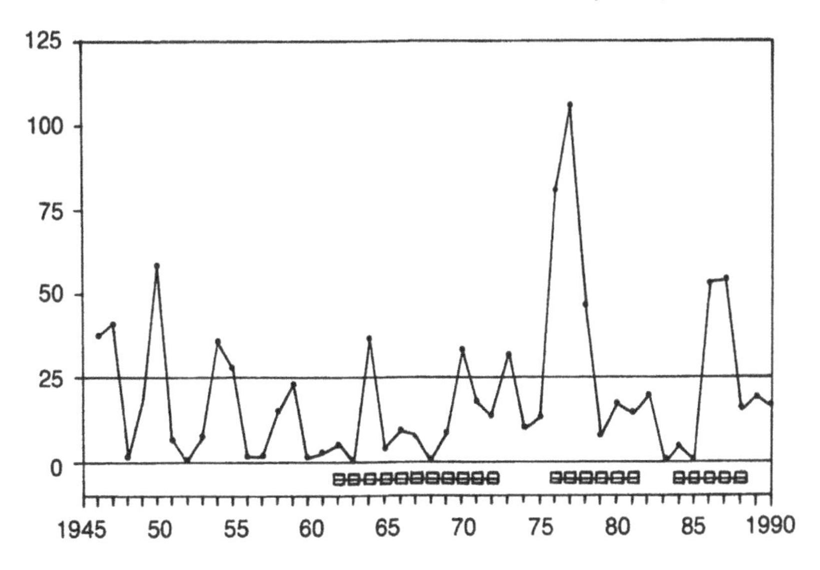

Figure 1.5 Year-to-year percentage changes (in absolute terms) in price and the presence of an agreement for coffee: -⊟-, International Coffee Agreement periods

price, which remained inoperative until 1980. Owing to frost in Brazil, prices doubled between 1975 and 1976 and, for a number of reasons, more than trebled in 1977 compared with 1975. Subsequent negotiations between producers and consumers failed as a consequence of the unwillingness of consumers to accede to producers' demands for high price levels. Eight Latin American producers then organized themselves in the Bogota Group for the purpose of preventing prices from falling by intervening on the New York and London markets. This operation failed, and consequently producers expressed their willingness to negotiate with consumers, resulting in the economic provisions of the 1976 Agreement being activated in 1980. Prices were kept within the agreed range by withholding some 12 million bags.

The setting in which the 1983 Agreement, the Fourth ICA, was concluded was the need for structural adjustment to avoid overproduction. By and large, it contained the same provisions as the 1976 Agreement. In the late 1980s it did not prove possible to negotiate a new agreement, because of serious disagreement between producers on the system of distribution of quotas between types of coffee and thus between producing countries and regions. There was

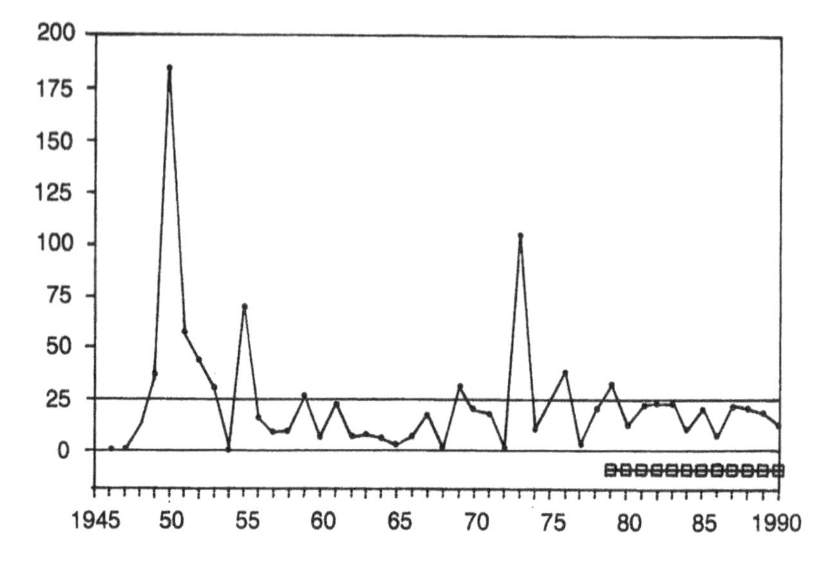

Figure 1.6 Year-to-year percentage changes (in absolute terms) in price and the presence of an agreement for natural rubber; -⊟-, International Natural Rubber Agreement period

no flexibility, either, in changing the market shares of different qualities in response to market demand for the better quality coffees. Another problem was the frustration of consumer countries because of sales at a substantial discount to non-member countries, in particular in the East European market. This led to suspension of the quota system in the middle of 1989, triggering a fall in prices in the year 1989 of about 50 per cent. A detailed evaluation of the early years of the ICA is given in Chapter 6. An impression of the volatility of prices can be obtained from Figure 1.5, which includes bars representing the presence of an agreement.

Natural rubber

As a result of UNCTAD's IPC in 1979, the INRA of 1979 was established. Thus, this Agreement became the first new international commodity agreement successfully negotiated under the IPC. An international natural rubber buffer stock was established that should keep prices within a range that could be changed on a regular basis. For further details see Chapter 7, in particular Figure 7.1. The INRA was extended for two years until 1987 when a new Agreement was negotiated on broadly the same terms as the previous Agreement.

In Figure 1.6 year-to-year percentage changes (in absolute terms) in price are shown, indicating the degree of instability. The bar in the figure represents the presence of an agreement.

After coming into force in 1980, the INRA was soon confronted with a weak market situation and heavy purchases were made by the buffer stock manager. Further purchases were made in 1985. In 1987 prices rose steeply and before the expiration date of the First Agreement a considerable part of the stock was sold by the buffer stock manager. This sale continued in 1988, and the last few thousand tonnes were sold in 1989. In the first half of 1990, prices dropped again, and the buffer stock manager purchased some 30,000 tonnes. To this was added another 70,000 tonnes in 1992. In Chapter 7, a description of the main economic elements of the First INRA is given. The impact is assessed, its performance is evaluated and some alternatives are also discussed.

Cocoa

A new 1976 Agreement came into force in a downward phase of the price cycle after the 1976–7 peak. A higher price range was accepted, but the market price was above the price range. In 1981, a new Agreement came into operation having only a buffer stock as the basic economic provision, with a maximum of 250,000 tonnes and a price range of 100–150 US cents per pound. Export or production controls were not included. The largest producer, Côte d'Ivoire, did not join because it wanted prices at a higher level, and it withheld cocoa from the market to achieve that aim. The USA, the largest consuming country, did not join either, because it considered the price range to be too high. Prices went down strongly, and buffer stock purchases of over 100,000 tonnes only provided a very temporary rise in prices and were insufficient to prevent a further fall afterwards, as purchases were less than that crop year's production surplus. Available finance did not permit more purchases by the buffer stock manager. Furthermore, the appreciation of the US dollar made operations even more difficult for the International Cocoa Organization.

After intensive negotiations, the Fourth ICCA came into force in 1986. New aspects were a price range in special drawing rights (SDRs) and a semi-automatic adjustment of the price range. Still, purchases of another 150,000 tonnes by the buffer stock could not keep prices within the range. The earlier high prices had contributed to large-scale planting in Malaysia and Indonesia, which now entered the market. Disputes over the clauses on automatic revision of the price range prevented further operations and the economic provisions were suspended in 1990. An analysis of the cocoa market and an evaluation of the performance of the cocoa agreement is given in Chapter 8. Figure 1.7 gives year-to-year percentage changes (in absolute terms) in price and includes bars indicating the presence of an agreement.

PROPOSED AND REALIZED COMPENSATORY FINANCING SCHEMES

The policy dialogue concerning export earnings stabilization schemes started later than that on price stabilization and commodity agreements. Whereas proposals for international price stabilization date back to the early 1930s, an intensive discussion on compensatory financing developed in the 1950s and 1960s. There were basically two reasons behind the proposals for export earnings stabilization at that time. First, a relatively sceptical view had emerged on price-stabilizing international commodity agreements. Their introduction had proved to be difficult because of varying national interests and, moreover, after being introduced, they had often failed to reach their

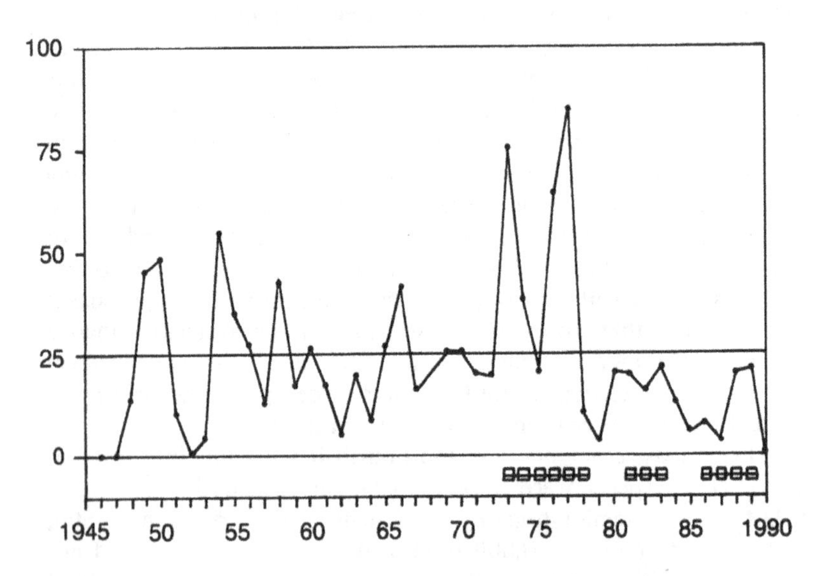

Figure 1.7 Year-to-year percentage changes (in absolute terms) in price and the presence of an agreement for cocoa: -⊟-, International Cocoa Agreement period

primary objectives. Second, the view had become widespread that export earnings instability has detrimental effects on the economic growth of developing countries. Thus, the view predominated that there is a need for some form of compensation of export earnings instability (Lovasy 1965; Expert Group 1985).

The export earnings stabilization schemes under discussion had included very different features regarding their transfer component, the earnings variable to be stabilized and the administration of the system (Hirschler 1978; Expert Group 1985). The discussion of the 1960s was dominated by three different types of proposal. The first one was to introduce something like an insurance system for export earnings shortfalls. In 1961, for example, an expert group at the United Nations suggested the creation of a Development Insurance Fund (United Nations 1961). It was designed like a social insurance system combining stabilization objectives with redistributive elements in favour of developing countries. The second type of proposal was directed at the short-term compensation of export earnings shortfalls by increasing the amount of international credit facilities. The scheme developed by an expert group of the Organization of American States (1962) belongs to this category, as does the International Monetary Fund's (IMF's) Compensatory Financing Facility (CFF) created in 1963. Both systems aimed at the short-term stabilization of national export earnings, i.e. balance-of-payments stabilization. A third type of compensatory financing scheme was oriented at longer-term stabilization of export earnings and was primarily advocated by the World Bank in the 1960s. The rationale was that a mere short-term stabilization of export earnings could not deal with cases where not only are export earnings temporarily low but medium-term efforts are necessary to reach a sustainable level of exports. The World Bank's approach was given serious attention in intergovernmental discussions between 1964 and 1973 but did not in the end lead to the implementation of an additional compensatory financing scheme.

Although the World Bank's proposals were not realized, renewed interest in compensatory financing arose in the 1970s owing to the increasing price instability in world commodity markets. The most important result was that STABEX came into force in 1975 with the new EC–ACP Lomé Convention. Different from the IMF's CFF, STABEX deals with shortfalls in export earnings for individual commodities and not with shortfalls in national export earnings. It aims at earnings stabilization, too, but also includes more redistributive elements than the IMF's CFF.

The major policy changes after the introduction of the IMF and the EC schemes were extensions of these two systems. The financial framework of the IMF's CFF was significantly increased over time, starting from a very limited access of up to 25 per cent of a member's quota from 1963 to 1966, and rising to 50 per cent (from 1966 to 1975) and 75 per cent (from 1975). It has been increased further in several recent extensions of the system. Since 1979, the facility has referred to shortfalls in receipts from tourism and workers' remittances in addition to traditional export earnings. In 1981, the scheme was extended by providing the option of being compensated for increases in cereal import costs, too. In 1987, the Compensatory and Contingency Financing Facility was established with the possibility of additional support in the case of balance-of-payments problems, provided that a country has joined IMF-supported adjustment programmes. The drawings under this new facility are now limited to 122 per cent of the national quota. All these modifications were important steps towards a comprehensive balance-of-payments stabilization policy.

Analogously, the coverage of STABEX has increased in the course of the various Lomé Conventions. It now includes forty-four products, and the list of potential user countries has risen to sixty-nine. The funds were raised, too, and with Lomé II a financial stabilization policy for the mining sector – SYSMIN – was created, besides the primarily agriculture-oriented STABEX scheme. Additionally, the basic elements of STABEX were brought into the so-called COMPEX scheme, which was founded in 1987 by the EC in order to stabilize commodity-related export earnings of non-associated least developed countries.

Apart from these modifications, the major difference between the IMF and the EC system remained. The IMF scheme aims at balance-of-payments stabilization, even more so nowadays, and STABEX is oriented at the stabilization of commodity export earnings.

Beyond the main policy actions, a continuous intergovernmental discussion has taken place on the issue of compensatory financing. Several initiatives were taken to increase the potential of compensatory financing, including separate proposals by the USA, Sweden and the Federal Republic of Germany. The USA recommended additional compensatory financing measures in 1975. In 1977 and 1978, Sweden and the Federal Republic of Germany respectively suggested the introduction of a new compensatory financing scheme in order to stabilize total export earnings arising from an aggregate of important commodities. UNCTAD participated actively in the discussion of export earnings stabilization, too. Compensatory financing was part of the IPC. In 1976, at UNCTAD IV in Nairobi, it was adopted as one of various measures meant to increase the stability of commodity markets. In Resolution 125 (V) in 1979, the Secretary General of UNCTAD was asked to prepare a detailed study for the operation of a complementary facility for commodity-related shortfalls in export earnings. Consequently, UNCTAD produced a series of reports on the issue (UNCTAD 1984a, 1986, 1988a) and an expert group ended up in 1985 with a proposal to introduce a new commodity-specific facility (Expert Group 1985; Lim 1991). It was argued by the expert group that existing programmes do not sufficiently deal with the causes of supply instability. Hence, non-automatic loans should be given to countries that are signatory to a multi-year programme addressing the causes of supply instability. This proposal has not yet been realized.

It is a general feature of the political discussion on compensatory financing that it was fairly benevolent. Governments of market-oriented economies viewed export earnings stabilization as a market-neutral alternative to more dirigistic commodity agreements. Proponents of commodity agreements such as the UNCTAD Secretariat regarded them as a necessary supplement to commodity market stabilization in order to reduce remaining instabilities in the balance of payments and in commodity earnings. A real opposition to compensatory financing did not exist.

CONCLUSIONS

In this chapter we have given a survey of prices, commodity agreements and compensatory financing in the past decades.

The brief overview showed that prices of major commodities like coffee and sugar have fluctuated much less in the 1950s and 1960s than in the last two decades. Their prices went up to fifteen times (coffee) and six times (sugar) the levels of 1946. For other commodities, like rubber and tea, the distinction was less pronounced. The maximum price was two or four times the 1946 price.

We have tried to relate the existence of commodity agreements to prices. The first question was whether instability has caused the participants to come together and decide on an agreement. Looking at Figures 1.3 and 1.4, it is clear that this is not likely. Especially in the early 1950s, the years around 1975 and around 1986, there were periods in which large price changes took place. But the starting of agreements did not follow suit. Nor were prices more stable during the periods in which agreements were operational. Thus, although agreements have stability of prices among their prime goals, no clear relationship between the two can be seen at first sight.

In this historical overview of commodity agreements, we have pointed to some other factors. Agreements before the Second World War were in general between a few contracting partners and had all the characteristics of cartels. Likewise, many of the later agreements had export control as their main instruments. If not combined with buffer stocks, either international or domestic, export quotas can only lead to higher prices. In spite of this tendency, many agreements that were negotiated in the post-war period were endorsed by consuming countries. Initially, many colonial powers approved on behalf of their colonies; later they may have done so out of regard for their former colonies, or as part of a more general development aid policy. We also indicated that geopolitical factors have played an important role, especially at the height of the cold war.

The international bodies that were established, especially UNCTAD, have greatly contributed to the debate on commodity price stabilization. They have also been instrumental in the negotiations on some of the agreements. But they have not been able to give commodity trade the place in the international economic coordination framework that was originally envisaged by Keynes. The Havana Charter and UNCTAD's IPC came some way, but were not made operational.

Keynes's selection of commodities in the 1930s (maize, sugar, coffee, rubber, cotton, wool and tin), however, was largely met by the later agreements. Cotton and wool were dropped from the list, no doubt because of their declining importance as synthetics came up. Maize was replaced by wheat. Cocoa has been added, as it gained in importance in later years, but has all the characteristics that make coffee eligible for intervention. And the same holds for tea. Hence, as to the selection of commodities, *nil novi sub sole.*

Whereas most of the commodity agreements lapsed after some time, one financial arrangement has been in continuous existence since 1963. The IMF's CFF has even gradually expanded over time to include more types of export revenues, import costs of cereals and a contingency facility. In this way, it should have provided some compensation for the lack of commodity price stability. The STABEX programme, started in 1975 between the EC and over sixty developing countries, is more directed towards commodities. Other proposals were made, aiming at financial support for more structural adjustment of commodity-producing countries, but have not been realized.

2 The economics of stabilization

A historical survey

INTRODUCTION

In this chapter we provide a survey of how economists have looked at the problem of instability. We shall distinguish between macroeconomics and microeconomics. The macroeconomic literature, focusing on benefits of stabilization at the country level, is reviewed in the following section. The microeconomic literature is discussed in the third section, where we start with the Waugh–Oi–Massell framework and then discuss nine reasons why this framework is too simple.

Whereas the earlier approaches, like Keynes's, dealt specifically with variability, i.e. changes over time, the later microeconomic approaches looked at the issue as being one of uncertainty. We shall first discuss some contributions in the field of macroeconomics or development economics. Although stability is probably among the goals of any government, its advantages are not clearly specified, let alone quantified. The early focus of the publications on primary commodity price stabilization appears to be on its contribution to mitigating the amplitude of the trade cycle and during the 1950s and 1960s on raising the purchasing power of the less developed countries. More recent contributions have focused on the optimal response to permanent and – still later – transitory shocks to the economy. While the older papers consider countries as the unit of analysis, these contributions clearly distinguish between the government and private sectors, thus providing a much richer picture. In addition, it appears that authors in the 1950s and 1960s looked at governments of less developed countries benevolently, contrary to present-day authors who consider the private sector as much more resembling *homo economicus* than the government.

Initially the microeconomics literature measured benefits from stabilization as Marshallian surpluses, and later used a more sophisticated expected-utility framework. The microeconomics of uncertainty is a strongly growing field of research and the development of adequate models, able to capture the individual's attitude towards present and future uncertainty, appears not to have reached maturity yet, fed as it is by a host of experiments in a mixed field of psychology and economics (see Machina's (1987) survey). Although the expected-utility approach lends itself perfectly to the analysis of stabilization issues, it is doubtful whether substantial arguments for or against world market price stabilization can be derived from it. This is not only because so many outcomes of this type of analysis can be of either sign, nor because eventual benefits are estimated to be so small, but rather because (a) individual producers do not experience as much variability as suggested by the variability of the prices, (b) what is experienced is the outcome of microeconomic and macroeconomic interaction of various economic agents, including the government and random events, and (c) the economic and social environment in which individuals find themselves (access to information, infrastructure, financial facilities, etc.) is much more important (see Kanbur 1984). This is not to say that stabilization of prices is unimportant. On the contrary, we think that the development of provisions that would enable individuals to mitigate the economic risks goes hand in hand with price stabilization.

MACROECONOMICS AND DEVELOPMENT ECONOMICS

When Keynes wrote in 1942 that 'we should aim at combining a short-period stability of prices with a long-period price policy which balances supply and demand and allows a steady rate of expansion to the cheaper-cost producers' (Keynes 1974: 301), he based his arguments on the experiences in the then recent past, in which prices had fluctuated enormously. The average annual price range (yearly high over yearly low) observed in the period 1928–37 for (natural) rubber, cotton, lead and wheat amounted in his calculations to no less than 67 per cent. The most volatile price, that of rubber, had a score of less than 70 per cent only in one year. When we compare this with present-day figures, it appears that 'the extent of the evil' has been much reduced: the highest scores for natural rubber in the recent past are 63 per cent in 1981 and 50 per cent in 1988.[1] Keynes suggests that the cause of the fluctuations in prices is on the supply side and that major contributors to the instability of prices are the reluctance of traders, manufacturers and retailers to hold stocks, because of uncertainty and high storage costs, and the practices of speculators. Compared with the 1930s, many improvements have been made in the field of information, futures markets have developed and specialized traders can benefit from economies of scale in storage. This must have been a major contribution to reducing the extent of short-term price fluctuations. Keynes mentions two advantages of price stabilization: it would enable an 'orderly programme of output' both of the raw materials and of their manufactured products and it would reduce the amplitude of the trade cycle by keeping up effective demand during the slump. The ideal was to combine short-term stability and medium-term stability via the contribution to effective demand in recessionary years and a 'long-period price policy which balances supply and demand'. But Keynes himself admitted that a great deal of trial and error would be required to find out what the equilibrium price should be.

The short-term aspects appear to have been back-stage in the 1950s and 1960s. After the Havana Charter of 1948 (which did actually recommend the introduction of buffer stocks, export restrictions and trade at fixed prices), the emphasis was on the supposedly declining terms of trade of developing countries, and Kaldor wrote in 1962, at the request of Raoul Prebisch, then Executive Secretary of the Economic Commission for Latin America, a proposal in which it was suggested that prices be 'stabilized at, say, 10% above their current level' (Kaldor 1964: 114). He also considered the sugar, tin and coffee agreements successful in 'stabilizing prices at a higher level than would have been attained without them' (p. 115). Enzo Grilli and Maw Cheng Yang (1988) have recently returned to the issue of the trend in terms of trade. They have shown that there is a long-run tendency for primary commodity prices, especially of agricultural raw materials, to decline over time relative to the price of manufactures, thus confirming the Prebisch–Singer findings, but that the increased demand for and production of these goods more than compensate for the relative decline in prices. Scandizzo and Diakosavvas (see Scandizzo and Diakosavvas 1987 and Diakosavvas and Scandizzo 1991) addressed the same issue and concluded that 'there is some justification in suspecting a negative bias in the movement of international trade in primary commodities and that the evidence is insufficient to warrant firm conclusions on the matter' (1987: 161).

Kaldor, Hart and Tinbergen, in 1964, emphasized again the contribution to attenuation of trade cycle effects in their paper on an international commodity reserve currency, reproduced in Kaldor (1964). Such a currency, expressed in the prices of a range of primary commodities, would provide stability to the export earnings of primary commodity producers and thereby enhance their purchasing power in recessionary periods. The effects would be 'supermultiplied' by induced investments in the primary producing sector during those years (p. 164). Although this idea came up from time to time in later years, it has never gained substantial political support from the developed countries.

With the establishment of the United Nations Conference on Trade and Development (UNCTAD) in 1965, numerous studies have been made on the potential contribution that stabilized export earnings could make to the economic growth of developing countries. In 1966, MacBean published his results on whether or not fluctuating export earnings are harmful to the growth of developing countries. His findings that no hard case could be made for positive effects of stability aroused great interest and the research has been replicated many times: see Knudsen and Parnes (1975), Adams and Behrman (1982) and Behrman (1987). Herrmann (1981, 1988a) provides a thorough discussion; a comprehensive overview of the literature on instability and economic growth is given by Love (1987). Most authors are reluctant to admit that stability would not contribute and gave stabilization the 'benefit of the doubt'. The discussion often centres on how investments are affected by instability of export earnings. On the one hand a more uncertain future deters investments, but on the other hand unstable income might induce more savings and thereby more investments. Lim (1991) surveys the issue again and concludes (again) that 'the results do not overwhelmingly support the case for or against export instability' (p. 49).

After the enormous changes in prices and exchange rates that occurred in the early 1970s, emphasis appears to have shifted from analyses in which less developed countries were treated as one block towards more disaggregated studies in which a further distinction was made within the country models themselves. In particular, the role of the government in reaction to a sudden change was emphasized more than before. The 'Dutch Disease' type of analysis dealt with the effects of a sudden change that was to be permanent, like the discovery of oil resources. See Corden (1984) for a good survey.

More relevant to the non-oil primary commodities is the 'trade shock theory', which is a further extension of the earlier analysis and is applicable to temporary changes. A recent survey of the issue is given by Bevan *et al.* (1990a). While the 'Dutch Disease' analysis distinguishes between a 'tradable' sector and a 'non-tradable' sector in addition to the booming sector, a further distinction is introduced in the trade shocks literature. Whereas the permanent shock theory would predict a price increase in all non-tradables, following a permanent positive shock in foreign exchange earnings, trade shock theory predicts a further increase in the price of non-tradable capital goods relative to non-tradable consumer goods. In particular, 'a temporary trade boom will generate large profits in the construction industry' (Bevan *et al.* 1990a: 39). Private agents are considered to recognize the shock as temporary and to adjust their consumption only marginally (in contrast to the case of permanent shocks). A large proportion of the windfall profits will then be saved, which leads to investments on the one hand and (temporary) foreign asset accumulation (if possible) on the other. The government will normally see its revenues rise, and more so if these revenues are collected from export taxes. If a government cannot recognize the temporary character, it will expand consumption by employing more people, but the correct response would be to save a substantial part (in foreign financial assets) and run them down gradually by means of government investments. Excessive investments immediately following a boom would be inefficient, as they will normally increase prices of investment goods.

In a survey of responses to positive trade shocks (in coffee prices) in the second half of the 1970s, J.M. Davis (1983) summarizes: 'the increase in producer prices was restricted, allowing substantial sums to accrue to the central government and commodity organizations. The counter-cyclical impact of fiscal policy was often limited by the rise in development spending.' By the end of 1978, he concludes, the reserve position of many of the countries was little better than before the windfall gain, and these countries were not in a position to buffer any further reductions in export proceeds. Cuddington (1989) in a later survey states that the few countries that managed booms well were those that limited increases in government spending to levels consistent with long-term trends in revenue collection and 'avoided indulging in wasteful investments'. Balassa (1986) notes that inward-oriented countries initially mitigated the shocks brought about by higher oil prices in the early 1970s and high interest rates around 1980. Outward-oriented countries suffered larger shocks but avoided reliance on foreign debts. Eventually, the countries that had an outward-oriented policy were much better off.

The great diversity in the types of policy and control regimes in the developing countries thus may provide an explanation of the weak regression results of the cross-country comparisons *à la* MacBean. Booms have often proved to be 'a mixed blessing' (Cuddington 1989). In the traditional analyses of fluctuating export revenues, booms were supposed to compensate for slumps. If the potential economic advantages of a boom are in general so badly exploited by the countries concerned, they can hardly be believed to play that role. In fact, both booms and slumps will be very demanding as far as government policy is concerned. And the optimal policy in the case of a boom is not symmetrical with that in the case of a slump. This is because saving foreign currency (the boom case) is not restricted, but borrowing hard currency in the situation with low export earnings often is. Furthermore, the interaction between government and private sector is important: as Bevan *et al.* (1990a) point out, the perception by the private sector of the signals provided by the government, such as changes in taxes or import licensing, can make a substantial difference to the allocation of their income. Even if government follows the prescriptions for optimal policy, if the private sector does not believe that this will be continued for some time to come, the effects may be drastically different from the optimal case. Calvo (1988) shows this in respect of trade liberalization without full credibility.

In a detailed analysis of the responses to the coffee boom in Kenya and Tanzania, Bevan *et al.* (1990b) conclude that the responses by the private sector are in general efficient, but that governments appear to react unwisely. In an epilogue, they make the suggestion that the private sector should be shielded from the government. At the micro-level shocks appear to be treated quite well, but not so at the macro-level. This would suggest that, if there must be fluctuations in world market prices, they should be transmitted to the producers, but at the same time government earnings should be stabilized. Actual practice is quite different, with producers more often than not 'protected' against price fluctuations at the cost of government exposure.

This being so, direct stabilization of revenues would have the advantage that a government would not need to go through all the difficulties of suddenly adjusting its policy. This suggests that prices might be left to the market if the balance of payments is stabilized. Financial compensation of countries for export shortfalls is the appropriate way to do this, rather than price stabilization. Export earnings stabilization is different from price stabilization because it cannot be captured in a demand–supply framework. Export earnings stabilization should aim at avoiding those year-by-year changes which would necessitate sudden changes of policy. This might imply extension of credit facilities and, in some instances, perhaps contraction of borrowing facilities. But as Eaton *et al.* (1986) argue, a major problem is the enforcement of a loan contract.

MICROECONOMICS

The pure microeconomics of stabilization has developed substantially since the first exercises along the lines of Marshallian surplus. The newer approach is the expected-utility approach. In the former approach, the basic framework is a demand–supply model where welfare calculations are used to assess desirability of stabilization; in the latter approach, which in general is more algebraic, consuming and producing agents are expected-utility maximizers and desirability of stabilization is dependent on whether a higher level of expected utility is achieved.

In the Marshallian approach, the basic reference is Massell (1969) who combined two earlier papers by Waugh (1944) and Oi (1961) into one framework. Massell's results can be summarized as follows.

1 Producers lose (gain) and consumers gain (lose) from price stabilization if the source of price instability is random shifts in demand (supply).
2 Total gains from stabilization are positive.

This is based on the graphical analysis shown in Figure 2.1. In Figure 2.1(a), the market price p can take on two values, depending on whether supply is high (S_2) or low (S_1). Given buffer stock intervention and equal probability for the two cases, prices can be stabilized at p_m. Without stabilization, consumer surplus over the cycle is $f + a + b + c + d + f$; with stabilization, this becomes $2(a + b + f)$; hence the gain from stabilization is $a + b - (c + d)$, which is

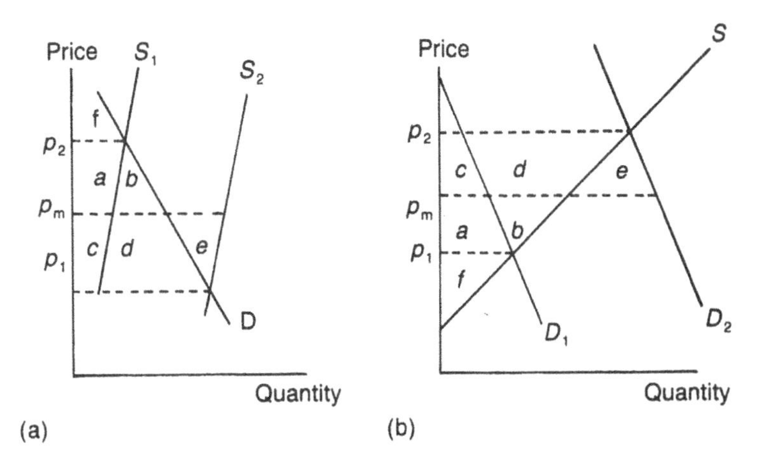

Figure 2.1 The Waugh–Oi–Massell diagram

negative. The change in producer surplus from the situation without stabilization to the stabilized case is $-a$ when supply is low and $c+d+e$ when supply is high. The gains to producers over the cycle are therefore $c+d+e-a$, which is positive. Total gains are therefore $b+e$ and positive.

In Figure 2.1(b), the source of uncertainty is on the demand side, with the demand taking the shape of D_1 or D_2 with equal probability. The gains from stabilization to the consumer over the cycle are now $c+d+e-a$, which is positive, and to the producers $a+b-(c+d)$, which is negative. Total gains over the cycle are again $b+e$ and positive.

However, the assumptions needed for these results are very strong:

1 linear demand curves and additive disturbances
2 free storage by the buffer stock and no private storage
3 prices are known at the time of consumption or production
4 the welfare measures are appropriate
5 homogeneous groups of producers and consumers
6 no other sources of instability
7 no dynamics
8 no general equilibrium effects
9 market equilibrium known

Subsequent literature has dealt with many of these assumptions and we shall discuss them one by one.

The assumption of linear curves and additive disturbances

Turnovsky (1976) has investigated what the effects are when non-linear functions are assumed together with multiplicative disturbances. As is also pointed out in Newbery and Stiglitz (1981), this is the more natural specification both of the random influence and of the curves themselves. The most important effect is the shift in the average price. It has been shown that a buffer stock cannot in general – in this environment – stabilize the price at the pre-stabilization mean price. Depending on the sizes of demand and supply elasticities and frequency distributions of the random factors, the stable price will lie above or below the original average. This and the curvature of the functions themselves are the causes for transfers to take place when prices are stabilized. In very general terms, if supply elasticity is low and demand elasticity is relatively high, producers tend to gain from stabilization. Turnovsky (1978: 127) 'hastens to add' that this will not hold in particular cases. If, for example, both demand and supply curves are loglinear (as they commonly are assumed to be), producers would gain only if the size of the demand elasticity exceeds unity, which is rare. Newbery and Stiglitz (1981: 125) examine this case more closely. If supply is random but not responsive to price changes and if demand has constant price elasticity $-e$ where e is positive, then the size of the transfers from producers to consumers relative to total sales equals approximately $\frac{1}{2}(1 - e)$ times the squared coefficient of variation of the prices.

A further outcome in the non-linear case is that the source of instability no longer plays a role in the distribution of any welfare gains. But, as pointed out by Ghosh *et al.* (1987), these welfare gains are now measured by comparing the situation without buffer stock with a situation where the buffer stock stabilizes prices at a feasible price, i.e. a price where expected sales from the buffer stock equal expected purchases. The above mentioned distribution refers only to the welfare gains not counting the transfer effects.

The assumption of costless storage and the role of private stockholders

A further comment by Ghosh *et al.* on the Turnovsky results refers to the surmised efficiency gains from stabilization. If there are benefits to derive from stabilization, why would these not be captured by private stockholders? A commodity that can be held in buffer stocks can certainly be held in private stocks. Wright and Williams (1982) have analysed the effects that private stock holding has on the distribution of the prices. Unlike, for example, A. Schmitz (1984: 18), but following Gustafson (1958), they include a non-negativity constraint in their analysis (stocks cannot be negative) and this has profound effects on the market prices. A rational stockholder will have an incentive to buy at prices below the expected price (minus storage costs) for the next period, but no incentive to buy when prices are above this level. Hence, in the above framework, there will be additional market demand when supply is high, but no change in demand when supply is low. This by itself will decrease the frequency of low prices and will increase the frequency of prices just below the average price. In addition, the frequency distribution of market supply will change. Extremely low production can still occur with the same probability, but there will now be extra supply coming from private stocks. Hence, the occurrence of very low market supply will be less frequent, whereas higher market supplies will occur more frequently. If there is no production response, the market supply distribution will be shifted to the right. Hence, the originally highest prices will occur

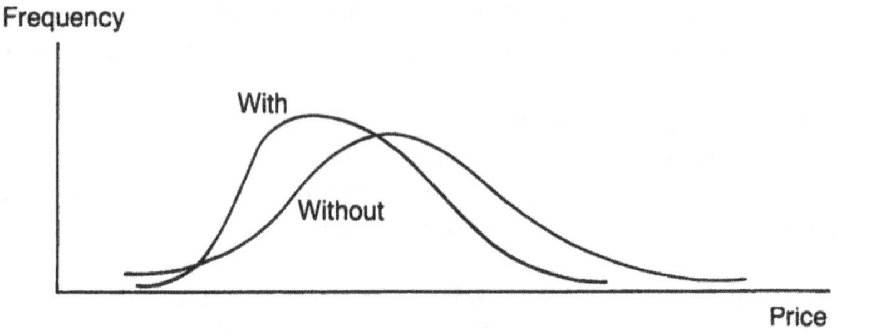

Figure 2.2 Price distribution with and without storage

less frequently. The overall price distribution will become more skewed to the right and moderately low prices will occur far more frequently than high prices, whereas very low prices are ruled out. See Figure 2.2 for a graphical illustration.

The asymmetry in the market-demand schedules that is introduced by private stockholders is also relevant for a buffer stock. When storage is costless, it may be reasonable to assume that very large stocks are held, so that a buffer stock will 'always' be able to intervene, but this is no longer true in the more realistic situation in which stocks are not held without cost. In this case, the positive chance that the buffer stock will lack stock to prevent prices from rising should be incorporated. This by itself enhances the skewedness of the price distribution, because low prices may still be avoided through intervention but high prices may not. If the buffer stock does not have unlimited funds available for purchases, a positive chance will exist that the authority is not able to make purchases, so that low prices are possible.

The effects of private storage are quite difficult to ascertain. On the one hand, the market-demand curve is now more curved than it was before. This would increase the potential gains from stabilization to consumers and indeed Wright and Williams suggest that the mere introduction of storage works to the advantage of consumers and to the disadvantage of producers. On the other hand, the change in frequency distributions makes it difficult to assess the expected values of consumer and producer benefits.

Recently, Deaton and Laroque (1990) have again analysed this problem. Assuming – in line with Wright and Williams – rational expectations held by private stockholders but no supply response, they arrive at frequency distributions of prices that resemble actual distributions of commodity prices fairly closely. This provides an explanation for the occurrence of sharp peaks and wide valleys (statistically expressed as positive skewedness) of many commodity price series.

Additional stabilization by a buffer stock in a world with private storage (and taking its asymmetry into account) has been analysed in Wright and Williams (1988) who conclude from simulations that producers would lose. It may be expected, as in the case of Newbery and Stiglitz (1981), that the incentive for private stockholders will diminish; thus more sales or purchases by the buffer stock will be required to achieve a given price change. The enhanced skewedness in the price distribution would induce transfers, which – depending on the supply responsiveness – tend to favour consumers.

In addition to private stockholding, the (concomitant) existence of futures markets further reduces the potential benefits from price stabilization. Although the futures market can be used to hedge a certain production against the influence of a change in prices, in general the benefits of futures markets to least developed countries are limited because substantial margin payments may have to be made, requiring dear hard currency, and because this does not resolve the uncertainty of production (see Gemmill 1985; Gilbert 1985). Futures markets may, however, play an important role in reducing the uncertainties during the marketing of the products. After harvest, traders may benefit from the futures market by hedging against price changes during transport. This may have its repercussions on their willingness to buy from smallholders. Futures markets provide hardly any insurance against price changes more than one year ahead.

The assumption that prices are known at the time of consumption or production

This was assumed to be the case in the earlier analyses of Waugh and Oi. In particular, it means that producers commit expenditures to the production process only after they know what price will be realized for the product. In agriculture, as anywhere else, production takes time, especially for tree crops and the like, so that heavy commitments are made without the eventual price of the product being known with certainty. In any particular year, supply can often hardly respond to the current prices and the more appropriate model appears to be one in which consumers may still adjust their consumption pattern to the prevailing price but producers cannot similarly adjust their supply. Welfare effects of stabilization will become quite different from the original Massell results, even under linear demand schedules. As A. Schmitz (1984) points out, with linear demand curves and additive disturbances on the demand side, but with supply now predetermined, producers may be indifferent to price stabilization, whereas consumers will gain. Both results are different from the original Massell outcome. If demand is non-random and follows a non-linear curve, but supply is random and not price responsive, consumers are likely to gain and producers may lose, both results depending on the size of the elasticities. If supply in a particular year is predetermined but can respond to price changes with a lag of one year (for annual crops) or more (for perennial crops and mining, for example), the issue is how to evaluate the effects that stabilization can have on future supply. In these cases, the supply response typically depends on how expectations of producers are affected by current price changes. This point will be taken up again in the section on the omission of dynamics.

A common and much analysed case is that of annual crops, for which yields are uncertain and decisions on resource allocation must be made well before harvesting time, so that supply is predetermined but uncertain. It may very well be the case that low overall yields coincide with high prices, thus stabilizing aggregate income to some extent. Price stabilization in this situation would only enhance income variability. Individual farmers may not be fully aware of this negative correlation between yields and prices, and may adjust their expectations of the prices according to last year's prices. Hazell and Scandizzo (1975) and Scandizzo *et al.* (1984) have shown the social inefficiency of this behaviour and use it in a plea for stabilization, not necessarily by buffer stocking but rather by the provision of adequate information to farmers about expected prices. They and others (e.g. Turnovsky 1974) also show that the gains from stabilization in this context critically depend on how expectations are formed.

As to perennial crops, very little has come out of research into the determinants of investment in tree stands. As we shall show in Chapter 7, present agreements on price stabilization can hardly be expected to add anything to the predictability of real prices, say ten years from now. Theoretically, the issue is how the provision of more stable prices in the future affects present allocation of resources. This issue will be taken up in the section on the omission of dynamics.

The assumption that these (Marshallian) welfare measures are appropriate

The measurement of consumer and producer surpluses, as the area below the demand curve and above the price line and the area between the price line and the supply curve respectively, does not take into account how the supply curve (and in some cases the demand curve) itself is affected by the uncertainty of the prices. More adequate measures are Hicks's compensating and equivalent variations. With price uncertainty, and risk-averse producers, the planned supply may be substantially lower than it would be without the uncertainty. Boussard (1990) estimates for sub-Saharan Africa that the difference between actual average gross margins and 'action certainty equivalent margins' may be as high as 50 per cent.

As the sub-title of their book (*A Study in the Economics of Risk*) suggests, Newbery and Stiglitz (1981) make clear that major benefits of commodity market stabilization could come solely from this effect of the reduction in variability of prices and income. This would be so if agents were averse to risk. Their analysis of commodity price stabilization is cast in the framework of expected-utility maximization. In the Massell framework, prices were assumed to be known at the time the relevant decisions were made. As pointed out earlier, this is hardly ever appropriate for producers and on many occasions inappropriate for consumers. If prices and/or production are not known for certain when land or other resources are allocated, such allocation must be made on the basis of expected-utility or profit maximization.

Expected utility was given its conceptual foundation by von Neumann and Morgenstern (1944), who show under what conditions preferences concerning uncertain events can be ranked like normal utility rankings of preferences. The types of function to be used differ however. Whereas the standard utility theory allows any monotonic transformation of a utility function without changing the results of the maximization, the type to be used in expected-utility maximization may only be transformed by a linear transformation. Applicability of one utility function for a group of agents has its limitations in the standard case, but is even more troublesome with this type of function. Arrow (1965) and Pratt (1964) developed a measure for risk aversion for these utility functions, using the ratio of the second-order derivative to the first-order derivative as a relevant measure of the curvature of a function. This approach enables comparison of uncertain events. Newbery and Stiglitz (1981: 93) derive the following approximate formula for the benefits B of having income Y_0 with mean m_0 and squared coefficient of variation (CV) s_0 instead of income Y_1 with mean m_1 and squared CV s_1:

$$B = (m_0 - m_1) - \tfrac{1}{2} m_1 R(s_0 - s_1) \tag{2.1}$$

where R is the Arrow–Pratt coefficient of relative risk aversion defined as

$$R = -\frac{Yu''}{u'} \tag{2.2}$$

and where u'' and u' are the second and first derivatives of the (von Neumann–Morgenstern) utility function with respect to Y. The first term in the expression for B is the transfer benefit and the second term captures the risk benefits.

In a trading environment with a loglinear demand curve depending on income and price, non-responsive supply and no storage, and with multiplicative disturbance terms added to consumer income and supply, Newbery and Stiglitz derive the following benefits from complete price stabilization:

1 For the producers (p. 94):

$$\text{transfer benefits} = \tfrac{1}{2} Y(e - 1)s \tag{2.3}$$

$$\text{risk benefits} = \tfrac{1}{2} YR^s(1 - 2e)s \tag{2.4}$$

where Y is the average pre-stabilization revenue from sales of the good, R^s is the producers' coefficient of relative risk aversion and s is the squared CV of the price. This squared CV is related to the two potential sources of disturbances by

$$s = \frac{s_q + f^2 s_y}{e^2} \tag{2.5}$$

where e and f are the price and income elasticity of demand and s_q and s_y are the squared CVs of production and consumers' income respectively.

2 For the consumers (p. 127):

$$\text{transfer benefits} = \tfrac{1}{2} X(1 - e)s \tag{2.6}$$

$$\text{efficiency benefits} = \tfrac{1}{2} X\left(es - \frac{2R^c f s_y}{e}\right) \tag{2.7}$$

where X is the average consumer expenditure on the good, which is equal to Y, the revenues of the producers.

Welfare benefits from complete stabilization are therefore

$$\text{total welfare benefits} = \tfrac{1}{2}X\left\{[R^s(1-2e)+e]s - \frac{2R^c f s_y}{e}\right\} \qquad (2.8)$$

Supposing that the coefficients of relative risk aversion are unity and that disturbances are from supply changes only, then relative total welfare benefits amount to $\tfrac{1}{2}(1-e)s$, which for a CV of the price of 0.25 and $e = 0.5$ (corresponding to a CV for production of 1/8) would equal only 1/64, which is 1.6 per cent. Transfer benefits accruing to consumers are in this case of the same size. If, in addition, $f = 1$ and income has a CV of 0.1, then the CV of the price increases to 0.32 ($s = 0.1025$), leading to total benefits equal to 0.56 per cent and transfers to the consumers of 2.56 per cent. These and other results have been derived by Newbery and Stiglitz for a range of commodities and their conclusion was that in general net benefits from stabilization are meagre.

The above formulae from Newbery and Stiglitz assume supply to be unstable but not responsive to prices. For the crops considered in the present book, i.e. coffee, cocoa and rubber, this is true to the extent that capacity is predetermined. The capacity utilization may still depend on the current price. If these responses were incorporated, price variability would be reduced as high prices would trigger increased production, thus reducing prices. For normal small values of the supply elasticities, the effects on transfer and risk benefits from stabilization would be mitigated, but the signs would remain the same. Producer benefits in this case, assuming all instability to be from supply disturbances, would be for a supply elasticity of z:

$$\text{relative transfer benefits} = \tfrac{1}{2}w(1-w)s_q \qquad (2.9)$$

$$\text{relative risk benefits} = \tfrac{1}{2}Rw(w-2)s_q \qquad (2.10)$$

$$\text{relative total benefits} = \tfrac{1}{2}ws_q[1-w+R(w-2)] \qquad (2.11)$$

where $w = (1+z)/(e+z) > 1$ for $e < 1$. Total benefits are only positive if

$$R(w-2) > (w-1) \qquad (2.12)$$

or, for $R > 1$,

$$z < \left(2-\frac{1}{R}\right)e - \left(1-\frac{1}{R}\right) \qquad (2.13)$$

These benefits still do not account for changes in the supply function owing to changes in the uncertainty about future prices. As mentioned earlier, this can only be done when assumptions are made on the formulation of expectations. Even if these are rational, i.e. if the expected price is the price generated by the model in the absence of new disturbances, Newbery and Stiglitz show that the market solution is not in general Pareto optimal. But one cannot deduce whether stabilization of prices would be beneficial. As to longer-run benefits for producers, they conclude:

> In the longer run, producers will adjust their effort, and this will affect the prices they receive. The magnitude of this response depends on the effects of price stabilization on the mean value of the marginal return to effort, and this need not move in the same direction as the mean value of utility.
>
> (Newbery and Stiglitz 1981: 334)

We shall come back to this in the section on the omission of dynamics.

The assumption of homogeneous groups of producers and consumers

The standard analysis only includes representative agents, who are either consumers or producers. The world markets for the major commodities, however, show a far from homogeneous picture. Crops such as coffee, cocoa and natural rubber are produced in many countries, but production is heavily concentrated in some of them. For all three crops, by far the major part is produced in only a few countries. If an analysis of stabilization effects shows that income is redistributed from 'producers' to 'consumers', it does not necessarily mean that all producers would lose and all consumers would gain. In particular, it has been shown that, if the source of uncertainty is in a major producing country, price stabilization may destabilize export earnings of this country (for example, because production shortfalls would no longer be compensated by higher prices), but other – more stable – producers may see their earnings stabilized. Herrmann (1983b) has demonstrated that it is possible that world export earnings are stabilized by partial price stabilization, but that some individual countries' export earnings are destabilized. Nguyen (1990), however, argues that such cases are fairly uncommon and the partial price stabilization would usually stabilize export earnings of all participants.

In addition to the possible differential impact of price stabilization on national exports due to different market shares and market-supply elasticities, domestic policies in the countries may differ substantially. In some countries, world market price changes are passed on to the producers; in other countries, domestic prices may fluctuate far less than world market prices. Hazell *et al.* (1990) conclude that

> in most cases the variability in export unit values has not been fully transmitted to producers in the prices they receive. Real exchange rates have played a major buffering role, but so too have domestic marketing arrangements and government interventions. In fact, most export producers face price variability that appears to be largely determined by factors other than variations in the local currency value of their country's export unit values.

But, to the countries themselves, nearly all variability has been transmitted in the US dollar values of the export unit values. Knudsen and Nash (1990) consider whether variability in domestic prices has been reduced by domestic policy compared with the world market prices. They find that beverages, in particular, appear not to have benefited so much from the variety of domestic policies (export taxes, marketing boards) that were in place in various countries. In 31 per cent of the cases, the variability of real producer prices exceeded that of real border prices. Mundlak and Larson (1990), on the other hand, claim that world market price variability is a good measure of producer-price variability. However this may be, there is a great variety of domestic policies that make producers in one country experience quite different variability of the real prices than producers in another. The same may hold for government revenues or those of parastatal organizations. The implication is that one world market price stabilization scheme would work out quite differently for the individual producers and producing countries and that, in order to assess the effects of stabilization, one should take each major producing country's policies into consideration.

The assumption that there are no other sources of instability

Clearly other sources of instability affect the producers of export commodities. To the extent that these other uncertainties are correlated with the prices paid to producers of the commodity concerned they cannot be ignored. Newbery and Stiglitz mention the case of crops chosen by the farmer so as to minimize the CV of his earnings. If the price of one of these crops was stabilized, it might destabilize his overall income, if the stabilizing effects of negative correlations were removed. Changes in the exchange rates are a common source of instability which does affect export crops to a greater extent than non-traded commodities. If this was the only source of uncertainty, producers would be faced with a random demand function with multiplicative inverse demand shifts (see Newbery and Stiglitz 1981: Figure 8.1(a)). But even in the case of uncorrelated random factors, other sources of instability can play a role. Zeckhauser and Keeler (1970) indicate that when the size of the total risk increases individuals may be prepared to pay a more than proportionally higher risk premium. This can also be understood to indicate that in a risky environment, after reduction of one risk, for example by stabilization of revenues from one commodity, individuals may be prepared to take greater risks in another, and vice versa: when forced to take one risk, they may be less prepared to take another (see Pratt and Zeckhauser 1987; Kimball 1990).

The omission of dynamics

We have considered earlier that in general prices are not known with certainty by the producers at the time when they take the relevant decisions. In the case of annual crops, this may lead to excess supplies in some years. When storage is included in the model, private stockholders carry over stocks to the next year and – if possible – to later years. Ghosh *et al.* (1987) show that permanent storage of commodities may be the outcome of the repetitive process. Shocks in supply will in this way be carried over to later years and stabilization of prices will also have longer-run effects. In the case of jute, for example, a shock of sudden high prices is followed by a huge supply one year later, yielding relatively low prices, followed by a relatively low supply but still lower prices, owing to large carry-over stocks. This is the worst year for farmers' income; later, production and prices will stabilize if no other shocks occur (see Burger and Wansink 1990).

In the case of perennial crops, resources are allocated and fixed for many years ahead and variable costs of production are but a small proportion of total costs. This leads to very low short-run supply elasticities. In the longer run, capacity may be adjusted to a change in prices. There is a considerable debate on the effect that price stabilization can have on such longer-term decisions. The issue is how future uncertainty will affect present decisions. Consider decisions on consumption and investment. The consumption decision is affected as reduced uncertainty in the future may lead to a decrease in precautionary savings. Investments, on the other hand, may be triggered by the prospect of more certain revenues. Depending on the efficiency of the capital market, these two decisions may be closely connected. In the development economics literature this trade-off has been extensively discussed in the analyses of the linkage between export earnings stability and economic growth. Friedman's permanent income theory provided the basis for the assumption that unstable export earnings would lead to higher saving rates (see Knudsen and Parnes 1975; Yotopoulos and Nugent 1976). In the past few years, some progress has been made in the analysis of these types of problem. The progress is in two directions.

One is the treatment of (precautionary) savings. As Leland (1968) has shown, the more uncertain future income is, the higher present savings will be (precautionary saving). This requires the third derivative of the utility function to be positive. Recently Kimball (1990) has proposed an elegant way of looking into this matter by applying the theorems concerning risk aversion to (the negative of) the marginal utility function. He derives a 'coefficient of absolute prudence' as the counterpart of the coefficient of absolute risk aversion and shows this to be related to the first derivative of the coefficient of relative risk aversion. If the coefficient of absolute risk aversion A is decreasing in Y, then the coefficient of absolute prudence H is greater than A. Kimball's coefficient governs the marginal propensity to save out of current wealth and $H > A$ can be interpreted as meaning that, if future income is uncertain, the amount of future wealth the consumer would need to bring present consumption back to levels equal to the situation with a certain future is greater than the amount that is required to compensate the consumer for accepting the future risk as such. In other words, when only comparing two 'lotteries' – one with uncertain future outcomes, the other with certain outcomes – the difference can be measured by the risk premium, compensating for the uncertainty. Kimball's contribution is to point out that, if $H > A$, this compensation still does not lead to the same level of savings in the present. To have this equivalence, more compensation should be offered.

The other direction in which advances have been made is in the distinction between a premium to compensate uncertainty and a parameter accounting for (certain) instability of income over time. If credit markets are perfect, there is no need for separate treatment of the latter, as this predictable instability can be compensated by borrowing and lending. With imperfect capital markets, this no longer holds. In the traditional analysis of intertemporal utility maximization, only one parameter accounted for the two characteristics, namely the substitution elasticity, to which the coefficient of relative risk aversion is closely linked. Attanasio and Weber (1988) and

Epstein (1988) make a distinction between, on the one hand, the substitution elasticity between the present and the certainty-equivalent future and, on the other hand, the relationship between future uncertain events and this certainty-equivalent utility. The first elasticity measures instability aversion, whereas the latter accounts for unpredictability of future situations. Stabilization of future revenues might have benefits not only in terms of increased predictability but also in terms of more stability. Powell (1990) has recently tried to estimate the combined benefits and arrives at much higher benefits from stabilization than the traditional estimates.

The omission of general equilibrium effects

At the micro-level, we have already alluded to the outside effects that commodity price stabilization may have. Other risks, other crops whose revenues may be correlated with those of the commodity concerned, prices of consumer goods – all these are excluded from the traditional analysis. In a wider economic context, there is even more that should be included. Changes in commodity prices can be so important, particularly for producers, that macroeconomic effects are far from negligible. For countries that specialize in exports of only some commodities, changes in revenues from these commodities will directly affect the balance of payments and hence exchange rates, government revenues, import demand, etc. Some recent advances in this field have been discussed in the previous section of this chapter.

The assumption that the market equilibrium is known

This aspect seems trivial, but in practice it is not. Implicit in the standard model is the assumption that an intervention authority knows at what price it should stabilize and how much it ought to buy to reach this level. In practice, the reference prices are the outcome of long and tedious negotiations between producer and consumer participants in an international agreement. Uncertainty about what is a longer-term equilibrium price leads to mechanisms such as adjustment of the reference price from time to time. This, of course, adds to the uncertainty facing producers and consumers even after commodity agreements are adopted. In an international context, the world market price is usually expressed in a number of currencies. For primary commodities the pound sterling and US dollar are commonly used. Owing to exchange rate changes and differential rates of inflation, producers and consumers in various countries will be differently affected by movements of the reference price over time. In the case of natural rubber, for example, real producer prices in Thailand were among the highest during the 1970s but among the lowest around 1990, whereas the situation for Indonesia is the opposite. For the outcome of the agreement itself, the currency chosen for the reference price can make quite a difference, as will be shown in Chapters 7 and 8.

CONCLUSION

Much progress has been made in the literature on the economics of stabilization. At the macro-level, it is now accepted that governments are often not able to deal properly with unstable income. Much domestic 'protection' of producers leads to inefficiencies and there appears to be a case for protecting governments from instabilities. Yet the economic environment of producers is more often the source of unstable incomes than are the prices of their products.

The traditional Marshallian analysis of benefits and costs of stabilization at the micro-level is too simple and therefore misleading. Important omissions are the neglect of storage, time and information. Furthermore, a realistic approach to stabilization should incorporate the economic environments of the producers and consumers. When this is done, it is unlikely that a case is left for international price stabilization or for export earnings stabilization *per se.*

Part II

Compensatory financing

An economic evaluation of current programmes

In this part, the performance of current compensatory financing schemes is evaluated. There are two major compensatory financing systems implemented in order to stabilize export earnings of selected beneficiary countries: the Compensatory Financing Facility (CFF) of the International Monetary Fund (IMF) and the STABEX scheme laid down in the EC–ACP Lomé Convention. These two programmes will be discussed first. Within the analysis of STABEX, an extension of the system which took place in 1987 will also be covered. The so-called COMPEX system was created to compensate for losses of export earnings of least developed countries not signatories to the Lomé Convention. As the objectives and the rules of STABEX and COMPEX are very similar, both programmes will be discussed in one chapter. The IMF's CFF was also extended when cereal import facility was combined with the traditional system to give an amended compensatory financing facilitiy in 1981. The cereal import facility includes a new idea in compensatory financing, since it is oriented towards food security. Its objective is to compensate for fluctuations in cereal import costs. In view of the new objective of the cereal import facility, we shall investigate its performance separately from the traditional CFF.

The analysis of the compensatory financing schemes will be based on their stabilizing, redistributive and allocative effects. Impacts on the systems' primary goal, export earnings stabilization, will be elaborated first. As the programmes are not purely stabilizing devices but also include redistributive elements, the implicit income transfers in compensatory financing are then measured. Although compensatory financing is often regarded as neutral with respect to factor allocation, this is not necessarily the case in current programmes. Possible impacts on resource allocation will also be discussed.

There are many important contributions to the literature on the pros and cons of compensatory financing and its design to stabilize export earnings or import costs effectively: Fleming *et al.* (1963); Lovasy (1965); Morrison and Perez (1975); de Vries (1975a); UNCTAD (1975, 1979); Goreux (1977, 1981); Hirschler (1978); Green and Kirkpatrick (1980); Koester and Valdés (1984); Expert Group (1985); Balassa (1989). These contributions either discuss compensatory financing schemes qualitatively or evaluate hypothetical compensatory financing schemes. Our analysis is complementary to this work, since our focus is on a quantitative analysis of the impact of current compensatory financing schemes.

3 The International Monetary Fund's Compensatory Financing Facility

INTRODUCTION

The International Monetary Fund's (IMF's) Compensatory Financing Facility (CFF) was established in 1963 and is the oldest of the existing compensatory financing schemes.[1] It is oriented towards the stabilization of national export earnings. The major objective of the CFF is to provide timely financial assistance to member countries which experience shortfalls of their aggregate export earnings because of external influences. Besides export earnings for commodities and manufactured goods, the definition of export earnings may, if a country so wishes, include earnings from workers' remittances and tourism since 1979. The CFF has been extended twice. Since 1981, excesses in the cost of cereal imports have also been covered in order to meet the stabilization needs of poor developing countries. More recently, in August 1988, the Compensatory and Contingency Financing Facility (CCFF) was founded. The new contingency element means that members with Fund-supported adjustment programmes can borrow *ex ante* in order to cope with various external shocks.

In this chapter, impacts on objectives of stabilization, redistribution and allocation will be elaborated for the traditional CFF, which is the core of the CCFF. We shall examine whether the CFF realizes its primary objective, the stabilization of export earnings, and how the economic performance of the system can be evaluated from the donor's as well as from the individual recipient country's point of view. Some observations regarding the contingency element are made in this chapter and the cereal import facility is discussed in Chapter 5.

Table 3.1 Major provisions of the traditional International Monetary Fund's Compensatory Financing Facility

Subject	*Provisions in the traditional CFF*[a]
Provisions with special importance for the CFF's stabilization effects	
Principle of administration	The speed of operations is a major concern in the system (Goreux 1980; 25)
Time-lags in cases of belated compensation	The maximum time-lag between the end of the year and the application of the country is six months
Advance payments	An advance payment is possible for the current year. Hereby, export earnings from merchandise exports can be estimated up to six months in advance and those of travel and workers' remittances up to twelve months in advance (Article 5, Decision No. 6224–(79/135))
Definition of the shortfall year	The shortfall year does not need to be a calendar year (Article 5, Decision No. 1477–(63/8)). For a more speedy compensation, a normal drawing may be reclassified within eighteen months as a drawing under the Compensatory Financing Facility (Article 9, Decision No. 1477–(63/8))
Linkage between repayments and export earnings	There is no binding linkage between repayments and overages in export earnings. However, the IMF suggests repaying half the difference between actual export earnings and the medium-term trend value in the first four years (Article 7, Decision No. 1477–(63/8))
Provisions with special importance for the CFF's redistribution effects	
Interest payments	For credits in the compensatory financing system, interest has to be paid by all countries. Since 1 May 1981, a uniform interest rate has been laid down for all countries and for the whole term of the drawing (see Appendix A.1)
Moratorium period	A moratorium period after borrowing does not exist
Currency of repayment	The repayment has to be effected in convertible currencies (Horsefield 1969: 450 ff.)
Service charge	A non-recurring service charge of 0.5 per cent of the gross amount of the credit is subtracted before the disbursement
Provisions with special importance for the CFF's stabilization and redistribution effects	
Degree of compensation	The deviation of actual export earnings from the reference value is compensated fully if it does not

Table 3.1 continued

Subject	*Provisions in the traditional CFF*[a]
	come up to the limitations stated under 'Limitations for compensation payments' below
Statistical computation of the amount of the compensation payment	The actual value of export earnings is subtracted from the geometric mean of export earnings for a five-year period, centred on the shortfall year. The IMF estimates the values of the two years following the shortfall by means of qualitative considerations. All calculations relating to the CFF are made in special drawing rights (SDRs) at current prices
Limitations for compensation payments	The maximum limit for CFF drawings is 100 per cent of the national quota. Drawings outstanding beyond 50 per cent will be met only if the Fund is satisfied that the member has been cooperating with the Fund in an effort to find appropriate solutions for its balance-of-payments difficulties (Article 3, Decision No. 6224–(79/135)). The total amount of drawings outstanding under all IMF facilities may not exceed 125 per cent of the national quota (Decision No. 6860–(81/81))
Amount and date of repayment	The amount of compensation has to be repaid fully within five years. Repurchases shall be made in equal quarterly instalments during the period beginning three years and ending five years after the date of purchase, unless the Fund approves a different schedule (Decision No. 5703–(78/39))
Provisions with special importance for the CFF's allocation effects	
National economic policy and compensation	The disturbance has to be temporary and largely beyond the member's control in order to qualify for a payment from the CFF. Moreover, the member must be willing to cooperate with the IMF in an effort to find appropriate solutions for its balance-of-payments problems

Sources: Own compilation on the basis of decisions of the IMF published in Horsefield (1969: 492 ff.) and Goreux (1980: Appendix I). The other information is taken from Goreux (1980); Horsefield (1969: 428 ff.); Herrmann (1983a: Tables 1 and 6); and UNCTAD (1983b: Chapter I)

Note: [a]The provisions are those which were in force in 1981 before excesses in cereal import costs were also taken into account. Some of the provisions above changed since the CFF was founded in 1963 and some have also changed later (see Chapter 5 and the sixth section of Chapter 3). A comparison with former provisions is given in Herrmann (1983a: Tables 1 and 6).

IMPORTANT RULES OF THE TRADITIONAL COMPENSATORY FINANCING FACILITY

Table 3.1 gives a survey of the provisions of the traditional CFF as they existed before the system was extended by the compensation of excesses in cereal import costs in 1981. Some of the provisions have changed since then but these changes will be discussed in the context of the cereal import facility in Chapter 5 and when the new Compensatory and Contingency Facility is introduced in the sixth section of Chapter 3. We concentrate here on the rules of the traditional CFF since these are more relevant for its impacts on the objectives of stabilization, redistribution and allocation. In general, export earnings shortfalls are compensated if certain conditions are met.

The disturbance has to be temporary and largely beyond the member's control. As it is a basic idea of compensatory financing schemes to be flexible enough to react quickly to instability, it is consistent that credits from the CFF have a lower degree of conditionality than credits from other IMF sources, for example from the stand-by facility. The Fund must be convinced that the member is willing to cooperate with the Fund in an effort to find appropriate solutions to its balance-of-payments problems. The member does not have to present a financial programme.

Despite this flexible element in the CFF, the provisions summarized in Table 3.1 do not ensure that a positive and high stabilization effect will occur, for the following reasons:

1. There are time-lags between the shortfall year and the compensation.
2. The calculation of the shortfall includes a forecasting element and forecasting errors may cause destabilizing effects as well.
3. Even if there is no forecasting error and no time-lag, a large stabilization effect may be hindered either by the existing limit on CFF drawings or by the missing link between overages in export earnings and repayments.

Moreover, the CFF contains redistributive elements. Interest is charged for credits under the CFF but at far below market rates. The grant elements involved in the stabilization payments are only lowered by a service charge of 0.5 per cent of the amount of the credit. This implies that the actual stabilization and redistribution effects of the CFF are *a priori* unclear. A quantitative analysis is necessary.

THE IMPACT OF THE COMPENSATORY FINANCING FACILITY ON EXPORT EARNINGS INSTABILITY

The following empirical measurement of the stabilization effects of the IMF system is based on a broad country basis and a comprehensive period of analysis. Ninety-two of the ninety-five countries which have received compensatory financing payments under the IMF system up to 1987 are taken into account.[2] The period of analysis is 1963–87.[3] We analyse whether the export earnings of countries participating in the IMF's CFF are more or less stable than those of countries without compensatory financing. The impacts of drawings under the CFF and of the countries' repayments are calculated separately. Additionally, the aggregate effect of all transactions under the facility is presented. In order to compute stabilization effects, yearly data on national export earnings[4] from the *International Financial Statistics* of the IMF are utilized.

Methodologically, the measurement of instability is based on the approach of Cuddy and Della Valle.[5] The measure of instability I is

$$I = v(1 - \bar{R}^2)^{1/2} \tag{3.1}$$

where v is the coefficient of variation (CV) of the time series and $\bar{R}^2$ is the coefficient of determination of the trend function with the best fit to the data adjusted by the degrees of freedom. This measure of instability is comparable for different trend functions and regressions with a differential number of explanatory variables. First, CVs of the time series are measured. If a trend exists in the time series, the CVs will overestimate the instability and they have to be corrected. A linear and a loglinear trend function are computed here so that three possible instability measures can be derived from (3.1):

$$I = v \tag{3.2}$$

$$I = v_L^* = v(1 - \bar{R}_L^2)^{1/2} \tag{3.3}$$

or

$$I = v_{LL}^* = v(1 - \bar{R}_{LL}^2)^{1/2} \tag{3.4}$$

where $\bar{R}_L^2$ and $\bar{R}_{LL}^2$ represent the corrected coefficients of determination for a linear and a loglinear trend function respectively. For all the time series, only one measure of instability is presented.[6]

The instability measure used in the following analysis can be interpreted as an indicator of uncertainty under specific assumptions. As was discussed in the economics literature, a measure of instability captures price uncertainty, too, if its deterministic and stochastic parts coincide with the expectations of the economic planner (Herrmann and Kirschke 1987). In our case, this implies that equations (3.1)–(3.4) can be interpreted as measures of uncertainty if national export earnings are expected to follow a linear or loglinear trend in the user countries of the CFF. This may or may not be the case; no empirical tests were performed here in order to investigate how economists in the respective countries actually form their expectations regarding the national export earnings.

Table 3.2 shows the quantitative results for the ninety-two recipient countries. The findings can be summarized as follows:

1 Export earnings instability varies widely across countries. It ranges between 10.4 per cent (Portugal) and 67 per cent (Laos, People's Democratic Republic of (PDR)) with an arithmetic mean of 24.5 per cent and a median instability of 21.9 per cent. The measurement of instability is mostly based on v^{*}_{LL}. This means that export earnings of many countries grew exponentially and the CV had to be corrected downwards.[7]
2 The overall impact of the IMF compensatory financing system on export earnings instability tends to be small. The median shows a destabilizing impact for the payments from the IMF (+0.10 per cent) as well as for the repayments to the IMF (+0.41 per cent). The median effect of payments and repayments combined on export earnings instability is destabilizing: +0.63 per cent. This implies that the CFF induced destabilizing influences for most of the drawing countries.
3 The payments from the IMF were only export-earnings stabilizing in forty-three out of ninety-two cases. When stabilizing effects existed, they were mostly low. They were higher than 3 per cent for twelve countries and higher than 5 per cent for only five countries: Côte d'Ivoire, Nepal, Zaire, Argentina and Dominica. The clear success case is Côte d'Ivoire where the export earnings instability was reduced by some 47 per cent. This country received relatively high payments in 1976 and 1981 when its export earnings were clearly below the exponential trend. The payments from the CFF were export-earnings destabilizing for the majority of countries (forty-nine). These destabilizing effects exceeded 3 per cent for eight countries and 5 per cent for three countries: Laos PDR, Panama and Somalia.
4 With regard to the stabilization of export earnings, the repayments to the IMF performed even worse. In twenty-eight recipient countries, less than a third of the total, export earnings

were stabilized. In all cases except Côte d'Ivoire, these stabilizing effects were lower than 3 per cent. On the other hand, destabilizing effects of the repayments exceeded 3 percent in twelve countries and 5 per cent in the following seven countries: Laos PDR, Argentina, Bangladesh, Panama, Madagascar, Gambia and Burma.

5 Consequently, the overall impact of both payments from the IMF and repayments to the IMF was export-earnings stabilizing for thirty countries and destabilizing for sixty-two countries. The stabilizing effect was higher than 3 per cent for eight countries and it exceeded 5 per cent only for the following five countries: Côte d'Ivoire, Dominica, Nepal, Sierra Leone and the Central African Republic. On the other hand, export earnings were destabilized by more than 3 per cent in seventeen countries and by more than 5 per cent in the following ten countries: Laos PDR, Panama, Madagascar, Bangladesh, Somalia, Sudan, Malawi, Ethiopia, Burma and Ghana. Destabilization was more than 10 per cent for the first three of these countries.

The overall performance of the IMF compensatory financing scheme can be generalized if the transactions up to 1987 are regarded as a representative sample for the future performance of the scheme. Then, given a 99 per cent level of statistical significance and a two-sided test, confidence intervals for the median stabilization effects can be computed.[8] These confidence intervals are

$$-0.59 \leq 100\frac{\Delta I}{I} \leq +0.66 \tag{3.5}$$

for the payments from the IMF,

$$+0.01 \leq 100\frac{\Delta I}{I} \leq +1.01 \tag{3.6}$$

for the repayments to the IMF and

$$+0.05 \leq 100\frac{\Delta I}{I} \leq +1.24 \tag{3.7}$$

for the sum of payments from the IMF and repayments to the IMF.

Given the historical performance of the CFF, we expect from these results that compensatory financing will lead to a median effect on export earnings instability which is *destabilizing* and lies between 0.05 per cent and 1.24 per cent. The median effect of the repayments alone can be expected to be destabilizing within a range of 0.01–1.01

Table 3.2 Effects of the compensatory financing system of the International Monetary Fund on the instability of export earnings of ninety-two recipient countries in the period 1963–87

Country	*Instability of selected variables*[a]				*Percentage change in export earnings instability*[b] *because of*		
	Export earnings	*Export earnings and payments from the IMF*	*Export earnings minus repayments to the IMF*	*Export earnings and payments from the IMF minus repayments to the IMF*	*payments from the IMF*	*repayments to the IMF*	*payments from the IMF minus repayments to the IMF*
Afghanistan[c]	22.80	22.67	22.98	22.85	−0.59	+0.79	+0.22
Argentina	22.73	21.56	24.46	23.16	−5.15	+7.64	+1.91
Australia	12.74	12.86	12.69	12.81	+0.93	−0.38	+0.56
Bangladesh[d]	14.71	15.27	15.67	16.06	+3.81	+6.51	+9.14
Barbados	37.76	37.63	38.52	38.39	−0.36	+2.00	+1.66
Belize	19.91	19.82	20.15	20.07	−0.43	+1.22	+0.81
Bolivia[e]	26.58	25.70	26.85	25.95	−3.33	+1.02	−2.40
Brazil	16.98	17.26	17.46	17.74	+1.63	+2.83	+4.47
Burma	38.62	38.92	40.55	40.87	+0.77	+5.01	+5.83
Burundi	31.41	32.02	31.75	32.38	+1.92	+1.09	+3.08
Cameroon[c]	22.03	21.98	21.92	21.87	−0.24	−0.50	−0.73
Central African Republic	19.21	18.47	18.99	18.22	−3.86	−1.16	−5.13
Chad[f]	24.85	25.13	24.81	24.95	+1.12	−0.16	+0.41
Chile	17.39	17.06	17.58	17.26	−1.90	+1.09	−0.72
Colombia	15.16	15.06	15.22	15.13	−0.61	+0.43	−0.16
Congo[g]	59.29	59.02	59.30	59.04	−0.45	+0.02	−0.43

Costa Rica	17.64	17.74	17.75	17.85	+0.56	+0.63	+1.19
Côte d'Ivoire[c]	31.20	16.59	16.46	16.61	−46.84	−47.24	−46.77
Cyprus	17.58	17.76	17.41	17.59	+0.99	−0.96	+0.06
Dominica[g]	31.57	29.97	30.63	29.08	−5.08	−3.00	−7.89
Dominican Republic	25.76	25.78	26.53	26.59	+0.08	+2.99	+3.21
Ecuador	26.50	26.33	26.89	26.73	−0.62	+1.47	+0.87
Egypt	15.60	15.48	15.91	15.78	−0.75	+1.98	+1.14
El Salvador[c]	21.76	21.58	22.38	22.22	−0.84	+2.85	+2.09
Ethiopia[c]	12.37	12.90	12.50	13.12	+4.26	+1.00	+5.99
Fiji[c]	19.72	19.90	19.74	19.93	+0.92	+0.11	+1.07
Gambia[c]	26.02	25.47	27.60	26.46	−2.13	+6.05	+1.66
Ghana[c]	41.68	42.50	43.50	44.09	+1.95	+4.35	+5.78
Greece	15.70	15.80	15.65	15.75	+0.66	−0.31	+0.36
Grenada	19.58	19.81	19.49	19.75	+1.17	−0.45	+0.87
Guatemala	21.03	21.26	21.42	21.65	+1.06	+1.82	+2.92
Guinea Bissau[g]	38.22	39.34	38.21	39.54	+2.93	−0.03	+3.45
Guyana	24.47	25.06	24.16	24.77	+2.42	−1.27	+1.24
Haiti	23.16	23.27	23.74	23.87	+0.45	+2.51	+3.06
Honduras[c]	13.21	13.25	13.44	13.49	+0.29	+1.72	+2.09
Hungary[h]	12.47	12.59	12.60	12.71	+0.90	+1.01	+1.90
Iceland	19.96	19.45	20.01	19.52	−2.53	+0.25	−2.22
India	16.01	15.99	16.14	16.13	−0.12	+0.79	+0.74
Indonesia	31.02	30.82	31.05	30.84	−0.66	+0.08	−0.58
Iraq	45.31	45.30	45.33	45.31	−0.03	+0.03	+0.00
Israel	10.69	10.86	10.59	10.76	+1.57	−0.93	+0.66
Jamaica	22.00	22.20	22.52	22.64	+0.92	+2.37	+2.93
Jordan	24.31	23.43	24.75	23.84	−3.62	+1.82	−1.94
Kenya	19.60	19.95	19.93	20.27	+1.77	+1.66	+3.40
Korea	20.10	20.12	20.12	20.14	+0.07	+0.09	+0.17
Laos, PDR[i]	67.01	78.95	78.93	90.45	+17.82	+17.78	+34.97

Table 3.2 continued

Country	*Instability of selected variables*[a]				*Percentage change in export earnings instability*[b] *because of*		
	Export earnings	*Export earnings and payments from the IMF*	*Export earnings minus repayments to the IMF*	*Export earnings and payments from the IMF minus repayments to the IMF*	*payments from the IMF*	*repayments to the IMF*	*payments from the IMF minus repayments to the IMF*
Liberia	19.84	20.19	19.89	20.25	+1.75	+0.23	+2.04
Madagascar[c]	15.76	16.47	16.72	17.44	+4.50	+6.06	+10.62
Malawi[j]	15.70	16.37	16.06	16.71	+4.25	+2.24	+6.42
Malaysia	19.61	19.65	19.58	19.63	+0.20	−0.12	+0.08
Mali	24.88	24.90	24.78	24.81	+0.11	−0.37	−0.25
Mauritania	25.18	24.93	25.22	24.94	−1.00	+0.15	−0.93
Mauritius[c]	25.70	25.02	25.34	24.66	−2.66	−1.43	−4.05
Morocco	16.88	17.09	17.06	17.29	+1.26	+1.10	+2.44
Nepal	19.60	18.04	19.76	18.30	−7.96	+0.79	−6.66
New Zealand	13.41	13.10	13.42	13.12	−2.34	+0.10	−2.18
Nicaragua	32.82	33.23	32.86	33.27	+1.24	+0.11	+1.39
Niger[g]	39.94	40.49	39.94	40.49	+1.39	+0.00	+1.39
Pakistan	24.12	23.92	23.87	23.70	−0.82	−1.03	−1.73
Panama	14.04	15.00	14.89	15.94	+6.83	+6.08	+13.53
Papua New Guinea	18.94	19.98	18.91	18.98	+0.22	−0.16	+0.20
Peru	24.36	24.53	24.34	24.51	+0.68	−0.11	+0.61
Philippines	17.23	17.13	17.36	17.24	−0.56	+0.72	+0.04

Portugal	10.44	10.07	10.31	9.95	−3.52	−1.28	−4.67
Romania[c]	12.25	12.49	12.27	12.52	+2.00	+0.18	+2.20
St Lucia[c]	22.25	22.38	22.22	22.36	+0.57	−0.16	+0.46
St Vincent[k]	43.83	44.47	43.83	44.47	+1.46	+0.00	+1.46
Senegal[c]	35.58	34.83	35.77	35.04	−2.10	+0.55	−1.51
Sierra Leone	15.05	14.36	14.68	14.09	−4.59	−2.48	−6.35
Solomon Islands[c]	21.14	21.27	21.15	21.26	+0.58	+0.03	+0.54
Somalia[g]	37.85	40.40	37.85	40.40	+6.74	+0.00	+6.74
South Africa	19.31	19.35	19.51	19.55	+0.21	+1.01	+1.24
Spain	12.94	12.97	12.93	12.95	+0.18	−0.08	+0.08
Sri Lanka	23.00	22.12	23.88	22.99	−3.80	+3.81	−0.05
Sudan[c]	21.93	22.35	23.00	23.39	+1.92	+4.86	+6.65
Swaziland	21.84	21.93	22.09	22.18	+0.40	+1.13	+1.55
Syria[c]	31.28	31.02	31.27	31.01	−0.83	−0.03	−0.86
Tanzania	21.40	22.40	21.41	22.43	+4.65	+0.01	+4.80
Thailand	17.07	17.21	17.04	17.18	+0.87	−0.16	+0.67
Togo[g]	24.54	24.37	24.32	24.15	−0.68	−0.89	−1.56
Trinidad/Tobago	38.88	38.88	38.88	38.88	+0.00	+0.00	+0.00
Tunisia	24.27	23.86	24.20	23.79	−1.67	−0.29	−1.95
Turkey	21.87	21.31	22.00	21.43	−2.57	+0.59	−2.04
Uganda[f]	20.82	20.57	21.47	21.20	−1.21	+3.13	+1.81
Uruguay	19.78	19.27	20.19	19.70	−2.56	+2.04	−0.41
Vietnam[k]	64.86	65.96	65.12	66.26	+1.69	+0.40	+2.15
Western Samoa	32.40	31.62	33.34	32.41	−2.41	−2.89	+0.05
Yemen, PDR[f]	55.70	55.62	55.71	55.63	−0.14	+0.01	−0.13
Yugoslavia[c]	11.92	11.91	11.86	11.87	−0.01	−0.43	−0.41
Zaire	29.63	27.60	30.99	29.04	−6.85	+4.56	−1.99
Zambia[c]	24.74	23.85	24.99	23.97	−3.59	+1.05	−3.08
Zimbabwe[l]	19.83	19.66	20.16	20.00	−0.86	+1.69	+0.86

Table 3.2 continued

Country	*Instability of selected variables*[a]				*Percentage change in export earnings instability*[b] *because of*		
	Export earnings	*Export earnings and payments from the IMF*	*Export earnings minus repayments to the IMF*	*Export earnings and payments from the IMF minus repayments to the IMF*	*payments from the IMF*	*repayments to the IMF*	*payments from the IMF minus repayments to the IMF*
Aggregate statistics							
Arithmetic mean	24.52	24.50	24.75	24.84	−0.42	+0.69	+0.76
Median	21.86	21.57	21.96	22.03	+0.10	+0.41	+0.63

Sources: Own computations. Data on export earnings are from IMF (b, 1988 issue). The payments of the IMF up to 1979 were taken from Goreux (1980: 52 ff.) and the additional payments of 1980 and 1981 from IMF (a, February 1980, 1981 and 1982 issues). The repayments up to 1975 were taken from IMF (a, February 1976 issue: 15). For the following years, the repayments were calculated by using data on payments and 'net compensatory drawings' of subsequent February issues of IMF (a)

Notes: [a]On the computation of the measures of instability see the text. Export earnings are expressed in million SDR. For Laos PDR, and Zimbabwe, the uncorrected CV was used. v_L^* was utilized for Burma, Guinea Bisau, Hungary, Mauritius, Papua New Guinea, Vietnam, Yemen PDR, and Zimbabwe. In all other cases, v_{LL}^* was the 'best' measure of instability.

[b]The percentage changes were computed from the non-rounded values underlying the instabilities.

[c]The calculations refer to the period 1963–86.

[d]The calculations refer to the period 1972–87.

[e]The calculations refer to the period 1966–87.

[f]The calculations refer to the period 1963–84.

[g]The calculations refer to the period 1963–85.

[h]The calculations refer to the period 1970–87.

[i]The calculations refer to the period 1963–81.

[j]The calculations refer to the period 1964–87.

[k]The calculations refer to the period 1963–82.

[l]The calculations refer to the period 1964–86.

per cent. The payments under the CFF can be expected to induce a median effect on export earnings instability which ranges between a stabilization by 0.59 per cent and a destabilization by 0.66 per cent. Generally, the probability of a destabilizing effect is higher than of a stabilizing effect.

Moreover, it can be concluded that it is very unrealistic to expect payments from the IMF, repayments to the IMF or all transactions under the CFF to have a strong effect on export earnings instability for many countries. Stabilization effects of a magnitude of 10 per cent or more are far outside the confidence intervals for the median impacts. These findings hold true as long as no significant change of system occurs. What are the reasons for this relatively poor performance of the CFF with regard to its primary objective – export earnings stabilization? At least four reasons are important.

First, the compensation payments are not prompt enough to stabilize national export earnings effectively. An analysis of the time-lags between the end of the shortfall years and the compensation payments under the CFF shows that these were relatively long in the period 1963–80 (Herrmann 1983a: Section 2.2). The mean time-lag was slightly above four months and less than 10 per cent of the compensation payments were advance payments. This pattern has not significantly changed since then. In 1985, for example, the mean time-lag was 4.7 months and an early drawing within the shortfall year occurred in only one out of thirteen cases. These time-lags in the compensation payments have caused destabilizing effects on export earnings of several countries under the CFF. This holds true, for example, for Somalia and Panama, where destabilizing effects of compensation payments were higher than 5 per cent. Payments to those countries in the 1980s were disbursed in the year following the export earnings shortfall. The payments arrived in years of 'high' export earnings and thus had destabilizing impacts.

Second, forecast errors led in some cases to a destabilization of national export earnings. Payments were then disbursed in the calendar year in which the shortfall year ended but were still destabilizing. Panama, which experienced a noticeable destabilization effect by the drawings under the CFF, received in 1976 a payment for a shortfall in that year. However, Panama's export earnings in 1976 were higher than the short-run trend of export earnings as implied in the IMF's calculation of shortfalls, and clearly higher than the medium-run trend as implied in the instability measurement used here. Forecasting errors occurred and they have led in this case to destabilizing payments. Similar cases were payments to Bangladesh in

1972 and 1976, which were excessive given the actual trend values of export earnings in these years.

Third, repayments often led to a destabilization of national export earnings, as they are not linked to excesses in export earnings. The rule that repayments have to be repaid between the third and fifth year is unsatisfactory. It leads in many cases to a destabilizing impact on the current account since it is often repaid in a period of 'low' export earnings. For example, Argentina, a country with relatively strong destabilization effects of the repurchases, repaid major parts of its debt in 1986 and 1987 which were years of low export earnings. The same holds true for Bangladesh in the same two years.

Fourth, the fact that stabilization payments are limited to a share of the national quota lowers the CFF's potential for stabilizing export earnings. Basically, this rule leads to the relatively low magnitude of both stabilization and destabilization effects by the CFF. The limitation was an especially binding rule in the early years. Under the 1966 decision of the IMF, individual credits were not allowed to exceed 25 per cent of the quota. Sixty-three per cent of the drawings under the CFF touched this 25 per cent limitation (Goreux 1980: 37ff.).

This empirical analysis has focused on the direct stabilization effects of the CFF on export earnings instability. The conceptual question could be raised whether it is appropriate to concentrate on these direct effects and to ignore indirect effects. To the extent that compensation payments under the CFF become predictable for the user countries and for the banking sector, the willingness of the banking sector to give short-term credits to potential CFF users could increase. In such cases, optimal adjustments by the users, including debt-management operations, could lead to export earnings stabilization even if the direct effects of the CFF are destabilizing. This would be an indirect and uncertainty-reducing effect of the CFF which might lead to a significantly more positive evaluation of the CFF from the stabilization point of view.

A study by the IMF (Kumar 1988) is based on this argument. Of course, such positive indirect effects are possible. There is no empirical evidence, however, that they actually do exist. Hence, our procedure to measure the direct effects of the CFF on earnings instability seems superior to the approach adopted by Kumar. He imposes the existence of the indirect effects on his model, whereas we do not. Some other arguments cast some doubt on the existence of the indirect effects and the necessity to deal with them. First, it is the philosophy of compensatory financing schemes that they ought to stabilize export earnings directly. It is not their philosophy that countries should adjust optimally to a destabilizing compensation and secure stability by themselves. Second, it seems impossible to predict the compensation payment exactly. The country does not know how the IMF predicts future earnings and the country's willingness to co-operate. Third, and most important, payments from the IMF are cheap credits, and this provides a major incentive to use the facility irrespective of whether the CFF succeeds in its primary goal – earnings stabilization.

REDISTRIBUTIVE IMPACTS OF THE COMPENSATORY FINANCING FACILITY

The CFF is not purely a stabilization scheme. It also induces income transfers towards the borrowing nations. This can be explained as follows. The benchmark situation, against which the CFF has to be evaluated, is a situation without this policy. We posit that a country with export earnings shortfalls would have to demand foreign exchange on the international credit market in the benchmark situation. Certainly, other forms of macroeconomic adjustment to an export earnings shortfall are conceivable (Bevan *et al.* 1990b). One might think of a cut in imports or of increased domestic savings in order to stabilize the purchasing power to import. Such alternatives are not dealt with here, since it is not possible to model the whole variety of adjustment policies across all user countries of the CFF. Within our benchmark situation, conditions for a drawing under the CFF are more favourable than those for a commercial credit from the banking system. A uniform interest rate across countries is charged which is clearly lower than the market rate. Income transfers towards the users of the CFF arise.

In the following, the hidden income transfers in all drawings from the CFF in the period 1963–87 are computed. The analysis draws heavily upon the methodology developed in an earlier study (Herrmann 1983a: Section 3.2). Calculated income transfers are taken from that study for drawings from the CFF which had already been repaid in 1980. For all other drawings from the CFF, new computations are presented.

Methodologically, the computation of income transfers in the CFF is based on the approach of 'grants economics' (Horvath and Minassian 1976; Pincus 1971). Grant elements will be calculated. The grant equivalent in a credit is defined as the difference between the nominal value of the credit minus the present value of future repayments and interest payments:

$$G = L - \sum_{j=1}^{T} \frac{C_j + I_j}{(1+r)^j} \tag{3.8}$$

where G is the grant equivalent in a credit; L is the nominal value of the payment; j is the year of repayment or interest payment; C_j is the repayment which becomes due at the end of year j; I_j is the interest payment which becomes due at the end of year j; and r is the opportunity interest rate.

The grant equivalent is zero when the credit is given on current market conditions. Then no implicit transfer compared with a free market is involved. The grant equivalent becomes highest when no repayments or interest payments are demanded from the borrower. Then, 100 per cent of the nominal value of the credit is a gift to the borrower ($G = L$). Applied to the CFF, the grant equivalent in a compensatory financing credit is that amount which is given to the borrower on more favourable conditions than on the credit market. *Ex post*, the grant equivalent in a credit from the CFF can be calculated with the following formula:

$$G = L^G(1-b) - \sum_{j=1}^{5} \frac{C_j + i_j(L^G - \sum_{i=0}^{j-1} C_i)}{(1+r)^j} \tag{3.9}$$

where L^G is the gross value of the drawing, which is equal to the nominal value of the compensatory financing payment; b is the service charge as a percentage of the drawing's gross value; $L^N = L^G(1 + b)$ is the net value of the drawing after subtracting the service charge; i_j is the interest rate as a percentage per annum for compensatory financing credits under the CFF; $\sum_{i=0}^{j-1} C_i$ is the sum of repayments for a compensatory financing credit up to year j; and $L^G - \sum_{i=0}^{j-1} C_i$ is the remaining debt for the compensatory financing credit at the end of year j.

Compared with (3.8), equation (3.9) takes into account the following special features of the CFF:

1 The gross drawing differs from the net drawing under the CFF as a service charge exists. It has been 0.5 per cent of the gross drawing since the very beginning of the CFF.
2 The term I_j of the general formula is specified. Under the CFF, it is equal to the product of the interest rate and the remaining debt of the stabilization credit. It is a further characteristic of the CFF

that the interest rates varied before 1 May 1981, whereas there is a fixed interest rate in the existing system. More specifically, it was

$$i_j = i_j(Q_j, j) \tag{3.10}$$

in the IMF system up to 1 July 1974, where Q_j is the national quota in year j. Thereafter, the interest rate was no longer dependent on the national quota. It was

$$i_j = i_j(j) \tag{3.11}$$

in the IMF system from 1 July 1974 to 1 May 1981, with an interest rate rising over time ($i_T > i_{T-1}$). Under the existing IMF system, a fixed interest rate $\bar{i}$ has been determined since 1 May 1981:

$$i_j = \bar{i} \tag{3.12}$$

The interest rate is fixed annually for one financial year, depending on the estimated income and expenditure of the Fund (IMF (c), 1983 issue: 96). It is then held constant over the whole term of the credit, i.e. it is no longer differentiated by category and maturity.

3 The repayment of a drawing under the CFF has to occur within five years after the payment, and therefore T is equal to 5 in equation (3.9).

Suppose now that the charged interest rate under the CFF is lower than the opportunity interest rate, and the grant equivalent in a CFF drawing is positive. Then equation (3.9) implies that the grant equivalent in a drawing from the CFF is higher

1 the higher the nominal value of the stabilization payment net of the service charge,
2 the lower the amounts of repayments and interest payments for the stabilization payments and the later they occur,
3 the higher the opportunity interest rate.

Equation (3.9) is the basic equation for the following computation of the implicit transfers under the CFF, combined with either equation (3.10), (3.11) or (3.12). Actual grant equivalents are calculated for all drawings from the CFF in the period 1963–87 which were repaid fully up to 1988. For those drawings which were not or not fully repaid up to 1988, minimum grant equivalents are computed on the basis of specific assumptions on the future repayment schedule. In order to measure the implicit transfers, data on L^G, the nominal value of compensatory financing credits, are taken from IMF sources (IMF (a) (b, 1988 issue); Goreux 1980) and are presented in Appendices A.3–A.5. Data on b and i_i are shown and explained in Appendix A.1.

Information on repayments, which is necessary for C_j and $\sum_{i=0}^{j-1} C_i$, is partly taken from IMF (a, February 1976 issue: 15) and thereafter
Information on repayments, which is necessary for C_j and $\Sigma_{i=0}^{j-1} C_i$, is partly taken from IMF (a, February 1976 issue: 15) and thereafter
derived from data on payments and 'net compensatory drawings' of subsequent February issues of the same source. In cases where several CFF drawings of one country have not been repaid, repayment is attributed to the earliest credit. This procedure corresponds to the fifo (first in, first out) principle in calculating the remaining charges and the implicit transfers in individual drawings. A crucial point in the calculation of grant equivalents is to determine national opportunity interest rates r. It would be an ideal procedure to use country-specific opportunity interest rates. Those country-specific rates would have to represent the most favourable interest rate at which a country could receive an additional credit on the international capital market. Unfortunately, such country-specific data are not available, in particular not as time series. Therefore, it is necessary to assume a uniform opportunity interest rate for all user countries of the CFF within a given year. Two additional assumptions are made on this uniform opportunity interest rate:

1 The most favourable alternative from the national point of view to finance export earnings shortfalls is a loan from the World Bank.
2 The World Bank transmits its own average credit costs without additional charge to the borrowing countries.

Based on these suppositions, the average credit costs of the World Bank as summarized in Appendix A.2 are interpreted as uniform opportunity interest rates for accepting a loan from the CFF.

It is common in grant economics to present the grant ratio in the gross value of a credit (g^G) additionally to the grant equivalent:

$$g^G = 100\frac{G}{L^G} \tag{3.13}$$

As the gross value differs from the net value of the drawing, the grant ratio is additionally presented as a percentage of the net value of the credit:

$$g^N = 100\frac{G}{L^N} \tag{3.14}$$

In general, the computation of the CFF's redistributive effects to be presented in the following is contingent upon the assumptions of our approach. The grants are approximations and should be interpreted rather as lower limits of actual income transfers. This is due to the fact that the opportunity interest rates used are quite low. Moreover, minimum rather than actual grant equivalents are measured for non-repaid drawings.

The results of the quantitative analysis are presented in Appendices A.3–A.5 and summarized in Table 3.3. Appendix A.3 indicates grant equivalents in credits under the CFF which were given before 1 July 1974. For these credits, the interest rate charged by the IMF was still dependent on the national quota and varied from year to year. Equations (3.9) and (3.10) are utilized and the results are taken from an earlier study (Herrmann 1983a). In Appendix A.4, grant elements in credits given between 1 July 1974 and 30 April 1981 are presented. The interest rates for these credits no longer depended on the national quota but did still increase from year to year. Equations (3.9) and (3.11) are applied. Some results of Appendix A.4 are taken from the same earlier study, but most numbers are computed with information on credit costs and opportunity interest rates given in Appendices A.1 and A.2. Appendix A.5 summarizes the grant equivalents in those purchases made under the CFF from 1 May 1981 up to the end of 1987. These are the purchases which are made at a fixed interest rate over the whole period of repayment. Equations (3.9) and (3.12) are used for these calculations.

A first comparison of the average levels of credit and the average grant equivalents per credit reveals that these levels increased significantly over the three phases of the CFF. The average CFF drawing rose from 19.6 million special drawing rights (SDR) in the first phase (before 1 July 1974) to 38.1 million SDR in the second phase (from 1 July 1974 to 30 April 30 1981) and to 97.7 million SDR in the third phase (from 1 May 1981). Analogously, the average grant equivalent per credit increased from 2.1 million SDR in the first phase to 3.5 million SDR and 6.1 million SDR in the second and third phases. This rise in the magnitude of credits and grant equivalents over time holds, although Appendices A.3–A.5 involve a declining grant ratio per credit. The average g^N is 12.71 per cent in the first phase, but 9.15 per cent and 6.58 per cent in the second and third phases respectively. These differences in grant ratios over time should not be exaggerated, however. On the one hand, the non-repaid payments to

Table 3.3 Income transfers under the International Monetary Fund's Compensatory Financing Facility in the stabilization payments, 1963–87[a]

Country	Grant equivalents in the IMF credits 1963–87		GNP per capita (1982) (SDR)
	Absolute value (1,000 SDR)	Per capita (SDR)	
Iceland	3,512.4	15.01	10,969
Australia	30,463.3	2.00	10,091
New Zealand	18,508.4	5.77	7,165
Spain	5,352.5	0.14	4,873
Israel	9,849.8	2.45	4,819
Greece	6,131.0	0.63	3,877
Cyprus	1,782.1	2.76	3,533
Barbados	1,317.9	5.25	3,469
Uruguay	7,874.2	2.67	3,080
Yugoslavia	19,091.2	0.84	2,808
Mexico	16,952.4	0.23	2,482
South Africa	59,013.7	1.94	2,400
Portugal	24.422.7	2.43	2,228
Hungary	4,776.5	0.45	2,047
Chile	37,979.2	3.31	1,984
Brazil	76,059.2	0.60	1,966
Panama	6,024.4	3.14	1,920
Argentina	79,008.0	2.78	1,875
Fiji	2,239.0	3.40	1,775
Korea	53,573.2	1.36	1,730
Malaysia	28,605.5	1.97	1,694
Jordan	2,034.0	0.65	1,531
Syria	2,148.2	0.23	1,522
Ecuador	6,569.1	0.82	1,458
Colombia	1,040.9	0.04	1,286
Tunisia	3,896.9	0.58	1,250
Congo	691.7	0.40	1,241
Turkey	20,201.3	0.44	1,232
Dominican Republic	11,396.6	1.98	1,214
Peru	52,988.9	3.04	1,141
Jamaica	17,606.6	7.84	1,123
Mauritius	5,863.8	5.95	1,114
Belize	228.4	1.52	1,051
Costa Rica	5,748.9	2.47	1,042
Guatemala	286.9	0.00	1,024
St Lucia	206.2	1.68	942
Dominica	327.9	4.10	851
Grenada	202.4	1.79	851
Swaziland	566.9	0.85	842
Côte d'Ivoire	17,361.5	1.94	824
Cameroon	1,722.1	0.19	797
Morocco	42,919.8	2.12	779

Nicaragua	2,322.0	0.81	779
Zimbabwe	3,424.8	0.46	770
Papua New Guinea	837.5	0.27	752
Philippines	39,009.1	0.77	743
Thailand	42,862.5	0.88	716
St Vincent	156.7	1.55	697
El Salvador	7,538.1	1.48	634
Solomon Islands	121.1	0.49	616
Egypt	20,289.7	0.46	607
Honduras	4,747.7	1.20	598
Zambia	26,483.2	4.38	580
Bolivia	2,815.0	0.48	553
Guyana	3,247.3	4.07	534
Indonesia	23,768.3	0.16	525
Liberia	5,897.4	2.93	444
Senegal	7,129.9	1.18	444
Mauritania	1,775.6	1.11	435
Yemen, PDR	265.0	0.14	426
Sudan	24,204.0	1.20	389
Kenya	19,128.4	1.06	353
Sierra Leone	2,961.3	0.93	353
Pakistan	24,309.4	0.28	344
Gambia	1,349.3	1.98	326
Togo	696.6	0.25	317
Ghana	6,497.4	0.53	308
Madagascar	6,291.3	0.68	290
Sri Lanka	12,299.5	0.81	290
Central African Republic	1,673.5	0.70	281
Guinea	823.9	0.14	272
Haiti	219.3	0.04	272
Niger	1,421.1	0.24	272
Somalia	1,004.5	0.22	263
Tanzania	6,460.1	0.33	245
India	46,516.4	0.07	236
Uganda	9,888.6	0.74	217
Burundi	1,157.0	0.27	217
Guinea Bissau	337.0	0.40	199
Malawi	4,043.6	0.63	190
Burma	7,174.5	0.21	172
Zaire	35,974.0	1.17	163
Mali	469.9	0.07	154
Nepal	1,752.6	0.11	154
Bangladesh	24,249.1	0.26	127
Ethiopia	5,126.8	0.16	127
Chad	1,553.1	0.33	72

Source: Own computations
Note: [a]The GNP per capita data are from World Bank (a, 1985 issue) and the 1982 exchange rate (0.9058 SDR/US dollar) is used to express these data in SDR rather than US dollars. In order to calculate the income transfers, the grant equivalents in the individual transactions as presented in Appendices A.3–A.5 were added up for each country. Population data for the computation of per capita transfers are again from World Bank (a, 1985 issue).

Kampuchea strongly raised the mean grant ratio in the first phase. On the other hand, grant ratios and grant equivalents are probably underestimated the most in the third phase. This is due to the fact that many recent CFF drawings had still not been repaid, and an orderly structure of repayments of the loans was assumed. Given the severe debt problems of many less developed countries, the assumed structure of repayments will probably be too optimistic. It can be expected, therefore, that the increase in grant equivalents over time will actually become more pronounced than calculated here.

Table 3.3 shows the GNP per capita for the user countries of the CFF. Additionally, income transfers to these countries contained in the CFF's stabilization payments in the period 1963–87 are presented in absolute and per capita values. Within this table, the results of Appendices A.3–A.5 are summarized country by country. In this way we can elaborate on how the income transfers are distributed across recipient countries with differential income classes. The allocation of implicit transfers in the CFF can be evaluated from a redistributive point of view. Moreover, the quantitative importance of the welfare gain induced by the income transfers is shown for individual countries. The following major results can be derived:

1 The highest income transfers went to two South American countries, Argentina with 79.01 million SDR and Brazil with 76.06 million SDR. Then followed South Africa with 59.01, Korea with 53.37, Peru with 52.99 and India with 46.52 million SDR. Seven more countries received an income transfer higher than 30 million SDR under the CFF: Morocco, Thailand, Romania, Philippines, Chile, Zaire and Australia.
2 In terms of per capita income transfers, Iceland ranked highest with 15.01 SDR, followed by Jamaica with 7.84, Mauritius with 5.95, New Zealand with 5.77 and Barbados with 5.25 SDR. Three other countries received a hidden income transfer of more than 4 SDR per capita: Zambia (4.38), Dominica (4.09) and Guyana (4.07). The arithmetic mean of grant equivalents per capita amounted to 1.54 SDR, with a standard deviation of 2.11 SDR in the cross-section of countries.

The distribution of per capita transfers does not appear to follow any distribution criterion. Countries with relatively high per capita income received per capita transfers of the IMF system that were either above average (Iceland, New Zealand) or sub-average (Mexico, Spain). Countries with lower per capita income also received transfers that were either above average (Guyana, Zambia) or sub-average (India,

Bangladesh). The income transfers arising from the compensatory financing system of the IMF are a by-product of export earnings stabilization and seem to be arbitrarily connected to distribution indicators like per capita income. This result is confirmed by correlation analysis. The correlation coefficient between GNP transfers and per capita income transfers received under the IMF's CFF is 0.59. This positive correlation coefficient is significantly different from zero at the 99.9 per cent level and it suggests an even stronger conclusion: countries with a higher per capita income got higher per capita transfers in the period 1963–87 than those with lower per capita income. A significantly positive correlation between per capita income transfers and per capita income exists within the highest income group as well.

Additional findings can be derived if income transfers under the CFF are shown for country groups with different income levels. The following country groups are distinguished: (a) countries with a per capita income of more than 1,500 SDR (group I); (b) countries with a per capita income between 750 and 1,499 SDR (group II); (c) countries with a per capita income from 300 to 749 SDR (group III); (d) countries with a per capita income under 300 SDR (group IV). Table 3.4 presents the results. It can be seen from the table that group I, the countries with the highest per capita incomes, have benefited the most from the CFF in absolute and in per capita terms. The mean grant equivalent per recipient country due to the IMF credits in the period 1963–87 was higher by more than 60 per cent for this group than for all recipient countries. The mean grant equivalent per capita increased with the income group. Moreover, the *t* test proves a significantly higher per capita transfer for the highest income class compared with the two lowest income classes. It can be seen, too, that grant equivalents for the lowest income group were significantly smaller than those for income groups II and III. Obviously, the redistribution effects arising under the CFF tended to favour richer countries.

NATIONAL INTERESTS IN THE COMPENSATORY FINANCING FACILITY: A WELFARE ECONOMIC APPROACH

In the previous sections, the effectiveness of the CFF in stabilizing export earnings was evaluated and redistributive impacts of the CFF were explored. The basic approach of these sections was to regard the CFF from a donor's point of view. A cross-country perspective was

Table 3.4 Indicators of the connection between income transfers under the Compensatory Financing Facility and the per capita income (GNPC) of the recipient countries, 1963–87[a]

Income class of the countries		*Countries with a per capita income*			
Indicator	*All countries*	*more than 1,500 SDR*	*between 750 and 1,500 SDR*	*between 300 and 750 SDR*	*less than 300 SDR*
Mean grant equivalent (G)					
Absolute value (1,000 SDR)	12,952	20,849	8,928	12,057	8,422
In per cent of $\overline{G}$ of all countries	100	161.0	68.9	93.1	65.0
Mean grant equivalent per capita (GC)					
In SDR	1.54	2.61	1.79	1.25	0.38
In per cent of $\overline{GC}$ of all countries	100	168.9	115.6	81.0	24.5
Correlation coefficient between grant equivalents per capita and per capita income	0.59***	0.65***	0.05	0.13	0.14
Comparison of grant equivalents per capita across income classes (*t* statistics)					
All countries	–	–	–	–	–
Countries with a GNPC of more than 1,500 SDR	1.55 (DF = 28)	–	–	–	–
Countries with 750 SDR ≤ GNPC < 1,500 SDR	0.50 (DF = 35)	1.06 (DF = 55)	–	–	–

Countries with 300 SDR ≤ GNPC < 750 SDR	0.88 (DF = 84)	1.96* (DF = 30)	1.09 (DF = 43)	–	–
Countries with a GNPC under 300 SDR	4.94*** (DF = 107)	3.43** (DF = 22)	3.29** (DF = 22)	3.39** (DF = 25)	–

Source: Own computations with data from Table 3.3

Notes: *** (**,*) Statistically significant at the 99.9 per cent (99 per cent, 90 per cent) level given a two-sided test.

[a]Those countries are considered for which data on GNPC and *G* were available.

chosen. In the following, the national interests of user countries of the CFF are highlighted. An individual country will usually receive an income transfer from participating in the CFF and will experience either a stabilizing or a destabilizing effect on its export earnings. In order to evaluate these effects jointly, a national welfare function has to be developed which allows an integrated assessment of the national transfers and the stabilization effects.

The level R of national export revenues, the instability I^R of national export revenues and the national costs CA of participating in the IMF may enter the welfare function of a potential recipient country of the IMF compensatory financing system. This gives

$$W = W(R, I^R, \text{CA}) \tag{3.15}$$

The way stabilization policies have an influence on welfare in the case of risk aversion has been analysed by Newbery and Stiglitz (1981: 57ff.).

Assuming their concept of producer's risk aversion applies to the planners in an exporting country too, the 'risk benefits' due to a lower instability in export earnings can be computed. Using national export earnings as a measure of welfare, these risk benefits (RB) are[9]

$$\text{RB} = -0.5\rho\Delta v_R^2 \tag{3.16}$$

where

$$\rho = -\frac{RU''(R)}{U'(R)}$$

and ρ is the coefficient of relative risk aversion as defined by Newbery and Stiglitz; $U'('')$ is the first (second) derivative of the social utility function with respect to the level of export earnings and v_R^2 is the squared CV of national export earnings.

With risk aversion ($\rho > 0$), a decreasing instability of export earnings increases the welfare level. Additionally, the effects of the change in export earnings, i.e. the so-called transfer benefit TB, and of the costs of making the application on national welfare have to be taken into account. The effect of a compensatory financing credit of the IMF on national welfare can then be measured by

$$\frac{\Delta W}{W} = \frac{\Delta R}{R} - 0.5\rho\Delta v_R^2 - \frac{\Delta CA}{R} \tag{3.17}$$

where $\Delta W/W$ is the relative change in the country's welfare position due to exports.

The gain in export earnings can be computed with the grant

element in the stabilization credit. Taking into account formulae (3.9) and (3.12) for the IMF system as it has been in force since 1981, equation (3.17) can be rewritten as

$$\frac{\Delta W}{W} = \left[L^G(1-b) - \sum_{j=1}^{5} \frac{C_j + i(L^G - \sum_{i=0}^{j-1} C_i)}{(1+r)^j} \right] \Big/ R$$

$$- 0.5\rho \Delta v_R^2 - \frac{\Delta CA}{R} \qquad (3.18)$$

Apparently, the following factors are essential for the net welfare impact arising from an IMF credit:

1 the difference between the opportunity interest rate and the interest rate for IMF credits;
2 the stabilizing or destabilizing impact of the CFF on export earnings as well as the degree of risk aversion of macroeconomic planners;
3 the relation between the marginal costs of making an application to the IMF and the amount of compensation.

The first and third factors are more likely to give rise to welfare gains for richer developing countries. The divergences between opportunity interest rate and repayment interest rate will be especially high in countries with a high degree of indebtedness. According to experience, these are countries which are already integrated into the international trade network and which are not the poorest countries. A statistical cross-country analysis confirms this presumption. By utilizing World Bank data for 1988 (World Bank (b), 1990 issue), it can be shown that those developing countries with a high average interest rate for external public borrowing tend to be richer in terms of the GNP per capita and tend to have higher shares of exports of goods and services in GDP. The respective coefficients of correlation are $r = 0.61$ and $r = 0.21$ respectively for eighty-eight countries, i.e. the relationship is statistically significant at least at the 95 per cent level. Assuming constant marginal costs of making an application which are independent of the amount of export earnings shortfall, these costs are more restrictive for countries with relatively small shortfalls. This connection may explain why countries with a relatively low per capita income applied proportionately less for IMF stabilization payments and received relatively low transfers.

In the following quantitative analysis for the period 1963–87, aggregate welfare impacts are computed for the user countries of the

IMF's CFF on the basis of formula (3.16) and the calculations on the system's stabilizing and redistributive effects shown above. Risk and transfer benefits are distinguished. Two assumptions have to be made, however:

1. An assumption is necessary on the costs of making an application. We posit that $\Delta CA = 0$.
2. The coefficient of relative risk aversion has to be determined. No empirical information is available on the magnitude of relative risk aversion. Similarly to a study by Kumar (1988), we base our computations on alternative values of ρ:

$$\rho = 0 \tag{3.19}$$

$$\rho = 1 \tag{3.19'}$$

$$\rho = \frac{I_i}{\bar{I}} \tag{3.19''}$$

where I_i ($\bar{I}$) is the instability of export earnings of country i (mean instability of export earnings across countries).

Table 3.5 contains the national welfare effects due to the CFF and breaks them down into transfer and risk benefits for $\rho = 1$. Aggregate welfare effects in the period 1963–87 are computed and expressed as a percentage of average national export earnings during this period. The following main results emerge from Table 3.5:

1. Given a coefficient of relative risk aversion of unity, it is striking that eighty-nine out of ninety-one countries gained from the participation in the IMF's CFF. This means that the transfer benefit, which was positive for all user countries, was in only two cases overcompensated by a negative risk benefit resulting from the CFF's destabilizing impact on national export earnings. In all but three countries (Côte d'Ivoire, Ghana, Guatemala), the transfer benefit was also the dominant source of the welfare change due to the CFF.
2. As a percentage of average national export earnings in the period 1963–87, the transfer benefits arising from the CFF in this period ranged between 0.01 per cent (Iraq) and 18.78 per cent (Laos PDR). The mean share of the transfer benefit in average national export earnings was 1.83 per cent. The risk benefit was on average negative, thus indicating a somewhat destabilizing impact of the CFF on national export earnings (−0.23 per cent). Consequently, the aggregate welfare increase due to the redistributive

Table 3.5 National welfare effects due to transfer and risk benefits under the International Monetary Fund's Compensatory Financing Facility, 1963–87[a] (per cent)

				Share in total welfare effects of	
Country	*Transfer benefits*[b]	*Risk benefits*	*Total welfare effects*	*transfer benefits*	*risk benefits*
Afghanistan	0.16	−0.01	0.15	107.62	−7.62
Argentina	2.00	−0.10	1.91	105.18	−5.18
Australia	0.28	−0.01	0.27	103.33	−3.33
Bangladesh	4.43	−0.21	4.22	104.92	−4.92
Barbados	1.13	−0.24	0.89	127.09	−27.09
Belize	0.49	−0.03	0.45	107.05	−7.05
Bolivia	0.65	+0.17	0.82	79.72	+20.28
Brazil	0.77	−0.13	0.64	120.61	−20.61
Burma	3.28	−0.89	2.39	137.48	−37.48
Burundi	2.40	−0.31	2.09	114.80	−14.80
Cameroon	0.34	+0.04	0.37	90.57	+9.43
Central African Republic	2.88	+0.19	3.07	93.96	+6.04
Chad	3.30	−0.02	3.27	100.76	−0.76
Chile	1.89	+0.02	1.92	98.82	+1.18
Colombia	0.06	+0.00	0.06	92.88	+7.12
Congo	0.19	+0.15	0.34	56.67	+43.33
Costa Rica	1.11	−0.04	1.07	103.49	−3.49
Côte d'Ivoire	1.36	+3.49	4.85	28.12	+71.88
Cyprus	0.73	−0.00	0.73	100.24	−0.24
Dominica	3.04	+0.76	3.79	80.08	+19.92
Dominican Republic	2.37	−0.22	2.16	110.07	−10.07
Ecuador	0.63	−0.06	0.57	110.76	−10.76

Table 3.5 continued

Country	*Transfer benefits*[b]	*Risk benefits*	*Total welfare effects*	*Share in total welfare effects of*	
				transfer benefits	*risk benefits*
Egypt	1.30	−0.03	1.27	102.22	−2.22
El Salvador	1.64	−0.10	1.54	106.58	−6.58
Ethiopia	2.28	−0.10	2.19	104.37	−4.37
Fiji	1.61	−0.04	1.57	102.66	−2.66
Gambia	5.05	−0.12	4.94	102.34	−2.34
Ghana	1.01	−1.03	−0.03	−3,733.56	+3,833.56
Greece	0.28	−0.01	0.27	102.88	−2.88
Grenada	1.79	−0.03	1.76	101.90	−1.90
Guatemala	0.05	−0.13	−0.09	−52.94	+152.94
Guinea Bissau	4.96	−0.51	4.44	111.55	−11.55
Guyana	1.79	−0.07	1.72	104.30	−4.30
Haiti	0.24	−0.17	0.07	324.71	−224.71
Honduras	1.28	−0.04	1.24	103.00	−3.00
Hungary	0.09	−0.03	0.06	152.71	−52.71
Iceland	0.86	+0.09	0.95	90.83	+9.17
India	1.02	−0.02	1.00	101.93	−1.93
Indonesia	0.29	+0.06	0.35	84.01	+15.99
Iraq	0.01	+0.00	0.01	100.00	+0.00
Israel	0.38	−0.01	0.37	102.03	−2.03
Jamaica	3.76	−0.14	3.62	103.95	−3.95
Jordan	0.76	+0.11	0.87	86.98	+13.02
Kenya	3.13	−0.13	3.00	104.46	−4.46
Korea	0.53	−0.01	0.52	101.54	−1.54

Laos PDR	18.78	−18.45	0.33	5,699.69	−5,599.69
Liberia	1.98	−0.08	1.89	104.34	−4.34
Madagascar	3.10	−0.28	2.82	109.88	−9.88
Malawi	2.96	−0.16	2.80	105.85	−5.85
Malaysia	0.48	−0.00	0.48	100.82	−0.82
Mali	0.43	+0.02	0.45	96.14	+3.86
Mauritania	1.19	+0.06	1.25	95.18	+4.82
Mauritius	2.79	+0.26	3.05	91.42	+8.58
Morocco	3.68	−0.07	3.61	101.94	−1.94
Nepal	2.36	+0.25	2.61	90.56	+9.44
New Zealand	0.66	+0.04	0.70	94.51	+5.49
Nicaragua	0.82	−0.15	0.67	122.13	−22.13
Niger	0.94	−0.22	0.72	130.56	−30.56
Pakistan	1.84	+0.10	1.94	94.82	+5.18
Panama	3.21	−0.28	2.93	109.73	−9.73
Papua New Guinea	0.19	−0.01	0.18	104.20	−4.20
Peru	3.28	−0.04	3.24	101.13	−1.13
Philippines	1.58	−0.00	1.58	100.11	−0.11
Portugal	1.03	+0.05	1.08	95.35	+4.65
Romania	0.79	−0.03	0.76	104.43	−4.43
St Lucia	0.98	−0.02	0.95	102.57	−2.57
St Vincent	2.01	−0.28	1.73	116.36	−16.36
Senegal	1.86	+0.19	2.05	90.72	+9.28
Sierra Leone	2.73	+0.14	2.87	95.13	+4.87
Solomon Islands	0.43	−0.03	0.40	106.34	−6.34
Somalia	1.50	−1.00	0.50	299.83	−199.83
South Africa	0.65	−0.05	0.61	107.70	−7.70
Spain	0.06	−0.00	0.05	102.39	−2.39
Sri Lanka	1.94	+0.00	1.94	99.88	+0.12
Sudan	6.46	−0.33	6.13	105.40	−5.40

Table 3.5 continued

Country	*Transfer benefits*[b]	*Risk benefits*	*Total welfare effects*	*Share in total welfare effects of*	
				transfer benefits	*risk benefits*
Swaziland	0.39	−0.07	0.32	123.71	−23.71
Syria	0.25	+0.08	0.33	74.67	+25.33
Tanzania	2.10	−0.23	1.87	112.04	−12.04
Thailand	1.36	−0.02	1.34	101.41	−1.41
Togo	0.67	+0.09	0.76	87.57	+12.43
Tunisia	0.46	+0.12	0.57	79.90	+20.10
Turkey	0.82	+0.10	0.91	89.54	+10.46
Uganda	3.65	−0.08	3.57	102.24	−2.24
Uruguay	1.60	+0.02	1.62	99.02	+0.98
Vietnam	1.57	−0.92	0.66	239.14	−139.14
Western Samoa	5.93	−0.00	5.93	100.05	−0.05
Yemen, PDR	0.10	+0.04	0.14	72.03	+27.97
Yugoslavia	0.44	+0.01	0.44	98.66	+1.34
Zaire	4.93	+0.17	5.10	96.61	+3.39
Zambia	3.36	+0.19	3.55	94.72	+5.28
Zimbabwe	0.50	−0.03	0.47	107.22	−7.22
Aggregate statistics					
Arithmetic mean	+1.83	−0.23	+1.60	+124.62	−24.62
Standard deviation	+2.23	+1.98	+1.46	+716.09	+716.09
Median	+1.28	−0.02	+1.07	+102.22	−2.22
Minimum	+0.01	−18.45	−0.09	−3,733.56	−5,599.69
Maximum	+18.78	+3.49	+6.13	+5,699.69	+3,833.56

Aggregate test statistics for an alternative relative risk aversion coefficient ($\rho I_i/\bar{I}$)					
Arithmetic mean	+1.83	−0.61	+1.22	+60.70	+39.30
Standard deviation	+2.30	+5.35	+3.83	+317.73	+317.73
Median	+1.28	−0.02	+1.07	+101.26	−1.26
Minimum	+0.01	−50.71	−31.93	−2,894.88	−191.79
Maximum	+18.78	+4.46	+6.16	+291.79	+2,994.88

Source: Own computations

Notes: [a]The computation of welfare effects is based on equation (3.16) in the text. A coefficient of relative risk aversion of $\rho = 1$ is assumed and the relative welfare effect is related to average national export earnings in the period 1963–87.

[b]The transfer benefits are equal to total welfare effects in the case of a relative risk aversion coefficient of zero.

> and stabilizing effects of the CFF amounted to 1.60 per cent on average for all ninety-one countries. When median shares of transfer and risk benefits in national export earnings are calculated, the respective values are 1.23 per cent and −0.02 per cent. The median welfare change across countries was as high as 1.07 per cent of national export earnings. For most countries, the welfare change was smaller than the transfer benefit, indicating that risk benefits were negative. Table 3.5 reveals in many cases that transfer benefits explained between 90 per cent and 110 per cent of the welfare change and the risk benefits between +10 per cent and −10 per cent.

The corresponding calculations for risk neutrality ($\rho = 0$) are included in Table 3.5 as a special case. When planners in the exporting countries are risk neutral and export earnings instability does not affect their utility functions, the welfare changes reduce to the transfer benefits. No risk benefits occur. The second column in Table 3.5 illustrates the aggregate welfare effects due to participation in the CFF, expressed as a percentage of average national export earnings in the period 1963–87.

Table 3.5 additionally includes some summarized statistics on risk benefits, transfer benefits and welfare changes for the relative risk aversion coefficient $\rho = I_i/\bar{I}$. This assumption on the coefficient of relative risk aversion implies that countries facing an export earnings instability that is above average (sub-average) will be more (less) risk averse than others. It can be seen that the extreme effects on risk benefits are strongly affected by this assumption compared with a relative risk aversion coefficient of unity. The aggregate welfare effect on user countries of participating in the CFF was also clearly worsened in individual countries (Laos PDR). However, the median welfare change due to participation in the CFF remained constant compared with $\rho = 1$, and still the overwhelming majority of countries realized a welfare gain due to participating in the CFF: eighty-six out of ninety-one. Moreover, the transfer benefits remain the dominant cause of the net welfare change in virtually all user countries of the CFF.

Summing up the discussion of national interests in the CFF, it can be stated that the welfare change that a country experiences as a consequence of the use of the IMF's CFF depends upon the difference between opportunity interest rate and repayment interest rate as well as on the relationship between the amount of compensation and the marginal costs of making the application. Both factors tend to mean that welfare gains can be expected primarily by countries with a strong foreign trade sector and a high indebtedness. Moreover, the national welfare impact is a function of the stabilizing effect of the CFF on national export earnings and of the relative risk aversion coefficient of the planner in the user country. In the quantitative analysis, transfer and risk benefits arising from the CFF for individual user countries were measured and added up country by country. The dominant source of the national welfare gains was the high transfer benefits.

THE EXTENSION OF THE SCHEME TO THE COMPENSATORY AND CONTINGENCY FACILITY

As outlined earlier in this chapter and in Chapter 5 below, there have been several important extensions of the CFF since its establishment in 1963. The CFF was broadened to include receipts from tourism and workers' remittances in calculating the export shortfall in 1979. A further extension in 1981 enabled the users to be compensated for an excessive rise in the cost of cereal imports. The most recent extension, however, is that the CCFF was established on 23 August 1988 (Decision No. 8955-(88/126)). The new facility kept all the essential features of the CFF but added a mechanism for contingency financing of member countries that had entered adjustment programmes supported by the IMF (Pownall and Stuart 1988; IMF (c), 1989 issue: 35–6; UNCTAD 1988a).

As before, the CCFF intends to help countries meet shortfalls in their export earnings and/or excesses in the cost of cereal imports. The new contingency element has to be seen in association with other arrangements of a member country with the Fund, i.e. a Stand-by or Extended Fund Facility arrangement or an arrangement under the Structural Adjustment Facility or the Enhanced Structural Adjustment Facility. For countries participating in such an arrangement, the Fund may rapidly provide additional funds under the contingency element in order to help countries in their efforts to cope with adverse external shocks. The external shocks may be related to key economic variables such as export or import prices or interest rates, provided that the variables cover a substantial proportion of the exogenous component of the member's current account. Deviations in the variables covered by a contingency mechanism are measured in comparison with baseline projections made at the start or the review of a Fund arrangement. The net sum of deviations of the key variables have to exceed a minimum threshold before external contingency purchases may be permitted (Decision No. 8955-(88/126), 19). This threshold is 10 per cent of the country's quota.

The following new limitations on access to the CCFF were introduced in 1988. Up to 40 per cent of the national quota is available under the traditional earnings stabilization component and under the contingency component respectively, and up to 17 per cent for the cereal-import component. Additionally, user countries may draw on an optional tranche of up to 25 per cent of the national quota to supplement any of the three components. These limitations add up to a maximum use of the CCFF of 122 per cent of the national quota for all three components or 105 per cent for two of three components. An additional limitation, of 70 per cent, refers to the share of contingency in total funds under the associated agreement with the IMF. Furthermore, not more than 35 per cent of the quota within the contingency funds is to be induced by changes in interest rates.

These limits are valid for countries using the new contingency element. Other countries, which have a satisfactory balance-of-payments position and do not need contingency financing, face an upper limit of 83 per cent of the quota for either of the two old elements, i.e. export shortfalls and excesses in cereal import costs. A joint limit of 105 per cent holds then for these two elements.

Separate from this major revision of the system in 1988, a decision was made in December 1990 to add an oil element to the CCFF (IMF (e), September 1991 issue). It was supposed to compensate members of the Fund for sharp rises in the cost of their imports of crude petroleum, petroleum products and natural gas. The overall access limit remained, however, at 122 per cent of a country's quota. Additionally, the range of services covered under an export shortfall was further widened and now includes most services.

The extension of the CFF to the CCFF has at least two important implications. First, the IMF system is now even more oriented towards the current account balance and macroeconomic stabilization. All major variables affecting the current account balance, including import prices and interest rates, are now covered, whereas the CFF started with a stabilization of export earnings for goods and services. Moreover, the system is now closely linked with the macroeconomic adjustment due to the contingency element. Second, the IMF stresses the *ex ante* compensation with the new contingency element rather than the *ex post* compensation of earnings shortfalls. Important implications for the stabilization, redistribution and allocation effects of the IMF system emerge from this. In general, the *ex ante* approach of the contingency financing is welcome from the stabilization point of view. However, baseline projections are needed, and the forecasts of deviations may perform well or badly. Consequently, the stabilization effects of the CCFF remain uncertain. With regard to redistribution, the grant ratios in contingency financing are the same as in traditional compensatory financing credits. Impacts on factor allocation become more important now since the contingency financing goes hand in hand with macroeconomic adjustment under an IMF programme. It will become more important in future evaluations to combine the welfare considerations of the CCFF with the analysis of macroeconomic impacts of the associated Fund programmes in the user country.

SUMMARY

It was investigated in this chapter whether the CFF has realized its primary objective, the stabilization of export earnings, which redistributive impacts have occurred and how the system's performance can be evaluated from the donor's as well as the recipient countries' points of view. We can summarize as follows:

1. CFF's success from the donor's point of view is very limited. The stabilizing impacts of the CFF are on average small, and for most countries a destabilizing impact occurred. Among other reasons, this is due to time-lags between export earnings shortfalls and compensation payments. Beyond the impact on export earnings instability, the CFF causes strong redistributive effects due to the grant elements in the CFF credits. From an international point of view, the allocation of these implicit aid flows seems untargeted. Per capita income transfers are positively correlated with indicators of need like per capita income.
2. From the national point of view of a recipient country, the CFF has to be evaluated more favourably. When welfare impacts are broken down along the lines of Newbery and Stiglitz, it can be shown that virtually all countries gained from participation in the CFF. This is due to the dominant impact of the transfer benefits the countries realized, whereas the risk benefits – either positive or negative – remained negligible. This empirical result implies that the major incentive to participate in the CFF is the implicit income transfer that the drawing country receives.

4 Commodity-related financial compensation by the European Community

INTRODUCTION

Various financial compensation schemes, which are commodity related, have been introduced by the European Community (EC) within its common development policy. STABEX, the most popular system, was introduced in 1975 under the First Lomé Convention (1975–9). It remained a major element of the Second (1980–4) and the Third (1985–90) Lomé Conventions as well as the Fourth (1990–9) which is currently valid for the twelve EC countries and sixty-nine African, Caribbean and Pacific (ACP) countries. STABEX is the major commodity-related export earnings stabilization scheme which is in force. It has often been discussed as a model for the future cooperation between developed and developing countries on the issue of commodity instability. Consequently, a parallel system of compensation for loss of export earnings (COMPEX) was established in 1987 for least developed countries not signatory to the Lomé Convention (Commission of the EC 1987a). This was in addition to the modifications of STABEX in the course of the Lomé Convention. In early 1982, it was reported that an extension of STABEX towards Latin American and Asian countries was additionally planned by the EC Commission. Different from STABEX and COMPEX is SYSMIN, which was established under Lomé II for mining-dependent ACP countries. It is not a compensatory financing system oriented towards export earnings stabilization, but projects are financed in order to strengthen the mineral sector or to diversify the economy.

It is the objective of this chapter to evaluate these financial compensation schemes from the donor's as well as the recipient countries' point of view. Primarily, the effects of STABEX on stabilization, redistribution and allocation goals will be investigated. The stabilizing, redistributive and national welfare impacts of STABEX will be

Table 4.1 Major provisions of the STABEX system in the Lomé Convention[a]

Subject	*Existing provisions in Lomé IV*
Provisions with special importance for the stabilization effects of STABEX	
Principle of administration	The ACP countries and the EC Commission shall take steps to ensure that payments are made rapidly. In order to realize this, statistical cooperation shall be instituted (Article 199, paragraph 1)
Deadline of applications	It is a pre-condition for a STABEX payment that the request including annual statistical data is sent to the Commission not later than 31 March in the year following that of application (Article 199, paragraphs 2 and 3)
Deadline for decisions	Cross-checking of statistics and consultations between the EC Commission and the ACP country on the application shall be concluded not later than 30 June of the year following that of application (Article 207, paragraphs 1 and 2). Then the Commission has to make the decision
Advance payments	Advance payments are possible (Article 207) and the same rules as for later payments apply then for the decision process and for cooperation between the EC and the ACP state on statistical issues (Article 205–207)
Definition of the shortfall year	The shortfall year is the calendar year (Article 197)
Provisions with special importance for the redistribution effects of STABEX	
Repayments	All STABEX payments are interest-free and non-repayable loans
Provisions with special importance for the stabilization and redistribution effects of STABEX	
Basic principle and objective	Commodity-related export earnings shortfalls of ACP countries are compensated with the aim of remedying the harmful effects of the instability of export earnings (Article 186, paragraph 1)
Products of the STABEX scheme	Forty-nine agricultural products or product groups are distinguished (Article 187). STABEX covers: groundnuts; groundnut oil; cocoa and various cocoa products; coffee and coffee products; cotton and cotton linters; coconuts; copra; coconut oil; palm products; raw hides and skins; leather; wood products; bananas; tea; raw sisal; vanilla; cloves; wool; mohair; gum arabic; pyrethrum; essential oils;

Table 4.1 continued

Subject	*Existing provisions in Lomé IV*
	sesame seed; cashew nuts and kernels; pepper; shrimps and prawns; squid, octopus and cuttlefish; cotton seed; oil cake; rubber; peas; beans; lentils; nutmeg and mace; shea nut products; mangoes
Subject of compensation	STABEX applies to export earnings of individual products or product groups to the EC, possibly also to other ACP states or to all destinations (Article 189, paragraph 1). Export shortfalls are defined in cost, insurance and freight (cif) terms
Magnitude of compensation	The transfer basis is the amount of a STABEX payment to an ACP country (Article 197, paragraph 5) and it is nearly equal to the measured export earnings shortfall. The transfer basis is defined as the difference between the reference level and actual export earnings minus 4.5 per cent of the reference level (Article 197, paragraph 3). The reference level is the average of export earnings during four of six calendar years preceding the application, where the two years with the lowest and highest figures are excluded (Article 197, paragraph 2). The 4.5 per cent reduction diminishes to 1 per cent for least developed ACP states or is dropped if the shortfall is lower than 2 million ECU (least developed or landlocked ACP states) or 1 million ECU (island ACP states) (Article 197, paragraph 3, 4)
Limitations for compensation payments	If the amount of resources available is lower than the total amount of the transfer bases, each transfer can be reduced (Article 194). The transfer basis can also be shortened if the shortfall is caused by trade-policy measures of the ACP country (Articles 201–204)
Pre-conditions for compensation payments	A dependence threshold must be exceeded. Export earnings of a STABEX product to all destinations must be higher than 5 per cent of total export earnings in the year preceding the year of application, and 4 per cent for sisal. The dependence threshold for least developed countries, landlocked and island ACP countries is 1 per cent (Article 196, paragraph 1, 2)
Financial means of STABEX	An amount of 1,500 million ECU is available for STABEX under the Financial Protocol 1990–5 of Lomé IV (1990–5). Under Lomé I, II and Lomé III, 380, 550 and 925 million ECU were available respectively

Subject	*Existing provisions in Lomé IV*
Provisions with special importance for the allocation effects of STABEX	
Conditions on the use of STABEX payments	Transfers shall be devoted to the sector that recorded the loss of export earnings or, where appropriate, to diversification, either for use in other appropriate productive sectors, in principle agricultural, or for the processing of agricultural products (Article 186, paragraph 2). The ACP state has to deliver a report on the use of the funds transferred within twelve months after the payments (Article 212, paragraph 1)

Source: Own compilation
Note: [a]All the cited provisions relate to Lomé IV. Many of these rules changed over time, for example those on repayment conditions. For earlier provisions, see *The Courier* (1979), Muller (1980) and Commission of the EC (1985).

assessed quantitatively with the same techniques as applied in the previous chapter.

IMPORTANT RULES OF THE STABEX SYSTEM AND TRANSACTIONS UNDER LOME I–III

It is the declared aim of STABEX to remedy

> the harmful effects of the instability of export earnings and to help the ACP states overcome one of the main obstacles to the stability, profitability and sustained growth of their economies, to support their development efforts and to enable them in this way to ensure economic and social progress for their peoples by helping to safeguard their purchasing power . . .
>
> (Article 186)[1]

Compensation is granted for shortfalls in export earnings of forty-nine agricultural products on which the ACP economies are dependent. The system applies to export earnings in trade with the EC or, upon request, to export earnings to all destinations or to other ACP countries. Table 4.1 gives a more comprehensive overview of the STABEX provisions that are important for the system's impact on goals of stabilization, redistribution and allocation.

As in the case of the International Monetary Fund's (IMF's) Compensatory Financing Facility (CFF), export earnings shortfalls are compensated after an ACP country's application if some pre-conditions are fulfilled. For each eligible shortfall, a transfer basis is computed and paid to the user country if the overall STABEX budget is sufficient to compensate the sum of all transfer bases. Apart from a 4.5 per cent cut (a 1 per cent cut for least developed countries), the transfer basis is equal to the difference between the reference level and the actual export earnings. It is certainly intended under STABEX that compensation payments should be made rapidly. Advance payments are possible.

Despite the obvious goal to stabilize export earnings, it is not clear *a priori* whether STABEX will lead to positive and high stabilization effects. Among other reasons, this is due to the fact that STABEX is a commodity-related compensatory financing system. Hence, the compensation of earnings shortfalls for individual commodities may or may not contribute to the stabilization of national export earnings. Moreover, time-lags between shortfalls and payments as a consequence of delayed applications or insufficient means of the STABEX fund may lead to stabilizing or destabilizing effects on national export earnings.

STABEX contains a strong redistributive element, too. This redistributive element has been particularly high since Lomé IV, where a grant equivalent of 100 per cent was introduced as a general rule for all user countries. Up to Lomé III, differential provisions had been valid for various country groups (see Articles 172, 173 of Lomé III). First, the least developed ACP states did not have to repay the compensation payments. Second, STABEX payments for all other ACP countries were interest-free loans. These loans had to be repaid, given that the following three conditions were fulfilled simultaneously. The export price had to be higher, the export quantity had to be equal to or higher and export earnings had to be at least 6 per cent higher than the average values of the respective variables in a reference period. The reference period was the four years prior to the shortfall year. The repayment should then occur after a two-year deferment period in five equal annual instalments (Article 174, Lomé III). These were already fairly soft repayment conditions.

For the allocative effects of STABEX, it is important that there is no binding obligation to use the compensation payment in the sector which caused the payment. Payments shall be devoted to the sector in question, or, for the purpose of promoting diversification, directed towards appropriate sectors. In principle, agricultural sectors or the processing of agricultural products are regarded as appropriate (Article 186).

Table 4.2 STABEX payments under Lomé I–III (1975–89) and the allocation of payments on beneficiary African, Caribbean and Pacific countries and on products

Allocation criteria	*Lomé I (1975–9)*	*Lomé II (1980–4)*	*Lomé III (1985–9)*	*Lomé I–III (1975–89)*
Total STABEX payments (million ECU)	389.812	669.362	1,457.682	2,516.855
Number of beneficiary countries	39	42	39	52
Number of products causing the payments	19	22	22	26
STABEX payments to most important user countries in million ECU (in per cent of total payments)				
Côte d'Ivoire	15.000 (3.85%)	93.417 (13.96%)	365.260 (25.06%)	473.677 (18.82%)
Senegal	65.106 (16.70%)	90.583 (13.53%)	106.953 (7.34%)	262.643 (10.44%)
Cameroon	4.065 (1.04%)	29.590 (4.42%)	198.764 (13.64%)	232.420 (9.23%)
Papua New Guinea	–	50.691 (7.57%)	110.006 (7.55%)	160.696 (6.38%)
Sudan	41.776 (10.72%)	40.695 (6.08%)	63.929 (4.39%)	146.401 (5.82%)
STABEX payments for most important products in million ECU (in per cent of total payments)				
Coffee	14.494 (3.72%)	246.583 (36.84%)	589.494 (40.44%)	850.571 (33.80%)
Groundnuts and groundnut products	139.360 (35.75%)	133.258 (19.91%)	168.023 (11.53%)	440.641 (17.51%)
Cocoa and cocoa products	1.521 (0.39%)	148.837 (22.24%)	202.941 (13.92%)	353.299 (14.04%)
Wood	39.992 (10.26%)	0.391 (0.06%)	107.111 (7.35%)	147.494 (5.86%)
Cotton	43.359 (11.12%)	36.534 (5.46%)	84.612 (5.80%)	164.506 (6.54%)

Sources: Commission of the EC (1988a, 1990b); own computations

In the general policy discussion, STABEX is seen as a major instrument of EC development policy. Although not being dominant in the overall Lomé budget, it is the most important financial stabilization arrangement within the Lomé Convention. A total of 1,500 million ECU is planned for STABEX, given an overall amount of

12,000 million ECU for the Financial Protocol 1990–5 of the Lomé IV Convention (Commission of the EC 1990a: 15). With this 12.5 per cent of the total budget, STABEX is much more important in quantitative terms than SYSMIN, the financing facility for mineral projects (with 480 million ECU or 4 per cent).

An overview of the transactions under the STABEX scheme up to the application year 1989 is given in Table 4.2. The magnitude of all STABEX transactions is shown separately for Lomé I, Lomé II and Lomé III. Moreover, total STABEX payments for Lomé I–III are shown as well as payments within this period disaggregated by the most important recipients and by the most important commodities which caused the payments. Some important conclusions can be drawn. First, a fairly broad group of ACP countries participated in the STABEX scheme. Up to the application year 1989, fifty-two ACP countries received STABEX payments. Apparently, most ACP countries were affected by export earnings shortfalls and viewed the system as beneficial.

Second, there is a much stronger concentration of STABEX payments on products than on countries. In the application years 1975–89, 65.4 per cent of STABEX payments were aimed at the compensation of export earnings shortfalls for three commodities: coffee (33.8 per cent), groundnuts and groundnut products (17.5 per cent) and cocoa and cocoa products (14 per cent). All other products covered by the STABEX system caused less than 10 per cent of the payments. The concentration on individual products was even greater when Lomé I, II and III were looked at separately. The share of coffee was as high as 37 per cent and 40 per cent under Lomé II and III and the share of groundnuts and groundnut products amounted to 36 per cent under Lomé I.

Third, the fact that a relatively large number of ACP countries export the three major STABEX commodities explains to a great extent why so many ACP countries participated in the scheme. The highest payments were received by Côte d'Ivoire with 18.8 per cent of total STABEX disbursements, Senegal with 10.4 per cent, Cameroon with 9.2 per cent, Papua New Guinea with 6.4 per cent and the Sudan with 5.8 per cent. In two of these countries, Côte d'Ivoire and Cameroon, the largest share of STABEX payments was caused by the coffee sector. Cocoa was also important for these two countries. In Senegal and the Sudan, export earnings shortfalls in groundnuts and groundnut products were most important. Papua New Guinea received most of its STABEX payments for earnings shortfalls in palm products. However, coffee and cocoa were also important and when taken together accounted for a similar magnitude to that of the palm products.

THE IMPACTS OF THE STABEX SCHEME ON EXPORT EARNINGS INSTABILITY

The following empirical analysis of the stabilizing effects of STABEX is based on aggregate export earnings of ACP countries. Forty-eight out of fifty-one countries[2] which received STABEX payments from the beginning of the Lomé Convention in 1975 up to 1987 are covered. Export earnings instability is analysed for the whole period 1975–87 on the basis of yearly data. This means that the quantitative analysis is far more comprehensive than in similar earlier studies.[3] As information on the extent and timing of repayments is not regularly published by the EC, and most ACP countries did not have to repay STABEX transfers, only the stabilization effects of disbursements from the EC are considered.[4]

The procedure is similar to that used for the IMF's CFF. We investigate whether the ACP countries' export earnings were more or less stable with STABEX payments than without them. Again, the measurement of instability is based on the approach of Cuddy and Della Valle and on the direct effects on export earnings instability rather than on indirect effects.[5] Table 4.3 shows the results for forty-eight ACP countries. This leads to the following conclusions:

1 Export earnings instability varied strongly between the ACP countries which used the STABEX scheme. Instabilities ranged between 5.7 per cent (St Lucia) and 60.9 per cent (Ghana). The arithmetic mean of instabilities was 26.4 per cent and the median 25.3 per cent. This implies that the average export earnings instability of STABEX users was of a similar magnitude to that of the users of the IMF's CFF. The median instability for the user countries of STABEX was higher by some percentage points than that of the countries under the CFF. The instabilities shown in Table 4.3 are in most cases based on the trend-corrected coefficient of variation v^*_{LL}. This implies that the export earnings of many ACP countries showed a statistically significant exponential growth in the period 1975–87 when export earnings are expressed in ECU.
2 The qualitative result on the stabilization effects of STABEX is similar to that reported for the IMF's CFF: the overall impact of STABEX was relatively weak. Table 4.3 reveals that the median

Table 4.3 Impacts of the STABEX scheme on the export earnings instability of forty-eight African, Caribbean and Pacific countries in the period 1975–87[a]

	Instability of selected variables		*Percentage change in export earnings instability due to STABEX payments*
Countries	*Export earnings* (1)	*Export earnings and STABEX payments* (2)	(3) = 100[(2) − (1)]/(1)
Belize[b]	18.68	18.68	+0.00
Benin[b,c]	58.48	57.97	−0.87
Burkina Faso[b]	18.84	19.30	+2.44
Burundi[b]	32.87	32.57	−0.91
Cameroon	24.11	24.11	+0.00
Cape Verde[b]	23.76	20.85	−12.25
Central African Republic[b,c]	13.40	13.12	−2.09
Chad[b]	30.83	29.04	−5.81
Congo, PDR[c]	34.66	34.68	+0.06
Côte d'Ivoire	17.89	17.58	−1.73
Djibouti[b,c]	29.26	29.44	+0.62
Dominica[b]	25.40	22.48	−11.50
Equatorial Guinea[b]	29.60	29.65	+0.17
Ethiopia[b]	18.60	18.60	+0.00
Fiji	16.40	16.38	−0.12
Gabon	34.43	34.42	−0.03
Gambia[b]	30.72	26.29	−14.42
Ghana	60.90	61.28	+0.62
Grenada[b]	9.83	10.32	+4.98
Guinea Bissau[b,d]	25.24	30.49	+20.80
Jamaica	16.47	16.50	+0.18
Kenya	18.99	19.07	+0.42
Lesotho[b]	38.80	38.92	+0.31
Liberia	18.17	18.07	−0.55
Madagascar	12.02	12.09	+0.58
Malawi[b]	19.97	19.82	−0.75
Mali[b]	17.38	15.98	−8.06
Mauritania[b]	27.10	24.88	−8.19
Mauritius	13.29	13.35	+0.45
Mozambique[b,e]	27.53	27.53	−6.54
Niger[b,c]	31.63	30.97	−2.09
Papua New Guinea	11.56	10.41	−9.95
Rwanda[b]	32.33	31.23	−3.40
St Lucia[b,c]	5.67	5.89	+3.88
St Vincent[b,f]	25.64	25.73	+0.35

Countries	*Instability of selected variables*		*Percentage change in export earnings instability due to STABEX payments*
	Export earnings (1)	*Export earnings and STABEX payments* (2)	(3) = 100[(2) − (1)]/(1)
Sao Tomé and Principe[b]	51.12	49.52	−3.13
Senegal	22.14	19.07	−13.87
Sierra Leone[b]	19.72	19.92	+1.01
Solomon Islands[b]	29.76	25.72	−13.58
Somalia[b]	26.37	26.54	+0.64
Sudan[b]	27.65	26.05	−5.79
Swaziland[b]	23.08	22.96	−0.52
Tanzania[b]	18.78	18.76	−0.11
Togo[b]	22.51	22.24	−1.20
Tonga[b]	34.73	36.46	+4.98
Uganda[b]	36.12	36.07	−0.14
Vanuatu[b]	48.14	44.72	−7.10
Western Somoa[b]	36.76	29.52	−19.70
General statistics			
Arithmetic mean	26.40	25.70	−2.33
Standard deviation	11.64	11.42	6.41
Median	25.32	24.50	−0.33

Sources: Own computations. Data on export earnings are from IMF (b, 1990 issue). Data on STABEX payments are taken from the Commission of the EC (1988a) and information on the dates of disbursement is from the Commission of the EC (a, b, 1981). The time series on the ECU-US dollar exchange rate needed to compute export earnings in ECU are from Deutsche Bundesbank (1990)

Notes: [a]The uncorrected CV was used for Djibouti, Gambia, Ghana, Jamaica, Liberia, Mozambique, Sao Tomé and Principe, Sierra Leone, Somalia, Tanzania and Vanuatu and v_L^* for the Central African Republic, Dominica, Equatorial Guinea, Mali, Mauritania, Papua New Guinea and Uganda. In all other cases, v_{LL}^* was used.

[b]These countries do not have to repay STABEX disbursements.

[c]The calculations refer to the period 1975–86.

[d]The calculations refer to the period 1975–85.

[e]The calculations refer to the period 1975–84.

[f]The calculations refer to the period 1975–82.

effect arising from STABEX payments on export earnings instability of recipient countries was slightly stabilizing (−0.33 per cent). In those cases where the stabilizing or destabilizing impact was at least 0.1 per cent, seventeen countries experienced a destabilization of their export earnings and twenty-seven countries a stabilization. Although the magnitude of most effects in either direction was comparatively low, the impact was still significant in some cases. In six cases, the stabilization effect of STABEX was larger than 10 per cent: in Western Samoa export earnings stability increased by 19.7 per cent, in Gambia by 14.4 per cent, in Senegal by 13.9 per cent, in the Solomon Islands by 13.6 per cent, in Cape Verde by 12.3 per cent and in Dominica by 11.5 per cent. In only one case was the destabilizing impact higher than 10 per cent: in Guinea Bissau STABEX payments increased export earnings instability by 20.8 per cent. In all other destabilizing cases, the destabilizing effect was lower than 5 per cent and ranged between 3 per cent and 5 per cent in three countries (Grenada, St Lucia, Tonga).

The overall performance of the STABEX scheme can be generalized when the payments during 1975–87 are treated as a representative sample for the future success of the system. Then, a median test can be applied, as in the case of the CFF, in order to derive confidence intervals for the stabilizing effects of STABEX disbursements. Given a 99 per cent level of statistical significance and a two-sided test, this confidence interval is

$$-3.13 \leq 100\,\frac{\Delta I}{I} \leq +0.17 \tag{4.1}$$

Starting from the performance of STABEX in the first thirteen years of the Lomé Convention, this implies that it can be expected that STABEX will induce a median effect on export earnings instability that lies between a stabilization by 3.13 per cent and a destabilization by 0.17 per cent. Consequently, the median effect can be evaluated as fairly small. Without any significant policy change, it is very unrealistic to expect that STABEX will affect the export earnings instability of ACP countries strongly. Stabilizing effects of 10 per cent or more are clearly outside the confidence interval for the median impact.

There are four reasons for the low success of the STABEX scheme in stabilizing ACP countries' export earnings:

1 Compensation payments are usually disbursed after a delay in the year following the shortfall. Requests for compensatory payments

can be made up to three months after the end of the shortfall year. Assuming a three-month duration for the consideration of the request, the time-lag between the middle of the shortfall year and the disbursement may be as much as twelve months. In this case, stabilization effects are coincidental, as they depend on the level of export earnings in the year following the earnings shortfall. An empirical analysis of delays in STABEX payments indicates that this is an important point. Under Lomé I, the mean time-lag between the end of the shortfall year and the compensation payment was higher than nine months (Commission of the EC 1981; Herrmann 1983a: Table 2). This implies that STABEX transfers were much less prompt than transfers under the IMF's CFF. The fact that less than 1 per cent of all STABEX disbursements under Lomé I were given as advance payments indicates, too, that transfers are not very prompt.

2 The EC compensates commodity-related export earnings shortfalls which need not be correlated positively with national export earnings shortfalls. Destabilizing effects on national export earnings may occur. Senegal, for example, the country which received the highest payments in the period 1975–84, got most of its STABEX transfers for shortfalls in the groundnut sector. As other important non-STABEX exportables exist, especially in the petroleum sector, even a prompt compensation of shortfalls in the groundnut sector may or may not stabilize aggregate earnings.

3 Stabilization impacts, according to our measure of instability, do not necessarily coincide with stabilization effects on the basis of the EC measure. The computation of the reference value under STABEX is oriented towards past values and does not take into account that a trend might underlie the time series of export earnings. Owing to the overestimation or underestimation of the 'normal' value, which includes the time trend, a destabilizing effect may occur for an ACP country that plans on the basis of detrended earnings.

4 Additionally, STABEX payments may be insufficient to compensate fully for export earnings shortfalls. This problem is the most severe when international coffee and cocoa prices fall drastically and many ACP coffee and cocoa exporters apply for compensation within the same year. In such cases, the STABEX fund proved to be too low to stabilize export earnings effectively. This was the case in 1980 and 1981. For the application year 1980, only shortfalls of less than 1 million ECU were compensated fully: 59.5 per cent of the higher shortfalls were covered for

the least developed ACP countries and 47.5 per cent for all other ACP countries. For the application year 1981, export earnings shortfals of the ACP countries exceeded the STABEX funds even more, and the transfer bases had to be restricted more tightly than in 1980 (Commission of the EC (b), 1982 issue). In such years, the stabilization potential of STABEX is obviously very limited.

It has to be borne in mind that these different reasons for the low stabilization success often coincide. The limited STABEX transfers for the export earnings shortfalls in 1980 and 1981, for example, were disbursed in the years following the shortfalls. A discretionary decision had to be taken on how to allocate the available funds to the ACP countries with earnings shortfalls. Additionally, a decision was taken in 1986 to compensate those parts of the shortfalls in 1980 and 1981 which were still uncompensated (Commission of the EC 1988a: 16ff.). Of course, compensation payments of this kind are purely coincidental in their stabilization effect. There are also discretionary elements in the decision process when overall financial resources are sufficient and time-lags are shorter. Consultations between the EC Commission and the ACP country which may become necessary (Article 200, paragraph 4, Article 203) are cases in point. Moreover, time-lags in the decision process may be from delays on the part of the ACP country, for example when sufficient information on the use of requested STABEX payments is not provided in time (Article 209, paragraph 1). All these arguments imply that STABEX is not an automatic stabilization scheme. It is regarded by the EC Commission as a kind of insurance system, which transfers resources to ACP countries after a discretionary decision process, given that commodity-related export earnings shortfalls exist.

The evidence of limited stabilization success confirms the results of earlier studies using a more limited data basis on STABEX transactions (Herrmann 1983a; Bachou 1986). It also confirms the results of a historical simulation of the STABEX scheme (Collins 1984). This simulation analysis with the rules of the STABEX scheme shows that relatively low mean stabilization effects would have been induced in the period 1960–80. This result is even arrived at under two assumptions that are relatively favourable for the system. First, it is assumed that a full compensation of export earnings would have been realized. Financial restrictions did not exist on the EC side. Second, it is assumed that shortfalls would have been compensated without any time-lag in the shortfall year. Additionally an empirical analysis of ten ACP countries and the period of Lomé I shows that the STABEX payments could not be seen as an effective instrument for short-term budget stabilization. They provided, however, significant budget support for the ACP governments (Hewitt 1983: 1017).

REDISTRIBUTIVE IMPACTS OF THE STABEX SYSTEM

As was argued above, STABEX contains elements of redistribution. As in the case of the IMF's CFF, these implicit transfers in the STABEX system will now be computed with the methodology of grant economics. The calculation of grant equivalents in STABEX payments is based on the provisions which were valid under Lomé I–III. During this period, STABEX payments were not in all cases full grants. The following equation is used in order to calculate grant equivalents in a STABEX payment (G^{ST}):

$$G^{ST} = L^{ST} - \sum_{j=t+p+d}^{T} \frac{C_j^{ST}}{(1+r)^j} \tag{4.2}$$

The grant equivalent in a STABEX payment is equal to the nominal value of the STABEX payment L^{ST} minus the present value of future repayments. In contrast to the IMF's CFF, STABEX payments bear no interest. t refers to the year of a STABEX disbursement and p to the additional years after a disbursement in which the EC Commission investigates the repayment obligation. d stands for the time-lag in years between the identification of a repayment obligation and the first year of repayment and T refers to the last year with a replenishment obligation. C and r are defined as they were in equation (3.8) for the IMF's CFF.

In the following, grant equivalents in the STABEX payments for the 1975–87 application period will be determined, based on information up to the payment year 1988. In order to determine empirically the grant equivalents in the STABEX payments, the variables in equation (4.2) must be defined. L^{ST} values are the actual STABEX payments ascertained from EC statistics. C^{ST} values are taken or derived from information contained in EC sources. As in the case of the IMF's CFF, no data are available on r, the national opportunity interest rates. Again, it is assumed that the interest burden of ACP countries for an alternative additional credit is equal to the average credit costs of the World Bank. This implies that the calculated grant equivalents have to be interpreted as lower limits of the income transfer through STABEX. Presumably, most countries will not have been able to receive loans on the capital market at such low interest rates. Given the rules laid down in Lomé III, the principle to determine p, t, d and T can be illustrated most easily with an example. Suppose that a country received a repayable STABEX payment in 1985. Between 1986 and 1992, the following seven years, the EC Commission will have checked or will check for a repayment obligation. If a replenishment obligation is identified in 1992, the years 1993 and 1994 will be the deferment years and the country will have to pay back the STABEX credit between 1995 and 1999 in five equal instalments. In this example, it holds that $t = 1985$, $p = 1, \ldots, 7$, $d = 3$ and $T = 1999$. This implies that $j = 1995, \ldots, 1999$.

On the basis of (4.2), actual grant equivalents are calculated for all STABEX payments in the application period 1975–87 which were non-repayable or repaid up to 1988. When STABEX payments were still not repaid by 1988 and the amount of repayment still depended on future development in export earnings, prices and quantities, minimum grant equivalents are calculated. These minimum grant equivalents have definitely accumulated from a 1988 point of view. The actual grant equivalent in these credits will increase with each additional year in which no repayment is made.

The calculated grant equivalents for the beneficiary ACP countries are derived from EC data on individual STABEX payments (Commission of the EC 1988a) and from calculated grant equivalents in individual STABEX payments (Herrmann 1990a: Appendix 3). The sum of STABEX payments under Lomé I–III was of the order of 12 per cent of all funds available for the Lomé Convention. Some 2,009 million ECU were paid in the period 1975–88 from the EC to the ACP countries for their export earnings shortfalls. Some 972 million ECU of the STABEX payments went to the least developed ACP countries. This means that 48.4 per cent of the STABEX payments in the period 1975–88 were *a priori* grant elements. Although nearly half of the stabilization payments were direct aid flows, this share had been even higher under Lomé I, at nearly 70 per cent. One reason for the declining share is that coffee and cocoa caused an increasing and major share of the STABEX payments under Lomé II and III. The beneficiary countries among the coffee and cocoa exporting ACP countries are to a substantial degree not least developed countries. Those 51.6 per cent of STABEX payments flowing to the countries which are not least developed also contain relatively high grant elements, although being repayable in principle. Given the information on repayment schedules until 1988, the grant ratio in the sum of all repayable STABEX payments was 32.3 per cent. This is a high magnitude, since the assumptions on the repayment pattern and on the opportunity interest rates tend to keep the calculated grant ratios at the lower limit. The major reason for high grant ratios in repayable stabilization payments is that the repayment conditions under Lomé I–III were already very soft. This caused at first a relatively large number of non-repaid credits under Lomé I. Moreover, the introduction of the deferment period and the splitting of repayments under Lomé II and Lomé III increased the grant elements in those credits where the repayment obligation was fulfilled. From Lomé IV, the grant ratio in STABEX payments is generally 100 per cent. Hence, it will significantly increase further for the ACP countries which are not least developed.

Table 4.4 shows the beneficiary ACP countries, the sum of grant equivalents the countries received in the period 1975–88, the per capita grant equivalents and the countries' per capita income. The highest income transfers went to the Sudan with 146.4 million ECU, Ethiopia with 117.3 million ECU, Senegal with 115.8 million ECU, Côte d'Ivoire with 70.9 million ECU and Tanzania with 50.5 million ECU. In per capita terms, the highest grants went to Vanuatu with 217.9 ECU, Solomon Islands with 139.7 ECU, Western Samoa with 108.5 ECU, Kiribati with 105.7 ECU and Sao Tomé and Principe with 92.3 ECU. The median of per capita grant equivalents is 3.27 ECU if all ACP countries are taken into account and 7.26 ECU if only the ACP countries with STABEX payments are considered.

The distribution of per capita transfers across the ACP countries does not appear to follow any distribution criterion. Countries with a lower per capita income than 300 ECU received per capita transfers from STABEX that were above average (Equatorial Guinea, Guinea Bissau) as well as below average (Ethiopia, Malawi) or zero (Zaire). Countries with a higher per capita income than 1,000 ECU also received transfers that were above average (St Lucia, Gabon) as well as below average (Jamaica, Burkina Faso) or zero (Trinidad and Tobago, Surinam). Relatively high income transfers accrued to island ACP countries with a medium per capita income (Dominica, Kiribati). It can be concluded that income transfers within STABEX represent a by-product of earnings stabilization and are only arbitrarily connected with distribution indicators like per capita income. This result is confirmed by correlation analyses based on the results of Table 4.4. The correlation coefficients between GNP per capita of ACP countries and STABEX grant equivalents in per capita terms is −0.15. This correlation coefficient is non-significant at the 5 per cent level of statistical significance.

As per capita income transfers under STABEX are uncorrelated with per capita income, it seems interesting to elaborate in a multiple-regression analysis which factors actually determine the international

Table 4.4 Income transfers from the STABEX scheme in the period 1975–88 and per capita income of ACP countries[a]

Country	*Grant equivalents in the STABEX payments, 1975–88*		*GNP per capita (1982) (ECU)*
	Absolute value (1,000 ECU)	*Per capita (ECU)*	
Trinidad and Tobago	0	0	7,063
Gabon	6,703.3	9.83	4,940
Bahamas	0	0	3,909
Barbados	0	0	3,909
Surinam	0	0	3,379
Seychelles	0	0	2,419
Fiji	1,750.9	2.66	2,001
Antigua and Barbuda	0	0	1,715
Congo	7,361.7	4.30	1,391
Burkina Faso	15,626.2	2.41	1,360
Jamaica	1,709.8	0.76	1,260
Mauritius	811.0	0.82	1,255
Belize	342.4	2.28	1,184
St Lucia	1,619.0	13.16	1,062
Grenada	4,930.1	43.63	959
Dominica	6,427.8	80.35	959
Swaziland	21,414.2	32.25	949
Côte d'Ivoire	70,900.6	7.93	929
Botswana	0	0	908
Cameroon	21,372.8	2.31	898
Zimbabwe	0	0	868
Nigeria	0	0	868
St Kitts and Nevis	0	0	847
Papua New Guinea	30,697.3	9.81	847
St Vincent and The Grenadines	913.3	9.04	786
Tonga	8,001.7	79.23	755
Tuvalu[b]	432.2	61.74	694
Solomon Islands	34,213.1	139.65	694
Zambia	0	0	653
Guyana	0	0	602
Lesotho	4,431.3	3.16	521
Senegal	115,834.6	19.22	500
Liberia	7,586.9	3.77	500
Djibouti[b]	691.9	2.10	490
Mauritania	37,000.5	23.15	490
Kiribati	6,341.0	105.68	480
Sudan	146,401.0	7.26	439
Sao Tomé and Principe	9,230.7	92.31	398
Kenya	20,524.6	1.13	398

Country	Grant equivalents in the STABEX payments, 1975–88		GNP per capita (1982) (ECU)
	Absolute value (1,000 ECU)	Per capita (ECU)	
Sierra Leone	18,328.4	5.74	390
Cape Verde	1,733.5	5.70	378
Gambia	36,614.7	53.69	367
Togo	45,983.7	16.70	357
Vanuatu[b]	26,803.4	217.91	357
Ghana	41,092.7	3.38	347
Comoros	15,964.0	43.38	347
Benin	37,423.0	10.14	337
Madagascar	8,184.5	0.89	327
Central African Republic	31,992.5	13.29	316
Niger	29,264.4	4.98	306
Guinea	0	0	306
Somalia	5,512.7	1.22	296
Tanzania	50,473.9	2.55	276
Mozambique[b]	21,451.2	1.66	276
Rwanda	35,299.0	6.38	265
Uganda	20,595.5	1.53	245
Burundi	39,817.5	9.16	245
Guinea Bissau	17,819.2	20.99	225
Malawi	16,870.0	2.61	214
Equatorial Guinea	4,506.4	12.77	185
Zaire	0	0	184
Mali	36,045.5	5.09	174
Ethiopia	117,325.5	3.56	143
Chad	47,348.9	10.19	82
Angola	0	0	n.a.
Western Samoa	17,246.5	108.47	n.a.

Sources: Herrmann (1990a: Table 4) and the data sources cited there
Notes: n.a., not available.
[a]The grant equivalents for the least developed countries are equal to the STABEX payments they received. The grant equivalents for those countries having a repayment obligation is computed on the basis of equation (4.2) in the text. For each country, the grant equivalents in the individual transactions were added. The three ACP countries which joined the Lomé IV Convention – the Dominican Republic, Haiti and Namibia – are not mentioned here.
[b]The GNP data are from 1980 (Mozambique) or from 1981 (Tuvalu, Djibouti, Vanuatu).

allocation of payments and income transfers under STABEX. The following hypotheses seem plausible:

1 The openness of an ACP country will positively influence the payments a country receives under STABEX. This is due to the fact that STABEX compensates export earnings shortfalls. Therefore, export-oriented ACP countries will receive more payments than inward-oriented ACP countries.
2 The structure of exports matters as well. Those countries where the most important STABEX commodities are important export goods will receive more STABEX payments than countries where these goods are less important. As Table 4.2 shows, the most important STABEX commodities until 1988 were coffee, groundnuts and groundnut products and cocoa and cocoa products.
3 Besides this, it might also be that more developed ACP countries receive higher payments under STABEX than less developed ACP countries. One reason is that more developed ACP countries tend to be more export oriented, and hence the STABEX system is more relevant for them than for less developed ACP countries. In this context, the degree of development is indicated by per capita income. Whether the suggested pattern is also valid for the distribution of payments in per capita terms, or for per capita income transfers, is *a priori* ambiguous.

On the basis of the above considerations, the following two regression models were estimated:

$$\begin{aligned}\ln \text{STAPAY} &= \underset{(57.92)}{7.44963} - \underset{(-0.02)}{1.01567 \times 10^{-4}}\ \text{OPEN} \\ &\quad + \underset{(2.24)}{1.55797}\text{COFX} + \underset{(3.79)}{13.3596}\text{GROX} + \underset{(2.22)}{1.45834}\text{COCX} \\ &\quad - \underset{(-2.17)}{0.257912}\text{GDPC} \\ &\quad (\bar{R}^2 = 0.53;\ F = 8.76)\end{aligned} \tag{4.3}$$

$$\begin{aligned}\ln \text{STAPAYC} &= \underset{(-0.14)}{-0.10509} + \underset{(3.00)}{1.04012}\ \ln \text{OPEN} \\ &\quad + \underset{(0.83)}{2.74031}\text{COFXC} + \underset{(3.25)}{25.8765}\text{GROXC} \\ &\quad + \underset{(2.91)}{22.9466}\text{COCXC} - \underset{(-0.57)}{0.20007}\ \ln \text{GDPC} \\ &\quad (\bar{R}^2 = 0.39;\ F = 5.28)\end{aligned} \tag{4.4}$$

STAPAY indicates STABEX payments to a beneficiary country in the period 1975–88 and OPEN is the openness of the ACP country, measured by the percentage share of export earnings in GDP on average for 1982 and 1983. COFX, GROX and COCX are the ACP country's export earnings for coffee, groundnut and groundnut products and cocoa and cocoa products respectively, on average for 1982 and 1983 and expressed in millions of US dollars. The extension C stands for per capita values and all per capita variables are measured in US$1,000. Values in parentheses are *t* values.

The following main conclusions can be drawn from the empirical analysis:

1. The international allocation of STABEX payments is primarily determined by the importance of coffee, groundnut and cocoa export earnings for an ACP country. The higher the coffee, groundnut and cocoa export earnings in an ACP country, the higher are the STABEX payments to this country.
2. In per capita terms, the magnitude of STABEX payments to an individual ACP country can be explained by the openness of the country and by its per capita exports of groundnuts and cocoa. According to equation (4.4), an increase in the share of export earnings in the country's GDP of 1 per cent leads to a rise in the STABEX payments per capita of 1.04 per cent. An increase in per capita groundnut exports of US$1 raises per capita STABEX payments by 0.03 per cent. If per capita cocoa exports rise by US$1, per capita STABEX payments grow by 0.02 per cent.
3. There is a negative relationship between per capita income and the magnitude of STABEX payments. *Ceteris paribus*, richer ACP countries within the group of STABEX users receive lower payments than poorer ACP countries. However, the more relevant relationship between per capita STABEX payments and the GDP per capita is insignificant.

The quantitative analysis suggests that per capita stabilization payments are not allocated to ACP countries according to neediness. The openness and the export structure, however, are crucial for the distribution of STABEX payments across ACP countries.

THE IMPACT OF STABEX ON RESOURCE ALLOCATION

It is often emphasized that a positive effect of compensatory financing is its 'market neutrality' in comparison with agreements on price stabilization. It must be kept in mind, however, that it is possible that

STABEX induces allocation effects because of its specific provisions. Export-monopoly marketing boards are very important on the STABEX markets, especially in Africa (Junginger-Dittel 1980; Knudsen and Nash 1990). Therefore it is possible that the marketing boards would pay the producers higher prices than in a non-STABEX situation if the STABEX payments were given to the sector in question. Producer prices would then contain a grant equivalent which is based on a mixed calculation: world market prices plus STABEX grants. This is more likely to be the case, the more STABEX payments contain elements of redistribution and are felt by the ACP countries to represent a long-term transfer of resources. This argument will become even more important under Lomé IV, since the grant ratio in STABEX payments has generally risen to 100 per cent. More factors would then be employed in the sector affected as a result of STABEX than in a situation where EC policy was not carried out.

Taking the reports of ACP countries on the use of STABEX payments as an indicator of the system's effect on allocation between sectors, there is evidence for some countries that the payments went to national stabilization funds or marketing boards. However, there is a broad variety of uses in the ACP countries, either in the triggering sector or in other sectors (Hewitt 1983). The variety of uses corresponds with the fact that the Lomé Convention fails to define whether the best use of the compensation payments is in the unstable sector or not. This lack of a definite rule, however, can be justified from an economic point of view. It depends on the specific national situation whether it pays more in terms of allocation goals to invest in the sector under consideration or to diversify. In general, soft repayments or full grants in various instruments of development aid tend to induce a waste of capital, since investment is made possible that would not pay under market conditions. Therefore, the high redistributive elements in STABEX do not conform with the objectives of factor allocation either.

NATIONAL INTERESTS IN THE STABEX SCHEME: A WELFARE ECONOMIC APPROACH

Thus far we have elaborated the impacts of STABEX on the export earnings instability of recipient ACP countries, as well as the redistributive and allocative effects of the scheme. These impacts have been evaluated primarily from a donor's point of view. We shall now concentrate on the national interests of STABEX user countries as was also done for the IMF's CFF. An individual user country will receive an income transfer due to the grant element in STABEX payments and will experience either a stabilizing or a destabilizing effect on its export earnings. In order to evaluate these impacts jointly, we can again use the method described in the fourth section of Chapter 3 and compute transfer benefits, risk benefits and total economic benefits for each user country.

It may be argued again that the level R of national export revenues, the instability I^{R} of national export revenues and the national costs CA^{ST} of applying for STABEX payments affect the economic welfare W of a potential recipient country. It follows that

$$W = W(R, I^{R}, CA^{ST}) \tag{4.5}$$

The relative impact of STABEX on the national welfare of that country can then be measured as

$$\frac{\Delta W}{W} = \frac{\Delta R}{R} - 0.5\rho\Delta v_{R}^{2} - \frac{\Delta CA^{ST}}{R} \tag{4.6}$$

Equations (4.5) and (4.6) are the counterparts of formulae (3.14) and (3.16) from the analysis of the IMF's CFF. The gain in national export earnings can be computed with the grant element in the STABEX payments, i.e. equation (4.2) has to be introduced into (4.6). Taking export earnings as an indicator for the welfare position in the export sector, this yields

$$\frac{\Delta W}{W} = \left[L^{ST} - \sum_{j=t+p+d}^{T} \frac{C_{j}^{ST}}{(1+r)^{j}}\right] \Big/ R - 0.5\rho\Delta v_{R}^{2} - \frac{\Delta CA^{ST}}{R} \tag{4.7}$$

The following quantitative analysis is based on equation (4.7). Aggregate welfare impacts as a consequence of STABEX are computed by means of the redistribution and stabilization effects of the system shown in the previous sections. As for the CFF, we posit that $\Delta CA = 0$ and the coefficient of relative risk aversion is alternatively set at zero, unity or $I_i/\bar{I}$. In the latter case, I_i is the instability of export earnings of the STABEX user country i and $\bar{I}$ is the mean instability of export earnings across all beneficiary ACP countries. Table 4.5 shows the national welfare effects due to the STABEX system in the period 1975–88. Moreover, total welfare effects are broken down for each country into transfer and risk benefits assuming a coefficient of relative risk aversion of unity. The main results are as follows:

1 All the forty-eight ACP countries considered gained from partici-

Table 4.5 National welfare effects of forty-eight African, Caribbean and Pacific countries owing to transfer and risk benefits under the STABEX scheme, 1975–88[a] (per cent)

Country	Transfer benefits[b]	Risk benefits	Total welfare effects	Share in total welfare effects	
				Transfer benefits	Risk benefits
Belize	0.42	+0.00	0.42	100.00	+0.00
Benin	57.58	+0.30	57.87	99.49	+0.51
Burkina Faso	22.95	−0.09	22.86	100.38	−0.38
Burundi	47.06	+0.10	47.16	99.79	+0.21
Cameroon	2.60	+0.00	2.60	100.00	+0.00
Cape Verde	52.96	+0.65	53.61	98.79	+1.21
Central African Republic	38.58	+0.04	38.62	99.90	+0.10
Chad	55.39	+0.54	55.93	99.04	+0.96
Congo, PDR	10.03	−0.01	10.03	100.07	−0.07
Côte d'Ivoire	2.98	+0.05	3.03	98.19	+1.81
Djibouti	5.08	−0.05	5.03	101.05	−1.05
Dominica	29.60	+0.70	30.30	97.69	+2.31
Equatorial Guinea	21.82	−0.01	21.81	100.07	−0.07
Ethiopia	33.74	+0.00	33.74	100.00	+0.00
Fiji	0.75	+0.00	0.75	99.56	+0.44
Gabon	0.42	+0.00	0.43	99.20	+0.80
Gambia	92.46	+1.26	93.72	98.65	+1.35
Ghana	4.18	−0.23	3.95	105.87	−5.87
Grenada	26.59	−0.05	26.54	100.19	−0.19
Guinea Bissau	161.49	−1.46	160.03	100.91	−0.91
Jamaica	0.24	−0.00	0.24	102.09	−2.09

Kenya	2.14	−0.02	2.13	100.72	−0.72
Lesotho	14.68	−0.05	14.64	100.32	−0.32
Liberia	1.74	+0.02	1.76	98.97	+1.03
Madagascar	2.69	−0.01	2.68	100.31	−0.31
Malawi	7.47	+0.03	7.50	99.60	+0.40
Mali	26.97	+0.23	27.20	99.14	+0.86
Mauritania	15.11	+0.58	15.69	96.32	+3.68
Mauritius	0.20	−0.01	0.20	104.06	−4.06
Mozambique	12.66	+0.00	12.66	100.00	+0.00
Niger	10.85	+0.21	11.05	98.13	+1.87
Papua New Guinea	3.90	+0.13	4.03	96.87	+3.13
Rwanda	34.73	+0.35	35.08	99.00	+1.00
St Lucia	4.10	−0.01	4.08	100.31	−0.31
St Vincent	6.50	−0.02	6.48	100.36	−0.36
Sao Tomé and Principe	80.07	+0.81	80.88	99.00	+1.00
Senegal	22.06	+0.63	22.69	97.21	+2.79
Sierra Leone	13.83	−0.04	13.80	100.29	−0.29
Solomon Islands	62.26	+1.12	63.38	98.23	+1.77
Somalia	6.06	−0.04	6.01	100.75	−0.75
Sudan	29.39	+0.43	29.82	98.56	+1.44
Swaziland	8.83	+0.03	8.86	99.69	+0.31
Tanzania	13.00	+0.00	13.01	99.97	+0.03
Togo	24.24	+0.06	24.30	99.75	+0.25
Tonga	138.34	−0.62	137.73	100.45	−0.45
Uganda	7.31	+0.02	7.33	99.75	+0.25
Vanuatu	99.32	+1.59	100.91	98.43	+1.57
Western Samoa	131.69	+2.40	134.09	98.21	+1.79
Aggregate statistics					
Arithmetic mean	30.15	0.20	30.35	99.69	0.31

Table 4.5 continued

Country	*Transfer benefits*[b]	*Risk benefits*	*Total welfare effects*	*Share in total welfare effects*	
				Transfer benefits	*Risk benefits*
Standard deviation	38.50	0.56	38.66	1.59	1.59
Median	14.26	0.01	14.22	99.77	0.23
Minimum	0.20	−1.46	0.20	96.32	−5.87
Maximum	161.49	+2.40	160.03	105.87	+3.68
Aggregate test statistics for an alternative relative risk aversion coefficient ($\rho = I_i/\bar{I}$)					
Arithmetic mean	30.15	0.27	30.41	99.78	0.22
Standard deviation	38.50	0.77	38.80	2.48	2.48
Median	14.26	0.01	14.22	99.77	0.24
Minimum	0.20	−1.40	0.20	96.23	−14.67
Maximum	161.49	+3.34	160.09	114.67	3.77

Source: Own computations

Notes: [a]The computation of welfare effects is based on equation (4.7) in the text. A coefficient of relative risk aversion of $\rho = 1$ is assumed unless otherwise indicated, and the relative welfare effect is related to average national export earnings in the period under consideration. Grant elements as shown in Table 4.4 underlie the computation of transfer benefits in the period 1975–88. The stabilization effects of STABEX come into the computation of risk benefits and are related to 1975–87 or a shorter period as indicated in Table 4.3.

[b]The transfer benefits are equal to total welfare effects in the case of a coefficient of relative risk aversion of zero.

pation in the STABEX system. In not a single case did negative risk benefits, which existed for several countries, outweigh the transfer benefits. Generally, transfer benefits were so important in their magnitude that they clearly exceeded risk benefits in all cases.

2 As a percentage of average national export earnings in the period 1975–87, the transfer benefits arising from STABEX ranged between 0.20 per cent (Mauritius) and 161.49 per cent (Guinea Bissau). The mean share of the transfer benefit in average national export earnings was 30.15 per cent. The risk benefit was on average positive but low when considered as a percentage of the average export earnings (+0.20 per cent). Consequently, the mean aggregate welfare increase due to the redistributive and stabilizing effects of STABEX amounted to 30.35 per cent of average export earnings. The comparison between the arithmetic mean and the median indicate, however, that the effects are not normally distributed across countries. When median shares of transfer and risk benefits in national export earnings are computed, the respective values are +14.26 per cent and +0.01 per cent. The median welfare effect was +14.22 per cent across all forty-eight ACP countries. These numbers reveal the overwhelming influence of the transfer benefits for overall welfare gains due to the participation in STABEX. The median share of transfer benefits in total welfare gains is 99.77 per cent and the median share of risk benefits is only 0.23 per cent. For all forty-eight countries, the share of transfer benefits in total welfare gains is somewhere between 96 per cent and 106 per cent.

It follows from the dominant role of transfer benefits under STABEX that the coefficient of relative risk aversion is not very important for the qualitative results. When planners in the exporting countries are risk neutral ($\rho = 0$), the transfer benefits are equal to the total welfare gain. Obviously, the median welfare impact changes from 14.22 per cent of national export earnings ($\rho = 1$) to 14.26 per cent ($\rho = 0$). Some summary statistics are also included in Table 4.5 for the relative risk aversion coefficient $\rho = I_i/\bar{I}$. The median effect remains unaffected compared with $\rho = 1$, but the extreme risk benefits and risk losses become much stronger. Nevertheless, all the forty-eight ACP countries remain gainers from the STABEX system and transfer benefits remain the dominant source of the overall welfare effect in all cases.

To summarize, the national interests of the user countries of

STABEX depend on the transfer benefits which the system generates. The redistributive impacts are much more important than the stabilization effects from the recipient countries' points of view. This is a surprising finding, given the fact that the postulated major objective of STABEX is export earnings stabilization and not redistribution. Although this result coincides with our findings for the IMF's CFF, the result is even clearer for STABEX. When the magnitude of the redistributive component under STABEX is compared with that under the CFF, it is much more important for STABEX. Expressed as a percentage of average national export earnings, the median transfer benefit amounted to 14.3 per cent under STABEX but to only 1.3 per cent under the CFF. This holds true although transfer benefits have been considered under STABEX for the much shorter period of 1975–88 as compared with 1963–88. The dominance of the transfer benefits for total welfare effects is also much more pronounced under STABEX than under the IMF's CFF.

OTHER FINANCIAL STABILIZATION MEASURES IN THE EUROPEAN COMMUNITY'S DEVELOPMENT POLICY: COMPEX AND SYSMIN

Besides STABEX, two other financial stabilization arrangements are part of the EC's development policy: COMPEX and SYSMIN. Like STABEX, SYSMIN is contained in the Lomé Convention, whereas COMPEX is not. COMPEX extends the coverage of STABEX to least developed countries which are not signatories of the Lomé Convention. Like STABEX, COMPEX is basically related to shortfalls in export earnings of agricultural commodities. This is a major difference from SYSMIN, which is oriented towards the mineral sector. SYSMIN offers the ACP countries the financing of mineral projects or suitable projects for diversification.

In 1987, the Council introduced the so-called COMPEX or STABEX-LLDCs system as a system of compensation for loss of export earnings for least developed countries not signatory to the Third EC–ACP Convention. Basically, the STABEX system has been extended with the introduction of this scheme to an additional group of countries. The discussion concerning COMPEX dates back to the Paris Conference on least developed countries, where the Community had expressed its willingness to investigate whether a STABEX-like arrangement could be offered to these countries. Later, at the UNCTAD meeting in October 1985, the Commission stated its intention of setting up such a system.

Table 4.6 Income transfers under COMPEX for least developed countries which are not signatories of the Lomé Convention, application years 1986–90, 1,000 ECU[a]

Recipient countries	*Product*	*Application year*	*Income transfer*
Yemen	Coffee	1986	379.0
Bangladesh	Jute	1986	4,389.1
		1987	3,089.9
		1988	3,108.4
		1989	291.6
	Tea	1986	1,228.0
		1987	1,850.9
		1989	2,344.7
Nepal	Hides and skins	1986	232.8
		1987	519.5
		1988	853.8
		1989	558.0
	Lentils	1988	108.1
		1989	112.7
Haiti[b]	Coffee	1987	4,854.9
		1988	4,069.9
	Cocoa	1987	278.9
		1988	1,859.7
Total			30,130.0

Sources: Commission of the EC (a), 1987–9 issues; Commission of the EC 1988b; unpublished information of the EC Commission

Notes: [a]As the grant ratio for the least developed countries is 100 per cent, the COMPEX payments imply a full income transfer to the user countries.

[b]The income transfers to Haiti for export earnings shortfalls in the application year 1990 in coffee, cocoa and essential oils are not counted here since Haiti became a member of the Lomé Convention in 1990.

COMPEX applies to selected countries among the non-signatories of the Lomé III Convention which are classified by the United Nations as least developed countries.[6] The costs of implementing COMPEX from the financial year 1987 to the financial year 1991 are estimated at 50 million ECU (Commission of the EC 1987a: Article 4). Four countries made use of the system in the fiscal years 1987–90: Bangladesh, Haiti, Nepal and Yemen. The COMPEX disbursements are summarized in Table 4.6. Generally, the provisions for the least developed countries under COMPEX are very similar to those applying to the least developed countries under STABEX. There are some differences between the lists of products covered, the most important one being that jute is included under COMPEX which is of major importance for Bangladesh (Commission of the EC 1987b: Annex 1). A further difference from STABEX is that COMPEX transfers, if they are used in the sector with the loss of export earnings, have to be used for projects, programmes or operations in that sector (Commission of the EC 1987a: Article 1). This means that, like STABEX, COMPEX can be evaluated from the donors' as well as the beneficiaries' point of view. COMPEX payments imply a grant ratio of 100 per cent for the user countries, and they may or may not stabilize export earnings of the recipients. Like STABEX, COMPEX may attract resources in the shortfall sector and is not necessarily neutral with regard to allocation goals. This applies in particular when the resource transfers for export earnings shortfalls are transmitted to the producers and when producer prices with COMPEX are raised above those in the case of non-intervention. From the individual user country's point of view, COMPEX has to be evaluated positively when the country is interested in the level of export earnings. Payments under COMPEX represent an untied form of aid and hence increase the country's welfare.

Table 4.7 SYSMIN payments by the EC Commission to individual African, Caribbean and Pacific countries under Lomé II, III and IV up to 1990 (million ECU)

Country	*Product*	*Amount*	*Share of total (%)*
Zambia	Copper and cobalt	83.000	24.40
Zaire	Copper and cobalt	81.000	23.81
Guinea	Aluminium	35.000	10.29
Guyana	Bauxite	34.500	10.14
Botswana	Nickel and copper	21.650	6.36
Papua New Guinea	Bauxite and copper	21.000	6.17
Mauritania	Iron	18.000	5.29
Togo	Phosphates	15.700	4.62
Senegal	Phosphates	15.000	4.41
Niger	Gold and coal	12.450	3.66
Rwanda	Tin	2.840	0.83
Liberia	Iron	0.049	0.01
Total		340.189	100

Sources: *The Courier*, various issues; Commission of the EC (a), 1989 and 1990 issues

SYSMIN was established under Lomé II for ACP countries which are dependent on their mining sectors. This special financing facility has also been an important element of Lomé III and IV[7]. It is the objective of SYSMIN 'to contribute towards establishment of a more solid and wider basis for the development' of the mining-dependent ACP countries. It is intended to support the countries' efforts:

1 'to safeguard their mining production and export sectors by remedial or preventive action' in order to cope with a 'decline in their production or export capacity and/or export earnings in the mining products sector following major technological or economic changes or temporary or unforeseeable disruptions', or
2 'for States heavily dependent on exports of one mining product, to diversify and broaden the bases of their economic growth, notably by helping them complete development projects and programmes under way ...' (Article 214, paragraph 2) which are seriously endangered by earnings shortfalls from the mining product.

The funds available were 282 million ECU under Lomé II and 425 million ECU under Lomé III, and they are 480 million ECU for the financial protocol 1990–5 of Lomé IV.

A major pre-condition for receiving a payment under SYSMIN is that 'the viability of one or more enterprises in the mining sector has been or is about to be seriously affected following temporary or unforeseeable difficulties... beyond the control of the State or undertaking concerned' (Article 215, paragraph 2). The damage to viability is assumed to be given when production or export capacities drop by around 10 per cent or more and/or when the external trade balance deteriorates. Not all ACP countries have access to SYSMIN funds. Only those which export to the EC and which fulfil one of the following conditions may apply (Article 215, paragraph 1):

1 The ACP country derives 15 per cent or more of its export earnings from a selected mining product.
2 The ACP country derives 20 per cent or more of its export earnings from all mining products (excluding oil, gas and precious metals other than gold).

The selected mining products covered under (1) were copper, phosphates, manganese, bauxite and aluminium, tin and iron ore in Lomé II and III, with uranium being added in Lomé IV. Analogously, gold was introduced under (2) in Lomé IV. The proportions mentioned above are lower for the least developed, landlocked or island ACP countries (10 per cent and 12 per cent respectively).

Given that a SYSMIN payment is granted by the EC Commission, the viability of the mineral sector is crucial for the suggested use of the funds (Article 216). When viability is deemed possible, 'aid shall be used to finance projects or programmes ... with a view to maintaining, re-establishing or rationalizing at viable levels the production and export capacity concerned'. Diversification projects or programmes shall be installed to broaden the bases for economic growth when viability cannot be maintained or restored. It is even possible to agree upon diversification when viability can be re-established but the parties prefer to reduce the dependence of the mining product in question. In the case of investment in the mining sector, this procedure implies that two decisions have to be made by the EC Commission: (i) the decision on the entitlement to SYSMIN funds; (ii) the financing decision on a project under SYSMIN.

With regard to the grant element in SYSMIN payments, the provisions of Lomé II and III were crucially different from those under Lomé IV. Before Lomé IV, the SYSMIN payments contained the same grant elements as special loans from the EC, since SYSMIN payments had to be 'reimbursed on the same terms and conditions as special loans' (Article 184, Lomé III Convention). Since Lomé IV, SYSMIN payments have been made on a full grant basis.

SYSMIN payments up to 1990 are summarized in Table 4.7. Some 340 million ECU were paid to ACP countries. The payments under Lomé II and III amounted to 19 per cent of the STABEX payments in the same period. Although SYSMIN is not as important as STABEX in aggregate quantitative terms, it is significant for individual beneficiary countries. The SYSMIN payments went to only twelve ACP countries. Zambia and Zaire received more than 80 million ECU respectively for their copper and cobalt sectors. This means that these two countries got nearly 50 per cent of all SYSMIN payments.

This brief overview of SYSMIN illustrates clearly that there are two major differences between STABEX (or COMPEX) on the one hand and SYSMIN on the other hand:

1 SYSMIN does not compensate the ACP country for losses in its export earnings from mining products but does so for losses of capacity. Hence, SYSMIN is not a system of compensatory financing, whereas STABEX is.
2 The utilization of SYSMIN funds is conditional on a project upon which the EC Commission and the ACP country agree. There-

fore, income transfers under SYSMIN represent a form of tied aid, whereas they are untied under STABEX.

There are additional differences between SYSMIN and STABEX, but Lomé II and III have to be distinguished from Lomé IV:

1 Under Lomé II and III, SYSMIN payments had to be used to the benefit of the mineral sector, whereas STABEX funds may or may not be used in the sector that caused the payment. Since the introduction of Lomé IV, diversification has also been possible.
2 As in STABEX, SYSMIN payments include a substantial grant element. Under the provisions of Lomé II and III, loans were given on concessionary terms. The interest rate for special loans was 1 per cent per year and only 0.5 per cent for the least developed countries. Moreover, there was a long maturity period of forty years, including a mandatory ten-year period of grace (Article 196, paragraph 2 in the Lomé III Convention). Despite these relatively soft repayment conditions, the grant ratio was lower under SYSMIN than under STABEX. STABEX payments generally bear no interest. Thus, the grant ratio is generally 100 per cent under STABEX and was lower than 100 per cent under SYSMIN. This difference is no longer valid under Lomé IV, however, since STABEX as well as SYSMIN payments are not now repayable for all ACP countries.

It can be concluded from the beneficiary ACP country's point of view that a SYSMIN payment contains a substantial element of income transfer. Up to Lomé III, a STABEX payment was superior to a SYSMIN payment of the same magnitude, however, since it contained an even larger grant element. Moreover, since SYSMIN implies a form of tied aid, the use of SYSMIN funds requires a closer cooperation with the EC Commission than the use of STABEX. This means that the policy options are more limited when SYSMIN rather than STABEX funds are utilized.

SUMMARY

We have analysed in this chapter how the commodity-related financial compensation schemes by the EC performed in economic terms. Although COMPEX and SYSMIN were discussed as well, the main focus was on the STABEX system laid down in the EC–ACP Lomé Convention. We have investigated how far STABEX has realized its primary objective, the stabilization of export earnings, which redistributive impacts occurred and how the system can be evaluated from the donor's as well as the recipient countries' point of view. The main results are as follows.

STABEX has had only modest success from the donor's point of view when effects of stabilization, redistribution and allocation are considered. The stabilization impacts are, on average, small and were in various countries destabilizing. This is due to time-lags between export earnings shortfalls and compensation and also to the commodity-related approach. STABEX contains strong redistributive elements and the aid flows seem untargeted. Per capita income transfers are influenced by the openness of the economy and the importance of commodity sectors, but not by neediness in terms of per capita income. Negative allocation impacts of STABEX may arise if marketing boards in the recipient countries forward the income transfers to the commodity producers.

A much more favourable evaluation of STABEX is appropriate from a recipient country's point of view. All countries gained from participating in STABEX, and this welfare gain was in each case dominated by the strong transfer benefit the countries realized. The magnitude of the transfer benefit as a percentage of national export earnings was clearly larger than under the CFF. As under the CFF, risk benefits were negligible. This implies that the major incentive for participating in STABEX is the implicit aid flow that the user country gets. STABEX payments are also more attractive than SYSMIN payments, since the grant ratio is higher and it is a form of untied aid.

5 Food security and compensatory financing

A discussion of the International Monetary Fund's cereal import facility

INTRODUCTION

It has been suggested several times in the economic literature that the issue of food security should be combined with existing compensatory financing schemes (Goreux 1981; Koester and Valdés 1984). In 1981, this idea was implemented within the International Monetary Fund's (IMF's) Compensatory Financing Facility (CFF). Excesses in cereal import costs were accepted as a new reason for drawing from the CFF, and this extension has often been called the 'cereal import facility'. In this chapter we shall evaluate the success of the cereal import facility. First, the origins, the justification and the new rules of the facility are briefly summarized. Second, the acceptance of the new rules is described and a theoretical explanation is provided as to why the use of the cereal import facility was relatively moderate. Third, impacts arising from the cereal import facility on food security are elaborated for those seven countries which made use of it in the period 1981–8.

THE CEREAL IMPORT FACILITY: ORIGINS, RATIONALE AND RULES

The term 'cereal import facility' refers to the extension of the IMF's CFF in 1981. Besides the traditional compensation for export earnings shortfalls, the possibility of compensating for excesses in cereal import costs was added at that point in time and an amended CFF was created. A new idea in compensatory financing was implemented with this extension of the CFF. For the first time, food security in developing countries and the issue of compensatory financing were directly linked. The IMF does speak of a cereal import facility and not of a food financing facility although the latter term has been used widely within the economic literature on compensatory financing (see Green and Kirkpatrick 1982). From the IMF's point of view, the term 'food financing facility' stands for the proposal of a separate facility, whereas the term 'cereal import facility' does not. This relates to the economic debate prior to the modification of the CFF in 1981. In discussing the possibilities of combining financial stabilization with food-security objectives, two alternatives had been considered: (i) a facility to stabilize food import costs and (ii) an integrated facility that covers export earnings and food import costs (Goreux 1981; Huddleston *et al.* 1984). This debate had ended up with the introduction of the cereal import component into the existing CFF, whereas the proposal of a separate food financing facility was rejected by the Fund's Board.

The creation of the cereal import facility is closely related to research findings and policy recommendations of the International Food Policy Research Institute (IFPRI) which were in favour of such a facility (Adams 1982). Hence, the rationale for a cereal import facility can be most easily derived from the analyses of the IFPRI.[1] The need for a food financing facility was justified by insufficiencies of other food policy options. The alternatives at the international level are international stockholding agreements and food aid. International grain reserves have not been agreed upon in the international discussion. Within economic analyses, they have been shown to represent an inefficient and expensive way of providing greater food security for developing countries (Morrow 1980; Reutlinger and Bigman 1981). This is partly due to the fact that variations in the food import bill of developing countries can be attributed more to fluctuations in food production than in the world price variable (Reutlinger 1977; Valdés and Konandreas 1981). Widespread production shortfalls cause high world prices which in the past have tended to shrink the magnitude of overall food aid (Taylor and Byerlee 1991). Relating to food aid, it is argued that actual food aid deliveries in the 1970s responded insufficiently to widespread production shortfalls and did not cope effectively with severe food crises (Siamwalla and Valdés 1980; Huddleston 1981). Moreover, it is well known that food aid may depress domestic food prices and lower self-sufficiency via the price-disincentive effect (Schultz 1960; von Braun and Huddleston 1988). A food financing system, on the other hand, might address the balance-of-payments aspect of food security much more directly. No interventions in the world grain market are necessary and food financing has the principal advantage of being targeted directly at the foreign exchange needed to buy food.

Furthermore, simulation analyses by Goreux (1981) had indicated that an enlarged coverage of the CFF to protect countries against fluctuations in the cost of cereal imports would not raise the sum of shortfalls any further.

The extension of the CFF in 1981 can be broadly characterized as follows.[2] It was supposed to be 'a means of providing assistance to members in the financing of temporary increases in the costs of cereal imports that are largely beyond a member's control' (IMF (c) 1981 issue: 84). Assistance with respect to temporary increases in the cost of members' cereal imports as well as temporary shortfalls in export earnings were integrated. IMF member countries were now allowed to request a purchase under the traditional conditions (Decision No. 6224-(79/135)) or under the new Decision No. 6860-(81/81) which integrated the compensation of export earnings shortfalls and of cereal import excesses.

The choice of the rule was binding for the next three years. The net shortfall under the new decision was defined as the sum of the export earnings shortfall and the excess in cereal import costs. The export earnings shortfall is the difference between actual export earnings and the geometric mean of export earnings for five years centred on the year under consideration. The cereal import excess is the difference between the actual costs of cereal imports minus the arithmetic mean of those costs for a five-year period centred on the respective year. The costs of cereal imports cover the SITC categories 041–046 including wheat, rice and coarse grains such as maize, barley, sorghum and millet. The outstanding purchases under the amended CFF were limited to 100 per cent of the national quota for export shortfalls and cereal import excesses respectively. The limit on total purchases was 125 per cent.

Some modifications of the provisions of the cereal import facility have occurred since 1981 (IMF (c) 1984, 1985 and 1989 issues). In 1983, following the introduction of new quotas, the separate limits of 100 per cent of the quota on outstanding purchases relating to export earnings shortfalls or excesses in cereal import costs were reduced to 83 per cent. The joint limit of 125 per cent relating to both export shortfalls and cereal import excesses was cut down to 105 per cent (Decision No. 7602-(84/3)). In May 1985, the Executive Board of the IMF reviewed the cereal import facility and decided to extend it for a further period of four years until May 1989 (Decision No. 7967-(85/69)). As described in Chapter 3, the compensation of export earnings shortfalls and of excesses in cereal import costs was adopted and supplemented by contingency financing within the

Compensatory and Contingency Financing Facility (CCFF). The CCFF was established on 23 August 1988 (Decision No. 8955–(88/126)). For all those countries which have a satisfactory balance-of-payments situation and do not use the contingency element, the limits of 83 per cent and 105 per cent remained in force. For countries using the contingency component the rules changed as follows. Borrowing for all three elements – export shortfalls, cereal import excesses and contingency financing – is limited to 122 per cent of the quota. This implies a rise in the credit limits of 17 percentage points. However, the maximum drawing for export earnings shortfalls is only 40 per cent of the national quota and for excess costs of cereal imports 17 per cent of the national quota. Additionally, the compensatory element of the CCFF may be extended by an optional drawing of up to 25 per cent if a country does not use this drawing for the contingency element. This means that the maximum drawing for the compensatory financing component is now 82 per cent of the quota if the country makes use of the contingency element (65 per cent for export earnings shortfalls or 42 per cent for excesses in cereal import costs). Thus, the establishment of the CCFF has cut down the importance of the export-shortfall component as well as the food-financing component to the benefit of the new contingency element.

THE LIMITED USE OF THE CEREAL IMPORT FACILITY: DESCRIPTION AND THEORETICAL EXPLANATION

Table 5.1 indicates how important the cereal import facility was within the overall CFF. It is revealed by Table 5.1 that the use of the cereal import facility was quite limited. In the period 1981–8, only 10.6 per cent of total compensatory financing credits were given under the rules of the cereal import facility. Among those transactions, one part is related to export earnings shortfalls and another to excesses in cereal import costs. When only the credits for excesses in cereal import costs are taken into account, only 4.6 per cent of total CFF drawings were given during the period 1981–8.

The question arises why the use of the amended CFF has been so limited since 1981. Even observers who stress the conceptual advantages of the cereal import facility cannot provide a rigorous answer to this question. Johnson (1985: 74) argues with two possibilities. First, he makes the point that some developing countries facing difficulty in importing enough cereals commercially might have been successful in obtaining the required aid. This argument is put forward by staff members of the IMF as well.[3] Second, he argues that it might be

Table 5.1 The importance of food financing transactions within the Compensatory Financing Facility, 1981–8[a]

Year	*Compensatory financing credits (million SDR)*	*Credits under the traditional rules (export earnings shortfalls) (million SDR)*	*Credits under the new rules (net export earnings shortfalls) (million SDR)*	*Credits for excesses in cereal import costs (million SDR)*	*Share of the credits in total credits*	
					Under the new rules	*For excesses in cereal import costs*
1981	1,242.5	1,230.5	12.0	12.0	1.0	1.0
1982	2,627.7	2,153.5	474.2	294.8	18.0	11.2
1983	2,838.65	2,826.45	12.2	0.0	0.4	0.0
1984	815.9	464.2	351.7	9.0	43.1	1.1
1985	929.4	664.05	265.35	189.25	28.6	20.4
1986	567.52	567.52	0.0	0.0	0.0	0.0
1987	1,181.765	1,181.765	0.0	0.0	0.0	0.0
1988[b]	730.48	690.48	40.0	0.0	5.5	0.0
1981–8	10,933.915	9,778.465	1,155.45	505.05	10.6	4.6

Source: Own computations with unpublished IMF data for 1982–8 and with data for 1981 derived from IMF (a), February 1981 and February 1982 issues.

Notes: [a]The credits under the traditional rules refer to the compensation of export earnings shortfalls. The credits under the new rules refer to those under Decision No. 6860–(81/81), adopted 13 May 1981. The new rules refer to the net export earnings shortfall, i.e. the sum of a shortfall in export earnings and excesses in cereal import costs.

[b]January–November.

easier and quicker to obtain credits through the CFF without resorting to the special provisions for cereal imports. We do not share these views. The relevant question for a user country of the amended CFF was whether it wished to use the old or the new rules. Even if aid became available for commercial food imports, it usually paid a country to use the CFF since the credits include an implicit income transfer. This casts some doubt on Johnson's first argument. With regard to the second argument, it is not convincing that it could be more costly to use the special cereal provisions, as only a few statistical numbers have to be provided additionally. Our explanation for the limited use of the CFF is somewhat different.

Assuming rationality of the users of the CFF, it can be gathered from the limited use of the net shortfall rule that it must have been relatively unattractive from the individual country's point of view. Why could this be the case? Under the traditional CFF, a country's export earnings shortfall S is defined as the difference between the 'normal' value of export earnings E^* and the actual export earnings E:

$$S = E^* - E \tag{5.1}$$

In the amended system of the CFF, the net export earnings shortfall S' was defined as the sum of the export earnings shortfall S and the excess in cereal import costs. The excess in cereal import costs is the difference between the actual cereal import costs IC and the 'normal' value of cereal import costs IC*. This implies

$$S' = S + (\mathrm{IC} - \mathrm{IC}^*) \tag{5.2}$$

The point can be made now that S' might be systematically lower than S. This holds true if cereal imports and thus cereal import costs rise with the availability of foreign exchange, i.e. export earnings. Note that the need for an international food insurance scheme was rationalized by the widespread foreign-exchange shortage in developing countries, thus leading to lower food imports. This argument implies that food imports are seen as dependent on the availability of foreign exchange. Suppose the following linear function of this relationship:

$$\mathrm{IC} = aE \tag{5.3}$$

or

$$\mathrm{IC}^* = aE^* \tag{5.4}$$

with $a > 0$. Introducing (5.3) and (5.4) into (5.2) and disaggregating S according to (5.1) yields

$$S' = (E^* - E) + (aE - aE^*)$$

or

$$S' = (1 - a)(E^* - E) \tag{5.5}$$

Since $a > 0$, it follows from the comparison between (5.1) and (5.5) that $S' < S$. Consequently, a user country would experience a reduction in its shortfall by selecting the net shortfall rule under the cereal import facility rather than the gross shortfall rule under the traditional CFF. The change in the export earnings shortfall owing to the selection of the net shortfall rule is

$$\Delta S = (S' - S) = -a(E^* - E) < 0, \text{ if } E^* > E \tag{5.6}$$

The implications of the argument for the use of the CFF are straightforward: a country which plans food imports as a function of national export earnings will expect a lower shortfall under the special provisions for cereal imports than under the traditional rules. Hence, it will expect to receive lower credits under the cereal import facility than under the traditional scheme and thus smaller income transfers. Consequently, it is rational for such a country to participate in the CFF on the basis of the traditional export earnings shortfall rule.

Certainly, the argument is built upon a highly stylized model. A more complete model of cereal import behaviour would have to incorporate the fact that cereal imports are price dependent and that other sources of liquidity do exist, for example foreign aid. Significant increases in world food prices might then raise cereal import costs, or decreasing foreign aid might lower the country's liquidity. Both aspects would provide additional arguments for utilizing the cereal import facility. Booms in the world grain market were lacking, however, in the period considered and significant increases in foreign aid did not exist. Under such conditions, the argument presented may be the major reason why it can be unattractive to participate in the cereal import facility, at least when outstanding CFF drawings do not approach the given credit limits. The situation is somewhat different for countries which have shortfalls driving the outstanding drawings beyond the limit. For those countries, the extension of the credit limits from 100 per cent of the national quota to 125 per cent under the cereal import facility might have created an incentive to use the special provisions for cereal imports rather than the traditional rule. Increased credits and increased income transfers might occur for such countries, although the net shortfall is expected to be lower than the gross shortfall.

It follows that it is an empirical question as to how far the limited use of the cereal import facility can be explained by the expected benefit from the use of the traditional rules rather than the special cereals provisions of the CFF. The evidence is strongly in favour of our hypothesis, however. At the end of 1983, a year with particularly high drawings from the CFF, not a single user country approached the limit of 100 per cent of the national quota (IMF (a), February 1984 issue). Most countries ranged clearly below this limit. This indicates that the majority of user countries did not experience a binding quota limitation under the CFF in the 1980s and made a conscious decision in favour of the gross shortfall rather than the net shortfall rule. Additionally, empirical evidence suggests that the link stated in equations (5.3) and (5.4) does actually exist. Goreux (1981) found a negative correlation between excesses in the costs of cereal imports and shortfalls in export earnings for forty-six countries in the period 1963–75. Translated into equation (5.3), a positive relationship between cereal imports and export earnings does exist. Quantitative analyses of developing countries' imports also indicate that the value of imports rises with changes in the availability of foreign exchange (Hemphill 1974) and that the availability of foreign exchange is a binding constraint to financing food imports (Diakosavvas 1989). This lends strong support to the presented rationale for the limited use of the cereal import facility.

Table 5.2 allows a deeper insight into the exceptional cases in which the special rules on cereal imports were utilized in the period 1981–8. In nine cases, countries decided to draw from the CFF under the amended rules. In six out of these nine decisions, the outstanding drawings exceeded the quota limitations that applied for export shortfalls alone: Malawi in 1981, Korea, Morocco and Kenya in 1982, Ghana in 1984 and Morocco in 1985. This implies that these countries were able to extend their credit limits under the CFF by referring to the special provisions for cereal imports. In one additional case, Jordan in 1985, outstanding drawings were quite close to the prevailing credit limit. This evidence on user countries lends support to the hypothesis that countries with binding quota limits have an incentive to participate in the cereal import facility. By selecting the net shortfall rather than the gross shortfall rule, they can increase their credits under the CFF and benefit from higher income transfers.

Table 5.2 Drawings under the cereal import facility and the restrictiveness of the quota rules in the months of purchase, 1981–8[a]

			Amount of purchases under the food financing facility (million SDR)			*Outstanding drawings in the month of purchase (percentage of quota)*		
Country	*Date of purchase*	*End of shortfall year*	*Total amount*	*Export component*	*Cereal component*	*Total amount*	*Export component*	*Cereal component*
Malawi[b]	9/81	6/81	12.0	0	12.0	108.8	66.7	42.1
Korea[b]	1/82	9/81	106.2	0	106.2	104.0	62.5	41.5
Morocco[b]	4/82	3/82	236.4	113.0	123.4	123.6	18.7	104.9
Kenya[b]	5/82	12/81	60.4	28.8	31.6	125.0	66.7	58.4
Bangladesh[b]	8/82	9/82	71.2	37.6	33.6	47.4	16.2	31.2
Malawi	2/83	9/82	12.2	12.2	0	102.2	54.1	48.1
Korea	6/84	12/83	279.7	279.7	0	103.8	81.1	22.7
Malawi	8/84	12/83	13.8	13.8	0	77.6	73.6	4.0
Ghana[b]	12/84	5/84	58.2	49.2	9.0	87.4	83.0	4.4
Jordan[b]	1/85	6/84	57.4	34.4	23.0	77.7	46.5	31.1
Bangladesh	4/85	12/84	54.95	0	54.95	50.0	23.0	27.1
Morocco[b]	9/85	6/85	115.1	41.7	73.4	104.9	45.9	59.0
Kenya[b]	12/85	6/85	37.9	0	37.9	58.6	15.2	43.4
Kenya	10/88	4/88	40.0	40.0	0	54.9	28.2	26.7

Source: The data on the purchases are from unpublished IMF data for 1982–8, and for 1981 are derived from IMF (a), February 1981 and February 1982 issues. The information on outstanding drawings is from IMF (a), various monthly issues.

Notes: [a]On the provisions of the CFF in their development over time, including the special cereal provisions, see the text.

[b]Those cases are indicated where a country had to decide that it would use the CFF for the following three years under the special cereal import provisions.

IMPACTS OF THE CEREAL IMPORT FACILITY ON FOOD SECURITY IN THE USER COUNTRIES

A more comprehensive evaluation of the cereal import facility has to assess economic impacts arising from the system. In Chapter 3, payments and repayments under the specific cereal provisions have been incorporated already in the analysis of the impacts of the CFF on the level and the stability of export earnings. This uniform procedure can be justified, since the rules determining the redistributive and stabilizing effect of a given CFF drawing are identical irrespective of whether the traditional rules or the specific cereal provisions are applied. However, the food-security objective had been introduced with the creation of the cereal import facility. Therefore, it is interesting to evaluate the effects of transactions under this facility on food security in the user countries. This will be analysed in the following. We argue that food security will be improved if the variability of per capita cereal consumption declines at the aggregate level of the recipient countries owing to transactions under the cereal import facility. In order to test this hypothesis, food security in the existing situation with transactions under the specific cereal provisions of the CFF is contrasted with that in the hypothetical situation without a policy. This implies that the hypothetical situation without a cereal import facility has to be modelled. We posit that the cereal import facility increases the country's liquidity in a period of a compensation payment and decreases it in the period of repayment. Hence, the amount of purchase or repurchase under the facility is subtracted from or added to the user country's liquidity in order to measure the hypothetical liquidity. A change in liquidity, i.e. in the availability of foreign exchange, will then affect cereal consumption and – by definition – food security if cereal consumption responds to a change in the availability of foreign exchange. Cereal import-demand functions are estimated first in order to elaborate the liquidity elasticity of cereal imports, and this variable is then used to model the hypothetical cereal imports and consumption.

Table 5.3 shows estimated cereal import-demand functions in the seven countries which used the specific cereal provisions in the period 1981–8. A standard import-demand model of the type

$$q = f(p, L, PR) \tag{5.7}$$

is estimated for all seven countries and the period 1968–88 in loglinear form. q is cereal import demand, p is the import unit value of cereals, PR is the domestic cereal production and L is the liquidity

Table 5.3 Cereal import demand functions in the period 1968–88 for seven user countries of the cereal import facility[a]

Country	Constant	Elasticity of cereal import demand with regard to price	liquidity	domestic production	R^2	F	DW
Bangladesh	−23.5420	0.2458	−1.1107*	3.3267	0.27	2.38	1.74
	(−1.26)	(0.61)	(−2.64)	(1.95)			
Ghana	11.1022	0.4209	−0.0051	−0.4252	0.00	1.01	1.60
	(1.40)	(1.02)	(−0.02)	(−0.87)			
Jordan	3.6107***	−0.8728***	0.7748***	−0.0326	0.91	70.42	2.04
	(4.84)	(−4.18)	(10.54)	(−0.45)			
Kenya	21.5233	−2.0765**	2.2002***	−2.9042*	0.70	16.48	2.21
	(1.98)	(−3.54)	(6.30)	(−2.79)			
Korea	13.6711*	−0.2520	0.3935***	−0.5800	0.84	36.69	1.87
	(2.71)	(−1.61)	(9.07)	(−1.25)			
Malawi	25.1547*	−0.8107	1.1265*	−2.6222*	0.26	3.20	1.32
	(2.36)	(−1.72)	(2.78)	(−2.23)			
Morocco	5.0010	0.1477	0.9704***	−0.2715	0.71	17.11	2.26
	(1.56)	(0.39)	(4.16)	(−0.92)			

Source: Own computations. Data on cereal import demand are from FAO (a, various issues). Cereal import prices are derived as unit values from the same source. Liquidity data are from lines 90c and 81z in IMF (b, 1990 issue). Exchange rate data are from the same source. Cereal production data are taken from FAO (1987) and from FAO (b, 1988 issue).

Notes: * (**, ***) Statistically different from zero at the 95 per cent (99 per cent, 99.9 per cent) level of significance.

[a]Owing to data limitations, the estimates for Bangladesh refer to 1973–84, those for Ghana to 1972–87 and those for Malawi to 1968–87. Liquidity is an indicator of the availability of foreign exchange and defined as the sum of exports of goods and services and grants received. R^2, F and DW are defined as usual and values in parentheses are t values.

Table 5.4 The impact of the cereal import facility on the instability of cereal imports and cereal consumption in seven user countries, 1981–8 (per cent)[a]

Country/variable	*Instability in the situation* with cereal import facility	*Instability in the situation* without cereal import facility	*Impact of the cereal import facility*
Bangladesh			
Cereal imports	33.26	33.26	±0
Cereal consumption	5.14	5.14	±0
Per capita cereal consumption	2.24	2.24	±0
Ghana			
Cereal imports	22.69	22.69	±0
Cereal consumption	23.83	23.83	±0
Per capita cereal consumption	20.12	20.12	±0
Jordan			
Cereal imports	16.91	17.27	−2.08
Cereal consumption	15.42	15.81	−2.46
Per capita cereal consumption	8.63	8.92	−3.33
Kenya			
Cereal imports	62.17	62.78	−0.98
Cereal consumption	14.89	14.87	+0.13
Per capita cereal consumption	13.39	13.31	+0.62
Korea			
Cereal imports	17.77	17.89	−0.69
Cereal consumption	9.11	9.16	−0.57
Per capita cereal consumption	7.37	7.42	−0.68
Malawi			
Cereal imports	56.25	55.80	+0.82
Cereal consumption	7.72	7.69	+0.41
Per capita cereal consumption	13.05	12.98	+0.52
Morocco			
Cereal imports	20.53	20.98	−2.13
Cereal consumption	23.88	24.19	−1.27
Per capita cereal consumption	19.81	20.03	−1.08

Source: Own computations. Additional to the sources cited in Table 5.3, population data were taken from IMF (b, 1990 issue)

Note: [a]The instability of cereal imports and cereal consumption is measured with the coefficient of variation. Estimated liquidity elasticities of cereal import demand taken from Table 5.3 were utilized in order to model the impacts of the cereal import facility. A zero elasticity was assumed for Bangladesh and Ghana.

variable indicating the availability of foreign exchange. It is defined as the sum of national export earnings and grants received. The hypotheses on the signs are

$$\frac{\delta q}{\delta p} < 0 \qquad \frac{\delta q}{\delta L} > 0 \qquad \frac{\delta q}{\delta PR} < 0$$

The results presented in Table 5.3 confirm in most cases the theoretical expectations. The liquidity elasticity of cereal import demand, in particular, has in five out of seven countries a positive sign and is statistically different from zero. It ranks between 0.39 and 2.20, i.e. changes in the availability of foreign exchange alter cereal imports fairly strongly. Based on these elasticities, the impacts of transactions under the cereal import facility can be measured. Table 5.4 indicates how the purchases and repurchases under the facility in the period 1981–8 affected the instability of cereal imports, cereal consumption and per capita consumption of the user countries. It can be seen that a stabilizing influence was induced by the transactions under the cereal import facility for Jordan, Korea and Morocco, ranging between 0.6 per cent and 3.3 per cent. Destabilizing effects on cereal imports and consumption occurred in Malawi. It is important to note that the stabilizing impacts are primarily due to the fact that the purchases from the cereal import facility were not fully repaid in 1981–8 and purchases exceeded repurchases. Therefore, liquidity of the users was raised and mean cereal imports and cereal consumption were increased. This implies that the denominator of the coefficient of variation (CV) grew and instability tended to decline. This effect overcompensated the effects of destabilizing time-lags in the payments that were present under the food financing facility as well as the normal CFF transactions. Again, it can be said in summary that the impacts of the cereal import facility on food security have been low in general.

CONCLUSIONS

The IMF's cereal import facility has integrated the objective of food security within a compensatory financing system. Its performance with regard to the food-security goal has been quite limited.

1 Only a few countries utilized the specific cereal provisions of the IMF's CFF. Whereas the traditional rules referred to export earnings shortfalls (gross shortfall rule), the cereal provisions refer to the sum of export earnings shortfalls and excesses in cereal import costs (net shortfall rule).

2. Given rational users, liquidity-dependent food imports and no binding quota limitations, the limited use can easily be explained. Expected shortfalls and therefore expected income transfers are higher when the gross shortfall rather than the net shortfall rule is selected.
3. The impact of the cereal import facility on the stability of per capita consumption was modest. A stabilizing impact occurred in only three out of seven user countries in the period 1981–8. It ranged between 0.7 per cent and 3.3 per cent, i.e. it remained weak.

Part III

Commodity arrangements

An economic evaluation of current programmes

In this part, the performance of current commodity arrangements is evaluated. The focus is on directly price-influencing commodity arrangements rather than on arrangements which foresee institutionalized meetings and dialogues among producing and consuming countries. Three price-influencing commodity agreements are currently in force or have been in force for some time in the 1980s: the International Coffee Agreement (ICA), the International Natural Rubber Agreement (INRA) and the International Cocoa Agreement (ICCA). Not all three commodity agreements fit perfectly into the concept of the United Nations Conference on Trade and Development's Integrated Programme on Commodities (IPC) which represented the core of the international discussion in the 1970s. It had been the objective of the IPC to stabilize real prices of ten core commodities on the basis of international buffer stock schemes. At present, two buffer stock agreements do exist, the INRA and the ICCA, but only the economic clause of the INRA is active. The ICA was in force until 1989 and was based on an export quota scheme. Moreover, there is ample evidence that various agreements were relatively unsuccessful and that the goals of the IPC were certainly not fulfilled as intended.[1] The International Tin Agreement broke down. Prices were enforced which exceeded the medium-run equilibrium price and the commodity authorities ran out of funds. The International Sugar Agreement has never been an effective market stabilizer, as major producing countries do not participate. No agreement was reached on the five other core commodities of the IPC: tea, cotton, jute, hard fibres and copper.

The following quantitative analysis on the impacts of commodity agreements concentrates on three recent or existing schemes – those for coffee, natural rubber and cocoa. The first two are often pointed to as the success stories. A brief overview of the agreements will be given. Then, a quantitative analysis on the impacts will be presented in order to judge the effectiveness of the agreements in reaching their primary objectives. It will be argued that the ICA was primarily oriented towards price support, i.e. income redistribution, and the INRA and ICCA towards price stabilization. Nevertheless, it will become clear that transfer elements are also important in the cases of the INRA and the ICCA.

Besides international commodity agreements, other commodity policies are realized at the international level. One example of such a policy relates to the commodity protocols which are part of the Lomé Convention. Four protocols exist – for sugar, beef, rum and bananas. The two most important, the sugar protocol and the beef protocol, are also discussed here. It will come out that these two protocols are instruments of international commodity policy which transfer considerable amounts of trade-tied aid to the beneficiary countries. A quantitative analysis of the major impacts of the sugar and beef protocols and an economic evaluation of the schemes will be presented. Finally, a comparison between the discussed schemes will be given.

6 The International Coffee Agreement

INTRODUCTION

The history of the International Coffee Agreements (ICAs) dates back to the 1960s, and all ICAs have been characterized by export quota policies. The following quantitative analysis refers to the economic performance of the Third and Fourth ICAs in the 1980s. In the following section, where the basic rules of the most recent ICA and the regulatory activities under the ICAs are described, it will be argued that the design of the ICAs was such that they were basically price-raising rather than price-stabilizing mechanisms. Moreover, it was a specific feature of the ICAs in the 1980s that they led to a parallel-market situation between the regulated quota market and the unregulated market. Given this background, it is a primary objective of this chapter to elaborate and evaluate the redistribution and allocation effects of the ICAs. This is the content of the third section. After a discussion of other effects of the ICAs in the fourth section, we aim to model national interests in the ICA within the described parallel-market framework. Two alternative approaches to modelling national interests in international agricultural policy are outlined in the fifth section and are applied to the situation of coffee-exporting and coffee-importing countries under the rules of the ICA. The most important findings of the chapter are summarized in the final section.

BASIC RULES OF THE INTERNATIONAL COFFEE AGREEMENT AND ITS PERFORMANCE IN THE 1980s

The stated objectives of the Fourth ICA of 1983 are diverse.[1] Generally, the ICA is supposed to achieve a reasonable balance between world supply and demand on a basis which will assure adequate supplies of coffee at fair prices to consumers and at remunerative prices to producers and which will be conducive to long-term equilibrium between production and consumption (Article 1, paragraph 1). Additional goals of the ICA are

1 to avoid excessive fluctuations in the levels of world supplies, stocks and prices which are harmful to both producers and consumers (Article 1, paragraph 2);
2 to contribute to the development of productive resources and to the promotion and maintenance of employment and income in member countries, thereby helping to bring about fair wages, higher living standards and better working conditions (Article 1, paragraph 3);
3 to increase the purchasing power of coffee-exporting countries by keeping prices in accordance with paragraph 1 and by increasing consumption (Article 1, paragraph 4);
4 to promote and increase the consumption of coffee by every possible means (Article 1, paragraph 5).

The 1983 ICA was based on an export quota scheme, as were the earlier agreements of 1962, 1968 and 1976. The quota system was valid for the market of the importing member countries. No quotas existed for the market of the importing non-member countries. The first market is called the member market; the second one is the non-member market. The International Coffee Council (ICC) set a global annual export quota for all exporting member countries as the maximum to be sold on the member market (Article 34). Annual national quotas were fixed, too, and allocated as quarterly quotas (Articles 35, 36 and 37). Annual national export quotas contained a fixed part, determined by the historical basic quota of each member, and a variable part, which was allocated among exporting members according to the share of the individual member's stocks in all exporting members' stocks. The fixed part should constitute 70 per cent and the variable part 30 per cent of the annual quota (Article 35). Various smaller countries, like Burundi and Rwanda, were exempt from basic quotas and had a joint 4.2 per cent share of the global annual quota or individually fixed quotas (Article 31, Annex 2). The quota scheme was controlled at the borders of importing member countries. These countries had to make sure that each coffee export of a member was covered by a valid certificate of origin (Article 43). The introduction, continuation or suspension of the quota scheme was bound by price rules. A crucial element of these price rules was whether the composite indicator price of the agreement, defined as the arithmetic mean of the indicator prices for Other Mild

Arabicas and Robustas, was higher or lower than minimum prices fixed by the International Coffee Organization (ICO) (Articles 33 and 38).

The history of the ICAs shows that there was an active quota policy in the 1960s, but no interventions by the ICO occurred from 1972 to 1980, partly because of high world coffee prices. In September 1980, coffee quotas were reintroduced and remained in force until February 1986. From October 1987 to July 1989, the quota system was again in force. The introduction of quotas in 1980 caused a market separation between the member and the non-member markets with clearly higher prices in the quota market (Pieterse and Silvis 1988: 79). Exporting members sold parts of their quota-induced oversupply in the non-member market and depressed prices there. The ICO responded in 1985 to this situation with Resolution 336, saying that exporting members should not accept any sales contracts for coffee to be exported to non-members at a price which is lower than that applying to coffee with the same specifications sold to a member country. However, the parallel-market problem is still unresolved and it shows up again each time the quota system is in operation.

Since May 1989, a free world coffee market has existed again and there have been official negotiations concerning a new, fifth ICA. The Fourth ICA expired officially on 1 October 1989, but the interventions had already stopped in July 1989. The negotiations for the new coffee agreement had proved unsuccessful at that point in time, and the downward price trend could not be stopped by further quota reductions. On 4 July 1989, the Fourth ICA was extended to 30 September 1991 in order to give the contracting parties sufficient time to develop a new coffee agreement. The economic provisions of the extended ICA have remained ineffective since then, however. At the meeting in September 1990, the ICC agreed upon a further extension of the remaining rules of the Fourth ICA to 30 September 1992. Within the negotiations and the ongoing discussion, major industrialized countries stress two central problems to be solved in a successful new ICA (Deutscher Kaffee-Verband e.V.):

1 They argue that the parallel market with its unintended resource transfers to non-member countries has to be removed under a new ICA.
2 Consumer countries argue that the allocation of quotas has not been in line with the structure of demand. High-quality Arabica coffees, so it is argued, ran short owing to artificially low quotas for this quality under the ICA. On the other hand, an abundant

> supply of lower-quality Robusta coffees has become available since producers' incentives were directed towards this quality. It is suggested that the quota policy led to an upward distortion of the price ratio between high-quality and low-quality coffee, making the Arabicas more expensive for the consumer countries.

Moreover, the distribution of export quotas has been contested among the producing countries for years. Brazil, in particular, has resisted cuts in its market share in a new quota arrangement. Other producing countries like Indonesia, Ecuador and others vote for a more flexible distribution of quotas which takes into account their growing potential to produce.

Some authors conclude from the ICA's objectives that it is primarily a price-stabilizing agreement (Pieterse and Silvis 1988: 47). This view is misleading, however. The instruments of the ICA, as valid in the first half of the 1980s, worked towards a price increase in the member market compared with a liberalized world coffee market. The quota mechanism is a price-support instrument in periods of 'low' world price, but the ICA has no instrument to drive down prices in 'boom' periods. Therefore, it is argued here that the ICA is a price-support rather than a price-stabilization scheme and we shall concentrate in the following on an analysis of the redistributive consequences of this price-support scheme.

THE ALLOCATIVE AND REDISTRIBUTIVE CONSEQUENCES OF PRICE SUPPORT UNDER THE INTERNATIONAL COFFEE AGREEMENT

As the ICA is primarily oriented at price support and redistribution, the main focus of the following analysis is how the ICA distributes income across countries. Hence, the cross-country aspect matters more than the ICA's impact over time. Therefore, the following procedure was chosen in order to determine the agreement's effects on factor allocation and the international distribution of income.

The short-run allocative and redistributive consequences are modelled for two typical years, 1982 and 1983, when the quota system was in operation. First, the ICA's aggregate impact on the world market and the consequential welfare implications for country groups are shown. Beneficiaries and losers from the ICA will be determined in aggregate terms. Then we shall investigate how hidden income transfers under the ICA are allocated among ninety-four exporting and importing countries, and policy conclusions will be drawn. The analysis is based on an econometric world coffee market model which is used to model the hypothetical non-quota situation (Herrmann 1986b) and on the procedure outlined in Herrmann (1988a).

The basic economics of the aggregate impact of an export quota arrangement in a parallel-market setting can be depicted by Figure 6.1. Figure 6.1(a) illustrates the situation on the member market and Figure 6.1(b) the situation on the non-member market. In the non-quota situation, a uniform world market price p_0 would be valid. The aggregate demand on the world market, i.e. the demand of member countries (D_M) and of importing non-member countries (D_N), would be equal to the aggregate export supply on both market segments (S_M and S_N) at p_0. Suppose now that a binding quota $\bar{q}$ is fixed for the exports of member countries to importing member countries. The export supply function on the member market (S_M) cuts off at $\bar{q}$ because of the policy and intersects the import-demand function at p_M. Hence, a binding export quota policy on the member market leads to a price increase on this market compared with the hypothetical non-quota situation. If the exports from member countries to importing non-members are not controlled or cannot be controlled owing to prohibitive costs, an incentive may exist for exporting countries to exceed their quotas by selling surpluses on the non-member market. This shifts export supply on the parallel market from S_N to S'_N and leads to a price decrease from p_0 to p_N. It can be concluded

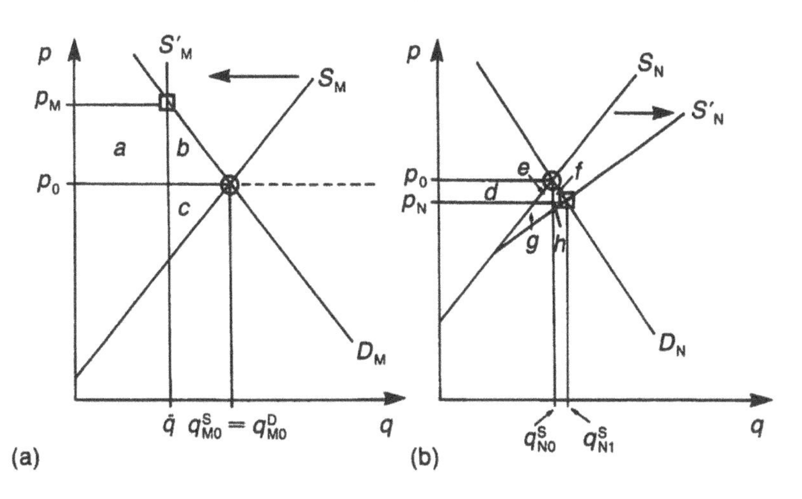

Figure 6.1 Economic impacts of an export-quota scheme in a parallel-market setting: (a) member market; (b) non-member market

that a binding export quota policy on a regulated market induces decreasing prices on the unregulated non-member market.

When we apply Marshallian welfare analysis to this market situation,[2] which was typical for the ICA in the 1980s, the following conclusions can be derived. Export quota policy increases the producer surplus on the member market by $a - c$ compared with the hypothetical non-quota situation. The consumer surplus of importing member countries is reduced by $a + b$, thus leading to an aggregate welfare loss of $b + c$ for producers and consumers on the member market. On the non-member market, export quota policy favours importing countries. They gain $d + e + f$ in consumer surplus. The exporting countries on the non-member market experience a welfare effect of magnitude $-d + g + h$ which may be positive or negative. The aggregate welfare gain on the demand and supply side of the non-member market is $e + f + g + h$. It can be shown that area $e + f + g + h$ in Figure 6.1 must be smaller than c and therefore also smaller than $b + c$. This can be explained as follows. The quota-induced oversupply on the member market is characterized by the horizontal difference between S_M and S'_M. It can be expected under the rules of the ICA that a certain share of this oversupply was transmitted to the non-member market. The horizontal difference between S_N and S'_N will then be less than the difference between S_M and S'_M. Consequently, $e + f + g + h$ will be less than c. This implies that the aggregate welfare impact of the discussed type of export quota policy is negative compared with the hypothetical non-quota situation. The aggregate welfare loss on the member market exceeds the aggregate welfare gain on the non-member market.

An econometric world coffee model was then estimated in order to derive price elasticities on the coffee market which allow it to compute the aggregate price, trade, earnings, expenditure and welfare effects of the ICA. Based on a two-stage least-squares procedure, the following import-demand and export-supply models were estimated for the world market and the member market in the period 1966–81:

$$\ln \hat{q}^S = \underset{(4.93)}{5.1789} + \underset{(4.03)}{0.0353} \ln \hat{p} + \underset{(9.01)}{0.6293} \ln \text{PR}_{t-1} \qquad (6.1)$$

$$\ln \hat{q}^D = \underset{(108.34)}{13.6310} - \underset{(-7.17)}{0.2678} \ln \hat{p} + \underset{(9.01)}{0.4926} \ln Y_{t-1} \qquad (6.2)$$

$$(\bar{R}^2 = 0.91;\ F = 60.72;\ \text{DW} = 2.69)$$

$$\ln \hat{q}^S_M = \underset{(4.18)}{4.9314} + \underset{(2.95)}{0.0295} \ln \hat{p}_M + \underset{(8.02)}{0.6413} \ln \text{PR}_{t-1} \qquad (6.3)$$

$$\ln \hat{q}_{M}^{D} = \underset{(96.96)}{13.5737} - \underset{(-7.08)}{0.2831} \ln \hat{p}_{M} + \underset{(8.37)}{0.5022} \ln Y_{t-1} \qquad (6.4)$$

$(\bar{R}^2 = 0.88;\ F = 46.16;\ DW = 2.65)$

Equations (6.1) and (6.2) stand for the export-supply and import-demand functions on the aggregate world coffee market, equations (6.3) and (6.4) for the corresponding functions on the member market. $\hat{p}$ indicates the estimated values of coffee prices from the first stage of the regression, depending on the predetermined variables of the system (Y_{t-1}, PR_{t-1}). q^S and q^D are export-supply and import-demand quantities on the world market. Analogously, p_M, q_M^S and q_M^D are prices and quantities on the member market. Y is a weighted income variable for the GNP data of the three main importing countries on the world coffee market (USA, Federal Republic of Germany, France), using the mean trade shares in 1969–72 as weights. PR is the world coffee production. Y_{t-1} and PR_{t-1} are the one-year-lagged values of Y and PR. The values in parentheses are t values. Data sources are FAO (a), FAO (b) and IMF (b). It can be seen that the elasticities have the expected signs and are statistically different from zero, at least at the 95 per cent level.

The estimated price elasticities and the Newton–Raphson algorithm were then utilized for computing the prices and quantities on the world coffee market in the hypothetical situation of not having an ICA. This benchmark situation was then confronted with the existing situation of the segmented coffee market for the years 1982 and 1983.[3]

Table 6.1 summarizes the ICA's aggregate impacts on the world market price, on trade, on export earnings and import expenditures and on economic welfare of major country groups. The following aggregate redistributive and allocative effects occurred:

1 Export quotas under the ICA raised the import price on the market of the importing member countries compared with a liberalized world coffee market. The price-increasing effect was 47 per cent in 1982, 17 per cent in 1983 and some 30 per cent on average for both years. This led to a reduction in the imports of member countries by 7 per cent and, owing to low price elasticity of import demand in this market segment (−0.28), to an increase in import expenditures by 21 per cent. The price rise on the quota market implies that income redistribution occurred under the ICA away from the importing member countries.
2 The effect arising from the ICA's quota policy on the market of the importing non-members was opposite to the effect on the

Table 6.1 Aggregate short-run impacts of price support under the International Coffee Agreement on world prices, trade, export earnings, import expenditures and economic welfare, average 1982 and 1983[a]

Variables	*Existing situation with ICA*	*Hypothetical situation without ICA*	*Impact of the ICA*
Price on the member market of the ICA (US dollars per tonne)	2,773.6	2,130.3	+30.2%
Price on the non-member market of the ICA (US dollars per tonne)	1,912.0	2,130.3	−10.2%
Price ratio between the non-member and the member market (%)[b]	68.7	100.0	−31.3%
Trade on the member market (1,000 tonnes)	3,337.1	3,605.3	−7.4%
Trade on the non-member market (1,000 tonnes)	590.6	581.7	+1.5%
Total world coffee trade (1,000 tonnes)	3,927.7	4,187.0	−6.2%
Relative size of the non-member compared with the member market (%)[b]	17.7	16.1	+9.5%
Import expenditures on the member market (million US dollars)	9,255.9	7,650.7	+21.0%
Import expenditures on the non-member market (million US dollars)	1,122.9	1,244.3	−9.8%
Export earnings of all exporting countries (million US dollars)	10,378.8	8,895.0	+16.7%
Economic welfare of importing member countries (million US dollars)	–	–	−2,239.0
Economic welfare of importing non-member countries (million US dollars)	–	–	+139.8
Economic welfare of all importers (million US dollars)	–	–	−2,099.2
Economic welfare of exporters on the member market (million US dollars)	–	–	+1,990.5

Economic welfare of exporters on the non-member market (million US dollars)	–	–	−58.1
Economic welfare of all exporters (million US dollars)	–	–	+1,932.4
Economic welfare on the member market (million US dollars)	–	–	−248.5
Economic welfare on the non-member market (million US dollars)	–	–	+81.7
Aggregate welfare of all exporters and importers (million US dollars)	–	–	−166.8

Sources: Various tables in Herrmann (1988a: Chapter 3) and the data sources cited therein

Notes: [a]The member market is the market of the importing member countries of the ICA; the non-member market is the market of the importing non-member countries of the ICA.

[b]Average price and trade ratios were calculated with the geometric mean.

quota market. Oversupply was transmitted to this parallel market and depressed the price by about 10 per cent compared with a liberalized world coffee market. Importing non-members raised their imports by 1.5 per cent and their import share by nearly 10 per cent. Owing to a price-inelastic import demand in the non-member market (−0.13), import expenditures fell by some 10 per cent in spite of increased imports. As a consequence of the price fall on the parallel coffee market, the ICA led to a redistributive impact in favour of the importing non-member countries.

3 Nearly all coffee exporters are members of the ICA. Hence, the coffee exporters were affected twofold by the export quota policy. They experienced a price support for their quotas on the markets of the importing members and they sold surpluses at a reduced price on the parallel market, compared with a uniform price on a liberalized world coffee market. Because of the large share of the member market in the aggregate world coffee market, the price-support element dominated. Although total exports declined, coffee exporters increased their export earnings by 17 per cent as a consequence of the ICA. The rise in the average export price implies that the group of exporting members of the ICA received a hidden income transfer because of the quota system.

4 Table 6.1 also records the magnitude of income transfers which were involved in the ICA's export quota policy. Implications of the ICA for economic welfare in Marshallian terms are elaborated for various country groups. The importing member countries were the welfare losers, with an aggregate loss of US$2,239 million. Welfare gainers were the exporting members, with an aggregate gain of US$1,932 million, and the importing non-member countries with US$140 million. The exporting member countries gained US$1,991 million on the member market and lost US$58 million on the non-member market.
5 As is well known from theory, the welfare effects of an export quota policy are not a zero-sum game. The welfare loss of importing member countries exceeded the combined welfare gains of the exporting members and the importing non-members. This implies that the ICA induced an aggregate welfare loss for all exporters and importers on the world coffee market. The magnitude of this welfare loss was US$167 million. When the parallel market is ignored, the net welfare loss on the quota market because of the ICA amounted to some US$250 million. This expresses the negative short-run allocation effect arising from the ICA's price-support policy. It results from the fact that coffee production was too high and world coffee consumption too low from the point of view of worldwide efficiency.

These redistributive and allocative impacts seem inconsistent with the goals of the ICA for the following reasons:

1 In general, the price-support character of the quota policy was not consistent with the declared objectives of the ICA, as it decreased consumption on the member market and also world coffee consumption. Article 1, paragraph 6, said, however, that coffee consumption should be increased by every possible means.
2 It did not conform with the objectives of the ICA that the importing non-member countries were net beneficiaries of the agreement. These countries realized lower import prices and import expenditures and a welfare gain in Marshallian terms. Several articles of and resolutions on the agreement indicated that welfare gains of non-members are undesired (Article 45; Resolution 336). The parallel-market problem and the welfare gains of non-members provided an incentive for importing members to leave the agreement and therefore endangered the stability of the agreement.

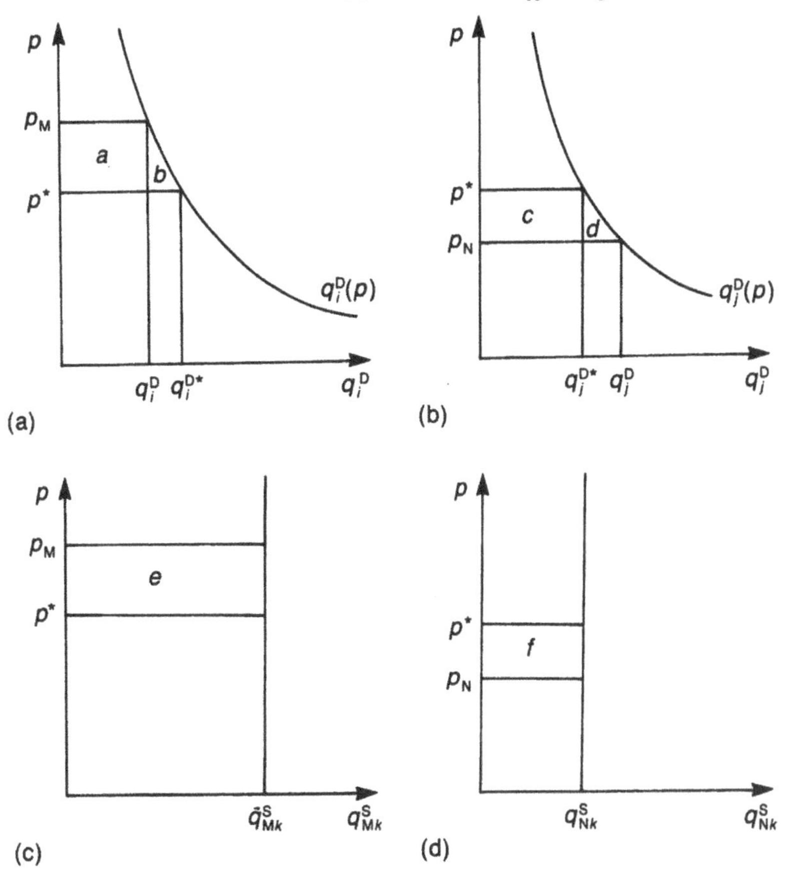

Figure 6.2 Implicit transfers to individual countries under the International Coffee Agreement: (a) importing member country; (b) importing non-member country; (c) exporting member country, member market; (d) exporting member country, non-member market

One might argue, however, that most coffee exporters are developing countries and the implicit transfer of the ICA might be justified from a redistributive point of view. The validity of this argument was tested in a quantitative analysis for ninety-four importing and exporting countries. On the basis of the aggregate price effects shown in Table 6.1 and econometrically estimated price elasticities of import demand and export supply for individual countries, the implicit aid flows under the ICA were determined.

Figure 6.2 illustrates the theoretical foundation of the empirical analysis. Given the segmented world coffee market, three different countries are distinguished:

1 the importing member country,
2 the importing non-member country, and
3 the exporting member country.

The national interests of each country are defined in economic welfare terms. It is assumed that national interests will be positively (negatively) affected if the country's economic welfare increases (decreases) because of the agreement. This means that the welfare positions of individual importing and exporting countries in the situations with and without the agreement have to be compared.

The importing member countries paid a higher import price under the ICA and imported less than under free-trade conditions. Figure 6.2(a) illustrates that an importing member country i imported the quantity q_i^D at the price p_M under the quota scheme, but would have imported q_i^{D*} at the price p^* in the non-quota situation. In Marshallian welfare terms, the country lost the area $a + b$ in consumer surplus. More generally, the welfare impact ΔW_i of the agreement on the importing member country i is measured as[4]

$$\Delta W_i = \int_{p_M}^{p^*} q_i^D(p)\mathrm{d}p \tag{6.5}$$

Again, p is price, q^D is import demand, subscript M stands for the member market and an asterisk indicates the hypothetical situation without the ICA.

The importing non-member countries gained from the ICA. Quota-induced oversupply of the regulated market was transmitted to the unregulated market. It depressed the import price and raised imports of importing non-member countries compared with a liberalized world coffee market. Figure 6.2(b) illustrates that an importing non-member country j imported the quantity q_j^D at the price p_N under the quota system and would have imported q_j^{D*} at the price p^* in the non-quota situation. This implies that the importing non-member country gained the area $c + d$ in Marshallian welfare terms because of the ICA. Generally, the welfare impact ΔW_j of the agreement on an importing non-member country j is given by

$$\Delta W_j = \int_{p_N}^{p^*} q_j^D(p)\mathrm{d}p \tag{6.6}$$

where N stands for the non-member market.

Exporting member countries selling in both market segments were affected twofold by the ICA. Given a price-inelastic export supply in the short run, they sold their quotas at a supported price on the regulated market, but supplied the difference between planned exports and their quota at a depressed price on the unregulated market. Figure 6.2(c) illustrates this.

The exporting member country k exported its quota $\bar{q}^{S}_{Mk}$ on the member market at the supported price p_M and its additional supply q^{S}_{Nk} at the price p_N on the non-member market. In the non-quota situation, the country would have sold all its exports at the uniform world market price p^*. This implies that the individual country gained area $e - f$ in export earnings and economic welfare because of the ICA. Generally, the impact ΔW_k of the agreement on export earnings and economic welfare of the exporting member country k can then be measured as

$$\Delta W_k = p_M \bar{q}^{S}_{Mk} + p_N q^{S}_{Nk} - p^* q^{S*}_{k} \tag{6.7}$$

where q^S is export supply and $\bar{q}$ is the national quota. All other symbols remain constant. For simplicity[5] it is assumed that

$$q^{S}_{k} = \bar{q}^{S}_{Mk} + q^{S}_{Nk}$$

Table 6.2 gives a summary of the quantitative results.[6] Large importing members like the USA and the Federal Republic of Germany were the most important welfare losers in absolute terms. Countries with the highest per capita consumption – Finland, Denmark and Sweden – experienced the highest welfare losses in per capita terms. Analogously, the highest welfare gains in absolute terms went to large coffee exporters like Brazil and Colombia and in per capita terms to countries with particularly high per capita exports: El Salvador, Côte d'Ivoire and Costa Rica. Within the group of importing non-member countries, the highest welfare gains were realized in absolute and per capita terms by the largest coffee importers, Algeria and the German Democratic Republic. The correlation analysis presented in Table 6.2 shows on a broad country basis that welfare effects in either direction increase with a country's net coffee trade position. This is consistent with theory: large importers are affected more negatively than small importers by a given price increase because of the ICA, and large exporters gain more than small exporters. It can also be seen in Table 6.2 that the welfare gains arising from the ICA are negatively correlated with per capita income as far as the total country sample is concerned.

Does the negative correlation of per capita welfare gains and per capita income imply that the ICA leads to a redistribution of income

Table 6.2 The international allocation of welfare gains and losses under the International Coffee Agreement, ninety-four countries, average of 1982 and 1983[a]

Indicator	Welfare effects – magnitude and correlations	
Highest welfare losses of importing member countries		
In absolute terms (million US dollars)	711.0	(USA)
	341.8	(Federal Republic of Germany)
	216.4	(France)
	162.9	(Italy)
	123.2	(Japan)
In per capita terms (US dollars)	8.50	(Finland)
	7.82	(Denmark)
	7.72	(Sweden)
	6.94	(Netherlands)
	6.85	(Belgium)
Highest welfare gains of exporting member countries		
In absolute terms (million US dollars)	581.6	(Brazil)
	332.0	(Colombia)
	151.0	(Côte d'Ivoire)
	94.4	(Uganda)
	87.3	(El Salvador)
In per capita terms (US dollars)	16.93	(El Salvador)
	16.41	(Côte d'Ivoire)
	15.16	(Costa Rica)
	12.19	(Colombia)
	8.23	(Guatemala)

Highest welfare gains of importing non-member countries:		
In absolute terms (million US dollars)	24.0	(Algeria)
	20.6	(German Democratic Republic)
	9.4	(Hungary)
	9.3	(Czechoslovakia)
	8.0	(Poland)
In per capita terms (US dollars)	1.22	(German Democratic Republic)
	1.19	(Algeria)
	1.08	(Israel)
	0.88	(Hungary)
	0.68	(Jordan)
Correlation between per capita welfare gains and GNP per capita		
All countries	–0.603*	(90)
Exporting members	–0.083 (n.s.)	(91)
Correlation between per capita welfare gains and net coffee exports in per capita terms		
All countries	0.929*	(43)
Exporting members	0.926*	(44)

Sources: Herrmann (1988b: various tables) and the sources cited therein. Net coffee exports are calculated on average for 1966–81 with data from FAO (a). GNP per capita data are computed on average for 1982 and 1983 with data from World Bank (a), 1985 issue.
Notes: *Statistically significant at the 99.9 per cent level; n.s. indicates not significant at the 90 per cent level. All tests are two-sided. The numbers in parentheses are degrees of freedom.
[a]Welfare effects are calculated for 1982 and 1983 in Marshallian welfare terms with the procedure outlined in Herrmann (1988b).

towards poor countries? The negative correlation coefficient for the total country sample implies that relatively rich coffee importers transfer hidden aid to relatively poor coffee exporters. This result of correlation analysis does not, of course, mean that a causal relationship exists between the per capita GNP and the welfare change that a country experienced under the ICA. A multiple-regression approach is necessary to test whether neediness helps to explain the allocation of implicit transfers under the ICA, when the most important economic determinants are also accounted for.

It is the objective of the following quantitative analysis to explain the cross-country distribution of welfare changes ΔW which ninety-four countries experienced as a consequence of the ICA on average for 1982 and 1983.

The theory of the determinants of welfare changes under the ICA outlined above suggests first that the net trade position of a country is significant for the direction and magnitude of the welfare impact. It can be seen from equations (6.5)–(6.7) that the exports or imports affect the welfare change that a country experiences under the ICA. Therefore, a variable characterizing the trade status (TS) of each country was introduced as an independent variable. It was measured by the countries' average net coffee exports for the period 1966–81.[7] The expected sign of the estimated coefficient is $(\partial(\Delta W)/\partial \text{TS}) < 0$. since the ICA redistributed income from importing to exporting members and the received aid (donated aid) will be higher the larger the member country's net export position (net import position).

Second, it follows from the different welfare considerations behind equations (6.5)–(6.7) that implicit aid flows to or from a country depending on whether it is an importing member country, an importing non-member country or an exporting member country. This is considered in the empirical analysis by introducing two dummy variables into the multiple-regression approach. D1 is the exporter/importer dummy which takes the value 1 if the country is an exporter and 0 if it is an importer. D2 is the member/non-member dummy with a value of 1 if the country is a member of the ICA and 0 if not. The countries' status in 1982 and 1983 is used. The expected signs of the estimated coefficients are $(\partial(\Delta W)/\partial \text{D1}) > 0$ and $(\partial(\Delta W)/\partial \text{D2}) < 0$. The positive sign with respect to D1 is due to the fact that the exporting countries gained in welfare terms from the ICA, whereas importing countries on average lost in economic welfare. The negative sign with respect to D2 arises from the fact that the average member country pays, as the implicit welfare losses of the importing members are higher than the implicit welfare gains of the exporting members. This has to be compared with the positive welfare gain of the average non-member country and, as the net donation of the member country dominates, a negative sign follows.

Beyond these determinants which theory suggests, a test was carried out to see whether the countries' neediness plays an additional role for the international allocation of trade-tied aid. The average per capita GNP (GNPC) in US dollars for 1982 and 1983 is used as an indicator of neediness.

On the basis of these considerations, regression equations of the type

$$\Delta \text{WC} = f(\text{TSC, D1, D2, GNPC}) \tag{6.8}$$

were estimated, where ΔWC and TSC indicate ΔW and TS in per capita terms. The following linear regression presents the empirical analysis of the cross-country analysis:

$$\begin{aligned} \Delta \text{WC} = {} & \underset{(3.74)}{0.9593} + \underset{(27.95)}{0.4163}\ \text{ESC} + \underset{(3.10)}{1.4238}\ \text{D1} \\ & \underset{(-5.13)}{-2.0518}\ \text{D2} - \underset{(-1.44)}{6.1314 \times 10^{-5}}\ \text{GNPC} \\ & (\bar{R}^2 = 0.94;\ F = 377.04;\ \text{DF} = 87) \end{aligned} \tag{6.9}$$

The per capita welfare change ΔWC resulting from the ICA is expressed in US dollars on average for 1982 and 1983. ESC, the net export status, is measured by average net coffee exports in kilogrammes per capita for 1966–81. Values in parentheses are t values.

The theoretical expectations are confirmed: equation (6.9) shows that the magnitude of the ICA's impact on a country's economic welfare depends on whether the country is an importing member country, an importing non-member country or an exporting member country. Within each group, the welfare impacts were stronger the higher the country's coffee imports or exports. After introducing these major determinants of the ICA's welfare impact, per capita income does not contribute significantly to the explanation of the cross-country distribution of welfare gains and welfare losses. This means that neediness does not matter when the major economic determinants of the ICA's welfare impacts are considered.

The result becomes even clearer when the distribution of trade-tied aid among the exporting member countries is analysed in more detail. The following regression equation was estimated for this country group:

$$\Delta WC = 0.4296 + 0.4057\ ESC - 0.80698 \times 10^{-4}\ GNPC \quad (6.10)$$
$$(1.68) \quad (24.68) \quad (-0.58)$$
$$(\bar{R}_2 = 0.93;\ F = 306.69;\ DF = 42)$$

Equation (6.10) shows that the most important determinant of a welfare gain resulting from the ICA is net coffee exports. An increase in per capita coffee exports by one kilogramme led to a rise in the per capita welfare gain by US$0.41. Neediness does not matter for the cross-country allocation of hidden aid to exporting member countries. This finding confirms empirically the well-known view from the economics of aid that trade-tied aid is inferior to well-targeted financial aid. The reason is that targeted direct aid does not depend 'on the accident of the distribution of those few commodities whose prices it is possible to support' (Little and Clifford 1965: 157). This statement is clearly valid for the ICA as it redistributes income according to the size of the coffee export sector which is uncorrelated with neediness.

It can be said in summary that the ICA contains strong redistributive elements. Income transfers are given as a form of trade-tied aid and this is a clearly suboptimal redistributive policy compared with targeted financial aid. Owing to the price-support effect, the ICA leads also to aggregate efficiency losses in the world coffee economy.

OTHER EFFECTS OF THE INTERNATIONAL COFFEE AGREEMENT

Price support and redistribution towards the exporting countries were regarded here as primary objectives of the ICA. The above analysis, as well as another recent study (Palm and Vogelvang 1991), indicates that a substantial redistribution occurred in the first half of the 1980s. Beyond that, a comprehensive economic evaluation of the international coffee policy has to take additional arguments into account. Recent contributions in the literature have stressed the following important aspects:

1 Bohman and Jarvis (1990) elaborated the economics of the non-member market further. Within a model of the segmented world coffee market, they analysed the recent proposals for reform of the 1983 ICA. Two primary mechanisms to eliminate the price differential between the member and non-member markets were discussed. The first proposal would allow sales to the non-member market but would impose tighter restrictions to make sure that the sales occurred only at the prevailing market price.

According to the second proposal, quotas would be implemented for the non-member market as well, either as a global quota valid for both market segments or as a separate quota for the non-member market. In their welfare analysis of the proposal, it is concluded 'that numerous exporters should oppose the allocation of quotas for the non-member market, unless they receive a large share of this market' (Bohman and Jarvis 1990: 99). Bohman and Jarvis argue that the benefits from selling to the non-member market were unequally distributed across countries. Moreover, they argue that the allocation of quotas among countries is the major problem of the ICA. Hence, they argue that sales to the non-member market may be a necessary 'escape valve', which probably has to be accepted as a price for the continuation of ICA export quotas.

2 Another interesting issue, which has not been discussed here, is the impact of the ICA on income distribution within exporting countries. Bohman *et al.* (1991) and Bohman (1991) argue that quota rents in coffee-exporting countries are created, thus encouraging directly unproductive behaviour by domestic groups. According to the authors, farmers and government will probably lose, whereas coffee-exporting firms and government officials may gain. With reference to Indonesia, it is also shown how domestic coffee policy determines the distribution of rents created by the ICA and what incentives exist for the groups to lobby for a favourable domestic policy.

3 The quantitative analysis of Akiyama and Varangis (1990) adds two important points to the discussion of the ICA: the ICA's impact on price stability and the dynamic effects of the ICA on the world coffee price. Akiyama and Varangis conclude that the quota system contributed to price stability in the early 1980s but will not be successful in redistributing income towards the exporting members in the medium run. Their basic argument is that price support in the quota market will increase supply and reduce coffee prices in the years when the quota system is not in operation. The rationale for this possibility is straightforward. When surpluses of the quota situation are partly withheld by exporting members and are not fully transmitted to the non-member market, these increased stocks might later, when the quota system is not in operation, shift the export supply curve to the right. In such years, world market prices would be lower than in a hypothetical free-market situation. Although this impact is possible, more work has to be done to clarify these issues. The

linkage between the member and non-member markets is not modelled by Akiyama and Varangis and this linkage is crucial for the price-stabilization and long-run redistributive impacts of the ICA.

MODELLING OF NATIONAL INTERESTS IN THE INTERNATIONAL COFFEE AGREEMENT

The above analysis focused on an evaluation of the ICA from an aggregate point of view where the effectiveness of the ICA in reaching its primary objectives was evaluated. The parallel-market framework which developed on the world coffee market in the 1980s makes it interesting, however, to analyse national interests in the ICA in more detail. Again, we start from the market situation illustrated in Figure 6.1, which was representative for those years when the quota mechanism was operating.

Two approaches to modelling national interests are distinguished, which we call descriptive policy modelling and decision-oriented policy modelling. Descriptive policy modelling is the traditional approach. Generally, the situation with an international policy is contrasted with a hypothetical situation without this policy. In order to measure the national effects of the policy, the values of economic variables in both situations are compared. Typically, conclusions are drawn from this approach concerning the impact of an international policy on important economic variables of an affected country. The methodoligical basis for the application of this approach to the ICA was presented in Figure 6.2 and equations (6.5)–(6.7). Changes in national interests which were caused by the introduction of the ICA in an otherwise unregulated world market were measured. The situations with and without an ICA were compared from the national welfare point of view. How the ICA affected the economic welfare of individual countries compared with a free-market situation was computed.

It is a limitation of the traditional approach that the benchmark situation rarely represents a valid option for national policy decisions. In that sense, this modelling of national interests is descriptive and not decision oriented. Under the ICA as it operated in the 1980s, for example, the 'average' country was not in a position to restore an unregulated world market without agreement. It could decide, however, as a member country, whether it wished to remain a member or to leave the agreement. Analogously, it had the choice as a non-member to stay outside or to join the agreement. Under the decision-

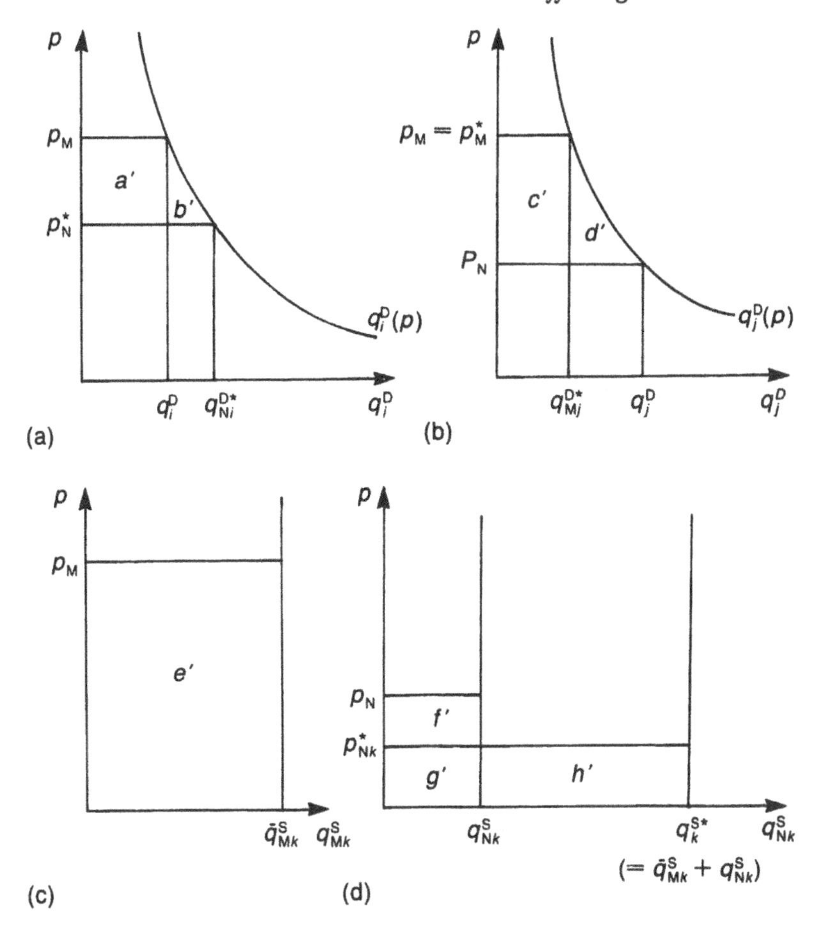

Figure 6.3 National interest in the International Coffee Agreement (decision-oriented policy modelling): (a) importing member country; (b) importing non-member country; (c) exporting member country, member market; (d) exporting member country, non-member market

oriented approach, in the following we shall measure changes in national interests that resulted from the country's decision to participate in the ICA or to stay outside. In this approach, the situation of participation in the ICA is compared with that of non-participation in the ICA.

In applying decision-oriented policy modelling to the ICA, it is assumed that national interests will be positively (negatively) affected if the country's economic welfare increased (decreased) because of the country's actual decision to participate in the agreement or to stay outside. This implies that an individual country's welfare position in the situations of making an actual decision or making a hypothetical alternative decision have to be compared.

For the importing member countries, the welfare impact arising from the decision to continue to participate in the agreement compared with the decision to withdraw have to be modelled. In the unobservable situation of a withdrawal, the country would have imported from the unregulated market. It can be expected that the price in the unregulated market would have increased because of the withdrawal. The reasoning is as follows. The aggregate import-demand curve, as a consequence of withdrawal, shifts to the left in the regulated market and, by the same amount, to the right in the unregulated market. Given a fixed price target of the ICO for the regulated market, quotas would have to be reduced and oversupply in the regulated market would increase. It was observed in the coffee market that only a part of the exporters' oversupply was transmitted to the unregulated market. Hence, the export supply curve in the unregulated market would have also shifted to the right, but to a lesser extent than the import-demand function. Consequently, the price in the unregulated market would have risen. These considerations have been taken into account in Figure 6.3(a), where p_N^*, the price in the unregulated market in the hypothetical situation of country *i*'s withdrawal, is higher than p_N in Figure 6.2(b). Figure 6.3(a) illustrates that the importing member country would have imported q_{Ni}^{D*} at the price p_N^* in the hypothetical case of its withdrawal from the agreement. The country lost the area $a' + b'$ in consumer surplus because of its membership decision, as it imported at a higher price than in the hypothetical situation of a withdrawal. Generally, the welfare impact arising from the decision to participate in the agreement instead of leaving it is for the importing member country *i*

$$\Delta W_i = \int_{p_M}^{p_N^*} q_i^D(p)\mathrm{d}p \tag{6.11}$$

Note that ΔW_i may be either negative or positive. A withdrawal would have increased the price in the unregulated market more the higher the net import position of the withdrawing country. Given the assumption that the commodity authority would still have succeeded in market segmentation if the price in the unregulated market had exceeded the price in the regulated market, a country's withdrawal could even have been welfare-decreasing ($p_N^* > p_M$). The quantitative results of the next section indicate that this argument is valid for some larger coffee-importing member countries of the ICA.[8]

For an importing non-member country, the welfare impacts of the decision to stay outside the agreement have to be compared with the hypothetical situation of entry. We posit that the ICO would have maintained the price in the regulated market in the case of a new member's entry by increasing export quotas ($p_M = p_M^*$). Then, it can be concluded that the importing non-member country would have gained because of its decision to stay outside the agreement, as the price in the member market would have been higher than that in the non-member market. Figure 6.3(b) illustrates the fact that the importing non-member country would have imported q_{Mj}^{D*} at the price p_M if it had joined the agreement. The country's gain in consumer surplus because of its decision to stay outside the ICA amounted to the area $c' + d'$. Generally, the decision to stay outside instead of entering the agreement induced a welfare impact for the importing non-member country j of

$$\Delta W_j = \int_{p_N}^{p_M^*} q_j^D(p)\mathrm{d}p \qquad (6.12)$$

Note that the calculated welfare gain is necessarily higher under the decision-oriented approach than under the descriptive approach, since $p_M < p^* < p_N$ was valid in the coffee market.

In applying decision-oriented policy modelling to an exporting member country, the welfare impact arising from the country's decision to participate in the agreement instead of leaving it can be computed. Again, it is assumed that export supply is price inelastic in the short run and that the aggregate exports of the country were not affected by the quota policy. Given these assumptions, a withdrawal implies that the observed exports of the member countries in both market segments would have been sold in the unregulated market. If an exporting member country withdraws, this will shift the export supply curve in the unregulated market to the right and will depress the price in this market segment. Figure 6.3(c) shows that the country k sells $\bar{q}_{Mk}^S$ at p_M and q_{Nk}^S at p_N as a member of the agreement and would sell $\bar{q}_{Mk}^S + q_{Nk}^S = q_k^{S*}$ at the depressed price p_{Nk}^* as a non-member. The welfare gain resulting from the country's membership of the agreement is then given by the area $e' + f' - h'$. Generally, the impact of the decision to participate in the agreement on the economic welfare of the exporting country k is measured as

$$\Delta W_k = p_M\bar{q}_{Mk}^S + p_N q_{Nk}^S - p_{Nk}^* q_k^{S*} \qquad (6.13)$$

As in equation (6.7), it is assumed that $q_k^{S*} = \bar{q}_{Mk}^S + q_{Nk}^S$. Note that the descriptive approach of equation (6.7) may reveal a negative impact on the national interests of the individual exporting member country, whereas the decision-oriented approach in equation (6.13) cannot. In any case, the welfare impact according to the decision-oriented approach is more favourable than under the descriptive approach.

The national interests of importing member countries in the ICA are measured with equations (6.5) and (6.11) as illustrated by Figures 6.2(a) and 6.3(a). Besides p^*, the unobservables p_N^*, q_i^{D*} and q_{Ni}^{D*} had to be quantified. p_N^* is calculated for each importing member country with the Newton–Raphson algorithm. The hypothetical import demand is calculated on the basis of point estimates of price elasticities of import demand taken from econometrically estimated import-demand functions. The price elasticities are presented in Table 6.3 as are the empirical results.

The following major results can be derived:

1 The calculated national interests in the ICA are strongly affected by the measurement approach. The calculated welfare effects according to descriptive modelling differ in magnitude and, for some countries, in direction from those under decision-oriented modelling.
2 The descriptive approach shows a uniformly negative influence of the ICA on the national interests of importing member countries. As the coffee price in the controlled market was raised above the liberalized world market price, economic welfare decreased in 1982 and 1983 for all importing member countries.
3 The results of the decision-oriented approach are less uniform. Under the model's assumption, the price in the uncontrolled market rises if an importing member country withdraws from the ICA. For some large countries, the price increase would have been so strong that the hypothetical price in the uncontrolled market would have exceeded the existing price in the controlled market. Taking the average for 1982 and 1983, this was the case for eleven countries which increased their economic welfare by participating in the ICA instead of leaving it. These countries gained in economic welfare because of their membership decisions, although the ICA worsened their welfare positions compared with the situation of a liberalized world market. The largest member countries, having the highest welfare losses according to the descriptive approach, realized the highest

Table 6.3 National interests of importing member countries in the International Coffee Agreement, 1982–3 (million US dollars)[a]

Member countries	*Price elasticity of import demand*[b]	*Descriptive policy modelling: the agreement's influence on economic welfare*	*Decision-oriented policy modelling: the membership's influence on economic welfare*
Europe			
Austria	−0.27	−39.9	−10.6
Belgium	−0.28	−67.6	+38.0
Cyprus	0	−1.7	−3.2
Denmark	−0.21	−40.0	−6.8
Finland	0	−41.2	−3.5
Federal Republic of Germany	−0.09	−341.8	+8,753.6
France	−0.10	−216.4	+2,068.1
Greece	−0.37	−13.7	−13.2
Ireland	0	−0.4	−0.6
Italy	−0.19	−162.9	+675.6
Netherlands	−0.31	−99.5	+137.4
Norway	−0.17	−27.0	−16.3
Portugal	−0.41	−12.6	−12.0
Spain	0	−78.1	+105.2
Sweden	−0.32	−64.3	+29.9
Switzerland	−0.40	−40.5	−8.9
UK	−0.16	−63.4	+34.7
Yugoslavia	0	−17.5	−18.2
Non-European member countries			
Australia	−0.26	−22.6	−15.1
Canada	−0.21	−59.3	+23.0
Japan	0	−123.2	+552.8
New Zealand	−0.39	−4.9	−5.8
USA	−0.39	−711.0	+7,119.1
Median impact	-	−41.2	−0.6

Sources: Herrmann (1989: Table 1); computed with data from FAO (a) and the ICO (1983, 1985) and using the method described in the text

Notes: [a]The calculations are based on equation (6.5) for the descriptive approach and on equation (6.11) for the decision-oriented approach. Average values are computed for 1982 and 1983.

[b]The national price elasticities of import demand are taken from estimations of national import-demand functions presented in Herrmann (1988a). A zero value implies that the elasticity coefficient is not significantly different from zero, given a 10 per cent level of statistical significance.

welfare gains according to the decision-oriented approach. Twelve countries, however, experienced a negative impact on national interests because of their membership decision. A withdrawal of these 'small' coffee-importing member countries would have increased the price in the non-member market but not beyond the actual import price in the member market. The highest welfare losses resulting from their membership decisions were realized by Yugoslavia (a loss of US$18 million), followed by Norway, Australia, Greece, Portugal, Austria, Switzerland, Denmark, New Zealand, Finland, Cyprus and Ireland. These countries lost in economic welfare not only as a consequence of the ICA's existence compared with a liberalized world market but also because of their decision to remain members of the ICA instead of leaving it. Note that the welfare losses of four of these eleven countries were higher under decision-oriented than under descriptive modelling, whereas for seven countries the reverse held true. This is mainly due to the fact that a withdrawal of the smallest countries would have left the price in the non-member market nearly unaffected. Hence, the hypothetical price under a withdrawal would still have been lower than the hypothetical price in the non-quota situation ($p_N^* < p^*$).

The national interests of importing non-member countries in the ICA are measured by equations (6.6) and (6.12) as illustrated by Figures 6.2(b) and 6.3(b). Besides p^*, the unobservables p_M^*, q_j^{D*} and q_{Mj}^{D*} had to be quantified. As mentioned earlier, it was assumed that $p_M = p_M^*$. Again, the hypothetical import demand was calculated by use of point estimates of price elasticities of import demand taken from econometrically estimated import-demand functions. The price elasticities and the calculated welfare impacts are presented in Table 6.4.

Table 6.4 contains the following major results:

1 How national interests in welfare terms are affected by the ICA is strongly influenced by the measurement approach. The calculated welfare impacts according to decision-oriented policy modelling are much stronger than those computed with the descriptive approach.
2 On average for 1982 and 1983, the importing non-member countries that imported in both years gained in economic welfare as a result of the ICA compared with a hypothetical non-quota situation. These gains, according to the descriptive approach, are due to the fact that the export quota system led to a price fall in

Table 6.4 National interests of importing non-member countries in the International Coffee Agreement, 1982–3 (million US dollars)[a]

Non-member countries	*Price elasticity of import demand*[b]	*Descriptive policy modelling: the agreement's influence on economic welfare*	*Decision-oriented policy modelling: the influence of non-membership on economic welfare*
Europe			
Czechoslovakia	−0.19	+9.3	+37.0
German Democratic Republic	0	+20.6	+78.3
Hungary	0	+9.4	+26.9
Poland	−0.25	+8.0	+20.2
Romania	0	+2.2	+12.1
USSR	−0.37	+6.4	+34.1
Africa			
Algeria	0	+24.0	+64.6
Egypt	0	+4.6	+11.6
Libya	0	+0.5	+1.8
Morocco	−0.57	+3.8	+13.6
Senegal	0	+1.0	+2.8
Somalia	−3.5106[c]	−0.6	+1.3
South Africa	−0.50	+2.6	+6.8
Sudan	−2.4010[c]	+1.3	+5.7
Tunisia	−0.6823[c]	+0.4	+2.9
Asia			
Hongkong	−0.88	+1.4	+4.0
Israel	−0.50	+4.4	+12.0
Jordan	−0.63	+2.2	+10.9
Korea, PDR	−1.30	+2.7	+9.8
Lebanon	−1.2654[c]	+1.9	+8.8
Saudi Arabia	0	+2.6	+17.6
Syria	0	+0.4	+4.2
Turkey	−1.20	+0.5	+2.2
South America			
Argentina	−6.0685[c]	+7.1	+26.4
Chile	0	+0.9	+5.3
Median impact	–	+2.6	+10.9

Sources: Herrmann (1989: Table 2); computed with data from FAO (a) and ICO (1983, 1985) and using the method described in the text

Notes: [a]The calculations are based on equation (6.6) for the descriptive approach and on equation (6.12) for the decision-oriented approach. Average values are computed for 1982 and 1983.

[b]The national price elasticities of import demand are taken from estimations of national import-demand functions presented in Herrmann (1988a). A zero value implies that the elasticity coefficient is not significantly different from zero, given a 5 per cent level of statistical significance.

[c]For these countries, the price coefficients of linear import-demand functions were used to calculate imports in the hypothetical situation.

the non-member market, and they have already been stressed in the context of Table 6.2.

3 The results for the decision-oriented approach show that national interests of all importing non-member countries were positively affected in 1982 and 1983. All the importing non-member countries increased their economic welfare by their decisions to stay outside instead of joining the agreement. A major result, however, is that the magnitude of the welfare impact was much more positive on the basis of the decision-oriented approach than with the descriptive approach. This result is caused by the fact that the export quota policy has raised the price in the regulated market beyond the hypothetical world market price. Hence, the gains from staying outside are even higher when the actual price in the non-member market is compared with the actual price in the member market rather than with the hypothetical free-trade price. The median welfare increase due to the decision to stay outside the agreement was US$11 million. This is more than four times as high as the median welfare gain shown by the descriptive approach. Analysis of the cases of individual countries makes the importance of the measurement approach even more obvious. Taking the average for 1982 and 1983, the decision-oriented approach shows the highest welfare gain, with US$87 million, for the German Democratic Republic. This gain due to non-participation is more than three times as high as the country's gain due to the introduction of the ICA (US$21 million). This extreme case shows that the change in the benchmark situation leads to a difference in the observed welfare impacts that amounts to nearly US$60 million.

The national interests of exporting member countries in the ICA are measured with equations (6.7) and (6.13) as illustrated by Figures 6.2(c) and 6.3(c). Besides p^*, the unobservable price p^*_{Nk} had to be quantified. It was calculated for each exporting member country on the basis of loglinear import-demand and export-supply curves in the unregulated market and by use of the Newton–Raphson algorithm. Table 6.5 presents the empirical results and shows how economic welfare and export earnings were affected in absolute and relative terms.

The following major results can be derived from Table 6.5:

1 Again, the calculated national interests in the ICA are strongly affected by the measurement approach. Both concepts indicate welfare gains and increasing export earnings for the exporting

member countries of the ICA, but they differ significantly in magnitude.

2 The descriptive approach shows that each individual member country increased its export earnings and its economic welfare as a consequence of the ICA. As described in the context of Table 6.2, the welfare gains from exporting at a supported price in the regulated market outweighed the welfare losses from exporting residual quantities at a depressed price in the unregulated market.

3 The decision-oriented approach shows, too, that the national interests of all exporting member countries were positively influenced in 1982 and 1983. All the exporting member countries increased their export earnings and their economic welfare as a result of their decisions to participate in the agreement instead of leaving it. An important difference between the decision-oriented and the descriptive approach, however, is that the welfare gains are clearly higher under the decision-oriented approach. The median exporting member realized a welfare gain of US$34 million as a result of its decision to participate in the agreement instead of leaving it. The median welfare gain as a percentage of actual export earnings was 77 per cent. These welfare gains are about twice (three times) as high as the welfare gains shown by the descriptive approach. The reason for this result is the following. Owing to a withdrawal, an exporting member would have received a lower price for each exported unit. It is not only that it would have lost the privilege to sell its quota at the supported price in the regulated market, but also that the selling price for its surplus in the unregulated market would have been further depressed. The price fall in the unregulated market due to an exporting member's withdrawal would have been higher the larger the withdrawing coffee exporter. Therefore, Table 6.5 shows that a withdrawal would have been most costly for large exporters like Brazil, Colombia, Côte d'Ivoire, Indonesia, Uganda and El Salvador. In terms of Figure 6.3(c), this implies that p^*_{Nk} would have been much lower for these large exporters than for small exporters. Consequently, there is a huge dispersion of hypothetical prices under the decision-oriented approach and, hence, of the membership's influence on export earnings and economic welfare in absolute and percentage terms. Under the descriptive approach, the dispersion is much smaller since a uniform hypothetical world market price would have been valid for all countries.

Table 6.5 National interests of exporting member countries in the International Coffee Agreement, 1982–3[a]

Member countries	*Descriptive policy modelling: the agreement's influence on economic welfare and export earnings*		*Decision-oriented policy modelling: the membership's influence on economic welfare and export earnings*	
	Million US dollars	*Percentage of export earnings*	*Million US dollars*	*Percentage of export earnings*
Angola	+9.2	+12.3	+22.1	+35.8
Benin	+1.7	+28.2	+2.6	+49.7
Bolivia	+4.3	+30.2	+6.5	+53.1
Brazil	+581.6	+30.0	+2,531.5	+70,876.7
Burundi	+17.0	+29.2	+32.6	+76.5
Cameroon	+49.8	+29.9	+140.2	+184.5
Central African Republic	+9.8	+27.8	+17.7	+64.7
Colombia	+332.0	+29.2	+1,447.9	+7,279.7
Congo	+1.5	+30.4	+2.1	+47.9
Costa Rica	+35.7	+16.3	+149.1	+140.6
Côte d'Ivoirc	+151.0	+29.0	+599.8	+824.8
Dominican Republic	+20.1	+29.0	+40.8	+83.6
Ecuador	+42.9	+27.0	+122.6	+155.4
El Salvador	+87.3	+27.1	+324.0	+378.6
Ethiopia	+50.0	+26.4	+156.4	+188.0
Gabon	+0.5	+31.9	+0.7	+44.6
Ghana	+0.5	+26.7	+0.6	+35.0
Guatemala	+64.3	+21.2	+261.2	+246.0
Guinea	+2.6	+24.6	+4.8	+57.6
Haiti	+11.3	+26.6	+23.3	+76.4
Honduras	+23.5	+16.2	+85.2	+102.4
India	+21.3	+12.8	+81.0	+76.0
Indonesia	+71.1	+14.2	+439.2	+331.7
Jamaica	+0.7	+30.1	+1.0	+46.5
Kenya	+50.5	+24.9	+160.6	+173.5
Liberia	+0.8	+4.2	+2.5	+15.1
Madagascar	+31.1	+27.9	+76.2	+114.6
Malawi	+0.3	+19.7	+0.6	+57.5
Mexico	+54.0	+15.9	+284.0	+261.0
Nicaragua	+23.0	+19.2	+67.3	+88.9
Nigeria	+1.3	+28.8	+2.0	+49.1
Panama	+2.5	+22.8	+4.3	+46.9
Papua New Guinea	+19.6	+19.4	+56.8	+88.6
Peru	+22.4	+21.4	+64.0	+101.4
Philippines	+15.2	+31.2	+27.8	+77.0

Rwanda	+17.5	+29.0	+35.5	+84.3
Sierra Leone	+4.4	+37.7	+5.3	+48.4
Sri Lanka	+1.9	+29.7	+2.8	+49.4
Tanzania	+27.8	+25.0	+70.5	+102.9
Thailand	+4.4	+21.1	+8.2	+48.9
Togo	+5.4	+33.9	+7.4	+53.0
Trinidad/ Tobago	+0.4	+16.7	+0.6	+27.9
Uganda	+94.4	+28.1	+337.9	+365.9
Venezuela	+0.8	+25.3	+1.4	+51.9
Zaire	+43.7	+29.6	+118.0	+161.4
Zimbabwe	+3.3	+21.3	+5.5	+41.8
Median impact	+17.3	+26.9	+34.1	+76.8

Sources: Herrmann (1989: Table 3); computed with data from FAO (a, b) and ICO (1983, 1985) and using the method described in the text

Notes: [a]The calculations are based on equation (6.7) for the descriptive approach and on equation (6.13) for the decision-oriented approach. Average values are computed for 1982 and 1983. The assumed short-run price elasticities of export supply are zero, and it is assumed for each individual country that the actual exports to the member and non-member markets would be equal to the hypothetical exports in the situation without quotas. Therefore the calculations indicate maximum welfare gains.

SUMMARY

It has been shown in this chapter that the ICAs have been price-raising rather than price-stabilizing policies. In the 1980s, the ICAs led to a parallel-market situation separating the member from the non-member market. The quantitative analysis of the redistribution and allocation effects for 1982 and 1983 revealed that the export quota policy under the ICA reduced world welfare and redistributed considerable amounts of income from the importing member countries to the exporting countries and the importing non-member countries. These redistributive impacts are due to the fact that the price on the member market was raised and the price on the non-member market was depressed. A cross-country analysis of the trade-tied aid under the ICA has illustrated that these aid flows are strongly affected by the net trade position of the individual country and by whether a country is a member of the ICA or not. Apart from these criteria, the cross-country allocation of aid is not oriented at indicators of need and is clearly inferior to a targeted financial aid policy.

Additionally, this chapter has provided a methodological basis for measuring national interests in international agricultural policy. Besides the descriptive approach showing the national welfare impacts due to the ICA compared with a liberalized world coffee market, a decision-oriented approach has been developed and applied to the ICA. We have investigated which welfare impacts occurred for an individual country as a result of its decision to participate in the ICA or to stay outside. From a decision-oriented point of view, the actual decision of most countries on their participation in the ICA could be justified. All importing non-member countries gained from their decision to stay outside the ICA; all exporting member countries gained from their decision to participate. In the case of importing member countries, some large members realized welfare gains because of their decision to participate; smaller members would have increased economic welfare by leaving the agreement. An important result is that the measurement of national interests in the ICA is strongly affected by the modelling approach.

7 The International Natural Rubber Agreement

INTRODUCTION

A brief review of international activities regarding natural rubber (NR) was presented in the seventh section of Chapter 1. In this chapter we analyse the International Natural Rubber Agreement (INRA) in detail. We start in the next section with a description of the main economic elements of the Agreement and a review of the history of the two agreements since 1979. A quarterly model of the NR market is presented in the third section, with which the performance of the INRA is evaluated in the fourth section. A full description of the model is given in Appendix B. The important questions are the following. Has the buffer stock been able to stabilize prices and/or incomes? Who are the losers or gainers from these operations? After a deterministic assessment of the impact of the INRA, we proceed to stochastic simulations to investigate the INRA's contribution to 'stability'. We shall employ two interpretations of stability: one referring to changes over time; the other related to uncertainty. In the latter interpretation, the question becomes: did the INRA reduce uncertainty? The answer to this question depends on the time perspective. We investigate the long term, the medium term and the short term in the fifth, sixth and seventh sections respectively. The eighth section discusses what the effects would have been of expressing the reference price in special drawing rights (SDRs). The final section draws conclusions.

A REVIEW OF THE INTERNATIONAL NATURAL RUBBER AGREEMENT

The United Nations Conference on Trade and Development (UNCTAD) at its Fourth Session in Nairobi in May 1976 adopted

Resolution 93 (IV) containing the Integrated Programme for Commodities (IPC). Pursuant to that resolution, UNCTAD convened a series of meetings to prepare for negotiation of an NR agreement and a United Nations conference for this purpose. At the end of the Fourth Session of the Conference, on 6 October 1979, the text of the INRA-1979 was established. Thus this Agreement became the first new international commodity agreement successfully negotiated under the IPC. Selected main features of the Agreement as regards stabilization are as follows:

1 The objectives of the Agreement are spelt out in Article 1. Selected sub-articles regarding price stabilization are as follows:

   (a) to achieve a balanced growth between the supply of and demand for NR, thereby helping to alleviate the serious difficulties arising from surpluses or shortages of NR;
   (b) to achieve stable conditions in the NR trade through avoiding excessive NR price fluctuations, which adversely affect the long-term interests of both producers and consumers, and stabilizing these prices without distorting long-term market trends, in the interests of producers and consumers;
   (c) to help to stabilize the export earnings from NR of exporting members, and to increase their earnings based on expanding NR export volumes at fair and remunerative prices, thereby helping to provide the necessary incentives for a dynamic and rising rate of production and the resources for accelerated economic growth and social development;
   (d) to seek to ensure adequate supplies of NR to meet the requirements of importing members at fair and reasonable prices and to improve the reliability and continuity of these supplies.

2 In order to achieve the objectives of the Agreement, an international NR buffer stock of 550,000 tonnes was established. This buffer stock consists of a normal buffer stock of 400,000 tonnes and a contingency buffer stock of 150,000 tonnes and is to be the sole instrument of market intervention for price stabilization in the Agreement.
3 For the operations of the buffer stock, the Agreement has established a price range consisting of a reference price with three price levels above and three price levels below it. The reference price that applied when the Agreement came into force was set at

210 Malaysian/Singapore cents per kilogramme. The upper and lower intervention prices are calculated as plus or minus 15 per cent of the reference price. The upper and lower trigger action prices are calculated as plus or minus 20 per cent of the reference price. For the first thirty months after the Agreement came into force, the upper and lower limits of the price range were set at 270 and 150 Malaysian/Singapore cents per kilogramme respectively. The upper limit is called the upper indicative price and the lower limit is called the lower indicative price.

4 A daily market indicator price (DMIP) was established which is a composite weighted average of daily official current-month prices on the Kuala Lumpur, London, New York and Singapore markets in respect of three quality grades, namely RSS1, RSS3 and TSR20. Depending on the level of the five-day average of the DMIP, the buffer stock manager is forbidden, allowed or forced to intervene in the market.

5 Under Article 28 of the Agreement, members commit themselves to financing the total costs of the international buffer stock of 550,000 tonnes. The financing of both the normal and contingency stock is to be shared equally between exporting and importing categories of each member. The total costs of the normal buffer stock of 400,000 tonnes are to be paid in cash.

6 The Agreement is for a period of five years, unless extended or terminated in accordance with the provisions of the Agreement.

The Agreement began to operate provisionally on 23 October 1980 and definitively on 15 April 1982. It was extended for two more years until 22 October 1987. On 20 March 1987, international agreement was reached on the continuation of the previous agreement under roughly the same terms. The new agreement, INRA-1987, became operational on 29 December 1988. Interesting is the change in the frequency of the price revision from once every eighteen months to once every twelve months. The reference price was revised upwards following the rules of INRA-1987.

The DMIP and the price ranges are presented in Figure 7.1. The area between the upper two lines is called the 'may-sell' range, while at the bottom a similar area is the 'may-buy' range. The top line shows the 'must-sell' price and the bottom line the 'must-buy' price. Early in 1980, prices had peaked; they fell to the may-buy level in 1981, stayed there in 1982, rose to the may-sell level in 1983, fell again to the may-buy range in 1985, then gradually rose to a level in mid-1988 above the upper limit of the Agreement. The last quarter

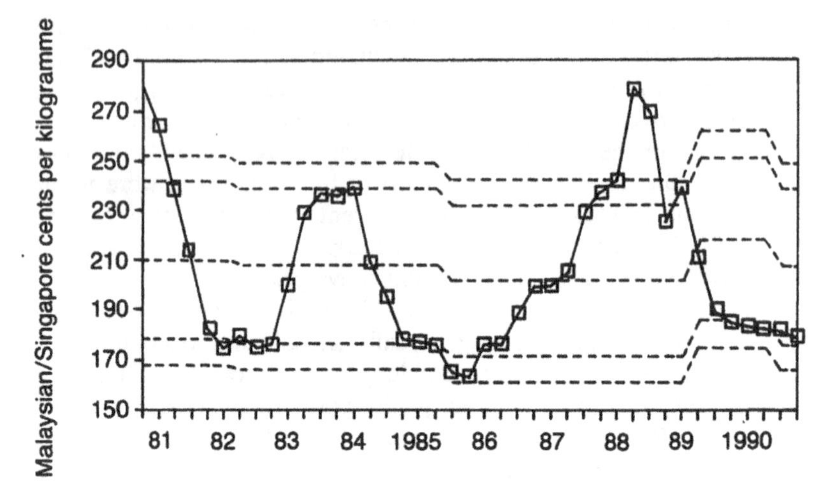

Figure 7.1 The daily market indicator price and the reference, intervention and trigger action prices: -⊟-, daily market indicator price

of 1988 gave prices which were again in the 'no-action' range. In 1989 prices dropped again and reached the may-buy range in the last quarter of the year. In 1990 prices stayed at this low level.

The buffer stock manager intervened in 1982 and 1985 and in September 1987 the buffer stock contained 362,000 tonnes. Later in the year prices rose to the may-sell level and just before the expiry date of the first agreement some rubber was sold by the buffer stock manager. Also, after 22 October 1987, substantial quantities of NR were sold by the buffer stock manager. Only some 25,000 tonnes was left in the buffer stock by the end of 1988. This was all sold in 1989. In the first half of 1990, the buffer stock manager is believed to have purchased some 30,000 tonnes again.

A STRUCTURAL MODEL OF THE NATURAL RUBBER ECONOMY IN VERBAL TERMS

The model of the NR economy, used for evaluating the INRA, is described in detail in Burger and Smit (1989). Here only the main features are reviewed. The equations of the quarterly model are presented in Appendix B.

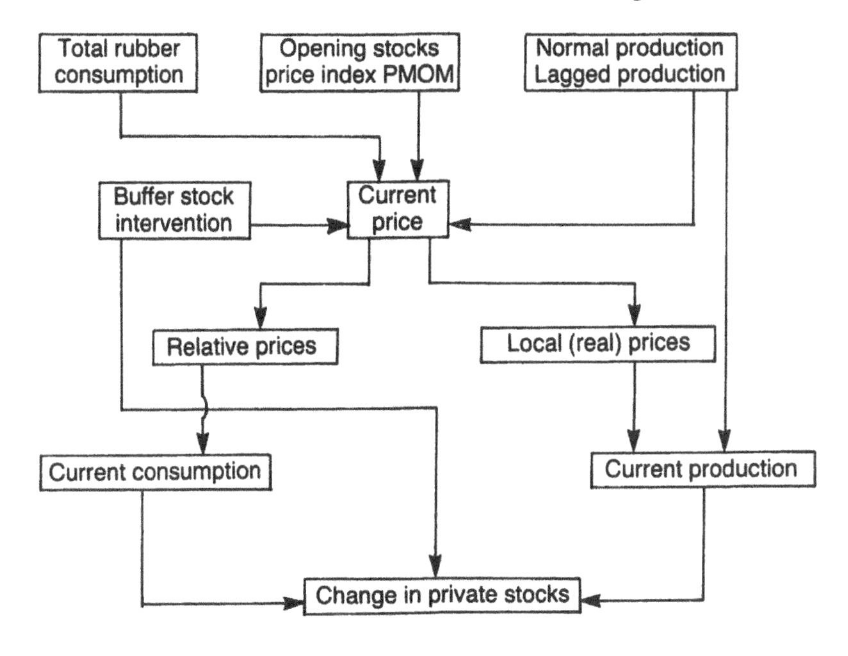

Figure 7.2 Schematic representation of the model

Broad structure of the natural rubber market model

The complete model consists of

1 the long-term analysis of NR production capacity, which is one of the long-term pillars for the short-term analysis;
2 the long-term analysis of total rubber demand, which is the other long-term pillar for the short-term analysis;
3 the quarterly model which is developed to describe short-term reactions of demand, supply and prices to each other, as well as in relation to behaviour of the buffer stock manager in the market. The model is depicted schematically in Figure 7.2.

Long-term production capacity of natural rubber

Rubber trees can reach the age of 60 years or older, but the yield per tree is not constant. Trees can be tapped after about six years, after which the yield normally increases, reaching its maximum when the trees are approximately 12 years old. As they grow older, yields normally decline, and at the age of 50 yields have decreased to almost nil. Besides, there has been an improvement in the quality of trees: recently developed trees yield better than, for example, trees developed in the 1950s. The supply of NR therefore depends not only on the area planted with rubber trees but also on their age composition and year of planting.

It will be clear to anybody familiar with NR statistics that data to carry out such an analysis are not available. The methodology for the analysis is shown in Smit (1984) and summarized in Burger and Smit (1989). The approach we used assumes a 'discarding function' that describes how the total discarded area is distributed over the various ages of the trees. Employing data on new planting, replanting, and discarding for the past sixty to ninety years, the age composition in more recent years can be fairly well established. The technical progress in the clones that are planted is assessed by relating theoretical production levels to actual production over the past twenty odd years and adjusting the yield parameters over time. After calibrating the outcome so as to equal the average production over this period, we arrive at what we call 'normal production'.

These long-term supply models are constructed for the three major producing countries. In Malaysia and Indonesia a further distinction is made between estates and smallholdings, as these groups may differ in yield level, technical progress and discarding behaviour. In Thailand, the third largest producer, the estate sector is too small to warrant separate treatment. Production trends for countries other than the above areas have been estimated using simpler models.

In the quarterly model, these trends and 'normal production levels' are used as the basis for short-term supply responses.

Long-term demand trends for all rubber

The volume of passenger cars and commercial vehicles on the road determines how many tyres are needed for replacement of those which are worn out. The increase in the number of vehicles on the road determines new sales (or new registrations) of vehicles, i.e. the net increase. The other element leading to new sales (or new registrations) is the discarding or scrapping of vehicles. From new registrations, it is a small step to determine the number of original equipment tyres. Also incorporated in the analysis is the number of retreaded tyres. Together with new tyres, they provide the need for rubber. Thus, consumption of total rubber in tyres for passenger cars and in tyres for commercial vehicles is arrived at by straightforward multiplication by the rubber weight per type of tyre. Elaborate models have been developed for all elements of this sequence.

Rubber consumption for such 'other tyres' as for tractors, aeroplanes, motorcycles, scooters and bicycles as well as tubes and retreading material, etc. has been derived separately. Some 40–50 per cent of all (natural plus synthetic) rubber is used, however, for products other than tyres. These products are grouped into a 'general products sector' and analysed separately as well.

By adding all elements of rubber consumption together, total demand for rubber (natural plus synthetic) is derived. This is the basis for short-term demand for all rubber. Short-term demand for NR is described below as being based among other things on total rubber demand and prices.

Short-term supply response to prices for natural rubber

In the short-term (quarterly) model, supply equations are estimated based on normal production levels. These normal production levels described above are derived on a yearly basis and are converted to quarterly figures. Consequently, quarterly supply behaviour refers to tapping only. A possible change in production capacity would be incorporated in the normal production levels and these are assumed in the short run not to depend on prices. As a dependent variable in the short-run supply equations, the ratio of actual and normal production has been used. A double logarithmic specification relates this ratio to seasonal dummies and to the ratio of the Singapore price of NR, converted into local currency and adjusted for export duties in Malaysia and Thailand, and the consumer prices. Quarterly supply elasticities are of the order of 0.13–0.20 for smallholdings and for Thailand and 0.10 for Malaysian estates (0.14 in the longer term). Production of the five groups represents some 75 per cent of world production. The production of other countries is analysed separately, using a simpler approach for deriving normal production levels and including real prices wherever possible.

Short-term demand response to prices for natural rubber

Demand for NR is related to total (natural + synthetic) rubber demand. As prices of rubber constitute only a very small portion of the costs of the end product (mainly tyres), they can be assumed to play no role in deciding the total use of rubber. Given a certain total demand for rubber, however, the share of NR in this aggregate depends on NR prices relative to synthetic rubber prices. The price of

RSS1-quality rubber has been taken as the representative price for NR expressed in US dollars in the Singapore market, and unit values of the US styrene–butadiene rubber (SBR) exports are used as competitive synthetic rubber (SR) prices. As an additional explanatory variable, a trend is used that first decreases and later increases. This reflects the technical changes that have taken place over the past decades: first the increases in new SR products; later the increases in radial tyres, the impact on NR consumption of which should be positive as radial tyres contain more NR than conventional tyres. This trend was assumed not to continue in the future. Estimated price elasticity of demand in the next quarter is 0.024; long-term elasticity, applicable to a one-year period, is 0.050.

Prices

Quarterly price determination on world markets is made between buyers (mostly NR-consuming tyre manufacturers) and sellers (mostly stockholders). Hence, the current quarter's production can hardly play a role, as this production cannot physically reach the consumers. The relevant considerations regarding the prices, therefore, are those of the NR consumers and those of the stockholders. Production plays a role only in as far as some indication is required for the stockholders about what future replenishment of their stocks is to be expected. The main determining endogenous factors of the prices are total world rubber consumption (NR + SR), opening stocks and expected production, the latter of which was represented by the four-quarter average, lagged by two quarters.

Prices are determined in a world market, influenced by changing rates of inflation, of interest and of currency exchange. These monetary influences on the price are captured in two additional variables, namely the price index of minerals, ores and metals (PMOM) and the US dollar–SDR exchange rates. The inclusion of the PMOM serves two ends. First, the prices pertain to commodities that are required by an industry that also uses rubber, and thus the PMOM complements the variable describing total rubber demand. Second, the commodity prices underlying the PMOM, like copper and aluminium prices, are sensitive to monetary changes. A declining US dollar, declining interest rates or rising inflation rates induce conversion of money balances into commodities (see Frankel 1984). The US dollar–SDR exchange rate lagged by one period has been found to have an effect of its own on the Singapore price of NR in US dollars.

In spite of the large seasonal fluctuations in supply and demand, prices do not show this cyclical pattern. Thus, stockholders appear to play their role of accommodating these short-term fluctuations well. In the price equation this is incorporated by de-seasonalizing the level of total consumption and the level of private stocks. See Appendix B for details on how this is done.

Finally, the purchases and sales of the buffer stock manager were to be included in the equation. Their influence on the prices proved to be modelled best when they were considered as a reduction of or as an addition to the private opening stocks of the quarter. Since these interventions are neither consumption nor production, this result is quite plausible.

The estimated (loglinear) equation corroborates the US dollar exchange rate effect, displaying an elasticity of about 0.23. Effects of consumption and production were of about equal size, showing elasticities of 1.7 and 2.0 respectively, whereas the direct effect of a change in opening stock was 0.9, measured as elasticity. The PMOM had an elasticity of 0.5. With 0.64 as the coefficient for the lagged price, longer-term elasticities are about 2.5 times as high as given above.

Inventories

The model is closed by an identity for stock changes, and private stockholders' behaviour, therefore, is modelled implicitly. Changes in the private stocks take place for seasonal reasons, as production and consumption do not match per quarter; they also occur after buffer stock intervention, as the buffer stock manager has hardly any alternative but to buy from private stockholders. Finding a positive influence of the US dollar–SDR exchange rate on the NR price indicates that private stockholders are less eager to sell – or others, for example speculators, are more eager to buy – stocks of NR when the US dollar falls (so that more US dollars must be paid for one SDR). Speculation has a positive effect on the size of stocks only to the extent that less is consumed and more is produced in a quarter. This effect is only minor. Speculation is more important for its effect on prices, and this effect is incorporated in the price equation. Larger opening stocks have a depressing influence on prices. Checks were made to investigate whether the total buffer stock should be included in these stocks or whether it is only the freely available stocks that directly impact on prices (in addition, of course, to changes in the buffer stock that do have an impact). The private opening stocks, after adjustment for current buffer stock manager purchases, appeared to be preferable. Buffer stock intervention thus reduces the quantity available for (other) sales in that quarter and in later quarters, but the accumulated quantity of NR, taken out of the market (but still stored somewhere), did not appear to have any further influence on the prices.

The estimated price equation can be used to simulate the behaviour of the buffer stock manager. The equation can be solved for that change in buffer stock that would bring prices to a certain, for example minimum, level. Simulations for the period 1982–8 showed that buffer stock management behaviour was apparently to defend a price positioned some 4 per cent above the minimum (must-buy) price of the agreement, i.e. at around the may-buy level.

PERFORMANCE OF THE INTERNATIONAL NATURAL RUBBER AGREEMENT IN 1982–9: DETERMINISTIC COMPARISON

In this section results as presented in Herrmann *et al.* (1990) are summarized. Results on the impact that buffer stock interventions in the period 1982–9 have had on the NR market are arrived at by comparing a dynamic simulation for all thirty-two quarters, in which the actual buffer stock purchases and sales are given, with a dynamic simulation in the event of no buffer stock intervention.

An assumption must be made on the disturbances that occur in the established relationships, particularly the supply and demand equations. The main results for the differences caused by the INRA will be assessed assuming that the disturbances as found in the static simulation will also occur in the dynamic simulation. A similar procedure was followed by Chu and Morrison (1986). In this deterministic run, therefore, an assessment of the effects of the INRA may be blurred by random factors. Precisely this aspect will be dealt with in the following sections.

Effects of the buffer stock

The main results on prices are depicted in Figure 7.3. This shows what the price is estimated to have been in a dynamic simulation with and without the buffer stock intervention so that it can be compared with the actually observed price. In 1982.1, the first quarter to be compared, the buffer stock manager bought 56,000 tonnes, thus increasing the price to S$1,800 per tonne, i.e. 3 per cent more than without intervention; production responds in the same quarter by a mere +2,481 tonnes, together bringing private stocks down by

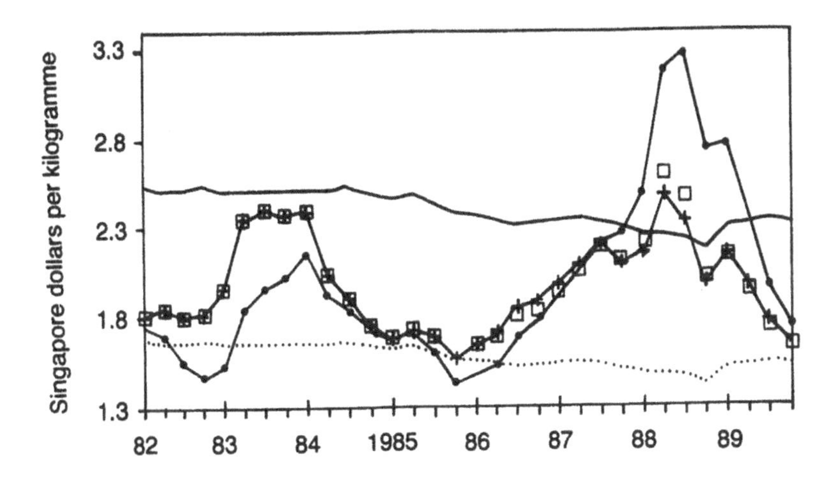

Figure 7.3 National rubber prices in a dynamic simulation with and without buffer stock: ----, lower limit; □, actual;-•-, without buffer stock;-+-, with buffer stock;—, upper limit

52,500 tonnes. In the following quarters, buffer stock purchases of 78,000, 53,000 and 44,000 tonnes respectively bring prices at the end of 1982 to a level of S$1,807 per tonne to be compared with S$1,648 in the case of no intervention. By this time cumulative additional production equals 46,000 tonnes and consumption over the year is 7,000 tonnes less than without intervention.

By mid-1983 prices are 27 per cent higher than without the buffer stock because of the earlier interventions. This effect fades away, and by the start of 1985 less than 1 per cent difference remains. The next - milder - interventions take place in the last two quarters of 1985 and the first quarter of 1986. By mid-1987 a mere 10,000 tonnes' difference in private stocks is left when comparing simulations with and without buffer stock intervention. When the buffer stock manager starts selling in 1987.3 (31,000 tonnes) and 1987.4 (66,000 tonnes), private stocks increase because these sales are temporarily added to the private stocks. The difference between the two simulations changes from −10,000 at the end of 1987.2 to +23,000 in 1987.3 and +81,000 at the end of 1987. Hence, for the major part, buffer stocks were merely relabelled to privately owned stocks.

Nevertheless, this had a strong impact on the prices. At the end of 1987, simulated prices in the case of non-intervention are 7.3 per

Table 7.1 Monetary transfers owing to the International National Rubber Agreement (million US dollars) with all trade evaluated at RSS1 prices, discounted to 1989.4 and after adjustment for initial buffer stock sales in 1988 and quality

Year	*Paid by buffer stock*	*Paid by consumers*	*Received by producers*	*Received by stockholders*
1982	196	352	405	143
1983	36	785	895	−73
1984	0	185	232	−46
1985	65	116	143	38
1986	4	321	372	−47
1987	−99	−77	−76	−100
1988	−278	−1,697	−1,932	−43
1989	−22	−807	−919	90
Total	−99	−822	−882	−39
Total[a]	−35	−483	−483	−35
Total[b]	+22	−124	−77	−25

Source: Own computations
Notes: [a]When discounted at 1 per cent per quarter to 1989.4.
[b]After further adjustment for the 1988 effect and quality.

cent below those in the case of intervention. Later sales by the buffer stock manager in 1988.1 and 1988.2 (of 99,000 and 104,000 tonnes respectively) increased private stocks to a level that is 230,000 tonnes higher than in the case of no intervention. Prices in 1988.2 are estimated to have been reduced by 22 per cent, but this was not enough to keep the prices from rising above the upper limit of the agreement. Because of the intervention, production in 1988 was decreased by 144,000 tonnes and consumption was increased by 27,000 tonnes. The last sales of International Natural Rubber Organization (INRO) rubber were made in the first half of 1989, but their effects still linger on. At the end of this year, prices were still 4 per cent below their non-intervention level and private stocks were 38,500 tonnes larger than they would otherwise have been. Of these 38,500 tonnes, 1,000 tonnes were from buffer stocks that were purchased in 1981.

Summed over the whole period 1982.1–1989.4, production was 10,200 tonnes higher and consumption 27,300 tonnes lower as a result of the buffer stock intervention.

During the earlier part of the period, prices were higher because of the intervention, whereas after 1987.2 prices were lower. Hence, initially transfers have taken place from consumers to producers.

Table 7.2 Buffer stock sales, natural rubber prices and estimates and estimated buffer stock sales required to reach actual price, 1987.3–1988.4

Year	*BS sales*	*Actual price*	*Given BS: estimated price*	*No BS sales: simulated price*	*Given price: BS sales required*
1987.3	31	2,169	2,199	2,219	51
1987.4	66	2,116	2,089	2,253	14
1988.1	99	2,210	2,150	2,493	99
1988.2	104	2,606	2,480	3,177	74
1988.3	17	2,477	2,329	3,278	12
1988.4	25	2,017	1,982	2,740	105

Sources: IRSG, INRO, own computations
Note: Volumes in 1,000 tonnes; prices in Singapore dollars per tonne; BS, buffer stock.

Later, the direction of this flow was reversed and consumers paid less than they would otherwise have done.

Table 7.1 indicates the size of the transfers made. Summed over the period 1982–9, producers have paid US$882 million and consumers received US$822 million, when all trade is evaluated at the (relatively high) RSS1 prices. Not counting storage costs, interest, overhead costs, etc., the buffer stock should have made a profit of US$99 million.

Because additional expenditures and revenues change over time and because of additional adjustments, the bottom rows of Table 7.1 indicate the new totals that would arise if a discount factor was introduced equal to 1 per cent per quarter and all values were discounted to their value in 1989.4. In this case, producers transfer 'only' US$483 million to consumers. Profits by INRO would likewise be lower. As a second case, some further adjustments are made because the effectiveness of INRO in 1988 was reduced and because the average price of traded NR is below the price of RSS1-quality rubber that is used in the earlier annual calculations. These final adjustments will be discussed below.

Rubber sold by INRO has been traded at considerable rebates of up to 30 per cent by reason of (alleged) diminished quality. Table 7.2 gives the actual and estimated values for the prices during the period 1987.3–1988.4, when prices peaked and (almost) all INRO rubber was sold.

The last column of Table 7.2 shows the sales from the buffer stock that would make estimated prices equal to actually observed prices.

Table 7.3 Changes in producers' revenues owing to the International Natural Rubber Agreement 1982–9 (million US dollars)

Year	*Malaysia*	*Indonesia*	*Thailand*	*Rest*	*Total*
1982	165	97	59	84	405
1983	348	227	131	188	894
1984	84	61	33	53	232
1985	49	37	24	33	143
1986	135	88	65	84	372
1987	−25	−21	−16	−14	−76
1988	−644	−489	−365	−434	−1,932
1989	−257	−239	−223	−200	−919
Total	−145	−238	−291	−207	−882
Total[a]	18	−139	−239	−123	−483
Total[b]	+144	−35	−155	−31	−77

Source: Own computations
Notes: [a]Discounted at 1 per cent per quarter.
[b]After further adjustment for buffer stock sales in 1988 and average price.

In 1987.3, sales should have been higher, or in other words actual sales had more impact than estimated. In this dynamic context, higher sales in 1987.3 increase private stocks by more than the original estimate; hence estimated prices in 1987.4 would become lower. As actual prices were above the originally estimated price, a further reduction of sales by the buffer stock manager would have been possible. Estimated required sales are only 14,000 tonnes.

Over the first four quarters of buffer stock sales, the actual sales amount to 300,000 tonnes, whereas their impact equals that of only 238,000 tonnes. This would indicate that the effectiveness of the sales is only 79 per cent. If, however, the buffer stock sales had achieved the simulated impact, private stocks would have increased by less than actually happened. This by itself would have had a price-increasing effect, explaining why in the final quarter, 1988.4, so many more buffer stock sales appear to be required to reach the actual lower price levels. It might be, therefore, as many observers have noted, that buffer stock sales are less effective at reducing prices, allegedly because of the low quality of the stored NR. If a longer period is considered, including the dynamic effects on private stocks levels, this reduced effectiveness is cancelled out.

For the effects on prices in 1988, it seems appropriate to reduce the estimates of Table 7.1 by something of the order of the calculated effectiveness, say 20 per cent. This leads to calculated transfers in

Table 7.4 Changes in import expenditures owing to the International Natural Rubber Agreement (million US dollars)

Year	*EC*	*OWE*	*EE*	*USA*	*China*	*Japan*	*Korea*	*Other*	*Total*
1982	86	13	42	72	17	48	14	60	352
1983	171	30	106	155	57	117	30	120	785
1984	39	7	23	40	11	27	8	31	185
1985	26	5	12	25	5	18	5	20	116
1986	72	13	28	65	19	48	16	61	321
1987	−17	−3	−7	−15	−7	−11	−4	−13	−77
1988	−354	−59	−106	−332	−152	−275	−99	−320	−1,697
1989	−172	−27	−56	−172	−74	−130	−45	−131	−807
Total	−148	−22	42	−163	−124	−160	−75	−173	−822
Total[a]	−69	−8	92	−94	−106	−113	−64	−121	−483
Total[b]	4	4	108	−24	−71	−6	−41	−52	−124

Source: Own computations
Notes: EE, Eastern Europe; OWE, other Western Europe.
[a]Discounted to 1989.4 at 1 per cent per quarter.
[b]After further adjustment for buffer stock sales in 1988 and average prices.

1988 that are around US$350 million lower than those given in Table 7.1, without substantially changing the calculated transfers of 1989.

Employment of the RSS1 price instead of the actual prices of various grades leads to the estimates being higher by 5 per cent on average. The bottom row of Table 7.1 gives the revised estimates of what the interventions have cost INRO, consumers, producers and stockholders. Calculated in this way, INRO has made a loss (not counting administrative overhead and storage costs); consumers received US$124 million, producers paid US$77 million and stockholders must have had extra expenditures of US$25 million.

Distributions among producers and consumers

The additional revenues and expenditures caused by INRO can be further divided over the major producing and consuming countries. On the producer side, we have taken the actual responses of Malaysian (peninsular) estates and smallholdings, Indonesian estates and smallholdings and Thailand separately. Table 7.3 provides details on monetary transfers to these three countries.

While the NR production in (peninsular) Malaysia was stagnant during this period, production in Indonesia and Thailand grew rapidly. This is the reason why the latter two countries incurred more costs because of the interventions: the lower prices at the end of the period affected larger volumes of exports than did the higher prices earlier in the 1980s. If the figures are discounted to the fourth quarter of 1989 at 1 per cent per quarter, peninsular Malaysia gained from the operation. Taking into account that the buffer stock manager has not been so effective in lowering the prices in 1988 as estimated in the basic version of the model, and taking into consideration that the prices of the average type of NR traded is some 5 per cent below the employed RSS1 price, a substantial gain for Malaysia results, while Indonesia and – in particular – Thailand have received less.

On the consumer side, a similar skewed distribution can be calculated. The basis for the calculation of Table 7.4 is the total change in world consumption expenditures. The yearly amounts were divided over the countries using their share in world net imports, however. This implies that countries are assumed to benefit or lose according to their participation in world trade. Thus, China's and India's domestically produced volumes of NR are not assumed to change in price in response to changes in the world market prices.

Those that have expanded imports of NR have benefited more from the lower prices in 1988 and 1989 than those that did not. Thus, Eastern Europe was a net loser, while all other regions have benefited from the interventions. After a reduction of the effects in 1988 by 20 per cent, a downward adjustment of average prices by 5 per cent and discounting all expenditures to the fourth quarter of 1989 by 1 per cent per quarter, tiny losses result for the whole of Europe (EC, other Western Europe and particularly Eastern Europe). Because of the large purchases of NR in recent years, China has benefited most.

PERFORMANCE OF THE INTERNATIONAL NATURAL RUBBER AGREEMENT: LONG-TERM UNCERTAINTY AND STABILIZATION

The previous section provided a deterministic assessment of the consequences of the INRA. The assumption was maintained that disturbances, as they occurred in the past, would also have occurred in the 'counterfactual' world without buffer stock intervention. This fails to acknowledge that the realized prices in the past are the outcome of a multitude of processes, many of which are far from deterministic. Production is subject to weather, prices are subject to exchange rates, real prices to inflation rates, consumption of car tyres to fuel prices, etc. This and later sub-sections aim at assessing the contribution that this INRA may have made to the stability of prices

Table 7.5 Projected and actual world rubber consumption

Source	*1980*	*1985*	*1990*
World Bank	13,040	16,100	21,000
Smit			
Low growth	–	13,486	15,178
Medium growth	–	14,356	17,422
High growth	–	15,288	19,920
Actual	12,445	13,295	14,950[a]

Sources: World Bank 1980; Smit 1982; actual data from IRSG
Note: [a]15,360 in 1989.

and earnings, taking into account that many exogenous factors are stochastic in nature and that the relationships employed by the model have a random component as well.

The long-term outlook for a commodity like NR critically depends on long-term demand, in its turn determined by car sales and income and by planting policies. Rubber trees remain immature for a period of some six years, and returns to investments in rubber are typically dependent on the average price levels ten to thirty years from the year of planting. The simulations above show that, after market intervention, prices of NR fairly quickly return to the levels that would rule in a free-market situation. This, the uncertainty about a continuation of any agreement after the five or seven years for which such agreements are made and the uncertainty about the price ranges if there were to be any continuation, make it very hard to believe that the INRA would have any significant impact on the long-term outlook for the NR market.

PERFORMANCE OF THE INTERNATIONAL NATURAL RUBBER AGREEMENT: MEDIUM-TERM UNCERTAINTY AND STABILIZATION

For a shorter period, say five to ten years ahead, a buffer stock agreement would have an appreciable impact on the stability of the market if it were able to cope with most of the changes in the relevant factors in the market. In the case of the NR market, there are medium-term prospects for overall rubber consumption and planting and therefore production capacity. What were these prospects at the time the INRA was negotiated, i.e. in 1980? Forecasts for total world rubber consumption at that time as presented by the World

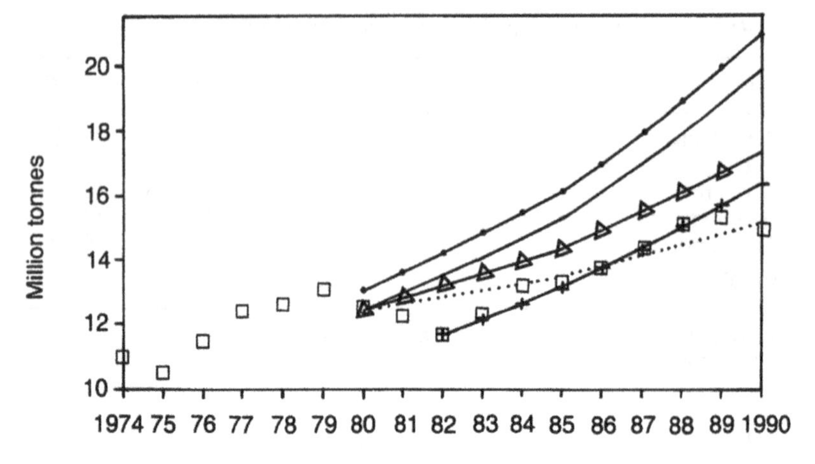

Figure 7.4 Estimates and actual values of total world rubber consumption: □ , actual; ----, low; —▲—, medium; ——, high; —•—, World Bank 1980; —+—, World Bank 1984

Bank (1980) and Smit (1982) are given in Table 7.5. As this table shows, there was apparent uncertainty about how future demand would develop and – with hindsight – projections were over-optimistic. Figure 7.4 shows the estimates and the actual values in the 1980s.

In addition to projections of demand, negotiators of the Agreement are faced with uncertainty about future supply and prices. Forecasts for supply at that time were all pointing upwards, but at various angles. Estimates ranged from 4.3 to 5.5 million tonnes in 1985. This is a huge spread, given that production in 1985 had to come from trees that had all been planted before 1980. Had people known the exact area and age distribution of the trees at that time, a much more precise estimate would have been possible. Smit (1982), in an extensive study including estimated vintages in the major producing countries, came to the correct estimate for 1985, as shown in Figure 7.5, but 1990 proved harder to predict. The reason is that, apart from price influences on the capacity utilization, the changes in the capacity itself need to be predicted. The capacity increases with new plantings and replantings and decreases when trees are discarded. New plantings and replantings have a late role to play at this term, as only trees planted in the early 1980s are tappable by 1990. This is a major reason for Smit's low prediction in 1990. Around 1980, rubber production from Malaysian smallholdings stagnated and the increase

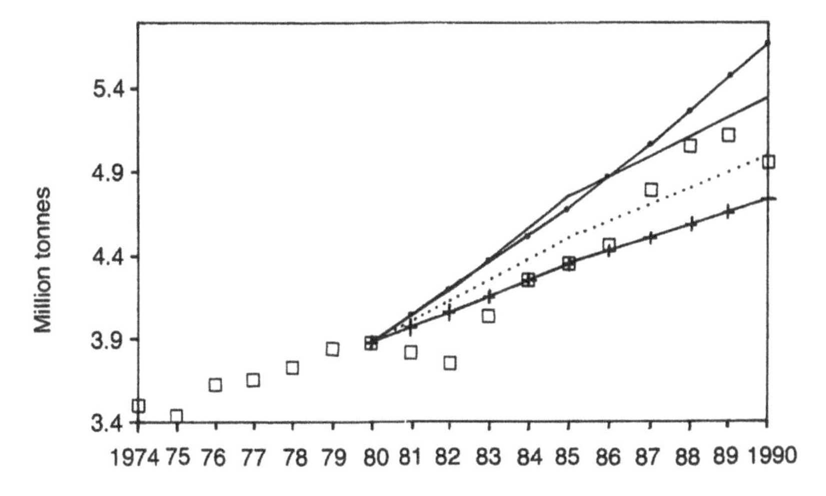

Figure 7.5 Estimates and actual values of world natural rubber production: □, actual; -•-, World Bank 1980; ----, IRSG-low; ——, IRSG-high; -+-, Smit 1982

in later years, owing to increased replanting after the high prices in 1980, was accountable for a large share of the prediction error. In addition, Indonesian smallholdings have increased their production by more than was expected in 1980. Indonesian figures are notoriously unreliable, and particularly so for the smallholdings. The high estimates of other forecasters apparently did not reckon with as much discarding as has taken place in this decade, particularly on Malaysian estates.

It is not only consumption and production which have to be forecasted when negotiating price stabilization. The price itself depends on other factors as well, notably the general price level prevailing in the world markets. These other prices in part reflect worldwide inflation and in part are themselves caused by supply and demand conditions. Price levels prevailing in the consuming and producing countries may differ as they are connected to the world market prices via a changing exchange rate. Thus forecasts at the time of negotiating the INRA were based on the inflationary trends that were apparent at that time. Figure 7.6 shows the level of the PMOM and the price outlook as published by the World Bank in 1980, 1982 and 1984. This price is relevant for rubber because rubber prices follow metals prices fairly closely (see Burger and Smit 1989).

Not surprisingly, in 1980 rubber prices were all predicted to go up.

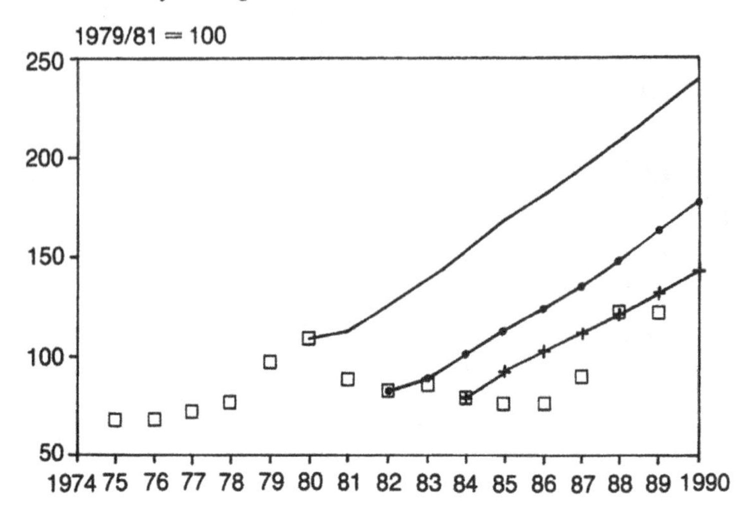

Figure 7.6 Estimates and actual values of the price index of minerals, ores and metals: □, actual; ——, World Bank 1980; -•-, World Bank 1982; -+-, World Bank 1984

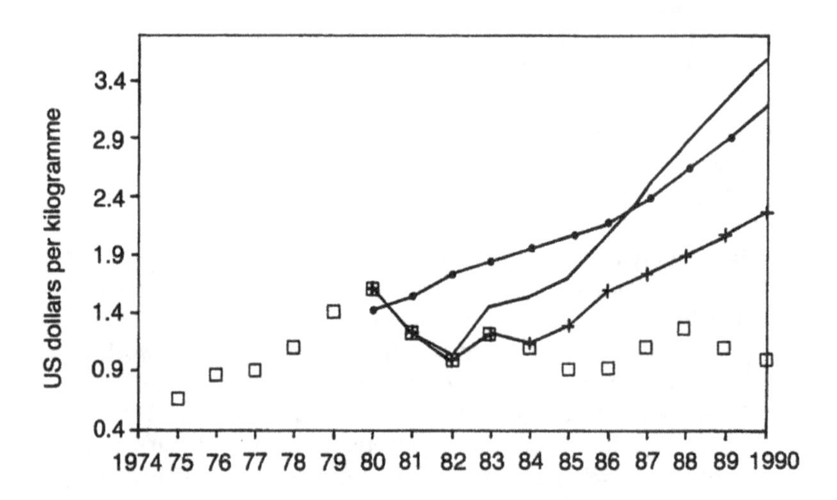

Figure 7.7 Estimates and actual values of natural rubber prices: □, actual; ——, Smit 1982; -+-, World Bank 1984; -•-, World Bank 1980

Figure 7.7 shows the forecasts made by Smit and the World Bank around that time.

This is the future that the negotiators of INRA-1979 were faced with: uncertain forecasts of world demand, supply and prices. What stability could an Agreement offer in this environment?

To quantify the extent to which uncertainty affected rubber prices, simulations were made with the same quarterly model of the world market as used in the previous section. The uncertainties are incorporated as follows:

1 *Demand*: an error term was included in the forecast of total world rubber consumption. The basic forecast was the average of the predictions as given in Table 7.5, but the average growth rate may differ from quarter to quarter in a random manner. The resulting spread in the forecasts for 1990 more or less equals the spread in the predictions of Table 7.5.
2 *Supply*: for the major producing countries, a base forecast of 'normal production' was made, which was taken to be the expected growth path. The actual path may deviate. The yearly change in 'normal production' was therefore included as a random variable. The error terms were largest for Indonesia and smallest for Thailand, whose growth of production should have been quite predictable. In addition, the production capacity of the rest of the world was assumed to follow the actual trend but with a random walk added to it. The total resulting spread of the forecast capacity was made equal to the actual spread as displayed by Figure 7.6.
3 *Prices*: the PMOM which is one of the explanatory variables of the rubber price, was likewise assumed to follow the predicted increasing trend (1.7 per cent per quarter), but with a relatively large random walk.
4 *Responses*: all behavioural equations in the model were assumed to have an error, of which the probability distribution matches the actual distribution shown in the past decade, including a correlation between errors in actual consumption and errors in prices equal to 0.31.
5 *Error distribution*: all forecasting errors in figures for total consumption, production capacity and exogenous prices were assumed to be homogeneous, so that 'high' has the same probability as 'medium' or 'low'. Behavioural errors in consumption, production and price equations were assumed to have normal distributions.

Table 7.6 Outlook, uncertainty and buffer stock intervention prospects as per 1980 (volumes in 1,000 tonnes)

	1985 mean	*1990 mean*	*CV–1*	*CV–2*
NR consumption	4,437	5,726	0.13	0.04
NR production	4,429	5,791	0.15	0.05
NR price (US dollars per tonne)	1,640	4,060	0.43	0.42
Buffer stock	14	0		
Chances of BS inability	*BS-400*	*BS-550*	*BS-0*	
Average over quarters	0.00	0.00	0.81	
In most likely quarter	0.01	0.01	1.00	

Source: Own computations
Note: BS, buffer stock.

The official buffer stock intervention rule is based on the DMIP, consisting of prices in various currencies and of various qualities of NR. This was endogenized in the model. The model covers only the price of RSS1, and a relationship between the DMIP and the RSS1 price was used to transform the must-buy and must-sell prices into the corresponding level of the RSS1 price. Buffer stock manager behaviour appeared to correspond to defending the may-buy price in 1982 and a slightly lower price in 1985 (when there was a danger of the buffer stock reaching its upper limit), and rubber sales were triggered by the must-sell price. In the model, changes in the buffer stock were restricted to a maximum of 100,000 tonnes per quarter. This had an impact only during the time when the buffer stock manager was selling. Without the constraint, the model would have simulated successful binding of the prices at the upper limit of the INRA until the depletion of the buffer stock, whereas this was not the case in reality. The reason was simply that the required amounts of NR could not physically be sold in one quarter.

A hundred simulations were made with this random model. The average values in each of the quarters and their standard deviations were measured. Two measures for uncertainty are reported. One is the coefficient of variation (CV) of the means per quarter (CV-1), which measures the variability over time; the other measure (CV-2) is a CV measured as the ratio of the average of the standard deviations per quarter to the overall mean of the variable. The first measure is affected by trends; the second coefficient is a better measure for the predictability of a variable in a quarter.

Effectiveness of buffer stock intervention can be assessed either by

Table 7.7 Outlook, uncertainty and buffer stock intervention prospects as per 1980, without inflationary trends

	1985 mean	*1990 mean*	*CV-1*	*CV-2*
NR consumption	4,438	5,740	0.13	0.04
NR production	4,395	5,772	0.15	0.05
NR price (US dollars per tonne)	1,260	2,970	0.40	0.43
Buffer stock	71	26		
Chances of BS inability	*BS-400*	*BS-550*	*BS-0*	
Average over quarters	0.01	0.01	0.59	
In most likely quarter	0.05	0.03	0.81	

Source: Own computations
Note: BS, buffer stock.

reduction in the standard deviation of the prices or by simple measures of the activity of the buffer stock. The chances are reported that the buffer stock could not intervene because of (a) BS-400, the buffer stock having reached its temporary upper limit (400,000 tonnes) when prices are at the lower limit of the Agreement; (b) BS-550, the buffer stock having reached its upper limit of 550,000 tonnes when prices are at the minimum level of the Agreement; or (c) BS-0, the buffer stock having no stock when prices breach the upper limit of the Agreement. The results of the simulations are given in Table 7.6.

The interpretation of the numbers in Table 7.6 is that consumption and production were expected to go up to around 5.75 million in 1990 and that prices would increase to 1.64 US$/kg in 1985 and 4.06 US$/kg in 1990. The statistic CV-2 measures the uncertainty about volumes or prices in any quarter. The average standard deviations of consumption and production are around 5 per cent of the overall means, whereas prices are highly unpredictable with an average standard deviation equal to 42 per cent of the overall mean. CV-2 is equal to CV-1, which means that variation in any quarter is as high as the variation over time. The buffer stock is inactive for most of the time. There is only a 1 per cent chance of reaching the 400,000 tonnes limit in the quarter in which it is most likely. On the other hand, in 81 per cent of all cases, the buffer stock manager should have been selling, but could not do so for lack of stocks.

Clearly, in this situation the Agreement could not be expected to contribute to the stability of the world market prices, and the negotiators apparently have agreed on a price range that looked quite low at that time. To a large extent, the inability of the buffer stock manager to intervene is because of the slow adjustment of the price band to prevailing world market price levels. The model has incorporated all 'automatic' changes which take place when the six-quarterly meetings of the Council cannot agree on another adjustment. This might not have been the case, of course, and, if the world had evolved in the way people in 1980 thought it would, the price bands might have been adjusted by more than is now simulated. To check whether it is the assumed rates of inflation that cause the buffer stock manager to be so passive, the effects of inflation were eliminated in a series of simulations, the results of which are reported in Table 7.7. For these simulations, inflation rates were again taken to be uncertain, but this time without any trend. Added in these simulations is uncertainty, although relatively little, about exchange rates. As shown in Table 7.7, forecasts and uncertainties of consumption and production are hardly affected. The reduced inflation has made buffer stock intervention much more likely, bringing the chance of the buffer stock manager being unable to defend the upper limit down on average from 81 per cent to 59 per cent. Prices are still on the increase, however, owing to demand trends outpacing supply trends until 1989.

In spite of the more frequent buffer stock intervention, the uncertainty about the prices in any quarter has not fallen. Simulations with the same random distributions, but without the possibility of buffer stock intervention, lead to higher average prices in 1990 (equal to US$3.30/kg), but the CV-1 and CV-2 of the prices are 0.41 and 0.42 respectively, indicating only an insignificant change compared with the situation with buffer stock intervention. This is understandable in view of the frequent inability of the buffer stock manager to prevent prices from breaching the upper limit.

Summarizing, the uncertainties facing governments and international bodies dealing with a commodity agreement are enormous. Forecasts available at any time can hardly serve to provide a basis for negotiations. With uncertainties in exchange rates, inflation rates, consumption and production trends and the behaviour of the agents, prices are so unpredictable in the medium run that no buffer stock agreement that has reasonable limits on its resources can be expected to reduce instability to a significant extent.

The uncertainties in prices as simulated here greatly exceed the common measures of instability. The CV-2, measured as the average standard deviation of prices per quarter divided by the average price over the period, underestimates the CVs applicable to end-of-period prices. Naturally, CVs per quarter at the start of the period are relatively low and increase over time. They appear to stabilize at a level around 0.5. Commonly, instability is measured on the basis of prices in the past. Thus, Newbery and Stiglitz (1981: 287) arrive at a CV (CV-1 in the above context) of de-trended real rubber prices over the period 1951–75 equal to 0.40; but they estimate the standard deviation of the relative difference of current price and a five-year moving average to be 0.19, and in Table 20.4 (p. 291) they give values for the CV of around 0.20. When negotiating the Agreement, the participants should be interested in the predictability of nominal prices in any of the quarters in the period for which the Agreement is negotiated. Hence, the measure that is employed here seems to be more appropriate.

The conclusion is that, when the Agreement was negotiated, the chances for the buffer stock to have any significant impact on the predictability of the prices were extremely low. In addition, as shown in the previous section, with increasing trends in consumption and production, successful intervention is likely to cost more to producing countries at times when prices are lowered by buffer stock sales than they benefit from extra revenues obtained when prices are raised by buffer stock purchases. This is because in the NR market high prices (and therefore buffer stock sales) are likely to coincide with high demand.

If there was so little chance for successful stabilization and, if successful, it was so likely that producers would lose, why did producing countries press so strongly for an Agreement? One reason may be that they expected to be able gradually to improve the regulations of successor-agreements to their advantage. Another reason is that, by their nature, buffer stock managers must purchase before they can sell, so that – if the buffer stock is effective – it will always raise prices before it will be able to lower them. When an agreement starts with an empty buffer stock, the probability that prices will be raised is therefore always greater than the probability that prices will be reduced. Of course, one reason may also be that analysts in the producing countries expected the general world economy to move in the (downward) direction that it actually did. As Malaysian production showed signs of stagnation at the time of negotiation, it may be that they expected to gain from an agreement, as indeed they eventually did, unlike the expanding producers. Finally, it may be that the preference of the governments in the producing countries for extremely low prices to be raised greatly exceeds their displeasure at having high prices lowered through market intervention. Technically, this would amount to a very high level of risk aversion. In view of their aversion to possible farmers' protests at low but not at high prices, this may take the form of simple down-side risk aversion.

Another question is why the price range that was agreed upon was set at such a low level. This reflects the outcome of negotiations with, on the one hand, the USA and the EC, who disliked the idea of running the risk of an unsaleable buffer stock and, on the other, the producers, who preferred a low floor to no agreement at all.

The final conclusion is that, given the forecasts available at the time of negotiation, the later success of the Agreement was largely fortuitous.

PERFORMANCE OF THE INTERNATIONAL NATURAL RUBBER AGREEMENT: SHORT-TERM UNCERTAINTY AND STABILIZATION

The INRA does not contribute to long-term predictability of rubber prices, nor to their predictability in the medium term, as we have seen in the previous section. In this section, we investigate what INRA's contribution is to short-term predictability. Have NR prices of, say, some quarters ahead become more predictable? In the previous section, we showed that most of future uncertainty about prices was because of the uncertainty about long-term trends in consumption and 'normal' production. In the nearer future, these may be fairly well predictable, but actual supplies may still be difficult to predict if effects of, for example, weather are substantial. In this section we investigate the importance of the variables that are included in the error terms of the quarterly model, such as weather influences or exchange rate changes not explicitly incorporated in the model. Does the INRA provide a buffer against the destabilizing influence of these minor variables?

The assessment is made on the basis of simulations, in which all the exogenous variables are at their actual values in the period 1982–9: the PMOM, the price of SR, the consumer price indices in the producing countries, the exchange rates, total world rubber (NR + SR) consumption and the production capacities. In addition, all discrepancies between actual values of the endogenous variables and their static (one-quarter) forecasts are calculated and set at the levels thus found. Simulations are then made in which error terms are added to the consumption and production function and to the price equation. The probability distribution of these error terms corresponds to the values found for the static residuals.

Two sets of basic dynamic simulations are made: one set in which

Table 7.8 Short-term uncertainty in the natural rubber price with and without buffer stock

	With BS	*Without BS*	
CV-1	0.124	0.238	
CV-2	0.108	0.140	
CV-avg	0.106	0.137	
Chances of BS intervention		*Buying*	*Selling*
Average over quarters		0.197	0.153
In most likely quarter		0.670	0.930
Relative to requirement		0.997	0.809

Source: Own computations
Notes: BS, buffer stock; CV-avg, average of the quarterly CVs.

all buffer stock rules apply in conformity with the automatic provisions of the Agreement and one set without any buffer stock. Table 7.8 summarizes the results of a hundred stochastic simulations under either assumption.

Under the assumptions mentioned above, the existence of the buffer stock agreement has contributed to the predictability of the prices. The variation over time has changed considerably, as shown by comparing the CV-1 in the situations with and without buffer stock, but the CV-2 of the prices has gone down as well. As before, CV-1 is defined as the standard deviation of the quarterly means divided by the overall mean price. CV-2 is defined as the average of the quarterly standard deviations divided by the same overall mean. CV-2 and CV-avg clearly indicate that prices have become more predictable. The buffer stock is almost always (99.7 per cent) able to meet its obligations of defending the lower limit (buying), but in about 20 per cent of the cases is unable to defend the upper limit. Overall, the buffer stock manager intervenes in 35 per cent of the cases – in 19.7 per cent to buy and in 15.3 per cent to sell.

Figure 7.8 shows the dampening impact of the interventions on the revenues of the producing countries. Revenue that would have been obtained in the case of no intervention is measured along the x axis and the (average) revenues obtained in any quarter with the INRA are measured on the y axis. The lower revenues have been increased and the higher revenues have been lowered by the INRA. Hence the spread has gone down from a range of 2.9 (1.4–4.3) to a range of 2.0 (1.4–3.4). This is what was indicated by the lower CV-1 in Table 7.8. The sums of the two series of revenues indicate that producers have

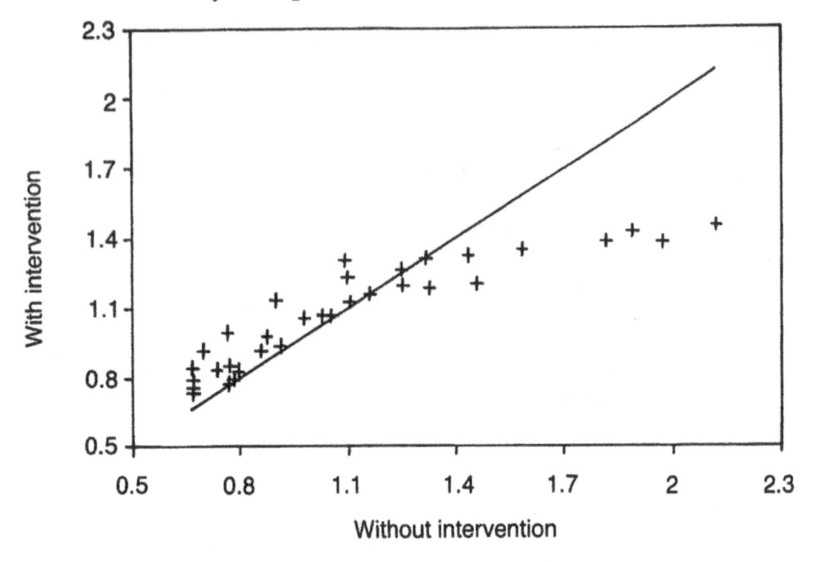

Figure 7.8 Impact of the buffer stock interventions on producers' revenues: export earnings, 1982.1–1984.4 (billion US dollars)

lost because of the INRA and some income has been transferred to consumers. But this is less than 1 per cent of the average quarterly revenues. Risk benefits due to the lower variance of the after-INRA series amount to approximately 0.5 per cent, assuming a coefficient of relative risk aversion of unity. Losses to the producers would have been much higher if the buffer stock had been able to keep the prices below the INRA upper limit.

THE EFFECT OF SPECIAL DRAWING RIGHTS AS THE BASIS FOR THE INTERNATIONAL NATURAL RUBBER AGREEMENT'S REFERENCE PRICE

The INRA has various rules which govern market intervention. Among these are the level of the reference price and the currency in which it is denominated. In this section, these parameters of the Agreement are assessed on their appropriateness for the NR market.

Table 7.9 gives the results of two simulations where the reference price is not expressed in Malaysian/Singapore currency, but in SDR. These are compared with simulations under the present rules. Present rules include a range of ±20 per cent, a maximum buffer stock size of 400,000 tonnes (and another to defend an even lower price at 550,000 tonnes) and a reference price in Malaysian/Singapore

Table 7.9 Natural rubber price, buffer stocks and intervention capability under different regulations: simulations over 1982–9

					BS intervention			
	Mean price (Singapore dollars per tonne)	*CV-2 in per cent*	*BS end 1989*	*BS-adjusted price*	*Percentage required*		*Percentage executed*	
					Lower	*Upper*	*Lower*	*Upper*
Present rules	1,992	10.8	72	1,998	19.8	19.0	99.7	80.9
Reference price in SDR, start 210	2,007	10.4	223	1,993	22.8	12.4	98.9	94.4
Reference price in SDR, start 200	1,993	10.6	119	1,990	16.3	15.7	100.0	74.3

Source: Own computations
Note: BS, buffer stock.

currency, which is revised once every eighteen months in normal circumstances. The starting level of the reference price was 210 Malaysian/Singapore cents per kilogramme.

The columns in Table 7.9 give the average price over a period 1982–9. CV-2 is the ratio of the average of the standard errors for all quarters and the average price. The third column gives the average size of the buffer stock at the end of 1990, and the fourth column contains the average price after adjustment for the differences in buffer stock size. This adjustment is simply made on the basis of a loglinear regression of average prices on buffer stock size, and the adjusted price brings the average prices to comparable levels by standardizing them on a buffer stock size of a hundred thousand tonnes.[1] The fifth and sixth columns indicate the probability of intervention required from the buffer stock manager, and the seventh and eighth columns give the percentages of the latter cases in which he is able to intervene.

Changing the denomination to SDRs (as in the International Cocoa Agreement) would have meant that the price range in US dollars would gradually have shifted upwards instead of downwards. The buffer stock manager, therefore, would purchase more rubber and more frequently meet the upper limit on the buffer stock size, but would run a chance of only 5.6 per cent of not being able to defend the upper limit. Owing to increased buying, the average price would have been higher. Prices would have been more predictable under this arrangement. If the stronger currency was compensated by a lower starting level of the equivalent of 200 Malaysian/Singapore cents, the buffer stock manager would buy still more, but the frequency of being unable to defend the upper limit would increase.

When negotiating the successor agreement INRA-1987, a proposal was made to have the reference price expressed in Malaysian currency only, instead of the average Malaysian/Singapore currency. As the Malaysian ringgit is the weaker currency, the effect of the proposal would have been that the reference price in US dollar terms would have gone down more than in the base simulation. And, opposite to the simulations with an SDR reference price, this would have led to fewer purchases and more frequent occurrence of lack of stocks.

Figure 7.9 shows the movements of the reference prices under two scenarios. One is the actual reference price, but expressed in equivalent US dollar terms for RSS1 quality. The other is the reference price, also expressed in US dollars, which would have prevailed if the initial fixing in October 1979 at 210 Malaysian/Singapore cents had

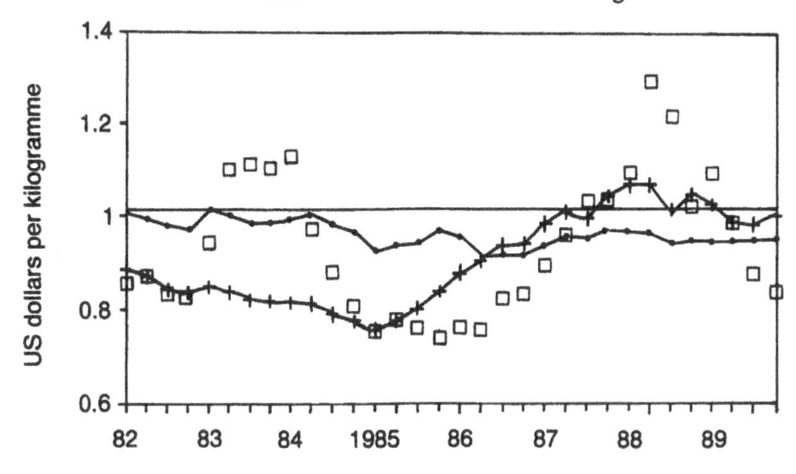

Figure 7.9 International Natural Rubber Organization reference prices under two scenarios, equivalents for RSS1 quality: —•—, fixed in Malaysian/Singapore dollars; —+—, fixed in special drawing rights; □, actual prices; ——, fixed in US dollars

been in SDR of the IMF. Clearly, the US dollar value of the reference price would have gone down more in 1979–85, but would have gone up by more in the period 1985–9, when the US dollar fell against the SDR. This conforms to the actual price movements of rubber in those years, and this reference price follows the actual price movements more closely.

Simulations were made with an SDR-based reference price, but starting at the equivalent of 210 Malaysian/Singapore cents of 1981.4 instead of holding the basis back to 1979.4. As the new reference price would start approximately equal to the present reference price in 1982, intervention would initially be approximately the same, but as actual prices have shown a movement similar to that of the US dollar–SDR exchange rate, the buffer stock would have had more scope for keeping prices within the price band. This leads to more predictable prices, given the values of all exogenous variables. In statistical terms, the CV-2 of the prices would have gone down from 10.8 to 10.4. More clear are the effects on the probability that the buffer stock manager would intervene. Taking together lower limit and upper limit interventions, under present rules this probability is 38.8 per cent, whereas with an SDR reference price this would only be 35.2 per cent, and even 32.0 per cent when starting at a lower value of the equivalent of 210 Malaysian/Singapore cents. The buffer stock's inability to defend the upper limit would fall from the current 19 per cent to 6 per cent in the simulation with an SDR-based reference price.

Summarizing this section, the simulations show that the predictability of NR prices, given full knowledge of all exogenous variables of the model, can be considerably improved by buffer stock intervention. The ratio of the average standard error over the quarters to the average price in the situation without a buffer stock is 14.0 per cent, and this reduces to 10.8 per cent under the present regulations. Variability over time is reduced by more: from 23.6 per cent to 12.4 per cent. Expressing the reference price in SDRs would make prices more predictable. But the gains from these changes are only a slight reduction in the average CV from 10.8 to 10.4 per cent.

CONCLUSIONS

A deterministic dynamic simulation was used to estimate the costs and benefits of the purchases and sales made by the buffer stock manager in the period 1982–9. After adjustment for average world market prices of grades of NR, after discounting all amounts by 1 per cent per quarter and after adjustment for the reduced efficiency of buffer stock sales in 1988 (estimated at 80 per cent), the following overall assessment results:

1. consumers have spent US$124 million less,
2. producers have received US$77 million less,
3. private stockholders have received US$25 million less, and
4. the buffer stock manager made a direct loss of US$22 million.

The direct effect of buffer stock manager intervention on producers' income is roughly that each US dollar spent by the buffer stock manager leads to US$7 extra revenues for producers. While producers are estimated to have received US$77 million less, Malaysia appears to have gained (US$144 million) and Indonesia (US$35 million) and Thailand (US$155 million) to have lost. These differences are because of differences in growth of production during the period.

A stochastic simulation was made to reflect the knowledge available at the time of negotiating the agreement. After quantifying the apparent uncertainty about the values of the exogenous variables, we showed that the CV of NR prices was no less than 0.42, and this would not be affected by the Agreement as it was very unlikely to become operational.

We then restricted the uncertainty to only the error terms in the model, so as to simulate short-term uncertainty. In this framework, the existence of the Agreement was shown to have a stabilizing impact on prices, in the sense that they have become more predictable. The CV goes down from 0.14 to 0.108.

Finally, we investigated whether a different currency for the reference price of the Agreement would have made much difference. We showed that an SDR reference price would follow the movements of the world market price better and reduce the need for intervention. The reduced need was quantified by the average probability of intervention, which was 38.8 per cent under the present rules of the Agreement and would go down to 32.0 per cent with an adjusted SDR reference price.

8 The International Cocoa Agreements

INTRODUCTION

The International Cocoa Agreements (ICCAs) and their performance were briefly presented in Chapter 1. In this chapter we analyse the agreements in more detail. We focus on the last two agreements, 1980 and 1986. Using an econometric model, we calculate their effects on quantities produced, consumed and stocked and on prices, revenues and expenditures. In addition, we investigate the importance of the choice of currency for the indicator price and – a special case for cocoa – the effects of full price transmission to producers in major exporting countries.

We start with a selection, in summary form, of the main stabilization aspects of the two agreements. A review of the history of the agreements and the evaluations by various authors regarding the agreements is given in the third section. The model that we apply is summarily described in the fourth section, paving the way for the evaluation of the performance of the agreements in the fifth section. The model is presented in full in Appendix C. In the sixth section, the results of alternative specifications are presented. Simulations are made with another currency and with full price transmission from the world market to producers in Africa. In the seventh section we give our conclusions.

THE AGREEMENTS OF 1980 AND 1986

Common to both agreements is the establishment of a buffer stock. Purchases and sales by the buffer stock manager should keep the world market prices within designated upper and lower limits for the indicator price. This indicator price is an average of London and New York price quotations for the nearest three active future trading months. In the 1980 agreement the indicator price is expressed in US dollars, in the 1986 agreement in special drawing rights (SDR). Price ranges for intervention were US$1.1–1.5 per kilogramme at the start of the 1980 agreement and 1.655–2.215 SDR per kilogramme (then equivalent to US$1.31–US$1.87) when the 1986 agreement came into force. The 1986 agreement had 'may-sell' and 'may-buy' ranges in which the buffer stock manager was allowed but not required to sell/buy. The 1980 agreement did not give him such discretionary powers.

In both agreements, price ranges can be revised by the Council. As these revisions are likely to cause conflicts between producers and consumers, the agreements provide for some automatism. In the 1980 agreement, prices are 'automatically' lowered by 4 per cent when 100,000 tonnes are purchased and again by 4 per cent when another 75,000 tonnes are purchased within a year. In the 1986 agreement the range is adjusted in such a way that the average market price per tonne of the preceding year falls within the range by at least 55 SDR. The condition for this adjustment is that the latest annual average market price falls outside the price band; the maximum adjustment is 115 SDR. The size of the buffer stock was 250,000 tonnes in both agreements. The 100,000 tonnes that were purchased under the 1980 agreement were carried over into the buffer stocks of the 1986 agreement.

The differences between the two agreements reflect (a) a general rise in prices leading to the upward shift in the price range; (b) a movement away from the US dollar towards SDR, on the apparent assumption that SDR reflect the supply/demand situation in the cocoa economy better (we shall see in the sixth section that this was not true); and (c) an enhanced automatism in the adjustment of the price range providing a closer link between the intervention prices and the world market prices. A difference of another type between the two agreements is the size of participation. In the 1980 agreement, the major producer (Côte d'Ivoire) and consumer (USA) did not participate, but in 1986 they did. As the International Cocoa Organization (ICCO) receives its funds from a levy (of one US$ cent per pound of cocoa beans on either imports or exports), revenues were seriously limited in the first period. In the following section a review is given of the assessments of these Agreements by various authors.

HISTORY OF THE TWO AGREEMENTS

Unlike the International Natural Rubber Agreement, the ICCA-1980 started at a time when the market prices were below the lower intervention prices. The ICCO itself, in a report to the United Nations Conference on Trade and Development states on the introduction of this ICCA:

> After the announcement, in late June 1981, that the Third ICCA would provisionally enter into force on 1 August 1981, prices recovered appreciably in the following months. Much of this recovery was subsequently discovered to be non-sustainable, having been brought about by speculative buying in anticipation of buffer stock intervention at levels around the lower intervention price. When buffer stock intervention actually commenced at the end of September 1981, market participants unloaded their stocks onto the ICCO and succeeded in putting extreme and early pressure on the buffer stock's resources.
>
> (UNCTAD 1985b)

The report goes on to state that, in the 1981–2 cocoa year, the imbalance between cocoa supply and demand worsened because of world economic recession, appreciation of the US dollar and high interest rates, resulting in a production surplus of the order of 135,000 tonnes and prices remaining consistently below the initial lower intervention price of 110 US cents per pound. Inadequate financial resources meant that the buffer stock could only siphon away some 100,000 tonnes. The inability to defend the price range was also caused by the limited membership. The ICCO paper concludes that a buffer stock scheme as the sole mechanism for attaining price stabilization is not adequate in a situation of structural over-production.

MacBean and Nguyen (1987a) agree that the required stock might have been much larger than the 100,000 tonnes purchased. However, a large buffer stock would have been an obstacle to reaching an agreement with consuming countries. In fact, the consuming nations in the ICCA did block attempts to raise further finance to purchase still more stocks. Gordon-Ashworth (1984) quotes the *Guardian* of 4 October 1982 reporting that producers and consumers failed to reach agreement on further measures to support cocoa prices under the auspices of the ICCO despite the US$75 million replenishment to the exhausted Buffer Stock Fund secured from Brazilian bankers in June 1982. Leading producers – Brazil, Ghana and Nigeria – all favoured higher prices, not least for domestic reasons. On 1 October 1982, world stocks were reported to stand at 688,000 tonnes, the highest level since 1965.

The purchase of 100,000 tonnes was made in two blocks, during the fourth quarter of 1981 and the first quarter of 1982, and did result in a significant but very temporary rise in the market price (Gilbert 1987). Since March 1982, the buffer stock has been inactive and, after a rise in the first half of 1984, the price dropped below the lower intervention level. Gilbert claims that the price fall in the 1980s is the direct effect of the high prices in the late 1970s, leading to dramatic new planting, in particular with the newer hybrid variety of cocoa. He states that the Third ICCA has been the least successful of current agreements, although its provisions create a better model than any other agreement. Its lack of success is a result of insufficient finance, he claims. However, in spite of this being 'a better model', parties were unable to agree on price revisions. The ICCO states:

> This lack of operational – as opposed to theoretical – flexibility in revising prices has been vividly demonstrated by the inability of the Council of the ICCO to consider dispassionately the effects of the sustained strength of the US$ on the price objective of the Agreements. Although the 1980 Agreement recognizes, in principle, that currency changes could have serious implications for its price provisions, the relevant Article 38 has been drafted in such vague terms that it can never be activated. . . . Indeed, if the price range of the Agreement had been adjusted to reflect currency movements and perhaps inflation in industrialized countries, the achievements of the 1980 Agreement would be perceived in a far more favourable light.
>
> (ICCO 1988)

The paper then illustrates that, if the prices had been denominated in SDR, prices would have stayed within the price range during a considerable part of the existence of the 1980 Agreement. If a basket of currencies had been used, based on the relative importance of each country in cocoa consumption, there would even have been sales by the buffer stock manager, leading to a healthier financial situation. It is finally estimated, but quoted in the paper with due caution, that the total gain to producers through increased value of exports of beans and products could have amounted to over US$1,000 million.

The ill fate of the 1980 Agreement was not unexpected. Menezes (1984), using a simple framework, found a clear trend towards oversupply in the second half of the 1980s. His prediction was that the buffer stock would have insufficient capacity to keep prices above the lower limit.

Akiyama and Duncan (1982b) used price-responsive supply and demand and prices simultaneously determined with the implied end-of-season stocks to simulate a world with and without a buffer stock agreement along the lines of the 1980 Agreement. Their basic simulation indicated an expected volume to be purchased by the buffer stock in 1981 and 1982 equal to 210,000 tonnes. In the simulation, this amount could be sold after 1987. However, they emphasized that 'a buffer stock operation cannot *per se* alter the long-term fundamentals' and warned against oversupply in the second half of the 1980s. This might be prevented if supply was responsive to the expected real decrease in prices. The rise in the value of the US dollar and the strongly reduced price transmission from the world market to the African producers were not to be foreseen.

So much for the 1980 Agreement, the Third Agreement, which expired in September 1985. Negotiations towards a Fourth ICCA broke down in March 1986 but met with surprising success in July 1986, when Côte d'Ivoire reached agreement with the EC on the terms for a new agreement which came into effect in January 1987. As in the Third Agreement, the intervention range was set too high. As a consequence, the cocoa price rose above the lower intervention level for a few months only. In the first half of 1987, 75,000 tonnes of cocoa beans were purchased. According to the Agreement, the price range could have been revised, but members had various interpretations of this rule and at the annual price review they were unable to reach an agreement on whether or not intervention prices should be lowered. Consumers were in favour; producers opposed. Consumers then refused to permit the buffer stock manager to purchase more cocoa. The issue was finally settled in January 1988. Intervention prices where lowered by the maximum of 115 SDR per tonne, and the buffer stock manager could purchase another 75,000 tonnes. No further agreement could be reached on what to do next. This stalemate finally led to the deletion of the economic paragraphs of the Agreement in 1990.

THE MODEL EMPLOYED FOR EVALUATING THE INTERNATIONAL COCOA AGREEMENTS

For the purpose of simulating a world without ICCO intervention, an econometric model has been constructed that incorporates the stylized facts of the world cocoa economy. In this section, we discuss these stylized facts. The analysis is based on an adjusted version of a model prepared by Pomp and presented in Pomp (1991). The equations can be found in Appendix C.

The supply of cocoa

Since cocoa is a perennial crop, production depends not only on decisions taken in the present and the recent past but also on decisions taken many years ago. The channel through which past decisions affect current production is the area under cultivation. The ideal approach to modelling cocoa supply would be to start with 'normal production', defined as the production level that will be forthcoming if prices and weather conditions are equal to their long-term trend. This normal production depends on the area under cocoa as well as on the age distribution of the trees. Changes in normal production are caused by planting and discarding decisions. These decisions are to be modelled separately.

Actual supply can differ from normal supply if a farmer decides to use smaller amounts of inputs. Particularly in Africa, where cocoa is produced on smallholdings, farmers may allocate less labour to pruning and picking if they expect to gain more from other activities. These other activities could consist of cultivating other crops or off-farm work. In Brazil and Malaysia, where cocoa is mainly produced on larger estates, low real prices may induce the owner to hire less labour than would be required to realize the full potential crop.

The way supply could be modelled in the present study only partly reflects the above considerations. Thus, the area under cocoa is

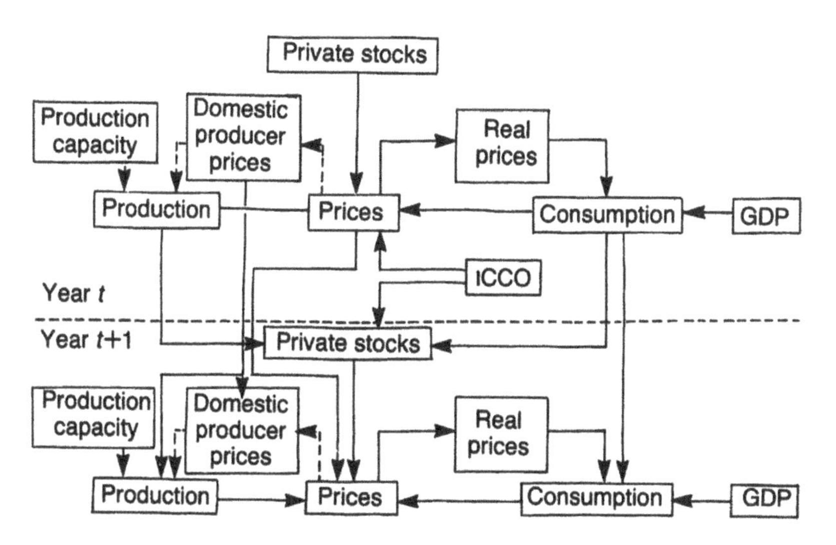

Figure 8.1 The structure of the model of the cocoa market

exogenous in the present version of the model. For the purpose of this study, this is not a serious limitation. The period considered, 1980–90, is too short to expect much impact of alternative planting decisions. In addition, the political uncertainty surrounding the ICCAs makes such agreements virtually irrelevant for investment decisions. Discarding area may have been influenced by prices (and therefore by the ICCA), but we shall see that this can only be applicable to a few countries. The estimates of 'normal' production are based on area only, without full consideration of changes in age composition etc. Ratios of actual to 'normal' production are related to real prices. In the model, no details on the appropriate deflator are incorporated and the overall consumer price index is used. The estimations gave reasonable results for Ghana, Côte d'Ivoire, Cameroon and Brazil (see Appendix C), showing real producer price elasticities of 0.30, 0.27, 0.42 and 0.35, respectively.

The demand for cocoa

Demand for cocoa beans depends on demand for final products. This demand will in turn be determined by consumer tastes, prices of cocoa products and substitutes, and income. Since tastes differ sharply across countries, consumption cannot appropriately be modelled on a world level. The same applies to income. If income per capita rises from a very low level, demand for cocoa will initially rise only mildly since the extra income will be spent on necessities. However, if income rises further, demand for luxury products, to which chocolate belongs, picks up. At still higher levels of income, saturation is reached and changes in income have little effect on demand for cocoa products. For this reason, a given change in income per capita on a world level may have different effects on cocoa consumption, depending upon where the change in income takes place.

For the present purpose, however, simplification is possible. Since no large stocks of intermediate and final products are held, demand for final products translates into grindings fairly rapidly (within one year). Thus, instead of modelling demand for final products, it is possible to model grindings directly. There is another reason for taking this route. The price of an important final product, chocolate bars, is not responsive to the price of cocoa. Nevertheless, demand for cocoa beans will vary with the price of cocoa beans, because manufacturers of chocolate products use more or less cocoa per unit of final product. The price per chocolate bar does not need to react very much, as size and contents may vary. In economic terms, grindings are more price elastic than the demand for final products. Therefore, changes in final demand for cocoa products are smaller than changes in demand for cocoa beans, and our concern is with the latter. A good deal of the variation in demand for beans can be explained by lagged consumption, real world GNP and the real world price of cocoa beans. See the first equation of Appendix C for details. Price elasticity of demand is −0.1 and income elasticity is 0.2.

The world market price of cocoa beans

The main international markets for cocoa beans are the New York Cocoa Exchange and the London Cocoa Terminal Market. Prices are quoted in US dollars and pound sterling respectively. Since prices on these markets do not differ very much when expressed in common currency, it does not matter which of these prices is taken as *the* cocoa price. However, since the world price is one of the explanatory variables in the demand equations, allowance has to be made for exchange rate fluctuations of the currencies of the main consuming countries *vis-à-vis* the US dollar and the pound. A crude but simple way of doing this is by expressing the cocoa price in the IMF's SDR. This is precisely the way the ICCO daily price is computed. Therefore, the yearly average of the ICCO daily price is taken as the relevant price variable.

A number of factors influence this price. Figure 8.1 gives the structure of the model. As indicated, current supply, demand and stocks play a role in determining the prices. If one abstracts from private stockholders and the operations of a buffer stock manager, the price will be low if supply is high and demand is low. However, this simple conclusion needs to be modified because of the effects of private stockholders and the buffer stock on the price. The influence of the buffer stock on the price is relatively straightforward, but the influence of the private stockholders (who could be traders, producers and/or consumers) is quite complicated. In the current version of the model, the behaviour of private stockholders has not been modelled explicitly. Instead, it is assumed that the price in any year depends on past prices, production, consumption, the opening level of private stocks and the operations of the buffer stock. The price flexibilities measuring the impact of a change in consumption or production on the prices were estimated to be around 2.4 (plus for consumption, minus for production), whereas the impact of opening stocks in a year has an elasticity of −0.13. After some checks, the impact of buffer stock intervention proved to be modelled best as corresponding to changes in the opening stocks. Lagged prices affect current prices with an elasticity of 0.86 in this context.

MEASURING THE PERFORMANCE OF THE INTERNATIONAL COCOA AGREEMENTS

In this section we measure the performance of the ICCA. We do this by using simulations with the model of a world in which there had been no agreements. The difference between two simulations (with and without agreement) or between the 'without case' and actual results provides a measure for the impact of the interventions. Some assumptions are needed before the simulations can be made. To these we turn first.

Unlike the market for natural rubber discussed in the previous chapter, the cocoa market is only to a minor extent a free market. In some major producing countries, like Côte d'Ivoire, Cameroon and, until recently, Ghana and Nigeria, national price intervention mechanisms exist. These are either through marketing boards or through 'caisses de stabilisation'. This effectively separates producer prices from world market prices. Hence, changes in world market prices brought about by buffer stock intervention are not necessarily passed on to the producers in these countries. For the simulation, it is important to assess what the domestic prices would have been if world market prices were different. This requires some assumption on government behaviour. As background information, Table 8.1 shows nominal price levels in some major producing countries during the 1980s. Of the countries listed in Table 8.1, only Brazil has a free-market system for cocoa, and the producer price follows the world market price fairly closely. Cameroon and Côte d'Ivoire show a tendency to fix nominal prices in terms of the Communauté Financière Africaine franc (CFA), as can be seen in the bottom part of the table, and thus move out of line with the fluctuating world market price, additionally influenced by changes in the US dollar–CFA exchange rate.

In 1989, the nominal prices in Cameroon and Côte d'Ivoire were reduced to CFA250 and later to CFA200. Ghana had an autonomous price policy and prices increased enormously in 1982 and 1983, only to collapse again afterwards when the country had to cope with high rates of inflation. Recently, Ghana moved to a free-market system and the marketing board is no longer operational. Nigeria took this step in 1986, but then saw producer prices of cocoa soar

Table 8.1 World market and producer prices in some countries in US dollars per tonne and in local currencies

	1980	*1981*	*1982*	*1983*	*1984*	*1985*	*1986*	*1987*	*1988*
World market price	2,603	2,077	1,742	2,119	2,396	2,255	2,068	1,996	1,585
Producer prices in US dollars per tonne in per cent of world market prices									
Brazil	62	67	61	66	74	66	65	68	81
Cameroon	53	54	55	45	36	41	59	70	89
Côte d'Ivoire	55	53	52	42	34	38	56	67	85
Ghana	56	93	250	246	30	36	40	40	49
Nigeria	86	102	111	90	78	76	57	81	106
Producer price in local currencies									
Brazil (Cr/15 kg)	1	2	3	12	49	138	276	800	5,032
Cameroon (CFA/kg)	293	303	315	360	380	413	420	420	420
Côte d'Ivoire (CFA/kg)	300	300	300	338	356	381	400	400	400
Ghana (cedi/30 kg)	120	160	360	540	763	1,332	2,195	3,513	4,638
Nigeria (naira/tonne)	1,217	1,300	1,300	1,375	1,425	1,525	1,600	6,500	7,500

Source: ICCO, ICC/36/14, 1988

owing to restrictions imposed on the convertibility of the naira: by buying and exporting cocoa, traders were able to convert local currency into foreign currency.

Of the major producing countries, only Brazil and Malaysia have a fairly rapid transmission of world market prices to producer prices. For the assessment of the buffer stock operations, Malaysia cannot be assumed to be very responsive to price changes because, at the time of the first interventions (1981), Malaysia was just starting to produce cocoa and in 1986, at the start of the Fourth ICCA, Malaysia had just entered the production phase on a major scale and many trees were at their peak production levels. For Brazil, a price transmission equation is included in the model. Because of the domestic market regulations, producer prices in West African countries are modelled as being independent of world market prices. In Malaysia, producer prices follow world market prices but do not significantly affect production in this period.

Performance of the International Cocoa Agreements

Using these assumptions on price and supply response in the period 1980–9, the model was used to simulate a world without an ICCA. Differences between the simulations with and without an ICCA are measures of the effects of the agreements. In 1981 and early 1982, the buffer stock was filled with 100,000 tonnes of cocoa. The model calculations show that this reduced private stocks by some 97,000 tonnes and decreased consumption by 3,000 tonnes in this crop year. The change in consumption is because of higher prices, which are estimated to have increased by 29 SDR per tonne (i.e. 2.1 per cent). In later years some production responses occur. These are weak because, as stated above, the major West African producing countries are assumed to maintain a policy that is not affected by the ICCA.

The slightly increased production widens the gap between prices in simulations with and without buffer stock intervention. Table 8.2 shows the estimated changes in prices and quantities. Actual prices in this period increased from 1,814 SDR per tonne in 1980 to 2,502 SDR per tonne in 1983 before declining to 950 SDR per tonne in 1989. Production and consumption steadily increased from around 1,600,000 tonnes in 1980 to 2,250,000 tonnes in 1989. Private stocks stood at 674,000 tonnes at the end of 1980 and had increased to 1,200,000 at the end of 1989–90.

As Table 8.2 shows, in the first year of intervention, prices are higher by 29 SDR; in the second year, some lagged supply response

Table 8.2 Changes caused by buffer stock intervention in world market price, consumption, production and stocks, from 1981–2 to 1989–90

Year	*Price (SDR per tonne)*	*Consumption (1,000 tonnes)*	*Production (1,000 tonnes)*	*Private stocks (1,000 tonnes)*	*Buffer stocks (1,000 tonnes)*
1981–2	+29	−3	+0	−97	+100
1982–3	+51	−6	+2	−90	+100
1983–4	+67	−8	+3	−78	+100
1984–5	+58	−10	+4	−64	+100
1985–6	+36	−10	+5	−50	+100
1986–7	+38	−10	+4	−111	+175
1987–8	+44	−13	+4	−169	+250
1988–9	+31	−15	+4	−150	+248
1989–90	+22	−14	+4	−131	+245
Total		−89	+30		

Source: Own computations

occurs, increasing supply by 2,000 tonnes; the lower level of private opening stocks (97,000 tonnes lower) pushes prices up to 51 SDR above the estimated level without intervention. Consumption is again lower, but now by 6,000 tonnes, caused by lagged endogenous effects and the higher prices. Private stocks in this (second) year are 90,000 tonnes lower than otherwise. The difference of 10,000 tonnes is accounted for by lower consumption (9,000 tonnes) and higher production (2,000 tonnes) (rounded figures). As production responses are weak because of regulated domestic markets in major producing countries and consumption responses are feeble by their nature, having an elasticity of only −0.1, it takes a considerable number of years before the initial drop in private (free) stocks of 100,000 tonnes is fully compensated for by higher production, lower consumption and building up new private stocks. At the end of 1985–6, the difference in private stocks is still 50,000 tonnes. But in 1986–7, the ICCO purchases another 75,000 tonnes, followed by the same amount in 1987–8. The resulting difference in private stocks increases to 169,000 tonnes at the end of 1987–8. This equals 25 per cent of actual stocks at this time. It would normally take another seven years or so before such a drop in private stocks had been restored. But prices move to their 'without-ICCA' levels sooner. This is because the price-increasing effect of lower private stocks is compensated by the price-decreasing effects of higher production and lower consumption. By 1991–2 the price effects of the buffer stock intervention should more or less have faded out.

Summed over the period 1981–2 to 1988–9, production has been some 30,000 tonnes higher and consumption 89,000 tonnes lower, because of the ICCAs. The balance is about 120,000 tonnes excess supply, which is more than compensated by the 250,000 tonnes that are stored in the buffer stock. Figure 8.2 shows the simulated prices in the simulations with and without an ICCA. Table 8.3 lists the changes in earnings caused by buffer stock intervention for various producing countries, assuming that all production is evaluated at world market prices.

The average increase in world market prices that is brought about by buffer stock purchases is between 2 per cent and 4 per cent. The exporting countries that do not adjust their supply to changes in world market prices experience an increase in the value of their production of the same order of magnitude. Countries like Brazil, that pass changes in world market prices onto farmers, benefit slightly more from the increased world market price. Brazil's additional production value does not exceed 4 per cent, however. In the cases of

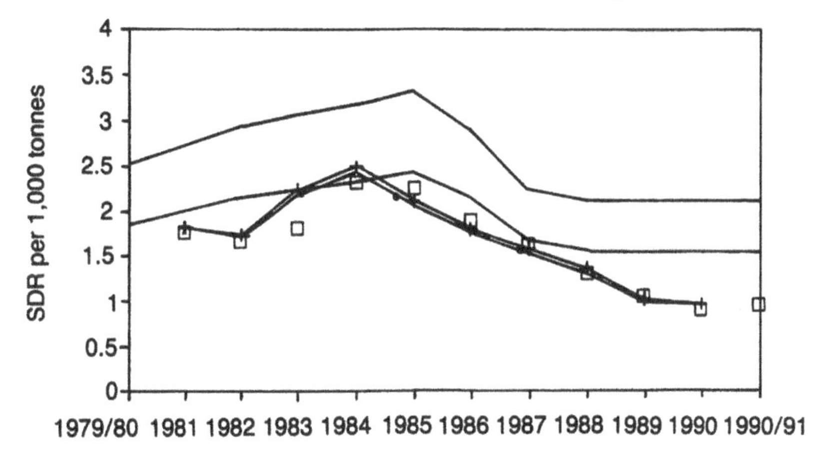

Figure 8.2 Price simulations with and without an International Cocoa Agreement: □, observed; —+—, simulated with International Cocoa Agreement; —•—, without International Cocoa Agreement; ——, International Cocoa Agreement range

Côte d'Ivoire and Ghana, and in other countries without production response, these additional revenues accrue to the government (or parastatal organizations like marketing boards and caisses). To the extent that these organizations have carried stocks that were lower than usual, their costs must have been reduced by the buffer stock, so that total gains (and welfare benefits) may have been higher than estimated here. In the case of Brazil, the extra benefits have not been realized at the country level because a large part of the production is used domestically. Approximately half of the additional production value is paid by Brazilian grinders.

Consumers have paid higher prices because of the intervention and have responded by slightly decreasing levels of consumption. This has led to income transfers to producing countries (including internal transfers, as in Brazil, from grinders to growers). Table 8.4 shows these transfers, including those involved in the buffer stock purchases themselves. The table shows that in 1981–2, for example, when the ICCO purchased 100,000 tonnes, this required 174 million SDR when evaluated at the prices after intervention. Producers benefited by 49 million SDR from the higher prices and consumers lost 43 million SDR because of higher prices combined with a volume that was only slightly reduced (see Table 8.2 for volume changes). As private storage was 97,000 tonnes lower, private stockholders must have received substantial amounts of money, here estimated at 167

Table 8.3 Change in revenues of producers caused by buffer stock intervention, from 1981–2 to 1989–90 (million SDR)

	1981–2	*1982*	*1983*	*1984*	*1985*	*1986*	*1987*	*1988*	*1989–90*	*Total*
Brazil	8	17	31	29	20	19	20	13	10	166
Côte d'Ivoire	13	18	27	33	21	23	30	25	16	206
Ghana	7	9	11	10	8	9	8	9	6	77
Nigeria	5	8	8	9	4	4	7	5	3	53
Rest of world	16	25	35	38	25	27	35	26	18	375
Total	49	77	111	119	77	81	99	79	54	747

Source: Own computations

million SDR. Overall, consumers have contributed 547 million SDR directly to the 747 million SDR received by the producers. The buffer stock purchases themselves have led to payments amounting to 388 million SDR. The balance of 188 million SDR (i.e. 547 + 388 − 747) has been received by stockholders, whose stocks by the end of 1989 are estimated to be 131,000 tonnes smaller because of the 250,000 tonnes purchased over time by the buffer stock manager.

In welfare terms, consumers have suffered a direct loss which is approximately equal to their extra payments (because of the low price elasticity). Distribution of these losses over consuming countries is difficult to estimate because the total loss will be distributed over grinders and final consumers of chocolate products. If we attribute all changes in consumption expenditure to grinders, on average some 12 per cent of extra payments are borne by Brazil and an equal amount by the USA. Germany contributes 11 per cent, The Netherlands 10 per cent, USSR 8 per cent and the UK 5 per cent. Other countries all account for minor shares.

To this must be added what the ICCO has spent on buffer stock purchases. This was given in Table 8.4. These expenditures are financed by an import levy, paid (almost fully) by the consumers. However, the ICCO still owns the buffer stock, which represents a value. At 1991 prices, the value is about 55 per cent of the total amount spent on its purchase. The rest, equal to some 180 million SDR, was and/or will be borne by the consumers, representing a welfare loss of about the same size.

Table 8.4 Change in revenues and expenditures owing to buffer stock intervention (million SDR)

	Received by producers	*Paid by buffer stock*	*Paid by consumers*	*Received by stockholders*
1981–2	49	174	43	167
1982–3	77	0	72	−5
1983–4	111	0	92	−19
1984–5	119	0	80	−38
1985–6	77	0	48	−29
1986–7	81	118	55	92
1987–8	99	101	70	72
1988–9	79	−2	51	−30
1989–90	54	−3	35	−21
Total	747	388	547	188

Source: Own computations

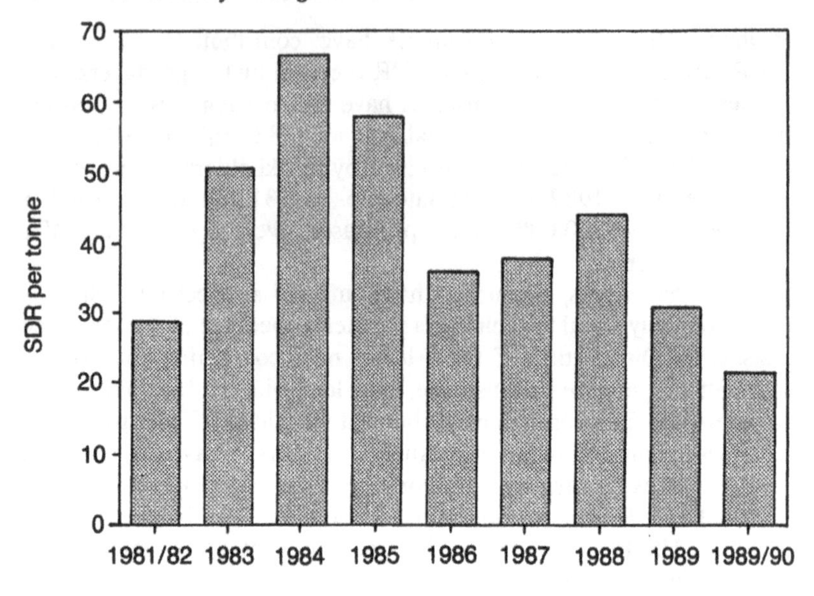

Figure 8.3 Cocoa beans price difference caused by International Cocoa Organization intervention

It is too early to make a full evaluation of the ICCA. Final assessment must await the sale of the buffer stock. When this takes place the transfer of income from consumers to producers will be reversed. But the world has changed. The stronger links between producer prices and world market prices would induce a quick supply response to any lowering of prices caused by buffer stock sales. This would mitigate the negative effects for the producing countries. Calculated in present discounted value terms, it is likely, therefore, that eventually producers will have net gains.

Figure 8.3 shows the differences in price that were caused by ICCO interventions. It is expected that by 1992 prices with the ICCA will have reached the levels that would have prevailed if the ICCO had not intervened. It is also expected that prices will not deteriorate from their present low levels but will rise later in the decade. Hence, the interventions of 1981–2 and 1985–6 have had only a temporary impact. They have not kept prices from falling to unprecedentedly low levels and have not been able to protect producers from low prices.

Because there is now a considerable quantity of cocoa beans in stock, a new agreement may be able to provide a buffer against high

Table 8.5 Producer prices and world market price with full price transmission, hypothetical relative to actual prices

	1981–2	*1982–3*	*1983–4*	*1984–5*	*1985–6*	*1986–7*	*1987–8*	*1988–9*	*1989–90*
Cameroon	141	208	208	185	122	75	65	63	104
Côte d'Ivoire	145	227	213	189	130	84	68	66	105
Ghana	84	44	38	222	145	125	120	119	133
Nigeria	118	152	161	132	108	132	91	86	116
World market price (model)	109	94	86	88	79	85	99	127	125

Source: Own computations
Note: 1980–1 = 100.

prices. In this case consumers would benefit. But until now the agreements have only caused transfers of income to producers and private stockholders. The major part of these transfers were not captured directly by the producers themselves but by their governments or parastatal organizations. These revenues have hardly contributed to the well-being of the cocoa economy in these countries, however. To some extent, this could be expected, as the domestic stabilization mechanisms that were operational have not worked effectively to the benefit of the sector. In addition, the ICCO-induced transfers were made in a period of strongly decreasing overall earnings. The international transfers have not been able to sustain the domestic stabilization measures: all major West African producers have drastically lowered their producer prices and/or abolished the domestic market intervention regulations.

ALTERNATIVES

Is this failure of the ICCAs because of circumstances outside the control of the participants or could more stabilization have been achieved?

As we indicated in the previous section, major cocoa-producing countries have shielded their producers from world market price changes, so that no supply responses were forthcoming from these countries. This has mitigated the extent to which reduced private stocks (because of transfer to the buffer stock) could be replenished. Through this lack of response, market prices have remained high for a longer period than would otherwise have been the case. The first alternative market situation investigated here is what would have happened if the West African producing countries had adopted a system of free price transmission to their producers.

For this simulation the assumption is made that in 1980–1 producer prices are equal to their actual values, but that in later years all changes in exchange rates and world market prices are transmitted immediately to producer prices. Table 8.5 shows how the hypothetical producer prices in those countries relate to the actual prices. We take Cameroon as an example. In 1981–2, the new prices would have been 41 per cent higher. This is because world market prices rose. This increase in world market prices was partly because of intervention. Actual Cameroon prices were kept constant at CFA303. Had these prices followed the change in world market prices, the producers would have received CFA427 per kilogramme. In 1982–3 the difference would have increased. Actual prices were CFA315, but as

Table 8.6 Changes in earnings and expenditures owing to buffer stock intervention with restricted and full price transmission (million SDR)

	Restricted transmission	*Full transmission*
Paid by		
consumers	547	351
buffer stock	388	384
Received by producers	747	539
of which		
Brazil	166	99
Côte d'Ivoire	206	164
Ghana	77	63
Nigeria	53	43
Stockholders	188	195

Source: Own computations

world market prices would have gone up because of the earlier intervention, and because of overall demand/supply conditions, producer prices would have been 108 per cent higher. Thus the table reflects the effects of full price transmission, including the extra repercussions on the world market prices of the interventions. In this hypothetical situation, world market prices would, of course, have been different. African producers are now assumed to be able to respond to world market price changes. The consequence is that, initially, supply would have been higher. In particular, supply from Cameroon and Côte d'Ivoire would respond positively to the higher producer prices. World market prices would therefore be lower. Shown in the bottom row of Table 8.5 are ratios of prices that would prevail in the new situation (still including all buffer stock intervention as in the old situation) and the actual prices.

World market prices in this new situation would have been lower throughout the period from 1982–3 to 1987–8. As of 1988, hypothetical world market prices are higher than actual prices. The reason is that, after 1985–6, hypothetical producer prices in Cameroon and Côte d'Ivoire are lower than they actually were, causing lower supply in later years.

The effects of buffer stock intervention in this new situation would also be different. Table 8.6 shows the summed changes in earnings and expenditures in the period 1981–9.

The calculations for Table 8.6 were made by simulating buffer stock behaviour in the new situation where all producers can respond to world market price changes. We incorporated the major regulations of intervention, including maximum buffer stock size and minimum prices. The simulations showed that, in the new situation, the ICCO would purchase the same quantities as it actually did. The effects of these purchases on consumer expenditures and producers' earnings are now less than in the earlier simulation, because world market prices change less. The reason for this is the enhanced sensitivity of producers to price changes. Transfers between consumers and producers are now some 70 per cent of what they were earlier. The conclusion is that 30 per cent of the ICCA-induced revenues of producers can be ascribed to the absence of world market price responsiveness of producers in major producing countries.

The stability offered by intervention in this new situation is only limited. By itself, more responsive supply reduces price fluctuations: the simulation with free price transmission leads to a coefficient of variation (CV) of the world market price in SDR per tonne of 21 per cent, compared with the actual CV of 27 per cent. But the interventions do not reduce the CVs of the price series because they are restricted to limited quantities only.

The world market price of cocoa is commonly expressed in SDR per tonne, because of the adoption of this denomination by the ICCO. Price movements in the 1980s have followed the US dollar rather than the SDR, however. The changes in the exchange rate between the US dollar and the SDR have caused prices in SDR to fall to a greater extent. This is also reflected in the CVs. Whereas the CV of the SDR price was 28 per cent, that of the US dollar price was only 19 per cent. If the reference price had been expressed in US dollars, there might have been more scope for stabilization. We have investigated this using the model.

US dollar or special drawing right price stabilization

The two agreements both suffered from a delay in implementation of the results of the negotiations. While the initial lower intervention price level of US$1.10 per pound seemed a reasonable price in 1979, in 1981 this proved much too high. In 1984–5, a may-buy price of 1,655 SDR per tonne was reasonable, but changes in the US dollar caused this to be too high in 1987 when it came into force.

In view of the above, we considered whether a fixed may-buy price of SDR 1655 would have been feasible after adjustment for US dollar–SDR exchange rate changes. This was implemented by first taking the exchange rate of 1984–5 and converting the 1,655 SDR to

US$1,646. This was then taken as the minimum price that was assumed to prevail from 1981 onwards. The model was run again, but now only US dollar price changes could trigger intervention. The results are surprising in that a substantial part of the changes in SDR price can be attributed to the exchange rate changes. Yet without intervention, prices would not have remained within the envisaged price band of ±550 SDR. A buffer stock size of 177,000 tonnes would have been sufficient in the early years of the 1980s, but to cope with the rising US dollar in 1987–8 an amount larger than the actual maximum of 250,000 would have been needed. In 1989–90, a buffer stock size of 606,000 tonnes would have been needed to keep prices above US$1,646.

The stabilization achieved with present limits on stock size and with the reference price expressed in US dollars is characterized by a CV of 20 per cent for the SDR price and of 13 per cent for the US dollar price, compared with 21 per cent for the SDR price and 15 per cent for the US dollar price in a situation without the buffer stock.

CONCLUSION

The ICCAs of 1980 and 1986 have not led to stabilization of the world market price of cocoa: the CV of the actual SDR prices was 27 per cent and this would not have been different without the buffer stock intervention; in addition, without these agreements the highest and lowest prices during the 1980s would have been the same. The interventions that have been made – 100,000 tonnes purchased in 1981–2, 75,000 tonnes in 1986–7 and 75,000 again in 1987–8 – have had short-term effects on prices and did not prevent a further drop in prices later. On average, SDR prices per tonne have been 46 SDR higher. This has led to transfers to producers of about 750 million SDR, to which consumers directly contributed some 550 million SDR. Expenditures by the buffer stock amounted to 390 million SDR, of which 200 million SDR was added to the flow to the producers and the remaining 190 million SDR was received by private stockholders. In early 1991, the buffer stock contained about 242,000 tonnes. When this is sold, it is likely to lead to transfers from producers to consumers that exceed the past transfers in the other direction. This is because of the larger volume of trade in the future and the increased responsiveness of producers to world market price changes, caused by the abolition of the marketing boards in Ghana and Nigeria.

A simulation assuming free transmission of world market price changes to producers in Cameroon, Côte d'Ivoire, Ghana and Nigeria as of 1981 indicated that, in that situation, transfers to producers would have amounted to only 540 million SDR, to which consumers would have contributed 350 million SDR. Although the absence of full price transmission caused the producing countries to benefit more from the ICCA, the drastic decrease of producer prices from CFA400 to CFA200 in 1989–90 in Cameroon and Côte d'Ivoire would not have been necessary. In a world with full price transmission, a price of around CFA250 would have prevailed. This analysis was made taking the relationship between producer prices and world market prices in 1980–1 as a benchmark.

Further analysis showed that interventions that aim at stabilizing US dollar prices, rather than prices in SDR, would have been easier in the sense of requiring less buffer stock capacity. Nevertheless, in a situation with a US dollar reference price and full price transmission, a buffer stock size of no less than 600,000 tonnes would have been required to keep prices within the band width of 560 SDR that was included in the 1986 Agreement.

A clear failure of the agreements was their neglect of regulations pertaining to changes in world market conditions between the time of negotiation and the time of the agreements themselves coming into force: particularly, changes in the exchange rates of the US dollar which have caused cocoa prices to diverge from the levels anticipated during the negotiations so that, when the agreements came into force, intervention prices proved too high. The fact that there was hardly any link between world market prices and producer prices in major producing countries was a major factor behind the persistence of the situation of oversupply. A buffer stock intervention cannot be expected to operate well under such conditions.

9 Commodity protocols

INTRODUCTION

International commodity policies do not only cover international commodity agreements and compensatory financing schemes. Besides the international commodity agreements discussed earlier, other international commodity policies exist. Among these policies, the so-called commodity protocols laid down in the Lomé Convention often receive much attention. It is the objective of this chapter to evaluate the economic performance of the most important commodity protocols from the donor's as well as the recipient countries' points of view. Lomé IV includes four commodity protocols: the banana protocol (Protocol 5), the rum protocol (Protocol 6), the beef and veal protocol (Protocol 7) and the sugar protocol (Protocol 8). Three of these protocols (the banana protocol,[1] the rum protocol and the sugar protocol) have been part of the Lomé Convention since the very beginning. The beef and veal protocol became an explicit part of the Lomé Convention under Lomé IV, although the rules on beef and veal had already been laid down earlier in correspondence between the European Community (EC) and African, Caribbean and Pacific (ACP) countries.

The sugar protocol is often regarded as the most important of the four. This is for two reasons. First, it affects more developing countries than the other three protocols. Seventeen ACP countries are mentioned in Protocol 8 of Lomé IV and similar arrangements exist with India as a non-ACP country. Second, the sugar protocol is the only one of the four which guarantees the ACP countries a specified quota at guaranteed prices. Hence, we shall primarily discuss the impact of the sugar protocol. Additionally, we shall review the beef protocol, which foresees a quota for beef to be sold on the EC market under preferential conditions. Our aim will be to analyse the impacts of the two protocols on the level and stability of prices and on the export earnings of the beneficiary ACP countries. Redistributive effects across countries will also be evaluated.

THE SUGAR PROTOCOL

The sugar protocol arose from the Commonwealth Sugar Agreement in which the UK guaranteed to purchase specified quantities of sugar from Commonwealth countries. The sugar protocol requires that the EC purchases and imports 'at guaranteed prices, specific quantities of cane sugar, raw or white, which originate in the ACP States and which these States undertake to deliver to it' (Article 1, paragraph 1).[2] Country-specific annual quotas of cane sugar, expressed in metric tons of white sugar, are fixed in Article 3 of the sugar protocol and in an annex for those countries which were not members of the ACP group in 1975).[3] Within certain limits, it is possible to modify these country quotas (Article 7). If, for example, a sugar-exporting ACP country is unable to deliver the agreed quantity, the Community may reallocate the quantity for one year or permanently between the other states which are mentioned in Article 3. When failure to deliver is due to reasons of *force majeure*, the ACP country may be allowed to deliver the quantity at a later period. Moreover, modifications of the quotas occurred in the sense that 'new' countries, Côte d'Ivoire and Zimbabwe, which had not been among the beneficiaries of the sugar protocol in 1975, received quotas. Besides fifteen ACP countries having quotas under the current provisions of the sugar protocol, there is a special treaty which guarantees India similar provisions. Table 9.1 summarizes the allocation of quotas under the sugar protocol since the Lomé Convention was founded, i.e. the sugar year 1975–6. It can be seen that Mauritius, Fiji, Guyana and Swaziland have received the largest sugar quotas.

On average across the potential users of the sugar protocol, the quotas cover a fairly substantial part of total sugar exports (Weiss 1991: 27). In the sugar years 1976–7 and 1987–8, the average share of the delivery quota in total sugar exports amounted to 52.5 per cent and 56.2 per cent respectively. When India (as a country with an exceptionally large domestic sugar market) is excluded, the average shares are even higher: 67.3 per cent and 56.8 per cent. The delivery quotas as a percentage of domestic sugar production were on average 16.6 per cent and 10.9 per cent in the same two sugar years. The respective shares increase significantly when India is excluded, to 49.5 per cent in 1976–7 and to 41.9 per cent in 1987–8. Because of very different shares of exports in domestic production of the sugar-

Table 9.1 Quotas of African, Caribbean and Pacific countries under the sugar protocol of the Lomé Convention[a]

ACP country	*Annual quota (tonnes)*	*Period*
Barbados	49,300	1975–6 to 1983–4
	50,049	1984–5 to 1985–6
	50,312	1986–7 to 1988–9
Belize	39,400	1975–6 to 1983–4
	40,105	1984–5 to 1985–6
	40,349	1986–7 to 1988–9
Congo, PDR	10,000	1975–6 to 1977–8
	4,957	1978–9 to 1982–3
	8,000	1983–4
	10,000	1984–5 to 1985–6
	10,186	1986–7 to 1988–9
Côte d'Ivoire	0	1975–6 to 1982–3
	2,000	1983–4
	10,000	1984–5 to 1985–6
	10,186	1986–7 to 1988–9
Fiji	163,600	1975–6 to 1983–4
	164,862	1984–5 to 1985–6
	165,348	1986–7 to 1988–9
Guyana	157,700	1975–6 to 1983–4
	158,935	1984–5 to 1985–6
	159,410	1986–7 to 1988–9
India	25,000	1975–6 to 1980–1
	0	1981–2 to 1982–3
	10,000	1983–4 to 1988–9
Jamaica	118,300	1975–6 to 1985–6
	118,696	1986–7 to 1988–9
Kenya	5,000	1975–6 to 1977–8
	93	1978–9 to 1981–2
	4,000	1982–3 to 1983–4
	5,000	1984–5 to 1985–6
	0	1986–7 to 1988–9
Madagascar	10,000	1975–6 to 1983–4
	10,573	1984–5 to 1985–6
	10,760	1986–7 to 1988–9
Malawi	20,000	1975–6 to 1983–4
	20,618	1984–5 to 1985–6
	20,824	1986–7 to 1988–9
Mauritius	487,200	1975–6 to 1983–4
	489,914	1984–5 to 1985–6
	491,030	1986–7 to 1988–9

Table 9.1 Continued

ACP country	*Annual quota (tonnes)*	*Period*
St Kitts and Nevis	14,800	1975–6 to 1983–4
	15,394	1984–5 to 1985–6
	15,591	1986–7 to 1988–9
Surinam	4,000	1975–6 to 1976–7
	3,199	1977–8
	2,667	1978–9 to 1979–80
	1,634	1980–1
	0	1981–2 to 1988–9
Swaziland	116,400	1975–6 to 1983–4
	117,450	1984–5 to 1985–6
	117,844	1986–7 to 1988–9
Tanzania	10,000	1975–6 to 1985–6
	10,186	1986–7 to 1988–9
Trinidad and Tobago	69,000	1975–6 to 1983–4
	43,500	1984–5 to 1985–6
	43,751	1986–7 to 1988–9
Uganda	5,000	1975–6 to 1977–8
	409	1978–9
	0	1979–80 to 1988–9
Zimbabwe	0	1975–6 to 1980–1
	6,000	1981–2
	25,000	1982–3 to 1983–4
	30,000	1984–5 to 1985–6
	30,225	1986–7 to 1988–9

Source: Own compilation with information from Wirtschaftliche Vereinigung Zucker e.V., various years
Note: [a]India is not a member of the EC–ACP Lomé Convention but benefits from a treaty with the EC which provides rules similar to those of the sugar protocol. The same held true for Belize and St Kitts and Nevis before these countries joined the Lomé Convention.

exporting countries, there is a considerable divergence of the quantitative importance of the sugar protocol for individual countries. For example, it is relatively important for Mauritius, which receives the largest sugar quota of all ACP countries and where the share of the quota in domestic production was 72.1 per cent in 1987–8. It is relatively unimportant for India, where the quota amounted to only 0.2 per cent of domestic sugar production in the same sugar year.

The central price rule of the sugar protocol is that the EC purchases the agreed quotas from ACP countries at a guaranteed price (Article 5, paragraph 3). The guaranteed price is fixed annually within the common market organization for sugar, 'taking into account all relevant economic factors' (Article 5, paragraph 4), and is expressed in ECU for unpacked sugar, cost, insurance and freight (cif) to European ports of the Community. The purchases at the guaranteed price are assured through the intervention agencies (Article 6).

On the basis of these fundamental rules, the impacts of the sugar protocol on export prices and on the level and instability of export earnings of the beneficiary ACP countries were computed. Table 9.2 compares the EC guaranteed price in the period 1975–88 with the respective world market price for sugar. In twelve out of fourteen years, the guaranteed EC price exceeded the world market price. This gave rise to an income transfer from the EC to the ACP countries in those twelve years. The only exceptions were the years 1975 and 1980, when the world price was higher than the EC price. Over the whole period 1975–88, the median percentage effect of the sugar protocol on the ACP countries' export prices was a fairly substantial price increase of 81.8 per cent.

Data on total exports and exports under the sugar protocol were combined with the price data contained in Table 9.2 in order to quantify the protocol's effects on national export earnings. The impact ΔE_i of the sugar protocol on national export earnings of an ACP country i is measured as the actual sugar quantity q_i^S delivered by the country under the sugar protocol, multiplied by the difference between the EC price p_{EC} and the world sugar price p_w:

$$\Delta E_i = q_i^S(p_{EC} - p_w) \qquad (9.1)$$

An underlying assumption in this computation is that total exports remain unaffected by the existence of the sugar protocol. This hypothesis follows the argument that the world price is the shadow price from an individual ACP country's point of view for the situations with and without the sugar protocol (Koester and Schmitz 1982: 194ff.). A domestic welfare maximum is realized when the aggregate marginal costs of sugar production are equal to the national shadow price. Countries realizing this welfare maximum will orient their producer price policies towards the world sugar price even in the situation with the sugar protocol, since they can sell an additional metric ton of sugar at the given world price. No effect on exports will then arise. It is clear that this assumption may be questioned for at least two reasons. First, when producer prices are set at the level of a mixed price between the EC and the world sugar price, impacts on

Table 9.2 Export prices for African, Caribbean and Pacific sugar in the situations with and without the sugar protocol, 1975–88 (ECU per tonne)[a]

			Difference between EC and world price	
Year	*EC guaranteed price*[b] *(p_{EC})*	*World market price*[c] *(p_w)*	*in absolute terms,* $p_{EC}-p_w$	*in percentage terms,* $(p_{EC}-p_w)100/p_w$
1975	255.30[d]	387.37	−132.07	−34.1
1976	261.15	202.44	58.71	+29.0
1977	269.75	175.92	93.83	+53.3
1978	275.30	151.81	123.49	+81.3
1979	309.70	178.47	131.23	+73.5
1980	350.10	486.49	−136.39	−28.0
1981	372.35	365.59	6.79	+1.8
1982	406.05	212.18	193.87	+91.4
1983	434.85	238.56	196.29	+82.3
1984	434.40	175.34	259.06	+147.7
1985	445.95	149.45	296.23	+197.9
1986	448.50	155.45	293.40	+188.7
1987	449.20	152.75	296.45	+194.1
1988	449.20	223.69	225.51	+100.8

Sources: Calculations explained in more detail in Weiss (1991) with data from Bartens and Mosolff, various years; Deutsche Bundesbank 1990

Notes: [a]The EC guaranteed price indicates the export price for sugar exported by ACP countries to the EC under the sugar protocol. The world market price for sugar is used to evaluate the actual sugar exports of ACP countries to non-EC markets and their hypothetical total sugar exports in the situation without the sugar protocol.

[b]Guaranteed price for ACP sugar covered by the sugar protocol, cif European ports, standard quality, recalculated from data for sugar years (July–June) into calendar year prices.

[c]London daily price (calculated as the arithmetic mean of daily prices), cif in bulk, recalculated in ECU with exchange rate data from Deutsche Bundesbank (1990).

[d]Sugar year 1975–6.

production and exports can be expected. Empirical evidence suggests that such a mixed price policy was realized at the level of individual ACP countries.[4] Second, the hypothesis implies risk neutrality. If producers are risk averse, the welfare implications of earnings-stabilizing or earnings-destabilizing impacts of the sugar protocol have to be taken into account as well. As information on producer price policies and on attitudes towards risk are not available, these risk benefits or risk losses are not discussed here.

The effects of the sugar protocol on export earnings according to

Table 9.3 Average annual income transfer to African, Caribbean and Pacific countries[a] benefiting from the sugar protocol, 1975–88[b]

Country	*Average annual income transfer*	
	in absolute value[c] *(1,000 ECU)*	*per capita*[d] *(ECU)*
Mauritius	73,573	71.59
Fiji	24,548	35.58
Guyana	23,698	28.92
Jamaica	18,055	7.76
Swaziland	16,648	22.55
Barbados	7,295	28.79
Trinidad and Tobago	6,797	5.82
Zimbabwe	6,713	0.79
Belize	5,987	37.00
Malawi	3,618	0.52
Côte d'Ivoire	2,408	0.23
St Kitts and Nevis	2,288	51.99
India	1,536	0.00
Madagascar	1,523	0.15
Tanzania	1,493	0.07
Congo, PDR	1,368	0.75
Kenya	350	0.02
Uganda	319	0.03
Surinam	163	0.45

Sources: Computations explained in more detail in Weiss (1991) on the basis of data from Wirtschaftliche Vereinigung Zucker e.V., various years; International Sugar Organization, various years; Bartens and Mosolff, various years; World Bank (a: Table 9.2)

Notes: [a]India is not a member of the ACP group and the reason for including it here is explained in footnote a of Table 9.1.

[b]The income transfer is measured as the gain in export earnings due to the sugar protocol. For those countries which did not ship sugar to the EC under the sugar protocol in certain years, only the years with actual deliveries were considered.

[c]Computed on the basis of the formula

$$\overline{\Delta E} = \frac{1}{n} \sum_{t=1}^{n} (E_t - E_t^*)$$

where E_t (E_t^*) is the actual (hypothetical) export earnings in year t in the situation with (without) the sugar protocol and E is the average annual income transfer. On details regarding the computation of E_t and E_t^* see the text.

[d]Computed with the formula

$$\overline{\Delta EC} = \frac{1}{n} \sum_{t=1}^{n} \frac{E_t - E_t^*}{\mathrm{POP}_t}$$

where POP_t is the population in year t and C indicates a per capita value.

equation (9.1) can also be interpreted as income transfers from the EC to an ACP country due to the sugar protocol.[5] These income transfers were computed for each individual year of the period 1975–88 and are documented in more detail elsewhere (Weiss 1991). The empirical analysis reveals that sugar export earnings of the beneficiary ACP countries and India were raised quite substantially in the total period 1975–88 as a consequence of the sugar protocol. The policy-induced increase in export earnings constituted some 24 per cent of total sugar export earnings. Put differently, the export earnings of all beneficiary countries in the situation without the sugar protocol were raised by about 31 per cent because of the existence of the sugar protocol (Weiss 1991: 40).

Table 9.3 summarizes the average annual income transfer of the sugar protocol to the individual user countries. It can be seen that the largest average income transfers per year went to Mauritius with 73.6 million ECU, Fiji with 24.5 million ECU, Guyana with 23.7 million ECU, Jamaica with 18.1 million ECU and Swaziland with 16.6 million ECU. In per capita terms, Mauritius again ranks highest with 71.6 ECU, followed by St Kitts and Nevis with 52.0 ECU, Belize with 37.0 ECU, Fiji with 35.6 ECU, Guyana with 28.9 ECU and Barbados with 28.8 ECU.

The comparison between per capita income transfers under the sugar protocol and the country's GDP per capita indicates that the transfers favour the richer among the beneficiary countries. Spearman's rank correlation coefficient between per capita income transfers and GDP per capita is 0.66 and the Bravais–Pearson correlation coefficient between the logarithms of both variables is 0.64.[6] Both correlation coefficients are different from zero at least at the 95 per cent level of statistical significance. It can be concluded from the donor's point of view that the income transfers under the sugar protocol must be evaluated as being arbitrary. They have their origin in the historical Commonwealth relationships and do not conform with the postulated redistributive objectives of the EC. Whereas the Community's development policy is oriented more towards the poorest developing countries, the hidden income transfers under the sugar protocol favour the most important sugar exporters to the EC. The correlation analysis suggests that this led to higher per capita transfers to the richer than to the poorer ACP sugar exporters. The rationale behind this finding is that the importance of an ACP country's sugar exports to the EC is a factor in determining the magnitude of the income transfer under the sugar protocol, whereas need is not.

Table 9.4 Effects of the sugar protocol on the instability of export earnings of beneficiary African, Caribbean and Pacific countries,[a] 1975–88[b] (per cent)

	Coefficient of variation		
ACP country	*Situation with sugar protocol* (1)	*Situation without sugar protocol*[c] (2)	*Effects of the sugar protocol on the instability of export earnings* (3) = 100[(1)–(2)]/(2)
Barbados	26.17	60.28	−56.59
Belize	26.46	48.20	−45.10
Congo, PDR	30.19	40.87	−26.13
Côte d'Ivoire[d]	87.65	108.26	−19.04
Fiji	32.26	53.98	−40.24
Guyana	39.27	55.31	−29.00
India	70.94	71.65	−0.99
Jamaica	16.88	38.79	−56.48
Kenya[e]	228.85	241.64	−5.29
Madagascar	46.25	75.62	−38.84
Malawi	51.39	63.84	−19.50
Mauritius	10.27	43.04	−76.14
St Kitts and Nevis	18.47	48.73	−62.10
Surinam[f]	46.54	36.52	+27.44
Swaziland	24.18	45.84	−47.25
Tanzania	34.08	63.78	−46.57
Trinidad and Tobago	12.95	34.94	−62.94
Zimbabwe	48.87	53.16	−8.07

Sources: Computations explained in more detail in Weiss 1991 on the basis of data taken from Bartens and Mosolff; Wirtschaftliche Vereinigung Zucker e.V.; International Sugar Organization, various years

Notes: [a]India is not a member of the ACP group and the reason for including it here is explained in footnote a of Table 9.1.

[b]The instability of export earnings is computed with the instability measure of Cuddy and Della Valle (1978) explained in the text. The data on export earnings are expressed in ECU. A linear trend correction was utilized for Mauritius, Trinidad and Tobago and Congo, PDR, in the existing situation with the sugar protocol. A loglinear trend correction was applied to Swaziland in the situation with the sugar protocol and for Jamaica, Trinidad and Tobago and India in the hypothetical situation without it. In all other cases, the instability measurement is based on the uncorrected coefficient of variation.

[c]It is assumed that total exports would be sold on the world market in a hypothetical situation without the sugar protocol.

[d]Export earnings data for 1977–88 were used.

[e]Export earnings data for 1977–84 were used.

[f]Export earnings data for 1976–80 were used.

Table 9.5 Instability of sugar export earnings in user countries of the sugar protocol and decomposition of export earnings instability,[a] 1975–88 (per cent)

		Decomposition of the instability of sugar export earnings into their regional components		
ACP country	*Export earnings instability*	*EC*	*Rest of the world*	*EC/rest of the world*
Barbados	26.17	37.09	91.21	−28.30
Belize	26.46	24.22	77.44	−1.66
Congo, PDR	30.19	53.20	73.65	−26.85
Côte d'Ivoire	87.65	17.73	199.51	−117.24
Fiji	32.26	18.59	73.93	7.48
Guyana	39.27	6.73	21.60	71.67
India	70.94	1.20	100.60	−1.80
Jamaica	16.88	7.28	90.96	1.76
Madagascar	46.25	7.13	113.72	−20.85
Malawi	51.39	8.06	80.08	11.86
Mauritius	10.27	48.72	97.12	−45.84
St Kitts and Nevis	18.47	3.05	91.63	5.32
Swaziland	24.18	2.86	77.38	19.76
Tanzania	34.08	82.05	44.93	−26.98
Trinidad and Tobago	12.95	28.60	126.04	−54.64
Zimbabwe	48.87	50.42	234.34	−184.76

Source: Computations explained in more detail in Weiss (1991) on the basis of the data sources cited in Table 9.4

Note: [a]The instability of export earnings is taken from column (1) in Table 9.4. The decomposition of export earnings is based on formula (9.3) in the text. The calculated values refer to the terms 100 var $(E_{ECi})/\text{var}(E_i)$, 100 $\text{var}(E_{RWi})/\text{var}(E_i)$ and 200 $\text{cov}(E_{ECi}, E_{RWi})/\text{var}(E_i)$. The footnotes a, b, c and d of Table 9.4 are valid again.

From the individual beneficiary country's point of view, transfers under the sugar protocol are a remarkable source of hidden aid. The average income transfers according to Table 9.3 constitute more than 1 per cent of GDP for six countries: Mauritius (3.64 per cent), St Kitts and Nevis (3.39 per cent), Belize (3.14 per cent), Guyana (1.97 per cent), Swaziland (1.65 per cent) and Fiji (1.23 per cent).

The above analysis has shown that the sugar protocol leads to a product-tied income transfer from the EC to ACP countries. This income transfer is substantial for several user countries. Beyond that, the instability of sugar export earnings is affected by the sugar protocol. These effects will be discussed now. It is well known from other studies that the market organization for sugar in the EC contributed to the stability of producer prices and earnings in sugar within the EC (Herrmann and Schmitz 1984). The provisions of the sugar protocol imply that the ACP countries participate in the stabilizing effect of guaranteed EC prices compared with highly volatile world sugar prices. It can be expected, therefore, that the sugar protocol contributed to the stability of the ACP countries' average export prices for sugar. This may or may not have led to a stabilizing effect on the national export earnings of sugar.

Tables 9.4 and 9.5 present empirical evidence on the stabilization effects of the sugar protocol. Table 9.4 compares the instability of the export earnings of the eighteen beneficiary countries in the two situations, with and without the sugar protocol. Again, it was assumed that the total exports would have been sold on the world sugar market in the non-protocol situation. The instability measure of Cuddy and Della Valle was used to calculate the instability of export earnings. The major empirical results are as follows:

1 The instability of sugar export earnings varied widely across countries. It was lowest for the country which had also benefited the most from the sugar protocol's income transfers, namely Mauritius with 10.3 per cent. The highest instability, for Kenya, is as high as 228.9 per cent. The median instability of sugar export earnings is 33.2 per cent, which is relatively high compared with other commodity markets.
2 The comparison of the two situations reveals that the sugar protocol reduced the instability of export earnings for all countries except Surinam. In the case of Surinam, the quota under the sugar protocol was continuously reduced between 1975–6 and 1981–2, as the country did not utilize its quota. Since 1981–2, the quota of Surinam has been zero. Owing to this special situation, the instability-raising effect for Surinam is only related to the period 1976–80. The stabilizing effect on the other user countries is fairly substantial. It is higher than 10 per cent in fourteen out of seventeen cases and higher than 25 per cent in twelve out of seventeen cases. The strongest stabilization effect of 76.1 per cent was realized by Mauritius. This means that Mauritius gained most as a consequence of the sugar protocol in terms of the level and stability of its export earnings in sugar. The instability of the sugar export earnings of four other countries was also reduced by more than 50 per cent: Trinidad and Tobago (by 62.9 per cent), St Kitts and Nevis (by 62.1 per cent), Barbados (by

56.6 per cent) and Jamaica (by 56.5 per cent). The median stabilization effect across all user countries was a reduction in the instability of sugar export earnings by 39.5 per cent.

3 The driving force behind the large stabilization effects is the fact that the guaranteed EC price was much more stable than the world sugar price, with a CV of 6.26 per cent as opposed to 45.05 per cent. This implies that a clear price-stabilization effect occurred for that part of total sugar exports which was directed towards the EC. Consequently, the EC-oriented part of sugar export earnings was much more stable than the world-market-oriented part. This holds true for all sixteen countries which utilized the sugar protocol during more than twelve years in the period 1975–88.

Table 9.5 gives a more detailed impression of the components of export earnings instability under the influence of the sugar protocol. The instability of sugar export earnings is decomposed into the instability of export earnings on the EC market and on the world market and the interaction between the two market segments. The methodology applied is variance decomposition, which has been used in various studies on the instability problem (Murray 1978; Brodsky 1980). The sugar export earnings E_i of an ACP country i can be defined as the sum of the export earnings E_{ECi} on the EC market and of the export earnings E_{RWi} on the rest-of-world market:

$$E_i = E_{ECi} + E_{RWi} \tag{9.2}$$

In variance terms, it can be written:

$$\text{var}(E_i) = \text{var}(E_{ECi}) + \text{var}(E_{RWi}) + 2\,\text{cov}(E_{ECi}, E_{RWi}) \tag{9.3}$$

This equation is valid when the variances and the covariance are defined around the respective arithmetic means and when they are defined around linear time trends of E_i, E_{ECi} and E_{RWi}. Table 9.5 presents this decomposition. The contributions of the components are measured in percentages of var(E_i).

It can be seen that the main component of the instability of total sugar export earnings is in all but one country (Tanzania) the instability of sugar export earnings on the world market. Owing to the fact that the guaranteed EC price is virtually constant, as is the quota under the sugar protocol, the instability of sugar export earnings on the EC market is in most cases much lower. It can be concluded that the quotas under the sugar protocol, combined with the guaranteed EC price, provided a stabilizing element for the ACP countries' sugar export earnings.

In the countries with the highest export earnings instability the described pattern is especially distinct. The contribution of the rest-of-world component of the variance of sugar export earnings was about ten times higher (for Côte d'Ivoire and Malawi) or even more than fifty times higher (for India) than the EC-market component.

When we compare the above results with earlier studies on the sugar protocol, major qualitative findings of earlier studies are confirmed and put on a broader data basis. Furthermore, one improvement of the preceding analysis compared with earlier studies is that data on actual deliveries rather than on delivery quotas were used in order to compute the impacts of the sugar protocol on the level and stability of national export earnings. The empirical analysis of Koester and Schmitz (1982) has already concluded, on the basis of calculated income transfers for four years, that fairly substantial income transfers arose for individual beneficiary countries because of the sugar protocol. They deduced that redistributive impacts across countries are related to the importance of the sugar sector but are arbitrary from a redistributive point of view. Our analysis suggests the even stronger conclusion that hidden income transfers are positively related to the countries' GDPs per capita. P.M. Schmitz (1982) computed the contribution of the sugar protocol to the stability of national export earnings for four countries. He concluded, on the basis of a different methodology, that substantial stabilization effects occur as a consequence of the protocol. Our results, which include data for the whole period of the Lomé Convention up to 1988–9, confirm this, although on a somewhat lower level. The median stabilization effect was 39.5 per cent in the above analysis compared with 65 per cent in the earlier study of Schmitz. Recent parallel studies by Koch (1989, 1990) come up with qualitative results similar to ours. He concludes, too, that the sugar protocol induced relatively high income transfers and relatively strong stabilization effects for the user countries and that Mauritius is the major gainer from the sugar protocol. Rather different from our results is the magnitude of export instability and of the stabilization effects in Koch (1989, 1990). This is due to the fact that no trend correction is applied to the CV by Koch, and this implies an overestimation of instability on the basis of the measurement concept utilized here.

Although the income transfers and the stabilization effects arising from the sugar protocol are important impacts, a comprehensive economic evaluation has to take additional arguments into account. The following other aspects are crucial.

First, the implications of the sugar protocol for world welfare have not yet been discussed. Leaving risk arguments aside, aggregate world welfare is lowered by the protocol since transport costs for a given traded quantity on the world market rise (Koester and Schmitz 1982: 201). The beneficiary countries ship sugar to the EC in order to receive the guaranteed price, whereas re-exports are then necessary for the EC owing to its net-export position.

Second, we have not yet considered the welfare implications of the sugar protocol for third countries. This might be justified as long as our basic assumption that beneficiary ACP countries do not respond to the incentives of the sugar protocol by increases in production is correct. Then, world prices are not depressed because of the sugar protocol. The hypothesis is certainly valid when world prices remain the guiding criterion for domestic price policy in the beneficiary ACP countries and when producers in those countries face the same producer prices in the situations with and without the sugar protocol. It might be that our basic hypothesis on the non-existence of world price effects has to be qualified by further research. World price effects might exist for two reasons. A first argument is that some of the preferred countries possibly apply a mixed price policy which guarantees their producers a higher price than in the hypothetical situation without the sugar protocol. Such a price policy is not guided by the national shadow price and, given risk neutrality, leads to welfare losses compared with a free-trade solution. Despite this obvious conflict with the allocative goal, such a policy is possible and was confirmed for individual countries. The second argument is that sugar producers might be risk averse and, if producer prices are faced with a lower price instability because of the sugar protocol, the supply curve of ACP producers might shift to the right. As a consequence of both cases, the beneficiary countries' production would increase and world sugar prices would fall. Thus, the sugar protocol would induce negative impacts on the export prices, export earnings and welfare of the non-preferred countries.

THE BEEF PROTOCOL

One basic difference between the EC's sugar trade policy and the beef trade policy is that the EC's trade preferences for beef are much more diverse than for sugar. Preferences exist for industrialized as well as developing countries, and bilateral arrangements with non-ACP countries are important besides the Lomé Convention (P.M. Schmitz 1984).

The regulations on beef and veal in the Lomé IV Convention are fixed in Protocol 7. The basic objective of the beef protocol is 'to enable ACP States which are traditional exporters of beef and veal to maintain their position on the Community market, thus guaranteeing a certain level of income for their producers'. The policy which is supposed to realize this objective is that 'import duties other than customs duties applicable to beef and veal originating in the ACP States shall be reduced by 90%' (Article 1) for specified beef quotas on the EC market.[7] According to Article 2, five ACP countries have access to the beef protocol: Botswana with 18,916 tonnes per calendar year, Zimbabwe with 9,100 tonnes, Madagascar with 7,579 tonnes, Swaziland with 3,363 tonnes and Kenya with 142 tonnes.[8] If one of the five countries cannot supply its quota during a year, it may waive its rights for that year and the EC may share the quota among the other ACP countries (Article 4). In cases of drought or animal diseases, the EC may also consider that the affected quantity can be delivered in the preceding or the following year. Different from the sugar protocol, the beef protocol does not include a duty to deliver the quota agreed upon.

An important additional rule in the period under consideration is that the EC lowered the import duty for the ACP countries only under the pre-condition that the ACP countries taxed their exports by the same amount. Given this additional rule, which was abolished under Lomé IV, the implicit transfers to the recipient countries can be calculated. Actual export earnings to the EC under the influence of the beef protocol are compared with those in the hypothetical non-protocol situation. Analogously to the case of sugar, the impact ΔE_i of the beef protocol on national export earnings of an ACP country i can be measured as the actual beef quantity q_i^S delivered to the EC multiplied by the difference between the price p_{EC} on the EC market and the world market price p_w for beef. Equation (9.1) is again valid. In the situation with the beef protocol, the beneficiary country receives a higher price on the EC market than in the hypothetical non-protocol situation on the world market. The price on the EC market is equal to the world price plus that part of the import duty which is waived by the Commission.

Table 9.6 presents the gain in export earnings or the income transfer which the beneficiary ACP countries received because of the beef protocol in the period 1975–88. As a consequence of significant product differentiation on the market for beef and veal, data collection on export prices in the two situations is difficult. Hence, the quantitative results have to be interpreted with some caution.[9] Export prices and export earnings for beef exports from the ACP countries to the EC are taken from NIMEXE statistics for the beef subcategories 0201.30-00, 0202.30-10, 0202.30-50 and 0202.30-90.[10] As an approximation for the hypothetical export price in the non-protocol situation, an average export price for all qualities of Argentine beef is used. In order to make the price series comparable, the average import unit values were converted from cif into free on board (fob) with cif/fob coefficients taken from IMF (b, 1987 issue). As in the case of sugar, the computations of the protocol-induced income transfers are based on actual beef deliveries by the beneficiary countries and not on the fixed quotas. Actual beef deliveries are taken from the annual publications of the Statistical Office of the EC.

The computations reveal that the gains in export earnings for the beneficiary countries owing to the beef protocol were relatively large. For the total period 1975–88, the four user countries together realized an income transfer of some 277 million ECU, i.e. 52.5 per cent of the actual beef export earnings of 528 million ECU. It can be seen from Table 9.6 that the beef protocol led to a positive income transfer for all four ACP countries in each year of the period 1975–88. It is the basic idea of the beef protocol that the export price under the EC preferences is higher than the world price.

Table 9.6 shows that the largest income transfer over the total period 1975–88 went to Botswana with 181.3 million ECU, followed by Zimbabwe with 52.5 million ECU, Swaziland with 28.1 million ECU and Madagascar with 14.8 million ECU. In per capita terms, the average annual income transfer is again the highest for Botswana with 14.03 ECU, followed by Swaziland with 3.33 ECU, Zimbabwe with 1.46 ECU and Madagascar with 0.16 ECU. Again, the income transfers induced by the beef protocol are quite substantial for the most important ACP beef exporters, in particular for Botswana.

The distribution of income transfers across the user countries is again not guided by targets of redistributive policy, but primarily by the historical beef export pattern. This means that Botswana's large export quota stems from its historical role as an important beef supplier to Great Britain under the Commonwealth (Wendt 1981: 156). Moreover, it depends on the country's ability to utilize the agreed quota. Here, Botswana again performed better than the other three ACP countries with a utilization of 63.5 per cent in the period 1975–88 (Weiss 1991: 81).

Besides the effects of the beef protocol on the level of national export earnings, the instability of national export earnings was affected. Table 9.7 presents an analysis of export earnings instabilities in ACP–EC trade and on the stabilizing or destabilizing impacts of

Table 9.6 Annual income transfers to African, Caribbean and Pacific countries benefiting from the beef protocol, 1975–88 (1,000 ECU)[a]

Year	*Botswana*	*Madagascar*	*Swaziland*	*Zimbabwe*	*ACP countries*[b]
1975	9,522	1,012	396	0	10,930
1976	15,344	404	1,880	0	17,628
1977	18,005	932	1,342	0	20,278
1978	8,608	1,890	3,467	0	13,964
1979	15,066	2,568	4,024	0	21,658
1980	861	2,980	2,298	0	6,139
1981	8,393	2,080	969	0	11,442
1982	17,809	553	1,187	0	19,548
1983	21,201	770	1,857	0	23,828
1984	17,482	1,013	900	0	19,395
1985	16,232	637	3,364	2,053	22,286
1986	13,831	0	4,546	10,962	29,339
1987	11,095	0	1,825	18,996	31,915
1988	7,841	0	0	20,458	28,299
1975–88					
Sum of income transfers	181,290	14,839	28,055	52,469	276,649
Average annual income transfers	12,949	1,349	2,158	13,117	19,761
Percentage of all income transfers to ACP countries	65.53	5.36	10.14	18.97	100
Average annual income transfer per capita (ECU)	14.03	0.16	3.33	1.46	1.84

Source: Computations explained in more detail in Weiss (1991)
Notes: [a]The income transfer or gain in export earnings (ΔE_i) for an ACP country i owing to the beef protocol is measured with the following formula: $\Delta E_i = q_i^S (p_{EC} - p_w)$. q_i^S stands for actual exports to the EC and p_{EC} for average import values in beef and veal for EC imports from the ACP country. For both variables, data are used from the Statistical Office of the EC. As an approximation for p_w, the average unit value of all Argentine beef, fob, carcass weight, is used. Data on p_w are from FAO, various years. Cif unit values of imports are converted into fob unit values with cif/fob coefficients taken from IMF (b, 1987 issue).
[b]The ACP countries included are Botswana, Madagascar, Swaziland and Zimbabwe. Kenya is excluded since it did not fulfil its quota.
[c]The average annual income transfer per capita is calculated as

$$\overline{\Delta EC} = \frac{1}{n} \sum_{t=1}^{n} \frac{E_t - E_t^*}{\mathrm{POP}_t}$$

where E (E^*) are export earnings to the EC in the existing (hypothetical) situation with (without) the beef protocol, POP_t is the population in year t and C indicates a per capita value. n indicates the number of years in which beef was delivered to the EC.

Table 9.7 Effects of the beef protocol on the instability of beef export earnings of beneficiary African, Caribbean and Pacific countries,[a] 1975–88[b] (per cent)

	Instability of export earnings			Instability of export prices			
ACP country	*Situation with beef protocol* (1)	*Situation without beef protocol* (2)	*Effect of the beef protocol* (3)=100[(1)−(2)]/(2)	*Situation with beef protocol* (4)	*Situation without beef protocol* (5)	*Effect of the beef protocol* (6)=100[(4)−(5)]/(4)	*Instability of export quantities in both situations* (7)
Botswana	45.78	52.97	−13.57	15.79	16.97	−6.95	44.88
Madagascar	69.43	76.95	−9.77	14.34	16.97	−15.50	64.74
Swaziland	53.36	48.01	+11.14	11.48	16.97	−32.35	52.23
Zimbabwe	64.35	65.06	−1.09	7.55	16.97	−55.51	66.96
ACP countries[c]	24.78	29.69	−16.54	9.71	16.97	−42.78	27.86

Source: Computations explained in more detail in Weiss 1991

Notes: [a]The computations are restricted to that part of the ACP countries' beef exports which are directed towards the EC.

[b]The instabilities are computed with the instability measure of Cuddy and Della Valle (1978) explained in the text. The data on export earnings are expressed in ECU. A linear trend correction was utilized for the aggregate export earnings of the four ACP countries and for the export prices of Swaziland and the ACP countries in the situation with the beef protocol. A loglinear trend correction was applied to the export prices of Botswana and Madagascar in both situations and of Swaziland, Zimbabwe and the ACP countries in the hypothetical situation without the beef protocol. In all other cases, the instability measurement is based on the uncorrected coefficient of variation.

[c]The ACP countries included are Botswana, Madagascar, Swaziland and Zimbabwe. Kenya is excluded since it did not fulfil its quota.

the beef protocol. In general, it is remarkable that the pattern of export earnings instability differs very strongly from the case of sugar. On the world sugar market, prices were extremely unstable. This implies that the sugar protocol led to a significant decrease in instability of sugar export prices of the beneficiary ACP countries and, consequently, to a clearly lower export earnings instability.

In the ACP–EC beef trade, export earnings instability as measured by the Cuddy and Della Valle instability index was fairly substantial even in the existing situation with the beef protocol. The highest instability of their beef export earnings from the EC was experienced by Madagascar with 69.4 per cent, followed by Zimbabwe with 64.4 per cent, Swaziland with 53.4 per cent and Botswana with 45.8 per cent. These export earnings instabilities are in all but one country (Swaziland) lower than in the hypothetical non-protocol situation. The stabilization effect was most distinct for Botswana with 13.6 per cent, followed by Madagascar with 9.8 per cent. The median stabilization effect, however, is clearly lower than under the sugar protocol. The most important reason for this is that the export earnings instability in the ACP–EC beef trade is primarily because of quantity rather than price instability. Therefore, price-stabilizing effects which were realized as a consequence of the beef protocol do not solve the problem of the instability in the quantities which remain.

For all beneficiary ACP countries, the beef protocol induced a stabilizing impact on beef export prices. The stabilizing effect was weaker, however, than under the sugar protocol when we compare median effects. The stabilization potential was also much lower since the instability of beef export prices on the world market was 17.0 per cent compared with 45.1 per cent for sugar. On the other hand, the instability of beef export quantities to the EC was substantial for all beneficiary ACP countries covered by Table 9.7. It varied between 67.0 per cent for Zimbabwe and 44.9 per cent for Botswana, with a median instability of 58.5 per cent. In the situations with and without the beef protocol, variance decomposition shows that for all four ACP countries quantity instability contributes significantly more to earnings instability than price instability. For Botswana, for example, the share of price instability in earnings instability is 14.7 per cent in the non-protocol situation, whereas the share of quantity instability is 99.0 per cent. Causes of these high quantity instabilities are various non-price factors, like adverse climatic conditions or phytosanitary problems. This quantity instability drives the high magnitude of export earnings instability in ACP–EC beef trade and it limits the potential for stabilization of national export earnings involved in the beef protocol.

SUMMARY

This chapter has shown that other important international commodity policies do exist besides international commodity agreements and compensatory financing schemes. The commodity protocols laid down in the Lomé Convention are cases in point, and their economic performance has been evaluated. We can conclude that the sugar and beef protocols imply significant welfare gains for the user countries owing to their hidden income transfers. Moreover, there has been an earnings-stabilizing impact for virtually all countries, but more so under the sugar protocol than under the beef protocol, since price instability tends to dominate for sugar, whereas quantity instability dominates for beef. From the recipient countries' point of view, the protocols represent an important countervailing instrument against the world price reducing and welfare-decreasing impact of the EC's Common Agricultural Policy for the ACP sugar and beef exporters.

Apart from the recipient countries' point of view, the economic success of the protocols has to be assessed more negatively. Overall welfare decreases, since trade diversion occurs and transport costs in world sugar trade rise. If there is supply response in the favoured nations, world market prices will be lowered and the economic welfare of non-ACP exporters will decrease. Additionally, the income transfers among ACP countries depend upon historical linkages and are untargeted, given the redistributive objectives of the EC.

10 A comparison and evaluation of the arrangements

INTRODUCTION

In this chapter we compare and evaluate the two financial compensation arrangements, the three commodity agreements and the protocols. In the following section, we start with the compensatory arrangements of the International Monetary Fund (IMF) and the European Community (EC). We shall compare the transfer and stabilization impacts of both arrangements. Furthermore, we shall see that the Compensatory Financing Facility (CFF), STABEX and the benefits of one of the commodity agreements often coincide. In the third section the common features and the differences of the commodity agreements and protocols are reviewed. In particular, the effectiveness of interventions in the various markets is discussed. Many countries are affected by more than one of the arrangements. Although we have no figures on the effects of the International Coffee Agreement (ICA) over time, we shall indicate the extent to which the benefits of various agreements correlate across countries. As to the International Cocoa Agreement (ICCA) and the International Natural Rubber Agreement (INRA), we shall investigate for some countries how the benefits and losses correlate over time. In the fourth section we shall draw conclusions on the performance of the stabilization arrangements and indicate routes towards improved international commodity policy.

COMPENSATORY FINANCING SCHEMES AND COMMODITY ARRANGEMENTS

A comparison of the compensatory financing schemes has to include common features as well as their differences. With regard to both aspects, some fairly surprising conclusions can be drawn from the findings of Chapters 3–5.

It is a common feature of the major compensatory financing schemes that their economic effects are crucially different from the impacts one would expect for theoretical *a priori* reasons. Chapters 3–5 have shown that the existing compensatory financing schemes are far from being perfect export earnings stabilizers. They redistribute, however, fairly substantial income transfers.

In many cases, existing compensatory financing schemes did not stabilize national export earnings as a consequence of substantial time-lags in the compensation payments. When stabilizing effects occurred, they were often small. Although compensation under the IMF's CFF is made more promptly than under the STABEX system, the overall impact of payments and repayments under the CFF was more often destabilizing than stabilizing. The median effect on export earnings instability was +0.63 per cent. Besides time-lags, unsatisfactory stabilization effects were due to quota limitations in the first years of the CFF, to the delinking of repayments and stabilization goals and in individual cases to forecasting errors. The median impact of STABEX payments on export earnings instability was −0.33 per cent. An important reason for the weak stabilization success of STABEX, besides time-lags, was limited funds in years of depressed coffee and cocoa prices. Without significant policy changes, it can be expected that the median stabilization effect of the existing compensatory financing schemes will remain negligible.

It is common to both major compensatory financing schemes, the CFF and the STABEX scheme, that they contain strong redistributive elements. Credits are given under more favourable conditions than on commercial markets. Significant grant elements are involved in the EC scheme, where earnings shortfalls under Lomé I–III were generally compensated by interest-free payments and, for many countries, even the absence of a repayment duty. In the period 1975–88, 48.4 per cent of all STABEX payments were *a priori* full grants and a minimum grant ratio of 32.3 per cent was found for the repayable STABEX credits, given the actual repayment patterns up to 1988. Since Lomé IV, the grant ratio has generally risen to 100 per cent. The grant ratios in the IMF scheme are lower but still important. From the donor's point of view, both compensatory financing schemes must be criticized in that the resulting income transfers appear arbitrary and untargeted. In particular, indicators of neediness appear to be unimportant for income redistribution under the compensatory financing schemes. For the CFF it was shown that the countries with the highest per capita incomes received significantly higher per capita transfers than countries in the two lowest income classes. For STABEX, cross-country regressions revealed that STABEX payments were allocated among users according to the openness of the recipient countries and the importance of major STABEX products in the export earnings of African, Caribbean and Pacific (ACP) countries, i.e. coffee, groundnuts and cocoa. There is no statistically significant relationship between the per capita income of the beneficiary countries and per capita STABEX payments. Thus, redistributive criteria are not important for the allocation of hidden aid under STABEX.

Differences exist with regard to the allocation effects of the existing compensatory financing schemes. The CFF is not commodity-oriented and therefore there is only a small possibility that producers' incentives are distorted owing to the existence of the CFF. STABEX, however, is not necessarily neutral with respect to allocation goals. In as far as income transfers are transmitted via higher prices to producers of the STABEX commodities, incentives for increased production in the affected sectors are provided. The same argument is valid for COMPEX. Under SYSMIN, allocation effects also exist. Investment in the mining sector, as opposed to other sectors, is fostered.

In a comparative evaluation of compensatory financing schemes, the individual user country's point of view has to be distinguished from the donor's point of view. From the national point of view, there is one further common feature of the CFF and the STABEX systems. The utility-theory approach of Newbery and Stiglitz for measuring risk and transfer benefits was applied. It was shown for a broad country sample that transfer benefits were much more important than risk benefits under the IMF's CFF as well as the STABEX scheme. Beyond this common feature there are major differences, however, between the two important compensatory financing schemes from the national points of view and between STABEX and the other financial stabilization schemes of the EC, i.e. COMPEX and SYSMIN. User countries will also recognize important differences between the food financing facility and the traditional export earnings stabilization scheme under the CFF. Most important are the following points:

1 Whereas the median risk benefit approaches zero under the CFF and STABEX, the median transfer benefit is clearly positive in both schemes, but it is much higher under STABEX than under the CFF. It reached 14.3 per cent of average national export earnings under STABEX in the period 1975–88 but only 1.3 per cent under the CFF in the longer period 1963–87.

2 A further advantage from the national point of view is that conditionality is much weaker for STABEX than for the CFF.
3 Participation in STABEX is more attractive than in SYSMIN; COMPEX, on the other hand, is a regional extension of STABEX and it can be evaluated like STABEX from an individual user country's point of view.
4 Within the CFF, the analysis has shown that the use of the traditional export earnings shortfall rule will in many cases be superior to the specific provisions on cereal imports introduced in 1981.

We can conclude that neither system offers much stabilization of export earnings, but they both transfer substantial amounts to the recipient countries. Grants under the STABEX and affiliated systems are much larger than those under the CFF.

Developing countries do not have to choose between the two systems but can apply for transfers under both arrangements. Transfers under the STABEX scheme can be taken into account when the IMF decides on applications for CFF transfers, however (see Goreux 1980: 81–2). Of the eighty-seven countries included in our survey of CFF drawings and the fifty-one countries that actually participated in the STABEX system, thirty-four countries received transfers from both sources. In addition, twenty of these countries benefited from the coffee agreement and eighteen from the cocoa agreement; eleven countries benefited from all four arrangements (CFF, STABEX, ICA and ICCA). For the thirty-four countries that participated in both the CFF and STABEX, a correlation coefficient was calculated between the transfers from either source to each of the countries. The value came out at 0.43, indicating a significantly positive relationship. Hence, countries that benefit more from STABEX also receive more net transfers from the CFF.

As we have shown in Chapter 3, STABEX transfers are closely related to whether the country exports cocoa or coffee. This is confirmed by two other measures: of the fifty-one STABEX countries, thirty-nine benefited from the ICA and eighteen from the ICCA. The correlation coefficient between STABEX transfers and transfers from the coffee agreement was 0.41 and between STABEX and ICCA-related receipts was 0.68.

From a donor's point of view, contribution to one system might compensate for that to another. For example, the transfer that the EC (as a cocoa importer) has made to cocoa-producing countries is substantial. But if the ICCA had not achieved this, the claims by the producing countries on transfers under STABEX regulations would have been higher. (It should be noted, however, that in practice only part of the claims by ACP countries have been granted by the EC.)

Links between CFF drawings and receipts related to the ICA or the ICCA are equally strong. Hence, many of the countries involved in commodity agreements make use of other facilities to stabilize – or at least augment – their export earnings. We have seen that no actual stabilization was achieved, but a well-designed Compensatory and Contingency Financing Facility (CCFF) system might go some way in this direction.

If so many countries can make use of financial compensation systems that in principle should stabilize their export earnings, is there a need for commodity agreements? Of the three agreements surveyed here, only the INRA has had a stabilizing impact on world market prices. But, as exchange rates and inflation rates differ between countries, the actual outcome for various producers of stable world market prices has been different. If countries were able to address their export earnings instability through the CFF or STABEX type of arrangement, the focus of commodity agreements would be on the provision of a stable environment for the individual producers. In view of the large differences across countries, this is a matter that could be addressed more directly at the country level.

COMMODITY ARRANGEMENTS COMPARED

The comparison between the commodity arrangements discussed in Chapters 6–9 includes their common features as well as their differences. There is an essential difference between the commodity agreements on coffee, natural rubber and cocoa on the one hand and the commodity protocols for sugar and beef on the other. The focus of the three commodity agreements is on the world market prices of the commodities concerned, whereas the protocols are restricted to the few countries concerned. In addition, the quantities in each of the countries are limited.

Within the group of commodity agreements, there are major differences as well. The coffee agreement stands apart because, unlike the other two agreements, it has no provisions for international price support through buffer stocking. Instead, coffee prices can be supported by export quotas allotted to the exporting members, as agreed in the ICA. Hence, the ICA is a price-supporting and not a price-stabilizing agreement. The ICCA and the INRA do have provisions for intervention through a buffer stock. The ICCA has so far turned out to be only price-supporting, because there has been no opportunity to sell any cocoa from the buffer stock. Only the INRA has been stabilizing prices through purchases and sales of natural rubber.

Unlike the other agreements, the ICA, by its provisions for national quotas, induced a distinction between members and non-members. This had serious repercussions on the world market, because the ICA thus introduced market fragmentation and two world market prices: a higher price in the member market and a lower price in the non-member market, as some of the supply surplus in the former market was transferred to the latter. The cocoa and natural rubber agreements did not have this unequal treatment of trading partners and even non-participating countries felt the effects of the agreements just like the countries that signed them.

The commodity protocols that we discussed in Chapter 9 provide stable (and high) prices for the commodities in the countries involved. They differ from international commodity agreements by their national focus and their restrictions on quota. The sugar protocol provided substantial stability to the sugar export earnings of the recipient countries. This was made possible by the stable and high prices offered. Had prices been lower, for example at the level of the average world market price for the period, countries might still have decided to participate. It would be tempting not to deliver in periods of high world market prices if there was no obligation to supply. Without the obligation, the protocol would be tantamount to a deficiency payment scheme with quota.

Effectiveness of intervention

By its design, the ICA should benefit producers. In 1982, prices were raised by 47 per cent because of the agreement and in 1983 by 17 per cent. Welfare transfers to exporters in this period amounted to US$1,932 million. As to cocoa, although the ICCA was hampered by lack of financial means, purchases for the buffer stock caused prices to rise by 2 per cent in the first year (1981–2) and by more in later years. Further purchases in 1986 kept prices above hypothetical non-ICCA levels until, finally, in 1991 the effects are estimated to have faded out. Transfers to producers (total, not just in welfare terms) amounted to 747 million SDR over the period 1981–2 to 1989–90 and were positive in all years. The peak year was 1984–5, when 119 million SDR was transferred, equal to 3.7 per cent of the production value. In contrast to these two agreements, by which income has been transferred to producers, the INRA has eventually benefited consumers more than producers. In the early 1980s, substantial additional income was enjoyed by the producers (in some quarters up to 23 per cent more), but sales from the buffer stock in 1987 and 1988 resulted in lower prices, leading to implicit transfers of income in the other direction (at maximum 23 per cent less revenues for producers). The latter flows exceeded the former, as both the volumes of trade and the effect on prices were larger.

We assess the relative effectiveness of intervention in the markets for coffee, cocoa and natural rubber by comparing the instrumental expenditure (like buffer stock purchases) with the results for producers' revenues.

The case of coffee is different in that the reduction of export supply was made 'by decree' rather than by something like buffer stock purchases. The increase in coffee producers' revenues by 17 per cent in 1982–3 was caused by a reduction in export supply of 260,000 tonnes, equal to 6.2 per cent (but 7.4 per cent on the member market). If some organization had done so, it would have had to spend US$721 million on the purchase. The reduction in export supply caused export earnings to go up by 17 per cent, or US$1,438 million. Hence, each US dollar 'spent on intervention' causes export revenues to rise by about US$2.

The increase in cocoa producers' earnings was estimated at 747 million SDR over the period 1981–2 to 1989–90. Further extra revenues after this period can be estimated at another 40 million SDR. These total additional revenues have been caused by buffer stock purchases amounting to 388 million SDR. Roughly speaking, therefore, each US dollar spent by the intervention authority causes producers' revenues to rise by US$2. Thus, the cocoa market shows a remarkable similarity to the coffee market.

In the first five years of intervention in the natural rubber market, the revenues of the producers have increased by US$2,047 million, caused by buffer stock purchases amounting to US$301 million. The implied impact ratio is 6.8. The sales by the buffer stock in later years represented a value of about US$400 million and led to losses of producers' revenues in the amount of US$2,927 million, implying a ratio of 7.3. Hence, interventions in the natural rubber market appear more effective in changing producers' revenues than those in the coffee and cocoa markets.

In a simple demand–supply framework, Spraos (1990: 301) shows that the impact ratio is equal to $(1 + s)/(s - d)$, where s is the supply elasticity and d the demand elasticity. In the cases of coffee and cocoa, this expression would equal 3 and 4 respectively. Here we have used the long-term values of the elasticities. The estimates are higher than the value of 2 that we found in the earlier calculations. In the case of coffee, the reasons are the mitigating influence of the non-member market and the time-horizon that was employed in Chapter 6. Only two years were considered there, and a longer-term simulation of the impact of the export quota might well lead to larger effects than those calculated above because of the presence of the lagged endogenous variable in the supply equation. In the case of cocoa, the difference is due to the impact of stocks. Buffer stock intervention was found to have an impact on prices equal to a similar reduction in opening stocks. In the cocoa market, the impact of stock changes on the prices is only minor. Hence prices, and therefore consumption, show only a very small alteration. The impact on the revenues of natural rubber producers is much stronger. Demand and supply elasticities would yield a value for Spraos's ratio equal to 7, which does not differ from our estimated impact. The mitigating influence of stocks that was found for cocoa is not applicable in the natural rubber market, because stock changes have strong effects on prices: the price flexibility of stocks is 0.90, compared with only 0.13 in the case of cocoa.

We can conclude that the natural rubber market is much more sensitive to interventions than the markets for coffee and cocoa. Hence, the natural rubber market lends itself better to intervention.

The effectiveness of intervention of the type in the Lomé protocol, that we have analysed here, is not large. If world market prices are not affected, the impact ratio is exactly equal to unity, and if more supply is induced the ratio is even less.

Specific aspects

A specific aspect in the case of coffee is the importance of the parallel market and the related issue of membership was analysed separately. The existence of the parallel market led to benefits accruing to non-members of the International Coffee Organization (ICO) and to (tiny) losses for exporters to this market. Many importing countries that are members of the ICO have suffered welfare losses because of the agreement. Only the smaller importers among these members would have gained, however, if they had cancelled their membership. Hence, the specific regulations of this agreement, involving the distinction between a member and a non-member market, provided a strong rationale for major trading partners to remain members of the ICA. This does not apply to the buffer stocking arrangements for cocoa and rubber, where free riding can occur easily.

A specific aspect of the ICCA is the change from a reference price in US dollars in the 1980 agreement to a reference price in SDR in the 1986 agreement. As shown in Chapter 8, the latter choice was unfortunate in that it would have been easier for the organization to keep prices within a band around a US dollar reference price. But, even in this case, the pressure from oversupply would be so strong that with the present size of the buffer stock the International Cocoa Organization (ICCO) would not have been able to keep prices above the lower bound. In the cocoa market, such persistence of oversupply can exist because many farmers have been shielded from the world market by domestic price regulations. In this situation, buffer stock interventions lead to persistent changes in world market prices, as producers in the major exporting countries hardly respond to induced world market price changes. This lack of response has led to substantial additional transfers to producing countries. Simulations with free price transmissions in these African countries showed that over the period 1981–90 more than 200 million SDR would not have been transferred if producers had responded to the change in world market prices caused by buffer stock purchases.

Contrary to the cocoa market, the market for natural rubber is quite open and all major producers have full transmission of world market prices to the farm gate level. Supply and demand elasticities are generally smaller, however, than in the case of cocoa. Hence, interventions by the buffer stock manager had substantial effects on prices. Although these deviations from free market levels tend to persist for only a year or two, they have contributed to the International Natural Rubber Organization's (INRO's) success in keeping prices above the lower bound level in the agreement.

A specific aspect of the natural rubber market is its use as an input in the manufacturing industry (mostly tyres). This renders the price of natural rubber relatively unimportant to the consuming industry and makes demand for natural rubber highly dependent on external factors, like demand for car tyres. The consequence is not only that the price elasticity of demand is low but also that demand itself is volatile: the consuming industry must order natural rubber well in advance of prospective tyre sales, and a small indication of an increase in demand for tyres may make the industry rush for additional natural rubber. The quality of natural rubber in the buffer stock – after some years of storage – was not suitable to meet the sudden upsurge in demand in 1987, and the INRO was therefore not able to keep prices from rising above the upper bound of the agreement.

The agreements on coffee and cocoa have both had a price-raising and not a price-stabilizing effect. This effect was natural in the case of the coffee agreement, as it has no provisions to decrease prices. The effect is only temporary for cocoa, because up to now the ICCO has not sold any cocoa. When it does, this will depress prices. Because supply responses to world market prices have become larger, now that Nigeria and Ghana have linked their prices to the world market, the market is in a better position to absorb such a buffer stock disposal. But any disposal is bound to lead to implicit transfers from producers to consumers that exceed the earlier transfers in the other direction.

The natural rubber market has witnessed both purchases and sales by the buffer stock manager. This has stabilized the prices around the level of the INRO reference price. Has it also made the prices more predictable? This question has been investigated in the case of the rubber market and the answer was 'no' for the long term but 'yes' for the short term. The uncertainty about the prices for more than a few years ahead is so great and the other forces so strong that the existence of the intervention mechanism makes hardly any difference to the prices. If the uncertainty about the future was limited to forces inside the natural rubber market, and excluded the uncertainties about overall rubber demand, exchange rates, inflation, etc., then the interventions would be shown to improve the short-term predictability of the prices.

Transfers

For all three agreements, the major effect is not stabilization but transfers: in the case of coffee from consumers to producers; in the case of cocoa in the same direction for the time being; in the case of natural rubber, at first from consumers to producers, but vice versa later. Gains and losses have therefore been felt by countries mostly in proportion to their share in the world market and according to their position of being an importer or exporter. It was shown for the coffee agreement that the substantial transfers due to the ICA, when calculated on a per capita basis, appear not to correlate with GDP per capita and do not, therefore, seem to be distributed fairly over the developing countries. The same holds for cocoa: when calculated across thirty-nine cocoa-exporting countries, the gains per capita resulting from the ICCO have a correlation coefficient with per capita GDP that is equal to only −0.03. In the case of natural rubber, this correlation coefficient is 0.23, indicating a significantly positive

Table 10.1 Correlations over time, means and standard deviations of transfers owing to the International Cocoa Agreement and the International Natural Rubber Agreement (1,000 US dollars) from 1981–2 to 1988–9

		Mean values		*Standard deviation*	
Country	*Correlation*	*Cocoa*	*Rubber*	*Cocoa*	*Rubber*
Brazil	−0.19	17,830	140	4,578	4,769
Cameroon	−0.32	5,948	−930	1,310	3,963
Côte d'Ivoire	−0.79	27,609	−1,663	7,571	7,555
Ghana	−0.63	10,109	−30	1,506	256
Guatemala	−0.00	100	−228	24	2,043
Indonesia	−0.91	1,835	−17,650	1,196	187,710
Liberia	0.57	298	−1,721	175	13,962
Malaysia	−0.95	6,433	−2,025	3,215	252,013
Nigeria	−0.02	7,049	−2,539	1,670	10,857
Papua New Guinea	−0.61	1,634	−59	341	556
Philippines	−0.68	297	−1,123	68	21,591
Sri Lanka	0.38	93	1,173	29	17,943
Zaire	−0.41	230	−96	49	2,886

Source: Own computations

relationship between the two. But, in the latter case of the INRO, the transfers involved are ultimately only small.

Cumulation of benefits/losses

Many countries export more than one of the commodities considered here. Of the forty-six countries exporting coffee, thirty-one countries exported cocoa as well and thirteen (out of the forty-six) exported natural rubber. Twelve countries exported all three commodities. Of the thirty-nine countries exporting cocoa, thirteen exported natural rubber too. The links between coffee and cocoa exports and participation in STABEX are also strong: of the forty-six coffee exporters, thirty-nine are ACP members receiving STABEX transfers; of the thirty-nine cocoa exporters, eighteen are beneficiaries of STABEX transfers. We know that the transfers per commodity are uncorrelated with GDP per capita, with the exception of INRA transfers. The same holds if the sum of all transfers is considered. Total transfers per capita resulting from participation in the ICO, the ICCO and the INRO are uncorrelated with GDP per capita (actually equal to −0.002). Including the receipts due to the sugar and beef protocols, the correlation coefficient hardly changes (to 0.023).

Transfers change over time. It might be, therefore, that the sum of the transfers is more stable than one series of transfers by itself. This was investigated for thirteen cocoa and natural rubber producing countries. Table 10.1 lists their average receipts, the standard deviations and the correlation between the two series. As shown in the table, most of the correlation coefficients are negative, indicating that while transfers from one agreement rose, those from the other declined. In particular, cocoa receipts rose and INRA transfers fell in this period. The standard deviations and mean values indicate, however, that there are enormous differences in the size of transfers between the countries and for the two commodities. A country like Indonesia, for example, although benefiting from ICCO, suffered so much (eventually) from the INRA that the negative correlation between the two series had negligible effects. Note that in these series, unlike in Chapter 7, the transfers due to the INRA have not been discounted.

CONCLUSIONS

Our prime conclusion must be a negative one: no stabilization, or hardly any, has been provided by the international arrangements that were designed to achieve this. The IMF's CFF has not stabilized export earnings, but has generated some transfers to the recipient countries. The STABEX system between the EC and ACP countries entails substantial transfers to the ACP countries but no stability to their export earnings. The coffee and cocoa agreements have led to considerable transfers from consuming to producing countries but not to stability in the world market for these products. Only the INRA has provided some stability to the world market price. Chapter 7 classified this success as 'fortuitous' however.

The arrangements have had substantial redistributive effects. Considerable amounts have been transferred from rich to poor countries. This applies in particular to STABEX, to the ICA and – for the time being – to the ICCA. The transfer effects of the CFF were only minor, and those eventually owing to the INRA were largely from producing to consuming countries and therefore negative for the poorer countries. Transfers under the five international arrangements have been distributed across less developed countries in a way that is not related to GDP per capita. Transfers from each arrangement separately were not related to GDP per capita, with the exception of the CFF and the INRA, of which the per capita transfers were positively related to GDP per capita. To a considerable extent the transfers under various arrangements coincide, and many countries benefit from more than one arrangement. The total transfers per capita, however, are also unrelated to GDP per capita.

From a donor's point of view, the arrangements have failed. They have not stabilized what they should stabilize, except in the case of the INRA. The transfers that are implicitly or explicitly the result of the arrangements have been distributed across the beneficiary countries in a way that does not appear to accord with the principles of development aid. From the recipient's point of view, too, the arrangements have failed, as no stabilization was achieved, except with the INRA. However, the countries will have appreciated the transfers received, again with the exception of the INRA.

Should commodity agreements be continued?

In Chapter 1, we surveyed the history of commodity agreements, which does not raise much hope for successful agreements. In Chapter 2, we indicated theoretical and empirical grounds for suspecting that government policy and the economic environment in the commodity-producing countries are much more important for producers than world market conditions. In the relevant chapters on the coffee, cocoa and natural rubber agreements, we showed how each of them led to substantial transfers. Although these transfers were – for the ICA and the ICCA – from richer to poorer countries, and therefore contributed to equity, the distribution of the transfer shows no sign of alleviating poverty or enhancing equity within the group of developing countries. In the chapters on cocoa and rubber, we also showed the large discrepancies between producer prices in the various countries and the feeble relationship to world market prices. In this final chapter, we showed how benefits from commodity agreements have largely accrued to countries that also have benefited from compensatory financing arrangements. We conclude that there is no reason to continue striving towards international commodity agreements of this type.

The compensatory financial arrangements have not been able to stabilize the export earnings and should be revised. The CFF has been revised into the Compensatory and Contingency Financing Facility and is now directed more to compensating balance-of-payments instability in countries adjusting their economy. The STABEX system has evolved more and more into a mechanism for transfer of considerable amounts of aid. It is doubtful, however, whether the aid flows under STABEX are efficiently allocated, based as they are on lagged changes in export earnings of primary commodities.

Given that many commodity-exporting countries are poor, there is every reason to continue the transfer of funds to these countries. But this is true for all the poor. Commodity producers should be equipped with stable economic environments. These are largely domestically determined by food prices and the prices for their products which are in turn influenced by export taxes and exchange rates. To some extent, the international community can help. International coordination of exchange rate and/or export taxes would be beneficial in creating the conditions for local stability. If aid, given under any flag, is used to create this local stability, it is used well.

Appendices

APPENDIX A.1: CHARGES ON DRAWINGS FROM THE INTERNATIONAL MONETARY FUND'S COMPENSATORY FINANCING FACILITY SINCE 1 MAY 1963

Table A1.1 Charges on credits effected after 1 May 1963 and up to 30 June 1974

	Annual charges[a] for portions of holdings in excess of quota by		
Kind of charge	*> 0%≤50%*	*> 50%≤100%*	*> 100%*
Service charge[b]	0.5	0.5	0.5
Interest rates[c] for different terms:			
0–3 months	0.0	0.0	0.0
3–6 months	2.0	2.0	2.0
½–1 year	2.0	2.0	2.5
1–1½ years	2.0	2.5	3.0
1½–2 years	2.5	3.0	3.5
2–2½ years	3.0	3.5	4.0[d]
2½–3 years	3.5	4.0[d]	4.5
3–3½ years	4.0[d]	4.5	5.0
3½–4 years	4.5	5.0	
4–4½ years	5.0		

Sources: IMF (a), 1974 issue: 99; IMF 1981: 13; IMF (b), various years

Notes: [a]Except for the service charge, which is payable once per transaction and stated as a percentage of the amount of transaction.

[b]No service charge was payable in respect of any gold tranche purchase effected after 27 July 1969. In the computation of income transfers, it is abstracted from this special provision.

[c]The CFF interest rates are utilized in the computation of the income transfers for the interest rates i_j. The assumption is made that interest payments occur only once a year, at the end of the year.

[d]Point at which the Fund and the member were consulted.

Table A1.2 Charges on credits effected from 1 July 1974 to 30 April 1981

	Annual charges[a] *(%)*	
Kind of charge	*1 July 1974 to 31 March 1977*	*1 April 1977 to 30 April 1981*
Service charge	0.5	0.5
Interest rates[c]		
for different terms:		
up to 1 year	4.0	4.375
1–2 years	4.5	4.875
2–3 years	5.0	5.375
3–4 years	5.5	5.875
4–5 years	6.0	6.375

Sources: See Table A1.1.
Notes: See Table A1.1.

Table A1.3 Charges on credits effected since 1 May 1981

Period	*Service charge (%)*	*Interest rate*[c] *(%)*
1 May 1981 to 30 April 1982	0.5	6.25
1 May 1982 to 30 April 1984	0.5	6.6
1 May 1984 to 30 April 1986	0.5	7
1 May 1986 to 30 April 1987	0.5	5.89
1 May 1987 to 31 January 1988	0.5	5.8
1 February 1988 to 30 April 1988	0.5	6.15
1 May 1988 to 31 October 1988	0.5	5.5
1 November 1988 to 31 December 1988	0.5	7.38

Sources: See Table A1.1.
Notes: See Table A1.1.

APPENDIX A.2: OPPORTUNITY INTEREST RATES USED FOR THE CALCULATION OF INCOME TRANSFERS IN CREDITS FROM THE INTERNATIONAL MONETARY FUND'S COMPENSATORY FINANCING FACILITY

Period	*Opportunity interest rates*[a] *(%)*	*Period*	*Opportunity interest rates*[a] *(%)*
1963.I[b]	4.04	1976.I	8.48
1963.II[b]	4.04	1976.II	7.85
1964.I	4.04	1977.I	7.85
1964.II	3.76	1977.II	6.95
1965.I	3.76	1978.I	6.95
1965.II	4.88	1978.II	6.54
1966.I	4.88	1979.I	6.54
1966.II	5.52	1979.II	8.1
1967.I	5.52	1980.I	8.1
1967.II	6.17	1980.II	9.1
1968.I	6.17	1981.I	9.1
1968.II	6.46	1981.II	10.93
1969.I	6.46	1982.I	10.93
1969.II	7.54	1982.II	8.75
1970.I	7.54	1983.I	8.75
1970.II	8.07	1983.II	8.42
1971.I	8.07	1984.I	8.42
1971.II	7.38	1984.II	7.98
1972.I	7.38	1985.I	7.98
1972.II	6.93	1985.II	6.93
1973.I	6.93	1986.I	6.93
1973.II	7.51	1986.II	6.73
1974.I	7.51	1987.I	6.73
1974.II	8.21	1987.II	6.70
1975.I	8.21		
1975.II	8.48		

Sources: World Bank (c), various years. Own calculations for the years 1963–5 from the information on credit amounts and interest payments in World Bank (c)
Notes: [a]The average yearly credit costs of the World Bank are used as opportunity interest rates for the compensatory financing credits drawn in the respective periods. It is assumed in the calculation of income transfers that the opportunity interest rate remains constant for the whole term of the IMF credit.
[b]I, 1 January to 30 June; II, 1 July to 31 December.

APPENDIX A.3: INCOME TRANSFERS IN THE CREDITS FROM THE INTERNATIONAL MONETARY FUND'S COMPENSATORY FINANCING FACILITY BEFORE 1 JULY 1974

Country	Month and year of payment	Credit position (percentage excess of quota)	Magnitude of IMF payments (million SDR)	Actual grant equivalent[a] in the IMF credits (SDR)	Grant ratio[a] (%) of	
					gross payment (g^G)	net payment (g^N)
Afghanistan	6/68	42	4.8	434,047	9.04	9.09
Argentina	3/72	40	64.0	8,196,167	12.81	12.87
Bangladesh	12/72	50	62.5	9,012,572	14.42	14.49
Brazil	6/63	35	60.0	1,381,870	2.30	2.31
Burma	11/67	25	7.5	844,160	11.26	11.31
	9/71	30	6.5	962,772	14.81	14.89
	2/74	61	15.0	1,845,739	12.30	12.37
Burundi	6/70	28	2.5	199,126	7.97	8.00
Chile	12/71	25	39.5	6,578,854	16.66	16.74
	12/72	50	39.5	5,699,833	14.43	14.50
Colombia	3/67	73	18.9	936,888	4.96	4.98
	4/68	90	1.9	103,963	5.47	5.50
Dominican Republic	12/66	76	6.6	536,171	8.12	8.16
Ecuador	10/69	49	6.25	444,488	7.11	7.15
Egypt	6/63	91	16.0	25,115	0.16	0.16
	3/68	48	23.0	2,137,624	9.29	9.34
	8/73	33	47.0	7,027,740	14.95	15.03
El Salvador	12/69	56	6.25	700,544	11.21	11.27
Ghana	11/66	65	17.25	1,298,621	7.53	7.57
Guatemala	2/68	54	6.25	[illegible]	[illegible]	[illegible]

	12/67	51	1.0	107,662	10.77	10.82
Iceland	11/67	25	3.75	356,933	9.52	9.57
	11/68	50	3.75	286,625	7.64	7.68
India	12/67	61	90.0	7,554,317	8.39	8.43
	2/74	53	62.0	4,641,162	7.49	7.52
Iraq	11/67	25	17.5	654,235	3.74	3.76
Jamaica	3/74	25	13.25	1,487,014	13.94	14.01
Jordan	11/71	20	4.5	413,877	9.20	9.24
	1/73	7	2.85	79,387	2.79	2.80
Kampuchea[b]	3/72	25	6.25	6,218,750	99.50	100.00
	4/73	50	6.25	6,218,750	99.50	100.00
New Zealand	5/67	76	29.2	736,752	2.52	2.54
Peru	6/72	25	30.75	1,935,009	6.29	6.32
Philippines	5/73	49	38.75	3,359,615	8.67	8.71
Sri Lanka	3/67	79	19.5	1,065,439	5.46	5.49
	4/68	117	19.3	1,527,260	7.91	7.95
	1/72	76	19.45	2,010,594	10.34	10.39
	6/73	75	18.6	2,039,265	10.96	11.01
	2/74	104	5.9	691,622	11.72	11.78
Sudan	6/65	33	11.25	126,454	1.12	1.13
Syria	9/67	45	9.5	1,102,507	10.66	10.71
	1/72	46	12.5	1,135,734	9.09	9.13
Uruguay	2/68	38	9.5	693,283	7.30	7.33
	5/72	53	17.25	2,003,991	11.62	11.68
Zaire	7/72	25	28.25	3,532,637	12.50	12.57
Zambia	12/71	25	19.0	2,871,821	15.11	15.19
	8/72	50	19.0	2,365,956	12.45	12.51

Source: Herrmann 1983, Table A.4, on the basis of data sources cited therein
Notes: [a]For the definitions of grant equivalents, grant ratios and the methodology to compute the grants, see the text.
[b]It is assumed that Kampuchea will not repay its debt in future.

APPENDIX A.4: INCOME TRANSFERS IN THE CREDITS FROM THE INTERNATIONAL MONETARY FUND'S COMPENSATORY FINANCING FACILITY DISBURSED BETWEEN 1 JULY 1974 AND 30 APRIL 1981

Country	*Month and year of payment*	*Magnitude of IMF payments (million SDR)*	*Actual grant equivalents[a] in IMF credits (1,000 SDR)*	*Grant ratio[a] (%) of*	
				gross payment (g^G)	*net payment* (g^N)
Argentina	12/75	110.0	10,711.69	9.74	9.79
	3/76	110.0	7,713.06	7.01	7.05
Australia	7/76	332.5	30,463.32	9.16	9.21
Bangladesh	8/76	39.1	4,025.70	10.30	10.35
Barbados	1/77	3.5	287.76	8.22	8.26
	10/77	3.0	172.46	5.75	5.78
Bolivia	7/78	15.0	668.69	4.46	4.48
Burundi	11/79	9.5	957.86	10.08	10.13
Cameroon	7/76	17.5	1,722.13	9.84	9.89
Central African Republic	2/76	5.1	612.28	12.01	12.07
	1/81	9.0	1,061.26	11.79	11.85
Chad	8/76	6.5	709.42	10.91	10.97
	1/81	7.1	843.70	11.88	11.94
Chile	6/76	79.0	7,692.94	9.74	9.79
Congo	2/77	6.5	691.69	10.64	10.69
Costa Rica	10/79	20.5	2,066.28	10.08	10.13

Côte d'Ivoire	3/76	26.0	600.95	2.31	2.32
Cyprus	5/76	13.0	1,356,39	10.43	10.49
	1/79	9.9	425.71	4.30	4.32
Dominica	12/79	0.95	95.44	10.05	10.10
	2/81	1.95	232.46	11.92	11.98
Dominican Republic	9/76	21.5	2,141.12	9.96	10.01
	1/79	6.0	91.93	1.53	1.54
	9/79	27.5	1,471.66	5.35	5.38
Egypt	6/76	94.0	11,099.18	11.81	11.87
Equatorial Guinea	7/80	6.4	767.08	11.99	12.05
	4/81	4.7	609.84	12.98	13.04
Ethiopia	8/79	18.0	1,672,76	9.29	9.34
	12/79	18.0	1,893.25	10.52	10.57
Fiji	7/77	6.5	325.60	5.01	5.03
Gambia	3/77	3.5	159.28	4.55	4.57
	11/78	4.5	204.30	4.54	4.56
Greece	9/76	58.0	6,131.03	10.57	10.62
Grenada	4/81	2.1	202.39	9.64	9.69
Guinea Bissau	4/79	1.1	48.20	4.38	4.40
Guyana	12/76	10.0	1,102.37	11.02	11.08
	7/78[b]	8.75	398.45	4.55	4.58
	1/80[b]	6.25	907.67	14.52	14.60
Iceland	3/76	11.5	1,317.83	11.46	11.52
India	8/80	266.0	34,320.89	12.90	12.97
Israel	8/76	65.0	6,621.10	10.19	10.24
	9/78	72.4	3,228.65	4.46	4.48
Jamaica	9/76	13.25	1,487.52	11.23	11.28
	11/76	13.25	1,487.52	11.23	11.28
	6/78	15.75	885.91	5.62	5.65
	9/79	31.75	2,748.21	8.66	8.70

Appendix A.4 continued

Country	*Month and year of payment*	*Magnitude of IMF payments (million SDR)*	*Actual grant equivalents[a] in IMF credits (1,000 SDR)*	*Grant ratio[a] (%) of*	
				gross payment (g^G)	*net payment* (g^N)
	4/81	37.05	4,119.23	11.12	11.17
Kenya	9/76	24.0	1,973.22	8.22	8.26
	10/79	69.0	7,045.80	10.21	10.26
Korea	6/76	40.0	4,755.91	11.89	11.95
	7/80	160.0	20,642.92	12.90	12.97
Laos, PDR	6/76	3.25	412.83	12.70	12.77
	12/76	3.25	413.66	12.73	12.79
Liberia	12/79	20.5	2,094.39	10.22	10.27
Madagascar	7/80	29.2	3,769.35	12.91	12.97
Malawi	8/79	9.5	746.97	7.86	7.90
	11/79	9.5	865.92	9.11	9.16
Malaysia	8/76	93.0	3,065.14	3.30	3.31
Mali	3/80	5.1	469.94	9.21	9.26
Mauritania	4/76	6.5	827.31	12.73	12.79
	1/80	10.5	948.33	9.03	9.08
Mauritius	7/77	11.0	641.40	5.83	5.86
	4/81	40.5	5,020.88	12.40	12.46
Mexico	11/76	185.0	16,952.36	9.16	9.21
Morocco	4/76	56.5	7,409.42	13.11	13.18
	8/78	56.0	2,497.05	4.46	4.48
Nepal	7/78	9.5	399.35	4.20	4.22
	9/80	10.49	1,353.29	12.90	12.97
New Zealand	7/75	50.5	6,243.71	13.11	13.18
	4/76	50.5	[illegible]	[illegible]	[illegible]

	12/76	50.5	5,523.60	11.89	11.95
Nicaragua	5/79	17.0	509.82	3.00	3.01
	10/79	17.0	1,812.22	10.66	10.71
Pakistan	7/76	90.5	9,627.52	10.64	10.69
	4/77	27.0	2,352.37	8.71	8.76
Panama	12/76	18.0	1,821.32	10.12	10.17
Papua New Guinea	6/76	10.0	837.49	8.37	8.42
Peru	5/76	61.5	6,884.70	11.19	11.25
	9/78	61.5	2,999.03	4.88	4.90
Philippines	4/76	77.5	8,353.83	10.78	10.83
	6/79	44.2	1,922.70	4.35	4.37
	3/80	93.3	8,599.70	9.22	9.26
Portugal	7/76	58.5	5,600.02	9.57	9.62
	7/77	29.25	1,719.91	5.88	5.91
Romania	4/76	95.0	10,733.34	11.30	11.36
	9/77	47.5	2,866.22	6.03	6.06
	4/79	41.25	1,794.20	4.35	4.37
	5/80	121.25	11,182.70	9.22	9.27
St Lucia	4/81	2.7	206.23	7.64	7.68
St Vincent	3/81	1.3	156.74	12.06	12.12
Senegal	11/78	21.0	953.10	4.54	4.56
Sierra Leone	3/76	7.0	789.25	11.27	11.33
	9/76	5.5	604.78	11.00	11.05
Solomon Islands	4/79	1.05	5.76	0.55	0.55
South Africa	11/76	160.0	13,154.76	8.22	8.26
Spain	2/78	98.75	5,352.49	5.42	5.45
Sri Lanka	11/76	15.8	1,673.63	10.59	10.65
Sudan	3/75	18.0	1,751.01	9.73	9.78
	5/76	26.7	3,309.94	12.40	12.46
	9/78	21.3	950.30	4.46	4.48

Appendix A.4 continued

Country	Month and year of payment	Magnitude of IMF payments (million SDR)	Actual grant equivalents[a] in IMF credits (1,000 SDR)	Grant ratio[a] (%) of	
				gross payment (g^G)	net payment (g^N)
	11/79	36.0	2,631.93	7.31	7.35
	11/80[b]	21.8	3,265.01	14.98	15.05
	4/81[b]	45.7	8,565.49	18.74	18.84
Tanzania	4/76	21.0	2,670.19	12.72	12.78
	5/79	20.25	870.50	4.30	4.32
	9/80	15.0	1,632.95	10.89	10.94
Thailand	8/76	67.0	7,309.41	10.91	10.96
	7/78	68.75	3,010.78	4.38	4.40
Togo	8/76	7.5	696.59	9.29	9.33
Tunisia	8/77	24.0	1,202.21	5.01	5.03
Turkey	11/75	37.75	4,870.56	12.90	12.97
	4/76	37.75	4,603.95	12.20	12.26
	5/78	74.5	4,261.84	5.72	5.75
	2/80	71.6	6,464.96	9.03	9.07
Uganda	4/76	20.0	2,543.04	12.72	12.78
	8/79	5.0	464.84	9.30	9.35
	1/80	25.0	2,250.86	9.00	9.05
Uruguay	3/76	25.9	1,993.27	7.70	7.73
Vietnam	1/77	31.0	2,837.91	9.15	9.20
Western Samoa	11/75	0.5	47.87	9.57	9.62
	11/76	0.5	52.96	10.59	10.65
	2/77	0.5	47.79	9.96	10.01
	11/78	1.25	56.13	4.49	4.51

Yemen, PDR	5/76	2.5	264.97	10.60	10.65
Yugoslavia	5/79	138.5	6,024.08	4.35	4.37
	2/80	138.5	13,067.08	9.43	9.48
Zaire	3/76	56.5	7,183.27	7.70	7.73
	5/77	28.25	2,532.03	8.96	9.01
Zambia	11/75	19.0	2,363.89	12.44	12.50
	6/76	19.0	2,261.53	11.90	11.96
	4/77	19.0	1,655.37	8.71	8.75
	5/78	48.75	2,793.83	5.73	5.76

Sources: Herrmann (1983: Table A.5), for those credits which had already been fully repaid by the end of 1981. For all other credits, information on credit costs and opportunity interest rates was taken from Appendices A.1 and A.2. Data on payments and repayments were taken from the sources cited in Table 3.2. Own computations

Notes: [a]For the definitions of grant equivalents, grant ratios and the methodology to compute the grants, see the text.

[b]In these cases, the repayment was still overdue in 1989 and no information was available about the repayment date. It was assumed that a full repayment of the debt occurred at the end of the first year for which no information on repayments was available (1989).

APPENDIX A.5: INCOME TRANSFERS IN THE CREDITS FROM THE INTERNATIONAL MONETARY FUND'S COMPENSATORY FINANCING FACILITY DISBURSED AFTER 1 MAY 1981

Country	*Month and year of payment*	*Magnitude of IMF payments (million SDR)*	*Actual grant equivalents*[a] *in IMF credits (1,000 SDR)*	*Grant ratio*[a] *(%) of*	
				gross payment (g^G)	*net payment* (g^N)
Argentina	1/83	520.1	31,747.92	6.10	6.13
	1/85	275.0	7,386.13	2.69	2.70
	7/87	518.765	13,253.02	2.55	2.57
Bangladesh	2/82	36.9	2,645.03	7.17	7.20
	8/82	71.2	4,928.36	6.92	6.96
	4/85	54.95	1,549.12	2.82	2.83
	2/87	88.9	2,088.40	2.35	2.36
Barbados	10/82	12.6	857.63	6.81	6.84
Belize	6/83	3.6	228.41	6.34	6.38
Bolivia	1/83	17.9	1,092.28	6.10	6.13
	12/86	64.1	1,054.06	1.64	1.65
Brazil	12/82	498.8	33,492.11	6.71	6.75
	3/83	466.25	30,323.92	6.50	6.54
	5/84	247.9	10,861.26	4.38	4.40
Burma	12/82	25.6	1,794.30	7.01	7.04
	8/83	29.15	1,727.55	5.93	5.96
Chad	9/85	7.0	0[b]	0[b]	0[b]
Chile	1/83	295.0	18,007.62	6.10	6.13
	8/85	70.6	0[b]	0[b]	0[b]

Costa Rica	6/81	30.1	2,610.02	8.67	8.71
	9/83	18.6	1,072.56	5.77	5.80
Côte d'Ivoire	9/81	114.0	16,760.53	14.70	14.78
Dominican Republic	5/82	36.0	4,407.40	12.24	12.30
	1/83	42.75	2,748.33	6.43	6.46
	12/85	15.5	0[b]	0[b]	0[b]
Ecuador	11/83	85.4	5,191.96	6.08	6.11
	8/86	39.7	932.65	2.35	2.36
El Salvador	7/81	32.25	4,622.38	14.33	14.40
	7/82	32.3	2,215.22	6.86	6.89
Ethiopia	5/81	18.0	1,560,78	8.67	8.71
	2/86	35.3	0[b]	0[b]	0[b]
Fiji	2/82	13.5	1,785.45	13.23	13.29
	1/85	4.75	127.90	2.69	2.71
Gambia	6/81	9.0	865.29	9.61	9.66
	9/86	4.71	120.42	2.56	2.57
Ghana	8/83	120.5	3,720.21	3.09	3.10
	12/84	58.2	1,478.57	2.54	2.55
Guinea Bissau	9/81	1.9	288.77	15.20	15.27
Guyana	11/82	5.9	613.33	10.40	10.45
Honduras	1/82	23.3	3,002.71	12.89	12.95
	11/82	23.1	1,745.03	7.55	7.59
Hungary	12/82	72.0	4,776.54	6.63	6.67
Iceland	12/82	21.5	1,550.97	7.21	7.25
Indonesia	8/83	360.0	11,481.38	3.19	3.21
	5/87	462.9	12,286.93	2.65	2.67
Jamaica	8/82	19.4	1,429.94	7.37	7.41
	6/84	72.6	3,000.44	4.13	4.15
	3/87	40.9	960.84	2.35	2.36

Appendix A.5 continued

Country	Month and year of payment	Magnitude of IMF payments (million SDR)	Actual grant equivalents[a] in IMF credits (1,000 SDR)	Grant ratio[a] (%) of	
				gross payment (g^G)	net payment (g^N)
Jordan	1/85	57.4	1,540.76	2.68	2.70
Kenya	6/82	60.4	10,109.35	16.74	16.82
	12/85	37.9	0[b]	0[b]	0[b]
Korea	1/82	106.2	16,438.52	15.48	15.56
	6/84	279.7	11,735.89	4.20	4.22
Liberia	6/82	7.0	1,249.86	17.86	17.94
	10/82	27.7	2,553.12	9.22	9.26
Madagascar	7/82	21.8	1,414.49	6.49	6.52
	6/84	14.4	596.11	4.14	4.16
	5/86	16.1	511.36	3.18	3.19
Malawi	9/81	12.0	1,295.53	10.80	10.85
	3/83	12.2	722.75	5.92	5.95
	8/84	13.8	412.41	2.99	3.00
Malaysia	9/81	189.8	25,540.40	13.46	13.52
Mauritius	3/85	7.5	201.55	2.69	2.70
Morocco	4/82	236.4	33,013.36	13.97	14.04
	9/85	115.1	0[b]	0[b]	0[b]
Niger	7/83	12.0	636.90	5.31	5.33
	10/83	12.0	784.22	6.54	6.57
Pakistan	8/82	180.2	12,329.47	6.84	6.88
Panama	6/83	58.9	4,203.10	7.14	7.17
Peru	6/82	199.9	37,354.93	18.69	18.78
	5/84	74.7	3,815.26	5.11	5.13

Philippines	3/83	188.55	11,508.92	6.10	6.13
	10/86	224.1	5,264.30	2.35	2.36
Portugal	10/83	258.0	15,602.69	6.05	6.08
	8/84	54.6	1,500.05	2.75	2.76
Romania	6/81	169.5	15,306.85	9.03	9.08
Senegal	9/81	42.0	6,176.79	14.71	14.78
Sierra Leone	2/83	20.7	1,567.30	7.57	7.61
Solomon Islands	10/82	1.6	115.37	7.21	7.25
Somalia	3/85	32.6	1,004.45	3.08	3.10
South Africa	11/82	636.0	45,858.96	7.21	7.25
Sri Lanka	6/81	25.3	1,140.19	4.51	4.53
	8/82	39.2	2,151.53	5.49	5.52
Sudan	3/83	39.1	3,603.86	9.22	9.26
Swaziland	6/83	9.0	566.89	6.30	6.33
Tanzania	6/81	15.9	1,286.45	8.09	8.13
Thailand	7/81	186.05	27,329.42	14.69	14.76
	6/85	185.0	5,212.84	2.82	2.83
Tunisia	11/86	114.71	2,694.69	2.35	2.36
Uganda	6/81	45.0	3,966.25	8.81	8.86
	6/87	25.0	663.65	2.65	2.67
Uruguay	8/82	55.3	3,183.69	5.76	5.79
	10/85	66.1	0[b]	0[b]	0[b]
Western Samoa	6/83	1.15	75.19	6.54	6.57
Zaire	3/82	106.9	14,144.00	13.23	13.30
	12/83	114.5	7,379.66	6.45	6.48
	5/87	45.3	1,202.41	2.65	2.67
Zambia	12/82	34.0	3,211.85	9.45	9.49
	5/83	97.2	8,958.96	9.22	9.26
	2/86	68.8	0[b]	0[b]	0[b]

Appendix A.5 continued

Country	*Month and year of payment*	*Magnitude of IMF payments (million SDR)*	*Actual grant equivalents[a] in IMF credits (1,000 SDR)*	*Grant ratio[a] (%) of*	
				gross payment (g^G)	*net payment (g^N)*
Zimbabwe	3/83	56.1	3,424.76	6.10	6.14

Sources: Own computations. Data on payments and repayments were taken from the sources cited in Table 3.2. Information on credit costs and opportunity interest rates is from Appendices A.1 and A.2

Notes: [a]For the definitions of grant equivalents, grant ratios and the methodology to compute the grants, see the text. Information on repayments of credits was available up to 1988. In many cases, credits were not or not fully repaid in 1988. When the repayment was overdue in 1988, it was assumed that a full repayment of the debt occurred at the end of 1989. This was the case for some of the 1982 and 1983 drawings. Partially repaid drawings of 1984 were also assumed to be repaid at the end of 1989. In as far as later drawings were not fully repaid until 1988, it was assumed that the repayment would take place in equal shares in the remaining years (1985 and 1986 drawings) or in the last three years of the duration of the credit (1987 drawings).

[b]A zero grant equivalent was introduced in these cases rather than a negative grant equivalent. The IMF's interest rate *i* exceeded the average credit costs of the World Bank in the relevant period.

APPENDIX B: THE QUARTERLY MODEL OF THE MARKET FOR NATURAL RUBBER

Statistical details of estimated relationships and the calculation of seasonal adjustment factors can be found in the appendices of Burger and Smit (1989).

Production

Malaysia

Estates Peninsular Malaysia

$$\text{lqqme}_t = -0.171 - 0.242d_1 - 0.293d_2 + 0.108\text{lprm}_{t-1} + 0.247\text{lqqme}_{t-1} - 0.124d_{843}$$

Smallholdings Peninsular Malaysia

$$\text{lqqms}_t = -0.667 - 0.054d_1 - 0.197d_2 + 0.253\text{lprm}_t - 0.142d_{854} - 0.112d_{843} + 0.115d_{834}$$

East Malaysia

$$\text{lqqmi}_t = -0.180 + 0.061d_1 + 0.115d_2 + 0.060d_3 + 0.060\text{lprm}_t + 0.863\text{lqqmi}_{t-1} + 0.158(d_{851} - d_{852})$$

Indonesia

Estates

$$\text{lqqie}_t = -0.026 - 0.119d_1 - 0.122d_2 - 0.045d_3 + 0.144d_{85} + 0.290\text{lqqie}_{t-1} - 0.104d_{803}$$

Smallholdings

$$\text{lqqis}_t = -1.741 + 0.201\text{lpri}_t - 0.285d_{794} - 0.241(d_{814} - d_{843} + d_{862} - d_{873})$$

Thailand

$$\text{lqqt}_t = -0.749 + 0.141d_1 - 0.166d_2 + 0.1521\text{prt}_t - 0.504d_{774} + 0.211d_{844}$$

Philippines

$$\text{lqqp}_t = -0.485 + 0.068\text{lpn}_t + 0.841\text{lqqp}_{t-1}$$

India

$$\text{lqqin}_t = 0.325 - 0.514d_1 - 0.428d_2 - 0.478d_3$$

Cameroon

$$\text{lqqca}_t = 0.264 - 0.450d_1 - 0.372d_2 - 0.332d_3$$

Brazil

$$\text{lqqbr}_t = -0.113 - 0.078d_1 - 0.173d_2 - 0.182d_3$$

Definition of the variables used for the supply equations

lqq (natural) logarithm of the ratio of actual production and 'normal' production of Malaysian estates (suffix me), Malaysian smallholdings (ms), East Malaysian (mi), Indonesian estates (ie), Indonesian smallholdings (is), Thailand (t), Philippines (p), India (in), Cameroon (ca) and Brazil (br). For the concept and calculation of 'normal' production see the main text in Chapter 7

lpr logarithm of the ratio of world market (Singapore, RSS1) prices, converted into local currencies and adjusted for export duties (Malaysia and Thailand) and the domestic consumer price index (1980 = 100); suffixes refer to Malaysia (m), Thailand (t) and Indonesia (i)

lpn logarithm of the above mentioned RSS1 price

d_1, d_2 and d_3 dummy variables taking the value of 1 in the first, second and third quarters of each year and the value 0 otherwise

d_{xxx} dummy variable equal to 1 in 19*xx.x* and 0 otherwise

Consumption

World as a whole

$$\text{lsnw}_t = -0.454 + 0.161\text{lsnw}_{t-1} + 0.366\text{lsnw}_{t-2} - 0.024\text{lpr}_{t-1} + 0.0032t - 0.0591t$$

with the following definitions:

lsnw logarithm of the natural rubber share in total world rubber consumption

lpr logarithm of the ratio of the Singapore RSS1 price of natural rubber (in US dollars) and the US export unit value of styrene–butadiene rubber (in US dollars)

t trend (1 in 1974.1). This trend was assumed not to continue in the future, but to remain at the level of 1988.4

lt logarithm of the trend t

Price

$$\text{lpsd}_t = 7.192 + 0.636\text{lpsd}_{t-1} + 0.537\text{lpmom} + 0.233\text{lxsdr}_{t-1} + 1.655\text{lctw}_t - 2.012\text{lsq}_{t-2} - 0.901\text{lzndzb}_t - 0.161d_{791}$$

with the following definitions:

lpsd logarithm of RSS1 price in Singapore (spot) in US dollars per tonne

lctw logarithm of world total rubber consumption (1,000 tonnes), adjusted for seasonal fluctuations

lxsdr logarithm of exchange rate between US dollars and SDR

lsq_t logarithm of average world production of quarters $t-3$ through t (1,000 tonnes)

lpmom logarithm of price index (current US dollars) of minerals, ores and metals (1979–81 = 100) since 1986.4 excluding tin

lzndzb_t logarithm of $\text{znp}_{t-1} - \text{zbw}_t + \text{zbw}_{t-1}$, where znp are private world stocks (1,000 tonnes), seasonally adjusted; zbw is the total INRA buffer stock (1,000 tonnes)

d_{791} dummy variable, taking the value 1 in the quarter 79.1 and 0 otherwise

For simulation purposes, a relationship was estimated between the INRA's Daily Market Indicator Price (DMIP) and the Singapore RSS1 price based on the following relationship:

$$\text{psm}_t = -70.99 + 10.86\text{DMIP}_t$$

where psm is related to the Singapore RSS1 price by

$$\text{psm} = \text{ps}/\text{xs} * (\text{xs} + \text{xm})/2$$

ps is the Singapore price in Singapore dollars per tonne and xm and xs are the exchange rates against the US dollar of Singapore and Malaysia respectively, so that psm is the RSS1 price expressed in 'Singapore/Malaysian' currency, which is the denomination of the DMIP.

To arrive at the minimum (maximum) price in terms of the RSS1 spot price in Singapore, DMIP in this equation was replaced by the lower (upper) trigger-action price. An automatic adjustment mechanism of the reference price is incorporated in the model in line with the arrangements in INRA-1979: every six quarters, the reference price is adjusted by 5 per cent, if the average price of the preceding two quarters was outside the price range.

Sources for the data are the *Rubber Statistical Bulletin*, published by the International Rubber Study Group, UNCTAD's *Monthly Commodity Price Bulletin* and the *International Financial Statistics*, published by the IMF.

APPENDIX C: THE MODEL FOR THE SIMULATIONS OF THE WORLD COCOA MARKET

Consumption

$$\log(c_t) = \underset{(3.3)}{3.025} - \underset{(4.3)}{0.107} \log(pr_t) + \underset{(3.7)}{0.554} \log(c_{t-1}) + \underset{(3.2)}{0.205} \log(Y_t)$$

$$(1965\text{–}86;\ R^2 = 0.91)$$

where c is world grindings in 1,000 tonnes, from ICCO; pr is the world market price in SDR per tonne deflated by the consumer price index in major consuming countries, with data and weights according to Table 1 in ICCO (1988); and Y is the real GDP in consuming countries, from ICCO (taken from Pomp 1991). Absolute t-values are given in parentheses.

Price

$$\log(p_t) = \underset{(0.6)}{0.920} + \underset{(4.2)}{2.509} \log(c_t) + \underset{(16.2)}{0.867} \log(p_{t-1}) - \underset{(5.8)}{2.383} \log(q_t)$$

$$- \underset{(1.2)}{0.132} \log[z_{t-1} - (BS_t - BS_{t-1})] + \underset{(5.1)}{0.547} d_{76}$$

$$(1971\text{–}89;\ R^2 = 0.97)$$

where p is the world market price in SDR per tonne from ICCO, q is world production in 1,000 tonnes, from ICCO; z is world stocks, end of crop year, in 1,000 tonnes, from ICCO; BS is buffer stocks, 1,000 tonnes; and d_{76} is a dummy variable taking the value of 1 in 1976–7 and 0 in other years.

This equation and the consumption equation above are both estimated by instrumental variables, with logarithms of p and c, the endogenous variables, replaced by their estimates in the right-hand sides of the two equations; these estimates result from auxiliary estimations using all exogenous variables in the system; the procedure results in approximate two-stage least-squares estimates.

Production

Brazil

$$\log(q_t) = -1.496 + 0.881 \log(\mathrm{at}_{t-9} + 1.6\mathrm{ah}_{t-5}) + 0.351 \log(\mathrm{pb}_{t-1})$$
$$(0.3) \quad (1.3) \qquad\qquad\qquad\qquad (4.9)$$
$$(1986\text{–}8;\ R^2 = 0.84)$$

where at is the area of traditional varieties (1,000 ha), from ICCO; ah is the area of hybrid varieties (1,000 ha), from ICCO; and pb is the real producer price, from ICCO (taken from Pomp 1991).

Other producing countries are assumed not to respond to world market price changes in the period considered here; the rest of the world production is related to the major producers by

$$\log(\mathrm{qr}_t) = 0.075 + 0.274 \log(\mathrm{q}^7{}_t) + 0.638 \log(\mathrm{qr}_{t-3,\,t-1})$$
$$(0.1) \quad (1.4) \qquad\qquad (2.1)$$

where the last term stands for the average production in the past three years and q^7 is the production of the seven major producing countries, including Brazil, Côte d'Ivoire, Nigeria, Ghana, Cameroon, Malaysia and Ecuador (taken from Pomp 1991).

Prices in Brazil are related to world market prices by

$$\log(\mathrm{pb}_t) = -2.422 + 0.743 \log(\mathrm{pw}_t) + 0.384 \log(\mathrm{pb}_{t-1})$$
$$(2.3) \quad (4.5) \qquad\qquad (3.0)$$
$$(1968\text{–}85;\ R^2 = 0.77)$$

where pw is the world market price in US dollars per tonne and pb is the real producer price in Brazil, from ICCO (taken from Pomp 1991).

The above equations constitute the model for the evaluation of the ICCAs of 1980 and 1986. In the evaluation, it was assumed that production in Cameroon, Côte d'Ivoire, Ghana, Nigeria and Malaysia did not respond to world market price changes. See the text for further justification. The intervention mechanism by itself was modelled, but not actively used as all the cocoa that the ICCO was allowed to buy was indeed bought.

For the simulation of the free price transmission situation, producer prices in the four West African countries were related to exchange rate changes and world market price changes, taking 1980–1 as the basis. Hence, a change in world market price by 10 per cent from 1980–1 to 1981–2 would, *ceteris paribus*, lead to an equal change in producer prices. No changes in (re)planting were assumed to occur.

Supply elasticities in thc above countries were taken from Pomp (1991) as well. He estimated the following relationships.

Cameroon

$$\log(q_t) = \underset{(0.8)}{-7.106} + \underset{(1.2)}{1.894} \log(\text{at}_{t-9} + 1.48\text{ah}_{t-6}) + \underset{(2.3)}{0.418} \log(\text{pc}_{t-1})$$

$$(1969\text{–}88;\ R^2 = 0.45)$$

Côte d'Ivoire

$$\log(q_t) = \underset{(-2.0)}{-4.953} + \underset{(4.1)}{1.694} \log(\text{at}_{t-9} + 1.494\text{ah}_{t-5}) + \underset{(5.7)}{0.470} \log(\text{pi}_t)$$

$$(1974\text{–}85;\ R^2 = 0.97)$$

Ghana

$$\log(q_t) = \underset{(2.4)}{-10.252} + \underset{(3.1)}{2.011} \log(\text{at}_{t-9} + 1.63\text{ah}_{t-7}) + \underset{(2.2)}{0.303} \log(\text{pg}_{t-1})$$

$$(1971\text{–}88;\ R^2 = 0.89)$$

Nigeria

$$\log(q_t) = \underset{(2.9)}{-13.686} + \underset{(3.8)}{2.773} \log(\text{at}_{t-10} + 1.039\text{ah}_{t-9}) + \underset{(2.5)}{0.3} \log(\text{pn}_{t-1})$$

$$(1971\text{–}88;\ R^2 = 0.75)$$

In these equations, px stands for the real producer price in country x. If these prices become linked to the world market, the supply from farmers in Côte d'Ivoire should be determined simultaneously with consumption and prices. The system was solved iteratively, after which the necessary intervention could be calculated. This led to changes in the price, requiring a new loop. For each year, this process was continued until convergence.

Notes

2 THE ECONOMICS OF STABILIZATION: A HISTORICAL SURVEY

1 Based on the maximum and minimum of the daily market indicator price of the International Natural Rubber Organization, provided by the International Rubber Study Group.

3 THE INTERNATIONAL MONETARY FUND'S COMPENSATORY FINANCING FACILITY

1 Detailed information on the CFF can be found in Goreux (1980). A quantitative analysis of the stabilizing and redistributive effects of the CFF up to 1980 can be found in Herrmann (1983a). Green and Kirkpatrick (1982) discuss the extension of the CFF in 1981. The importance of the IMF financial facilities for the food-deficit countries is elaborated in Kaibni (1988). The extension in 1988 to a CCFF is discussed in Pownall and Stuart (1988).
2 Equatorial Guinea, Guinea and Kampuchea are excluded since no data on export earnings were available.
3 Herewith, the analysis is much more comprehensive than in earlier studies. The analysis of Herrmann (1983a) is based on a selection of twenty recipient countries which had received either the largest or the most compensatory financing payments up to 1980. The stabilization effects were calculated for the shorter period 1967–80 in this earlier study. Finger and DeRosa (1980) refer to all countries which made purchases through January 1979. The study is based on data for the period 1961–77. The paper by Kumar (1988) is based on all countries which made purchases from the CFF between 1975 and 1985. The latter study differs from this study since the drawings are distributed over the shortfall and the drawing year. Consequently, the stabilization effects that Kumar calculates are more favourable than those computed here.
4 The compensation year under the CFF is the most recent twelve-month period for which data are available. Hence, the compensation years under the CFF partly diverge from calendar years but only data for calendar years are available in published form.
5 See Cuddy and Della Valle (1978: 82 and Della Valle (1979: equation

(2)). See also the contributions of Duggan (1979) and Brown (1979) on this measure of instability.

6 The presented measure of instability is selected as follows. If at least one F value of the two regression equations is significant at the 5 per cent level, either v_{L}^{*} or v_{LL}^{*} is chosen according to whether $\bar{R}^2$ is higher for the linear or the loglinear trend. If the F value of both regression equations is insignificant at the 5 per cent level, the uncorrected CV is used.

7 In no case was the 'best' trend of export earnings changed by transactions under the CFF.

8 On the method, see Sachs (1984: 201).

9 The following analysis draws heavily upon Herrmann (1983a: Section 5.1). The methodology utilized there is applied here to a much broader country sample and to a comprehensive period of analysis (1963–87) and it is extended by a computation of risk benefits and transfer benefits. On the concept of risk benefits and its utility-theoretical foundation, see Newbery and Stiglitz (1981: Chapters 6 and 20).

4 COMMODITY-RELATED FINANCIAL COMPENSATION BY THE EUROPEAN COMMUNITY

1 All the cited articles refer to Lomé IV as far as earlier versions of the Convention are not mentioned explicitly. On the text of Lomé IV, see Commission of the EC (1990a). For details on STABEX and the STABEX-related text of the Third Lomé Convention, see Commission of the EC (1985). A very comprehensive overview of the transactions under STABEX is given in Commission of the EC (1981, 1988a). The most recent survey of STABEX transactions (Commission of the EC 1990b) was not yet available when the computation on the impacts of STABEX were carried out.

2 For the Comoros, Kiribati and Tuvalu, data on export earnings were insufficient. Hence, these countries were excluded.

3 The analysis in Herrmann (1983a: 19–22) refers to a selection of nineteen African, Caribbean and Pacific (ACP) countries, which received the highest or most payments under Lomé I, and to the relatively short period 1974–80. Bachou (1986: Chapter 5) reports some similar calculations but he restricts himself to twelve countries and covers the period 1975–83. Collins (1984) provides a historical simulation of the STABEX scheme for a selected country and product sample in the period 1960–80 where she abstracts from financial limitations and time-lags in the disbursements.

4 The payments under STABEX and their timing, which underlie the following computations, are presented in Herrmann (1990a).

5 The concentration on the direct effects of STABEX seems even more justified than in the analysis of the IMF's CFF. The magnitude and timing of STABEX payments is hardly predictable for ACP countries and for the banking sector given the limited resources in years of low world commodity prices. Additionally, the grant element under STABEX was so high that ACP countries had a strong incentive to use the system as a source of untied aid irrespective of its stabilization effects. The latter argument is even more valid under Lomé IV since the grant ratio is now

100 per cent for all ACP countries.

6 For detailed information on COMPEX, see Commission of the EC (1987a, b, 1988c). In general, COMPEX does not automatically cover all least developed countries as defined by the United Nations. There is a case-to-case decision for each individual country.

7 The provisions of SYSMIN under Lomé IV are contained in Part 3, Title II, Chapter 3 starting with Article 214. An overview of SYSMIN is given in Commission of the EC and European Investment Bank (1988: 11ff.).

5 FOOD SECURITY AND COMPENSATORY FINANCING: A DISCUSSION OF THE INTERNATIONAL MONETARY FUND'S CEREAL IMPORT FACILITY

1 For a broader discussion of alternative food insurance schemes, see Huddleston *et al.* (1984) and the earlier study of Konandreas *et al.* (1978). For an interesting theoretical analysis of the possibilities and difficulties of introducing food stabilization objectives in a compensatory financing scheme, see Green and Kirkpatrick (1980).

2 The food financing facility is described and analysed in Green and Kirkpatrick (1982). The provisions of the 1981 extension of the CFF are contained in Decision No. 6860 (81/81) which is published and summarized in IMF (b, 1982 issue).

3 Kaibni (1988) is even more distinct on this point. He blames 'the growth in global food output, especially in the food deficit countries themselves, and the large cereal stocks held in industrial countries which have contributed to low prices and facilitated food aid flows' for the limited use of the food financing facility. Since these flows will not necessarily last forever, he views the IMF policy as an important insurance policy contributing to world food security. A similar and positive evaluation of the food financing facility is given by Sahn and von Braun (1987: 324).

PART III COMMODITY ARRANGEMENTS: AN ECONOMIC EVALUATION OF CURRENT PROGRAMMES

1 A discussion of the merits and demerits of international commodity agreements is given in Gilbert (1987) and Gordon-Ashworth (1984). Earlier surveys on the performance of international commodity agreements include UNCTAD (1983b), Nappi (1979: 31ff.), Senti (1978: 19ff.), Law (1975: Sections 3 and 4), Reynolds (1978), Rowe (1965: Part II, Sections 10–13), Baranyai and Mills (1963: 87ff.). In particular, Nappi, Law and Rowe present long-term analyses of interventions on commodity markets dating back as far as 1930. The commodity agreements in the period 1902–45 are surveyed in J. S. Davis (1946). The experience with international commodity agreements after 1945 is discussed in Radetzki (1970: 38ff.) and US International Trade Commission (1975). It is a common feature of this literature that the effectiveness of agreements is evaluated, but the hypothetical situations without agreements are not explicitly modelled.

6 THE INTERNATIONAL COFFEE AGREEMENT

1 For details on the 1983 ICA, see ICO (1982). Various ICAs are discussed in Pieterse and Silvis (1988) and Economist Intelligence Unit (1987). Important studies on the world coffee economy include Fisher (1972), Parikh (1974), de Vries (1975b), Ford (1977), Akiyama and Duncan (1982a), Marshall (1983) and Vogelvang (1988). Important data sources on the world coffee economy included ICO (1988a, b, c, d).
2 On the traditional surplus concept and its extensions, see Just *et al.* (1982) and Boadway and Bruce (1984).
3 On the details of the computations, see Herrmann (1986a, 1988a).
4 The fact that a purely stabilizing agreement also includes redistributive elements is ignored here. For an analysis of this issue, see Turnovsky (1978: 119ff.).
5 This assumption means that exports in the hypothetical situation of not having an ICA would not be higher than in the existing situation with quotas. Clearly, this is a restrictive assumption, as individual exporting member countries might withhold potential exports under the quota scheme and possibly would not transmit their whole oversupply to the unregulated market. This is due to the fact that increasing exports to the non-member market are penalized indirectly. They reduce national stocks and therefore future quotas in the regulated market (Article 35 of the 1983 ICA). Hence, the calculated gains in economic welfare according to equation (6.7) have to be interpreted as maximum welfare gains in the short-term analysis.
6 The following empirical analysis draws heavily upon Herrmann (1988b) where the international allocation of aid under the ICA is elaborated in much more detail.
7 TS is specified for an earlier period than 1982 and 1983 because this helps to avoid causal relationships between TS and GNPC, which is measured as an average of 1982 and 1983. Because of a positive income elasticity of coffee demand, TS would otherwise be a function of the GNP variable.
8 The welfare impacts arising from the ICA and from participation in the ICA are elaborated in Herrmann (1988a). Implications of a potential withdrawal of importing member countries are also analysed in Jaramillo (1986), based on aggregate world price effects of the ICA taken from an earlier version of Herrmann (1986b). Optimal national pricing policies from the individual coffee-exporting country's point of view are discussed in Jaramillo (1989) and Bohman (1991).

7 THE INTERNATIONAL NATURAL RUBBER AGREEMENT

1 The following regression was employed. Let lp be the log of the average price in Singapore dollars per tonne, and ls be the log of the size of the buffer stock (in 1,000 tonnes). The various simulation results reported in Table 8.5 are used to estimate the relationship

$$\text{lp} = 1.558 + \underset{(5.8)}{0.00845}\text{ls}$$

with a t value as indicated and R^2 equal to 0.81. The adjustment of the actual average prices is

$$p\text{-adj} = \frac{p\text{-actual}}{p\text{-estimated} \times p(100)}$$

where p-estimated follows from the regression and $p(100)$ is the estimated value of the price at a buffer stock size of 100. This value is 1992.8.

9 COMMODITY PROTOCOLS

1 An interesting recent analysis of the banana protocol, especially on policy implications of the EC Single Market as from 1993, is provided by Matthews (1992). See also the literature cited therein.
2 All articles mentioned in this section, unless otherwise stated, are part of Protocol 8 under the Fourth Lomé Convention. Economic analyses of the sugar protocol include Schmitz and Koester (1981), Koester and Schmitz (1982), Schmitz (1982, 1984), the country study of Strangmann (1981) and Koch (1989, 1990). An analysis of the implications of the sugar protocol for Mauritius is given in Wolffram and Beckers (1989). A description of the sugar market and the EC sugar policy is included in Bureau of Agricultural Economics (1985), Grosskopf (1979) and Fennell (1987). The political background of the sugar and beef protocols is discussed in Gruber (1987).
3 The countries mentioned in Article 3 are Barbados, Fiji, Guyana, Jamaica, Kenya, Madagascar, Malawi, Mauritius, Congo, PDR, Swaziland, Tanzania, Trinidad and Tobago and Uganda. Special rules in the annex refer to Belize, St Kitts and Nevis and Surinam.
4 Evidence on a mixed price policy of this sort is reported in Strangmann (1981: 122) and analysed in more detail in Schmitz and Koester (1981 42ff.).
5 It has to be borne in mind that the income transfers are computed on the basis of gross export earnings rather than net export earnings. Cif import prices, as shown in Table 9.2, are utilized as an approximation for export prices. Hence, export prices include cost, insurance and freight.
6 It can easily be seen from Table 9.3 that the per capita income transfers are not normally distributed. Hence, the Bravais–Pearson correlation coefficient is not applicable to the original data of per capita income transfers and GDPs per capita. GDP per capita data are taken from Summers and Heston (1988).
7 All articles mentioned in this section are part of Protocol 7 under the Fourth Lomé Convention. There are fewer economic analyses on the impacts of the beef protocol than on those of the sugar protocol. Relevant studies include P.M. Schmitz (1984) and von Massow (1983, 1984). The study of Tangermann and Krostitz (1982) includes the beef protocol within a more general analysis of protectionism in the livestock sector.
8 The quota for Kenya is more a symbolic one, since this country does not fulfil the animal health regulations set by the EC (Schnoor 1989: 35, 56).
9 The computations are documented in much more detail in Weiss (1991).
10 The NIMEXE numbers are those which have been used for the relevant sub-categories of beef and veal since 1988. The corresponding categories up to 1987 were 0201.15, 0201.24, 0201.25 and 0201.27.

Bibliography

Adams, F.G. and Behrman, J.R. (1982) *Commodity Exports and Economic Development. The Commodity Problem and Policy in Developing Countries.* Lexington, MA: Heath.

Adams, R. (1982) 'IFPRI research and the creation of the IMF cereal import facility', Note, International Food Policy Research Institute, Washington, DC.

Akiyama, T. and Duncan, R.C. (1982a) 'Analysis of the world coffee market', World Bank Staff Commodity Working Paper 7, Washington, DC.

—— and —— (1982b) 'Analysis of the world cocoa market', World Bank Staff Working Paper 8, Washington, DC.

Akiyama, T. and Varangis, P. (1990) 'Impact of the international coffee agreement's export quota system on the world coffee market', *World Bank Economic Review* 4(2): 152–73.

Anderson, R.W. and Gilbert, C.L. (1988) 'Commodity agreements and commodity markets: lessons from tin', *Economic Journal* 98: 1–15.

Arrow, K.J. (1965) *Aspects of the Theory of Risk Bearing,* Yrjö Jahnsson Lectures, Helsinki: Academic Bookstore.

Attanasio, O.P. and Weber, J. (1988) 'Intertemporal substitution, risk aversion and the Euler equation for consumption', *Economic Journal* 99 (supplement): 59–73.

Bachou, S.A. (1986) 'An evaluation of trade preference and compensatory financing arrangements in the framework of the Lomé regime', Ph.D. Thesis, University of Notre Dame, Notre Dame, Indiana.

Balassa, B. (1986) 'Policy responses to exogenous shocks in developing countries', *American Economic Review* 76(2): 75–8.

— (1989) 'Temporary windfalls and compensation arrangements', *Weltwirtschaftliches Archiv,* 125: 97–113.

Baranyai, L. and Mills, J.C. (1963) *International Commodity Agreements,* Mexico: Centro de Estudios Monetarios Latinamericanos.

Bartens, A. and Mosolff, H. (eds) *Zuckerwirtschaft-Zuckerwirtschaftliches Taschenbuch,* Berlin, various years.

Behrman, J.R. (1978a) *Development, The International Economic Order, and Commodity Agreements,* Perspectives on Economics Series, Reading, MA: Addison Wesley.

—— (1978b) 'International commodity agreements: an evaluation of the UNCTAD Integrated Programme for Commodities', in F.G. Adams and

S.A. Klein (eds) *Stabilizing World Commodity Markets*, Lexington, MA: Heath, pp. 295–321.

—— (1987) 'Commodity price instability and economic goal attainment in developing countries', *World Development* 15: 559–73.

Behrman, J.R. and Tinakorn-Ramangkura, P. (1982) 'Evaluating integrated schemes for commodity market stabilization', in F.A. Adams and J.R. Behrman (eds) *Econometric Modeling of World Commodity Policy*, Lexington, MA: Toronto, pp. 147–74.

Bevan, D., Collier, P. and Gunning, J.W. (1990a) 'Economic policy in countries prone to temporary trade shocks', in M. Scott and D. Lal (eds) *Public Policy and Economic Development, Essays in Honour of Ian Little*, Oxford: Clarendon Press.

—— and —— (1990b) *Controlled Open Economies*, Oxford: Clarendon Press.

Bird, G. (1987) 'Commodity price stabilization and international financial policy', in H.W. Singer, N. Hatti and R. Tandon (eds) *International Commodity Policy (Part II)*, New Delhi: Ashish Publishing House, pp. 805–33.

Boadway, R.W. and Bruce, N. (1984) *Welfare Economics*, Oxford: Blackwell.

Bohman, M.E. (1991) 'The impact of the International Coffee Agreement on policy in exporting countries', Ph.D. Thesis, University of California, Davis.

Bohman, M.E. and Jarvis, L. (1990) 'The International Coffee Agreement: Economics of the nonmember market', *European Review of Agricultural Economics* 17: 99–118.

Bohman, M.E., Jarvis, L. and Barichello, R. (1991) 'Domestic rent seeking effects of the International Coffee Agreement: an Indonesian case study', Poster paper presented at the XXI International Conference of Agricultural Economists, 22–9 August, Tokyo, Japan.

Boussard, J.-M. (1990) 'Les stratégies anti-risques des producteurs, limitent-elles leur productivité?', paper presented at Club du Sahel/CIRAD seminar, 12–14 September, Montpellier.

Braun, J. von and Huddleston, B. (1988) 'Implications of food aid for price policy in recipient countries, in J.W. Mellor and R. Ahmed (eds) *Agricultural Price Policy for Developing Countries*, Baltimore MD: The Johns Hopkins University Press, pp. 253–62.

Brodsky, D.A. (1980) 'Decomposable measures of economic instability', *Oxford Bulletin of Economics and Statistics* 42: 361–74.

Brown, A. (1979) 'On measuring the instability of time series data: a comment', *Oxford Bulletin of Economics and Statistics* 41: 249–50.

Bureau of Agricultural Economics (1985) *Agricultural Policies in the European Community, Their Origins, Nature and Effects on Production and Trade*, Policy Monograph 2, Canberra.

Burger, K. and Smit, H.P. (1989) 'Long-term and short-term analysis of the natural rubber market', *Weltwirtschaftliches Archiv* 125 (4): 718–47.

Burger, K. and Wansink, D. (1990) 'An integrated model of the markets for jute and jute goods', *Tijdschrift voor Sociaalwetenschappelijk Onderzoek van de Landbouw* 5 (4): 350–72.

Calvo, G.A. (1988) 'Costly trade liberalizations. Durable goods and capital mobility', *IMF Staff Papers* 35: 461–73.

Carr, J.D., Jumpasut, P. and Smit, H.P. (1988) *The World Rubber Economy, Changes and Challenges*, International Rubber Study Group, London.

Chandavarkar, A.G. (1984) *The International Monetary Fund. Its Financial Organization and Activities*, IMF Pamphlet Series 42, International Monetary Fund, Washington, DC.

Chhabra, J., Grilli, E. and Pollak, P. (1978) 'The world tin economy: an econometric analysis', in *World Bank Commodity Models* 1, World Bank Staff Commodity Working Paper 6, Washington, DC: World Bank.

Chu, K.–Y. and Morrison, T.K. (1986) 'World non-oil primary commodity markets, a medium-term framework of analysis', *IMF Staff Papers* 33: 139–84.

Collins, M. (1984) 'Die Stabilisierung der Exporterlöse in der AKP-EWG-Konvention von Lomé. Eine ökonomische Analyse des bestehenden Systems und Vorschläge zu seiner Verbesserung', Ph.D. Thesis, Bonn.

Commission of the EC (1981) 'Zusammenfassender Bericht über das mit dem Abkommen von Lomé eingeführte System zur Stabilisierung der Ausfuhrerlöse in den Anwendungsjahren 1975 bus 1979', SK (81), 1104, Brussels.

—— (1985) *Stabex Users' Guide, Third ACP–EEC Convention*, Brussels.

—— (1987a) 'Council Regulation (EEC) No. 428/87, February, setting up a system of compensation for loss of export earnings for least-developed countries not signatory to the third ACP–EEC convention', *Official Journal of the European Communities*, 13 February.

—— (1987b) 'Council Regulation (EEC) No. 429/87 of 9 February 1987 laying down detailed rules for the implementation of regulation (EEC) No. 428/87 setting up a system of compensation for loss of export earnings for least-developed countries not signatory to the third ACP–EEC convention', *Official Journal of the European Communities* L43/3, 13 February.

—— (1988a) 'STABEX-Relevé des Transferts Effectués au Titre des Années d'Application 1975–1987', Brussels.

—— (1988b) *Bulletin of the EC* 12, Brussels.

—— (1988c) 'Report from the Commission on the Administration during 1987 of the system of compensation for loss of export earnings for least-developed countries not signatory to the third ACP–EEC Convention', COM (88) 82 final, Brussels, 1 March.

—— (1990a) 'Lomé IV Convention', *The Courier Africa–Caribbean–Pacific–European Community* 120, March–April.

—— (1990b) 'STABEX, 1975–1989 transfers', unpublished document, November, Brussels.

—— (a) *Gesamtbericht über die Tätigkeit der Europäischen Gemeinschaften*, Brussels, Luxembourg, various years.

—— (b) *Bericht der Kommmission an den Rat über das Funktionieren des mit dem AKP–EWG–Abkommen und dem Beschluss über die Assoziation der ÜLG mit der EWG eingeführten Systems zur Stabilisierung der Ausfuhrerlöse*, Brussels, various years.

Commission of the EC and European Investment Bank (1988) 'Financing of mining projects', *The Courier African–Caribbean–Pacific–European Community* 109 (May–June): 11–14.

Corden, W.M. (1984) 'Booming sector and Dutch Disease economics: survey and consolidation', *Oxford Economic Papers* 36: 359–80.

The Courier Africa–Caribbean–Pacific–European Community, Brussels, various issues.
Cuddington, J. (1989) 'Commodity export booms in developing countries', *World Bank Research Observer* 4(2): 143–65.
Cuddy, J.D.A. and Della Valle, P.A. (1978) 'Measuring the instability of time series data', *Oxford Bulletin of Economics and Statistics* 40: 79–85.
Davis, J.M. (1983) 'The economic effects of windfall gains in export earnings, 1975–1978', *World Development* 11(2): 119–39.
Davis, J.S. (1946) 'Experience under intergovernmental commodity agreements, 1902–1945', *Journal of Political Economy* 54: 193–220.
Deaton, A. and Laroque, G. (1990) 'On the behaviour of commodity prices', NBER Working Paper 3439.
Della Valle, P.A. (1979) 'On the instability index of time series data: a generalization', *Oxford Bulletin of Economics and Statistics* 41: 247–8.
Desai, M. (1966) 'An econometric analysis of the world tin economy, 1948–1961', *Econometrica* 34: 105–34.
Deutsche Bundesbank (1990) 'Statistische Beihefte zu den Monatsberichten der Deutschen Bundesbank', Reihe 5, *Die Währungen der Welt*, February issue, Frankfurt a.M.
Deutscher Kaffee-Verband e.V., *Jahresbericht*, Hamburg, various years.
Diakosavvas, D. (1989) 'On the causes of food insecurity in less developed countries: an empirical evaluation', *World Development* 17(2): 223–35.
Diakosavvas, D. and Scandizzo, P.L. (1991) 'Trends in the terms of trade of primary commodities, 1900–1982: the controversy and its origins', *Economic Development and Cultural Change* 39 (2): 231–64.
Duggan, J.E. (1979) 'On measuring the instability of time series data', *Oxford Bulletin of Economics and Statistics* 41: 239–46.
Eaton, J., Gersovitz, M. and Stiglitz, J.E. (1986) 'The pure theory of country risk', *European Economic Review* 30: 481–513.
Economist Intelligence Unit (1987) *Coffee to 1991, Controlling a Surplus*, EIU Commodity Outlook Series, Special Report, 1086, London.
Epstein, L.G. (1988) 'Risk aversion and asset prices', *Journal of Monetary Economics* 22: 179–92.
Expert Group (1985) 'Compensatory financing of export earnings shortfalls', Report of the Expert Group, UNCTAD, TD/B/1029/Rev.1, New York.
FAO (Food and Agricultural Organization) (1985) *Sugar: Major Trade and Stabilization Issues in the Eighties*, FAO Economic and Social Development Paper 50, Rome.
—— (1987) *World Crop and Livestock Statistics 1948–1985*, Rome.
—— (a) *FAO Trade Yearbook*, Rome, various issues.
—— (b) *FAO Production Yearbook*, Rome, various years.
—— (c) *Commodity Review and Outlook*, Rome, various years.
Fennell, R. (1987) *The Common Agricultural Policy of the European Community*, 2nd edn, London: Granada.
Finger, J.M. and DeRosa, D.A. (1980) 'The compensatory financing facility and export instability', *Journal of World Trade Law* 14: 14–22.
Fisher, B.S. (1972) *The International Coffee Agreement, A Study in Coffee Diplomacy*, Praeger Special Studies in International Economics and Development, London: Praeger.
Fleming, M., Rhomberg, R. and Bouissonneault, L. (1963) 'Export norms

and their role in compensatory financing', *IMF Staff Papers* 10: 97–149.
Ford, D.J. (1977) 'Coffee supply, trade, and demand: an econometric analysis of the world market, 1930–69', Part 1 and 2, Ph.D. Thesis, University of Pennsylvania, Philadelphia.
—— (1978) 'Simulation analyses of stabilization policies in the international coffee market', in F.G. Adams and J.R. Behrman (eds) *Econometric Modeling of World Commodity Policy*, Lexington, MA: Heath.
Fox, W. (1974) *Tin: The Working of an Agreement*, London: Mining Journal Books.
Frankel, J.A. (1984) 'Commodity prices and money: lessons from international finance', *American Journal of Agricultural Economics* 66 (5): 560–6.
Gardner, B.L. (1979) *Optimal Stockpiling of Grain*, Lexington, MA: Heath.
Gemmill, G. (1985) 'Forward contracts or international buffer stocks? A study of their relative efficiencies in stabilizing commodity export earnings', *Economic Journal* 95: 400–17.
Ghosh, S., Gilbert, C. and Hughes Hallett, A. (1987) *Stabilizing Speculative Commodity Markets*, Oxford: Clarendon Press.
Gilbert, C.L. (1985) 'Futures trading and the welfare evaluation of commodity price stabilization', *Economic Journal* 95: 637–61.
—— (1986) 'Commodity price stabilization: the Massell model and multiplicative disturbances', *Quarterly Journal of Economics* 100: 635–40.
—— (1987) 'International commodity agreements: design and performance', *World Development* 15 (5): 591–616.
Gordon-Ashworth, F. (1984) *International Commodity Control, A Contemporary History and Appraisal*, Croom Helm Commodity Series, London: Croom Helm.
Goreux, L.M. (1977) 'Compensatory financing: the cyclical pattern of export shortfalls', *IMF Staff Papers* 24: 613–41.
—— (1980) *Compensatory Financing Facility*, IMF Pamphlet Series 34, International Monetary Fund, Washington, DC.
—— (1981) 'Compensatory financing for fluctuations in the cost of cereal imports', in A. Valdés (ed.) *Food Security for Developing Countries*, Boulder, CO: Westview Press, pp. 307–32.
Green, C. and Kirkpatrick, C. (1980) 'Insulating countries against fluctuations in domestic production and exports: an analysis of compensatory financing schemes', Discussion Paper 16, Department of Economics, University of Manchester, Manchester.
—— (1982) 'The IMF's food financing facility', *Journal of World Trade and Law* 16: 265–73.
Grilli, E. and Maw Cheng Yang (1988) 'Primary commodity prices, manufactured goods prices, and the terms of trade of developing countries: what the long run shows', *The World Bank Economic Review* 2(1): 1–47.
Grosskopf, W. (1979) *EG-Zuckermarktpolitik*, Landwirtschaft-Angewandte Wissenschaft, Heft 224, Münster-Hiltrup.
Gruber, L. (1987) *Landwirtschaftliche Kooperation zwischen Europäischer Gemeinschaft und Afrika im Rahmen der Lomé-Abkommen.* Fallstudien zum Zucker- und Rindfleischhandel, Hamburger Beiträge zur Afrika-Kunde 30, Institut für Afrika-Kunde, Hamburg.
Guitian, M. (1981) *Fund Conditionality*, IMF Pamphlet Series 38, Inter-

national Monetary Fund, Washington, DC.
Gustafson, R.L. (1958) 'Implications of recent research on optimal storage rules', *Journal of Farm Economics* 40: 290–300.
Hazell, P.B.R. and Scandizzo, P.L. (1975) 'Market intervention policies when production is risky', *American Journal of Agricultural Economics* 57: 641–9.
Hazell, P.B.R., Jaramillo, M. and Williamson, A. (1990) 'The relationship between world price instability and the prices farmers receive in developing countries', *Journal of Agricultural Economics* 41 (2): 227–40.
Hemphill, W.L. (1974) 'The effect of foreign exchange receipts on imports of less developed countries', *IMF Staff Papers* 21: 637–77.
Herrmann, R. (1981) *Exportinstabilität auf agrarischen Rohstoffmärkten-Situationsanalyse und Eingriffsmöglichkeiten*, Agrarökonomische Studien, Band 4, Kiel: Wissenschaftsverlag Vauk.
—— (1983a) *The Compensatory Financing System of the International Monetary Fund, An Analysis of its Effects and Comparisons with Alternative Systems*, Forum 4, Kiel: Wissenschaftsverlag Vauk.
—— (1983b) 'The effects of partial international price stabilization on the stability of national export earnings', *The Developing Economies* 11: 207–24.
—— (1986a) 'Evaluation of the buffer stock policy in the world cocoa market: a Box/Jenkins approach', *Studies in Economic Analysis* 10 (1): 34–59.
—— (1986b) 'Free riders and the redistributive effects of international commodity agreements: the case of coffee', *Journal of Policy Modeling* 8: 597–621.
—— (1988a) *Internationale Agrarmarktabkommen. Analyse ihrer Wirkungen auf den Märkten für Kaffee und Kakao*, Kieler Studien 215, Tübingen.
—— (1988b) 'The international allocation of trade-tied aid: a quantitative analysis for the export quota scheme in coffee', *Weltwirtschaftliches Archiv* 124(4): 675–700.
—— (1989) 'National interests in international agricultural policy', in S. Bauer and W. Henrichsmeyer (eds) *Agricultural Sector Modelling*, Proceedings of the Sixteenth Symposium of the European Association of Agricultural Economists (EAAE) Bonn, April 14–15 1988, Kiel: Wissenschaftsverlag Vauk, pp.183–92.
—— (1990a) 'Economic effects of financial stabilization schemes in the Convention of Lomé: STABEX, COMPEX and SYSMIN', Discussion Papers in Agricultural Economics 4, Institute of Agricultural Policy and Market Research, University of Giessen, Giessen.
—— (1990b) 'National interests in international commodity agreements: a theoretical framework and quantitative results for the export quota scheme in coffee', in A. Maunder and A. Valdés (eds) *Agriculture and Governments in an Interdependent World*, Proceedings of the Twentieth International Conference of Agricultural Economics, Buenos Aires, Argentina, August 24–31, 1988, Aldershot: Dartmouth Publishing Company, pp. 697–707.
Herrmann, R. and Kirschke, D. (1987) 'The analysis of price uncertainty: theoretical issues and empirical measurement on the world coffee market', *Asian Economies* 62: 24–44.

Herrmann, R. and Schmitz, P.M. (1984) 'Stabilizing producers' revenue by fixing agricultural prices within the EC?', *European Review of Agricultural Economics* 11: 395–414.

Herrmann, R., Burger, K. and Smit, H.P. (1990) 'Commodity policy: price stabilization versus financing', in L.A. Winters and D. Sapsford (eds) *Primary Commodity Prices: Economic Models and Economic Policy*, Cambridge: Cambridge University Press, pp. 240–90.

Hewitt, A.P. (1983) 'Stabex: an evaluation of the economic impact over the first five years', *World Development* 11: 1005–27.

—— (1990) 'Stabex: the scope for alternative systems', in K. Kiljunen (ed.) *Region-to-Region Cooperation between Developed and Developing Countries. The Potential for Mini-NIEO*, Aldershot: Avebury, pp. 129–43.

Hirschler, H.S. (1978) 'Kompensatorische Finananzierungsmodelle und ihre Bedeutung für die wirtschaftlich weniger entwickelten Länder', Ph.D. Thesis, Frankfurt a.M.

Hoffmeyer, M., Schrader, J.V. and Tewes, T. (1988) *Internationale Rohstoffabkommen. Ziele, Ansatzpunkte, Wirkungen*, Institut für Weltwirtschaft an der Universität Kiel, Kiel.

Hofman, P.S. (1988) 'Regulering van Grondstoffenmarkten: Internationale Overeenkomsten en Multinationale Ondernemingen (Regulation of Primary Commodity Markets: International Agreements and Transnational Corporations)', Working Paper 1, SOMO, Amsterdam.

Horsefield, J.K. (1969) 'Charges, repurchases, selection of currencies', in J.K. Horsefield (ed.) *The International Monetary Fund 1945–65. Twenty Years of International Monetary Cooperation. Vol. II: Analysis*, Washington, DC: IMF, 428–67.

Horvath, J. and Minassian, D.P. (1976) 'Appendix: the proportion of true grant in foreign aid: a mathematical formulation', in J. Horvath *Chinese Technology Transfer to the Third World. A Grants Economy Analysis*, Praeger, pp. 86–93.

Huddleston, B. (1981) 'Responsiveness of food aid to variable import requirements', in A. Valdés (ed.) *Food Security for Developing Countries*, Boulder, CO: Westview Press, pp. 287–306.

Huddleston, B., Johnson, D.G., Reutlinger, S. and Valdés, A. (1984) *International Finance for Food Security*, Baltimore, MD: The Johns Hopkins University Press.

ICCO (International Cocoa Organization) (1988) *The World Cocoa Economy: Review of Recent Developments and Outlook for the Next Three Years*, London, September.

—— *Quarterly Bulletin of Cocoa Statistics*, London, various issues.

ICO (International Coffee Organization) (1982) 'International Coffee Agreement 1983', Copy of the authenticated text, London, October.

—— (1983) 'Imports and exports by non-members and comparisons between imports by non-members and export by exporting members to non-members, 1971 to 1982', EB 2272/83(E) London, 7 June.

—— (1985) 'Unit values of exports of coffee to members and to non-members by quarter in coffee years 1981/82 to 1983/84', EB 2382/84 (E) Rev.4, London, 8 January.

—— (1988a) 'Stocks, production and availability of coffee in exporting member countries, crop years and coffee years 1968 to 1988', WP Agree-

ment 11/88 (E), Rev.2, London, 20 February.
—— (1988b) 'Exports, quotas and value of exports, coffee years 1965/66 to 1987/88', WP Agreement 13/88 (E), Rev.2, London, 21 February.
—— (1988c) 'Imports, re-exports and disappearance, coffee years 1965/66 to 1987/88', WP Agreement 14/88 (E) Rev.2, London, 17 February.
—— (1988d) 'Indicator prices, unit values and retail prices, long term series', WP Agreement 15/88 (E), Rev.2, London, 22 February.
IMF (International Monetary Fund) (1981) *Der internationale Währungsfonds*, Washington, DC: IMF.
—— (a) *International Financial Statistics*, February issues, Washington, DC: IMF, various years.
—— (b) *International Financial Statistics: Yearbook*, Washington, DC: IMF, various years.
—— (c) *Annual Report*, Washington, DC: IMF, various years.
—— (d) *Direction of Trade Statistics: Yearbook*, Washington, DC: IMF, various issues.
—— (e) *IMF Survey*, Washington, D.C., various years, various issues.
International Bank for Reconstruction and Development (1973) 'A review of the world tin market: problems and prospects, commodities and export projections division', Commodity Paper 3(7/73) Washington, DC.
International Rubber Study Group (1986) *World Rubber Statistics Handbook*, vol. 3, London.
—— *Rubber Statistical Bulletin*, various issues.
International Sugar Organization (ed.) *International Sugar Year Book*, London, various years.
International Tin Council (1979) *Tin Production and Investment*, London: The International Tin Council.
International Tin Research Institute (undated) *A Guide to Tin*, Publication 540, London: International Tin Research Institute.
International Trade Center (1987) *Cocoa – A Trader's Guide*, Commodity Handbook, International Trade Centre, Geneva: UNCTAD/GATT.
Jaramillo, C.F. (1986) 'EC Mercado Mundial del Café: Efectos del Retiro de Paises Importadores de la OIC', *Coyuntura Económica* 16(4): 179–94.
—— (1989) 'Supply response and optimal pricing for a perennial crop: the case of Colombian coffee', Ph.D. Thesis, The Food Research Institute, Stanford University, California.
Johnson, D.G. (1985) 'Alternatives to international food reserves', in FAO (ed.) *World Food Security: Selected Themes and Issues*, Rome, pp. 67–84.
Junginger-Dittel, K.-O. (1980) 'Marketing boards für Agrarexportgüter in Entwicklungsländern', Kieler Arbeitspapiere 105, Institut für Weitwirtschaft, Kiel.
Just, R.E., Hueth, D.L. and Schmitz, A. (1982) *Applied Welfare Economics and Public Policy*, Englewood Cliffs, NJ.
Just, R.E., Lutz, E., Schmitz, A. and Turnovsky, S.J. (1978) 'The distribution of welfare gains from price stabilization: an international perspective', *Journal of International Economics* 8: 551–63.
Kaibni, N.M. (1986) 'Evolution of the Compensatory financing facility', *Finance and Development* 23: 24–7.
—— (1988) 'Financial facilities of the IMF and the food deficit countries', *Food Policy* 13 (1): 73–82.

Kaldor, N. (1964) *Essays on Economic Policy, Vol. II*, London: Duckworth.

Kanan, N., Smit, H.P., Bade, J., Burger, K., Pomp, M. and Wansink, D. (1989) 'Supply management of commodity exports by developing countries', report for UNCTAD, Geneva.

Kanbur, S.M.R. (1984) 'How to analyse commodity price stabilization? A review article', *Oxford Economic Papers* 36: 336–58.

Keynes, J.M. (1974) 'The international control of raw materials', *Journal of International Economics* 4: 299–315.

Kim, H.K., Goreux, M.G. and Kendrick, D.A. (1975) 'Feedback control rule for cocoa market stabilization', in W.C. Labys (ed.) *Quantitative Models of Commodity Markets*, Cambridge, MA: Ballinger.

Kimball, M.S. (1990) 'Precautionary saving in the small and in the large', *Econometrica* 58(1): 53–74.

Kimmig, M. (1989) *Der Weltzinnmarkt: Einflussgrössen und Stabilisierungsmöglichkeiten eines internationalen Rohstoffmarktes*, Schriften zu Regional- und Verkehrsproblemen in Industrie- und Entwicklungsländer, Band 51, Berlin: Duncker & Humblot.

Knudsen, O. and Nash, J. (1990) 'Domestic price stabilization schemes in developing countries', *Economic Development and Cultural Change* 39: 539–58.

Knudsen, O. and Parnes, A. (1975) *Trade Instability and Economic Development*, Lexington, MA: Heath.

Koch, T. (1989) 'The sugar protocol: an appraisal,' *Intereconomics* 24 (6): 293–7.

—— (1990) *Das AKP-Zuckerprotokoll im Rahmen des Lomé-Vertrages*, Europäische Hochschulschriften, Reihe V, Volks- und Betriebswirtschaft, vol. 1128, Frankfurt a.M.: Verlag Peter Lang.

Koester, U. and Herrmann, R. (1987) *The EC-ACP Convention of Lomé*, Forum-Reports on Current Research in Agricultural Economics and Agribusiness Management 13, Kiel.

Koester, U. and Schmitz, P.M. (1982) 'The EC sugar market policy and developing countries', *European Review of Agricultural Economics* 9: 183–204.

Koester, U. and Valdés, A. (1984) 'The EC's potential role in food security for LDCs: adjustments in its STABEX and stock policies', *European Review of Agricultural Economics* 11: 415–37.

Kofi, T.A. (1977) 'The International Cocoa Agreements', *Journal of World Trade Law* 11(1): 37–51.

Konandreas, P., Huddleston, B. and Ramangkura, V. (1978) *Food Security: An Insurance Approach*, International Food Policy Research Institute, Research Report 4, Washington, DC.

Kumar, M.S. (1988) 'The stabilizing role of the compensatory financing facility: empirical evidence and welfare implications', IMF Working Paper WP/88/108, Research Department, Washington, DC.

Labys, W. and Pollak, P.K. (1984) *Commodity Models for Forecasting and Policy Analysis*, Beckenham: Croom Helm.

Law, A.D. (1975) *International Commodity Agreements. Performance and Prospects*, Lexington, MA: Heath.

Lee, S. and Blandford, D. (1980) 'An analysis of international buffer stocks for cocoa and copper through dynamic optimization', *Journal of Policy Modeling* 2 (3): 371–88.

Leland, H.E. (1968) 'Saving and uncertainty: the precautionary demand for saving', *Quarterly Journal of Economics* 82: 465–73.

Lim, D. (1976) 'Export instability and economic growth: a return to fundamentals', *Oxford Bulletin of Economics and Statistics* 38: 311–22.

—— (1991) *Export Instability and Compensatory Financing*, New York, London: Routledge.

Lister, M. (1988) *The European Community and the Developing World*, Aldershot: Avebury.

Little, I.M.D. and Clifford, J.M. (1965) *International Aid*, London: Allen & Unwin.

Lovasy, G.(1965) 'Survey and appraisal of proposed schemes of compensatory financing', *IMF Staff Papers* 12: 189–223.

Love, J. (1987) 'Export instability in less developed countries: consequences and causes', *Journal of Economic Studies* 14 (2): 3–80.

MacBean, A.I. (1966) *Export Instability and Economic Development*, London: Allen & Unwin.

—— (1980) 'Commodity policies in a new international order', in A. Sengupta (ed.) *Commodities Finance and Trade*, Oxford: Centre for Research on the New International Economic Order, pp. 59–73.

MacBean, A.I. and Nguyen, D.T. (1987a) 'International commodity agreements, shadow and substance', *World Development* 15(5): 575–90.

—— (1987b) *Commodity Policies: Problems and Prospects*, London: Croom Helm.

Machina, M.J. (1987) 'Choice under uncertainty: problems solved and unresolved', *Journal of Economic Perspectives* 1(1): 121–54.

Maizels, A. (1968) 'Review of export instability and economic growth', *American Economic Review* 85 (1): 50–73.

—— (1982) 'Selected issues in the negotiation of international commodity agreements: an economic analysis', Report for UNCTAD, TD/B/C.1/224, Geneva.

—— (1987) 'Commodities in crisis: an overview of the main issues', *World Development* 15 (5): 538.

Marshall, C.F. (1983) *The World Coffee Trade, A Guide to the Production, Trading and Consumption*, Cambridge: Woodhead-Faulkner.

Massell, B.F. (1969) 'Price stabilization and welfare', *Quarterly Journal of Economics* 83: 284–98.

Massow, V.H. von (1983) 'On the impacts of EEC beef preferences for Kenya and Botswana', *Quarterly Journal of International Agriculture, (Zeitschrift für Ausländische Landwirtschaft)* 22 (3): 216–34.

—— (1984) *Einfuhrbegünstigungen und Ausfuhrpolitik der EG bei Rindfleisch, Eine Analyse der Wirkungen mit einer Diskussion entwicklungspolitischer Aspekte am Beispiel der AKP-Quote*, Agrarökonomische Studien, Band 6, Kiel.

Matthews, A. (1992) 'The European Community's banana policy after 1992', Discussion Papers in Agricultural Economics, 13, Institute of Agricultural Policy and Market Research, University of Giessen, Giessen.

McKinnon, R.I. (1967) 'Futures markets, buffer stocks, and income stability for primary producers', *Journal of Political Economy* 75: 844–61.

McNicol, D.L. (1978) *Commodity Agreements and Price Stabilization*, Lexington, MA: Heath.

Menezes, J.A. de Souza (1984) 'The International Cocoa Agreement: the consequences of attempting to reduce price instability in the 1980s', Ph.D. Thesis, Cornell University, Ithaca, NY.

Mengel, W. (1991) 'Effekte von kompensatorischen Finanzierungssystemen unter besonderer Berücksichtigung von Stabilisierungswirkungen', Master's Thesis, University of Giessen, Giessen.

Morrison, T.K. and Perez, L. (1975) 'Export earning fluctuations and economic development', AID Paper, Washington, DC.

Morrow, D.T. (1980) *The Economics of the International Stockholding of Wheat,* International Food Policy Research Institute, Research Report 18, Washington, DC.

Muller, J.-C. (1980) 'The Stabex system in Lomé II', *The Courier Africa–Caribbean–Pacific–European Community* 62 (July–August): 30–6.

Mundlak, Y. and Larson, D.F. (1990) 'On the relevance of world agricultural prices', PRE Working Paper WPS 383, World Bank, Washington, DC.

Murray, D. (1978) 'Export earnings instability: price, quantity, supply, demand?', *Economic Development and Cultural Change* 27: 61–73.

Nappi, C. (1979) *Commodity Market Control, A Historical Perspective,* Lexington, MA: Toronto.

von Neumann, J. and Morgenstern, O. (1944) *Theory of Games and Economic Behaviour,* Princeton: Princeton University Press.

Newbery, D.M.G. and Stiglitz, J.E. (1981) *The Theory of Commodity Price Stabilization: A Study in the Economics of Risk,* Oxford: Oxford University Press.

Nguyen, D.T. (1980) 'Partial price stabilization and export earning instability', *Oxford Economic Papers* 32: 340–52.

—— (1990) 'Partial price stabilisation and national export earnings instability', *Journal of Economic Studies* 16 (3): 57–69.

Oi, W.Y. (1961) 'The desirability of price instability under perfect competition', *Econometrica* 29: 58–64.

Organization of American States (1962) 'Final report of the group of experts on the stabilization of export receipts', Doc. 59, Rev. 4, Washington, DC.

Palm, F.C. and Vogelvang, B. (1988) 'Policy simulations using a quarterly rational expectations model for the international coffee market', paper presented at the XXVth International Conference of the Applied Econometrics Association on International Commodity Market Modeling, World Bank, Washington, DC.

—— (1991) 'The effectiveness of the world coffee agreement: a simulation study using a quarterly model of the world coffee market', in O. Guvenen, W.C. Labys and J.B. Lesourd (eds) *International Commmodity Market Models. Advances in Methodology and Applications,* International Studies in Economic Modelling, London: Chapman and Hall, pp. 103–20.

Parikh, A. (1974) 'A model of world coffee economy: 1950–68', *Applied Economics* 6: 23–43.

Payer, C. (ed.) (1975) *Commodity Trade of the Third World,* London: Macmillan.

Pieterse, M.Th.A. and Silvis, H.J. (1988) *The World Coffee Market and the International Coffee Agreement,* Wageningse Economische Studies 9, Wageningen: Pudoc.

Pincus, J.A. (1971) 'Benefits and costs of aid', in G.M. Meier (ed.) *Leading*

Issues in Economic Development. Studies in International Poverty, 2nd edn, Oxford: Oxford University Press, pp. 257–68.
Pomp, J.M. (1991) 'Modelling and policy formulation in the case of cocoa', in United Nations' Economic and Social Commission for Asia and the Pacific, *The Use of Econometric Models for Commodity Policy Formulation*, New York: United Nations.
Powell, A. (1990) 'The costs of commodity price uncertainty', preliminary paper, Nuffield College, Oxford.
Pownall, R. and Stuart, B. (1988) 'The IMF's Compensatory and Contingency Financing Facility', *Finance and Development* 25: 9–11.
Pratt, J.W. (1964) 'Risk aversion in the small and the large', *Econometrica* 32: 122–36.
Pratt, J.W. and Zeckhauser, R. (1987) 'Proper risk aversion', *Econometrica* 55 (1): 143–54.
Radetzki, M. (1970) *International Commodity Market Arrangements, A Study of the Effects of Post-War Commodity Agreements and Compensatory Finance Schemes*, London: Hurst.
—— (1990) *A Guide to Primary Commodities in the World Economy*, Oxford: Basil Blackwell.
Raffer, K. (1987) 'Unfavorable specialization and dependence: the case of peripheral raw material exporters', *World Development* 15 (5): 701–12.
Rangarajan, L.M. (1978) *Commodity Conflict*, London: Croom Helm.
Reutlinger, S. (1977) 'Food insecurity: magnitude and remedies', World Bank Staff Working Papers 267, Washington, DC.
Reutlinger, S. and Bigman, D. (1981) 'Feasibility, effectiveness, and costs of food security alternatives in developing countries', in A. Valdés (ed.) *Food Security for Developing Countries*, Boulder, CO: Westview Press, pp. 185–212.
Reynolds, P.D. (1978) *International Commodity Agreements and the Common Fund. A Legal and Financial Analysis*, New York: Praeger.
Ridler, D. (1966) 'Stabilization of international trade in cocoa: a technical note', unpublished paper, International Monetary Fund.
Robertson, W. (1982) *Tin, its Production and Marketing*, London: Croom Helm.
Rote, R. (1986) 'A taste of bitterness – the political economy of tea plantations in Sri Lanka', Ph.D. Thesis, Amsterdam: Free University Press.
Rowe, J.W.F. (1965) *Primary Commodities in International Trade*, Cambridge: Cambridge University Press.
Sachs, L. (1984) *Angewandte Statistik. Anwendung statistischer Methoden*, 6th edn, Berlin: Springer-Verlag
Sahn, D.E. and Braun, J. von (1987) 'The relationship between food production and consumption variability: policy implications for developing countries', *Journal of Agricultural Economics* 38: 315–27.
Salant, S.W. (1983) 'The vulnerability of price stabilization schemes to speculative attack', *Journal of Political Economy* 91: 1–38.
Scandizzo, P.L. and Diakosavvas, D. (1987) *Instability in the Terms of Trade of Primary Commodities, 1900–1982*, FAO Economic and Social Development Paper 64, Rome: FAO.
Scandizzo, P.L., Hazell, P. and Anderson, J. (1984) *Risky Agricultural Markets*, Boulder, CO: Westview Press.

Schmitz, A. (1984) 'Commodity price stabilization. The theory and its applications', World Bank Staff Papers 668, Washington, DC.

Schmitz, P.M. (1982) 'Exporterlösstabilisierung durch AKP-Präferenzabkommen', Diskussionsbeiträge 47, Institut für Agrarpolitik und Marktlehre, Universität Kiel, Kiel.

—— (1984) 'European Community trade preferences for sugar and beef', in Deutsche Forschungsgemeinschaft and the Institute for Scientific Co-operation *Recent German Research in International Economics*, Weinheim, pp. 106–25.

Schmitz, P.M. and Koester, U. (1981) *Der Einfluss der EG-Zuckerpolitik auf die Entwicklungsländer*, Diskussionsbeiträge 42, Institut für Agrarpolitik und Marktlehre, Universität Kiel, Kiel.

Schnoor, A. (1989) 'Die Lomé-Politik der Europäischen Gemeinschaft gegenüber afrikanischen Rindfleisch–Exportstaaten', Master's Thesis, University of Göttingen, Göttingen.

Schultz, T.W. (1960) 'Value of U.S. farm surpluses to underdeveloped countries', *Journal of Farm Economics* 42: 1019–30.

Schulz, M. (ed.) (1991) *ACP–EEC: Partners in Cooperation*, Spektrum – Berliner Reihe zu Gesellschaft, Wirtschaft und Politik in Entwicklungsländern, Band 32, Saarbrücken: Breitenbach, Fort Lauderdale.

Senti, R. (1978) *Internationale Rohprodukteabkommen*, Diessenhofen: Verlag Rüegger.

Siamwalla, A. and Valdés, A. (1980) 'Food insecurity in developing countries', *Food Policy* 5: 258–72.

Smit, H.P. (1982) 'The world rubber economy to the year 2000', unpublished Ph.D. Thesis, Department of Economics, Free University, Amsterdam.

—— (1984) *Forecasts for the World Rubber Economy to the Year 2000*, Globe Industry Report 2, London: Macmillan.

Smit, H.P. and Burger, K. (1986) 'Cooperation in marketing of natural rubber: a simulation analysis of supply alternatives', UNCTAD/ST/ECDC/34, Geneva.

Spraos, J. (1990) Discussion on Herrmann *et al.* (1990) in L.A. Winters and D. Sapsford (eds.) *Primary Commodity Prices: Economic Models and Economic Policy*, Cambridge: Cambridge University Press, pp. 295–302.

Statistical Office of the EC, *Analytische Übersichten des Aussenhandels*, NIMEXE, Band A, Luxembourg, various years.

Strangmann, U. (1981) *Lieferabkommen für Agrarprodukte. Darstellung und Beurteilung aus der Sicht ausgewählter Entwicklungsländer am Beispiel des AKP-Zuckerprotokolls*, Europäische Hochschulschriften, Reihe V, Volks– und Betriebswirtschaft, vol. 310, Frankfurt a.M., Bern.

Summers, R. and Heston, A. (1988) 'A new set of international comparisons of real product and price levels, estimates for 130 countries, 1950–1985', *The Review of Income and Wealth* 34: 1–25.

Tan, C. Suan (1984) 'World rubber market structure and stabilization', World Bank Staff Commodity Papers 10, Washington, DC.

Tangermann, S. and Krostitz, W. (1982) *Protectionism in the Livestock Sector with Particular Reference to the International Beef Trade*, Göttinger Schriften zur Agrarökonomie, Heft 53, Göttingen.

Taylor, D. and Byerlee, D. (1991) 'Food aid and food security: a cautionary note', *Canadian Journal of Agricultural Economics* 39: 163–75.

Thomas, V. (1990) 'Discussion opening', in A. Maunder and A. Valdés (eds) *Agriculture and Governments in an Interdependent World*, Proceedings of the Twentieth International Conference of Agricultural Economists, Buenos Aires, Argentina, August 24–31 1988, Aldershot: Dartmouth Publishing House, pp. 707–10.

Turnovsky, S.J. (1974) 'Price expectations and the welfare gains from price stabilization', *American Journal of Agricultural Economics* 56: 706–16.

—— (1976) 'The distribution of welfare gains from price stabilization: the case of multiplicative disturbances', *International Economic Review* 17: 133–48.

—— (1978) 'The distribution of welfare gains from price stabilization: a survey of some theoretical issues', in F.G. Adams and S.A. Klein (eds) *Stabilizing World Commodity Markets*, Lexington, MA: Toronto, pp. 119–48.

US International Trade Commission (1975) 'International commodity agreements', report of the US International Trade Commission to the Subcommittee on International Trade of the Committee on Finance, United States Senate, Washington, DC.

UNCTAD (United Nations Conference on Trade and Development) (1975) 'An integrated programme for commodities. Compensatory financing of export fluctuations', report by the UNCTAD Secretariat, TD/B/C.1/195, Geneva: UNCTAD, 16 October.

—— (1976a) 'Elements of an international agreement on rubber', report by the UNCTAD Secretariat, TD/B/IPC/Rubber/L.2, Geneva: UNCTAD.

—— (1976b) 'Elements of an international agreement on jute, kenaf and allied fibres', report prepared jointly by the Secretariats of FAO and UNCTAD Secretariat, TD/B/IPC/Jute/L.2, Geneva: UNCTAD.

—— (1976c) 'Copper: The elements of an international stabilization arrangement', report by the UNCTAD Secretariat, TD/B/IPC/Copper/L.2, Geneva: UNCTAD.

—— (1979) 'Compensatory financing: issues and proposals for further action', TD/229/Supp.1, Geneva: UNCTAD, 7 March.

—— (1981) 'The processing before export of cocoa: areas for international co-operation', TD/B/C.1/PSC/18, Geneva: UNCTAD.

—— (1982a) 'Marketing and processing of tea: areas for international co-operation', TD/B/C.1/PSC/28, Geneva: UNCTAD.

—— (1982b) 'Review of STABEX and SYSMIN', TD/B/C.1/237, Geneva: UNCTAD, 22 November.

—— (1983a) 'Complementary facility for commodity-related shortfalls in export earnings. Review of the operation of the Compensatory Financing Facility of the International Monetary Fund', report by the UNCTAD Secretariat, TD/B/C.1/243, Geneva: UNCTAD, 11 January.

—— (1983b) 'International activities outside UNCTAD concerning individual commodities. A review of recent intergovernmental activities outside UNCTAD with respect to individual commodities', note by the UNCTAD Secretariat, Geneva: UNCTAD.

—— (1984a) 'Studies in the processing, marketing and distribution of commodities', TD/B/C.1/PSC/31/Rev. 1, Geneva: UNCTAD.

—— (1984b) 'Marketing and distribution of tin: areas for international co-operation', TD/B/C.1/PSC/38, Geneva: UNCTAD.

—— (1985a) *International Natural Rubber Agreement, 1979: An Analysis of its Development and Effectiveness*, contribution by the International Natural Rubber Organisation, TD/B/C.1.260, Geneva: UNCTAD, February.

—— (1985b) *Operation of the International Cocoa Agreements of 1972, 1975 and 1980*, an appraisal by the secretariat of the International Cocoa Organization (ICCO) TD/B/C.1/261, Geneva: UNCTAD, February.

—— (1986) 'Commodity earnings shortfalls and an additional compensatory financing facility', TD/B/AC.43/2, Geneva: UNCTAD, 23 April.

—— (1988a) 'The IMF Compensatory and Contingency Financing Facility', TD/B/AC. 43/7, Geneva: UNCTAD, 19 December.

—— (1988b) *Communication from the Executive Director of the International Cocoa Organization (ICCO)*, TD/B/C.1/L.89, Geneva: UNCTAD.

—— (1989) 'Recent developments in existing compensatory financing facilities and various institutional options, bearing in mind the balance-of-payments and/or commodity-related approaches', report by the UNCTAD Secretariat, TD/B/AC.43/8, Geneva: UNCTAD, 18 January.

United Nations (1961) 'International compensation for fluctuations in commodity trade', report by a Committee of Experts appointed by the Secretary–General, Department of Economic and Social Afairs, E/3447–E/CN.13/40, New York.

—— (1980) *International Cocoa Agreement 1980*, Geneva, TD/COCOA.6/7/Rev. 1.

—— (1984) *Studies in the Processing, Marketing and Distribution of Commodities: The Processing Before Exports of Cocoa: Areas for International Cooperation*, New York.

—— (1986) *International Cocoa Agreement 1986*, Geneva.

Valdés, A. and Konandreas, P. (1981) 'Assessing food insecurity based on national aggregates in developing countries', in A. Valdés (ed.) *Food Security for Developing Countries*, Boulder, CO: Westview Press, pp. 25–51.

Vellutini, R. and Alba, P. (1986) 'Simulacão Econométrica de Estoques Mundais para cacau', *Rivista de Econometria* VI (1): 137–56.

Vingerhoets, J.W.A. (1982) 'Ontwikkelingslanden als Grondstoffenexporteurs: Internationaal Grondstoffenbeleid en Oligopolistische markten, (Developing Countries as Primary Commodity Exporters: International Commodity Policy and Oligopolistic Markets)', Ph.D. Thesis, Gianotten BV, Tilburg.

Vogelvang, B. (1988) *A Quarterly Econometric Model of the World Coffee Economy*, Ph.D. Thesis, Free University, Amsterdam: Free University Press.

Vries, J. de (1975a) 'Compensatory financing: a quantitative analysis', World Bank Staff Working Paper 228, Washington, DC.

—— (1975b) 'Structure and prospects of the world coffee economy', World Bank Staff Working Paper 208, Washington, DC.

Wassermann, U. (1980) 'Breakdown of International Cocoa Agreement', *Journal of World Trade Law* 14 (3): 360–1.

—— (1981) 'UNCTAD: International Cocoa Agreement 1980', *Journal of World Trade Law* 15(2): 149–50.

Waugh, F.V. (1944) 'Does the consumer benefit from instability?', *Quarterly Journal of Economics* 58: 602–14.
Weiss, D. (1991) *Ökonomische Analyse des Zucker- und Rindfleischprotokolls im Rahmen des Lomé-Abkommens*, Materialien 20, Zentrum für regionale Entwicklungsforschung der Justus-Liebig-Universität Giessen, Giessen.
Wendt, H. (1981) *Aussenhandelspräferenzen und Entwicklungsförderung diskutiert am Beispiel der Zollpräferenzen für Agrarprodukte im Lomé-Abkommen*, Sonderhefte der Agrarwirtschaft 95, Hannover.
Weymar, F.H. (1968) *The Dynamics of the World Cocoa Market*, Cambridge, MA: MIT Press.
Williams, J.C. and Wright, B.D. (1991) *Storage and Commodity Markets*, Cambridge: Cambridge University Press.
Wirtschaftliche Vereinigung Zucker e.V. (ed.) *Jahresbericht*, Berlin, various years.
Wolffram, R. and Beckers, K. (1989) *Das AKP-Zuckerabkommen. Beurteilung aus entwicklungs- und finanzpolitischer Sicht: Fallstudie Mauritius*, Europäische Hochschulschriften, Reihe V, Volks– und Betriebswirtschaft 1018, Frankfurt a.M., Bern, New York, Paris.
World Bank (1980) 'Price prospects for major primary commodities', report 814/80, Washington.
—— (a) *World Bank Atlas*, Washington, DC, various years.
—— (b) *World Development Report*, Washington, DC, various years.
—— (c) *Annual Report*, Washington, DC, various years.
Wright, B.D. and Williams, J.C. (1982) 'The economic role of commodity storage', *Economic Journal* 92: 596–614.
—— (1988) 'The incidence of market stabilizing price support schemes', *Economic Journal* 98: 1183–98.
Yotopoulos, P.A. and Nugent, J.B. (1976) *Economics of Development. Empirical Investigations*, New York: Harper.
Zeckhauser, R. and Keeler, E. (1970) 'Another type of risk aversion', *Econometrica* 38 (5): 661–5.

Index